Accelerated Silverlight 2

Jeff Scanlon

Apress®

Accelerated Silverlight 2

Copyright © 2008 by Jeff Scanlon

ISBN-13 (pbk): 978-1-4302-1076-4

ISBN-10 (pbk): 1-4302-1076-1

ISBN-13 (electronic): 978-1-4302-1075-7

ISBN-10 (electronic): 1-4302-1075-3

Printed and bound in the United States of America 9 8 7 6 5 4 3 2 1

Lead Editor: Ewan Buckingham
Technical Reviewer: Fabio Claudio Ferracchiati
Editorial Board: Clay Andres, Steve Anglin, Mark Beckner, Ewan Buckingham, Tony Campbell, Gary Cornell, Jonathan Gennick, Michelle Lowman, Matthew Moodie, Jeffrey Pepper, Frank Pohlmann, Ben Renow-Clarke, Dominic Shakeshaft, Matt Wade, Tom Welsh
Project Manager: Richard Dal Porto
Copy Editors: Damon Larson, Ami Knox
Associate Production Director: Kari Brooks-Copony
Production Editor: Jill Ellis
Compositor: Kinetic Publishing Services, LLC
Proofreader: Linda Seifert
Indexer: Julie Grady
Artist: Kinetic Publishing Services, LLC
Cover Designer: Kurt Krames
Manufacturing Director: Tom Debolski

Distributed to the book trade worldwide by Springer-Verlag New York, Inc., 233 Spring Street, 6th Floor, New York, NY 10013. Phone 1-800-SPRINGER, fax 201-348-4505, e-mail orders-ny@springer-sbm.com, or visit http://www.springeronline.com.

For information on translations, please contact Apress directly at 2855 Telegraph Avenue, Suite 600, Berkeley, CA 94705. Phone 510-549-5930, fax 510-549-5939, e-mail info@apress.com, or visit http://www.apress.com.

Apress and friends of ED books may be purchased in bulk for academic, corporate, or promotional use. eBook versions and licenses are also available for most titles. For more information, reference our Special Bulk Sales–eBook Licensing web page at http://www.apress.com/info/bulksales.

The source code for this book is available to readers at http://www.apress.com. You may need to answer questions pertaining to this book in order to successfully download the code.

To Corey Chang, for showing me just how much patience can pay off.

Contents at a Glance

Contents

About the Author

JEFF SCANLON is an independent Microsoft consultant with extensive experience developing software using a variety of technologies. He designs and implements software across all layers with a focus on web-based applications. Jeff has lead developer training sessions on software engineering practices and introductions to new technologies at nearly every company he has worked with. He is the author of *Professional Java Programming with JDK 5,* and has written a number of articles on .NET for *Software Development* magazine. He holds several Microsoft certifications and a bachelor's degree in computer science from George Mason University.

About the Technical Reviewer

■FABIO CLAUDIO FERRACCHIATI is a senior consultant and a senior analyst/developer. He works for Brain Force (www.brainforce.com/) in its Italian branch (www.brainforce.it/). He is a Microsoft Certified Solution Developer for .NET, a Microsoft Certified Application Developer for .NET, and a Microsoft Certified Professional.

Fabio is a prolific author and technical reviewer. Over the past ten years, he has written articles for Italian and international magazines, and has coauthored more than ten books on a variety of computer-related topics. You can read his LINQ blog at www.ferracchiati.com/.

Acknowledgments

Thank you for deciding to buy this book. Without readers, a book is nothing more than an actor on an empty stage. I hope this book successfully helps you gain proficiency with Silverlight.

I had several publishers in mind when I first decided to pitch a book on Silverlight. After sending out several e-mails, I received a response from Ewan Buckingham in a mere matter of hours. This fast response encouraged me, since Apress was my top choice. Ewan impressed me from the beginning by seeing where this book could fit and helping get the project off the ground. He also saw this book through to the end, despite an issue during the middle of the project. I can't thank him enough for bringing me into the Apress author family and sticking with me on this project.

There are many other people at Apress that helped create this book and each deserves a great deal of appreciation. I couldn't have asked for a better project manager than Richard Dal Porto. Despite deadline slips and repeated schedule revisions that I'm sure would stress out any PM, Richard gave me plenty of space to work without constantly asking for status reports. Ewan and Richard trusted me to get the work done and I'm indebted to them for seeing this project through to the end.

Damon Larson was the copy editor for this book. Without his feedback, many ideas in this book would be unclear and the structure of the language might seem inconsistent. I think I gave him a lot of work to do, but the book is much better for his careful combings-through of my writing.

Jill Ellis worked as production editor. She helped the book through its final stages, ensuring the book looked how it should before it was sent to the printer. She was helpful in putting the extra polish on the book that will be evident when you read its pages.

Other people from Apress who helped along the way (in no particular order) are Joohn Choe, Ami Knox, Linda Seifert, Nancy Wright, and Dominic Shakeshaft. Compared to the hard work of all the people at Apress, I feel like my job was minor!

Fabio Claudio Ferracchiati, technical editor, was also of vital importance to this book. He offered a significant amount of feedback that helped improve the chapters. Based on his feedback, some sections were completely rewritten to improve structure and quality of information.

Any imperfections in this book are solely my responsibility, not Apress' or my technical editor's. I encourage you to leave feedback online or contact me directly so they can be addressed if necessary.

Claudia Holland from George Mason University helped ensure I had the required permissions to use the name of the university and video/pictures of the Fairfax campus.

I would also like to thank the people in my life who helped make this book possible. My parents deserve credit for letting me pursue what I want in life, regardless of the craziness of some pursuits. My closest friends deserve endless appreciation for their support: Corey Chang, for inspiring me and supporting me despite being the only person busier than I am; Phill Alexander, for his continual support and help with random snippets of language, despite a busy schedule as a PhD student; and Dave Nelson, for getting me into this intense, incredible field all those years ago.

Introduction

Silverlight is an exciting technology. There are technological aspects to Silverlight that convince me it will be a viable platform in the years ahead. I think Silverlight and its Linux implementation, Moonlight, will prove interesting to all developers, regardless of whether they have .NET experience. Silverlight brings the advantages of XAML and a CLR, and a set of useful platform libraries, to operating systems other than Windows. Someone once commented that Silverlight is where I placed my bet, and this is definitely true. I've upped the ante by investing the time and energy to write this book. *Accelerated Silverlight 2* aims to get you up to speed as efficiently as possible on Silverlight, and I hope you find what you're looking for within its pages. If you have any questions or problems, please get in touch with me using the contact information at the end of the Introduction, and I'll help. I also have a site specifically devoted to this book, `www.acceleratedsilverlight.net/`, which provides a place for readers to get questions answered and extend some of the topics discussed in this book.

Who This Book Is For

This book assumes you have a reasonable degree of familiarity with .NET, such as under-standing what assemblies are and how to develop on the .NET platform using C#. The goal of this book is to get you up to speed on Silverlight as efficiently as possible. Although Windows Presentation Foundation (WPF) also uses XAML (which you'll learn about in Chapter 2, in case you're unfamiliar with this term), you do not need to be familiar with WPF.

How This Book Is Structured

This book covers a significant amount of Silverlight, from the new Extensible Application Markup Language (XAML), to creating user interfaces, to the building of a real world–style application. The following subsections more specifically detail what is covered in each chapter.

Chapter 1, "Introducing Silverlight"

This chapter discusses some of the background of cross-platform applications to help you understand where Silverlight fits into the overall technological picture. There may not be much history to Silverlight, but it did start as a version 1.0 product that featured a basic XAML parser (but no managed execution engine). This chapter concludes with using Visual Studio 2008 and Expression Blend to create your first Silverlight application.

Chapter 2, "Getting to Know XAML"

XAML is a new declarative language. It provides an easy way to create and configure object hierarchies and relationships in markup. This chapter introduces important concepts, such as markup extensions to support handling resources and data binding, type converters for interpreting property values, dependency properties, attached properties, events, and other important aspects of XAML and Silverlight.

Chapter 3, "Creating User Interfaces"

Silverlight provides important controls for organizing user interfaces, displaying information, and receiving user input. After discussing the important aspects of the Silverlight object hierarchy, we get right into creating user interfaces. The major layout controls are explored—the Canvas for absolute positioning, the StackPanel for organizing controls horizontally or vertically, and the Grid for placing controls in HTML-like tables. Next, all the standard user interface controls are covered, including those for creating text entry boxes, check boxes, radio buttons, and list boxes.

Chapter 4, "Network Communication"

An online application that does not talk to other systems (or even back to its hosting server) is a rare case, so Silverlight must provide ways to interact with other systems. Unsurprisingly, Silverlight provides functionality to invoke web services and download data (such as ZIP files) from a web server. However, it might surprise you that Silverlight includes support for raw network communication, though it is subject to security restrictions.

Chapter 5, "Working with Data"

Communicating over the network is important for getting data—but once you have data, what do you do with it? This chapter details how to connect data from a data source to the user interface using the data binding architecture. Data can be stored in a collection in the code-behind or in XML. Silverlight provides the ability to use LINQ expressions (introduced in .NET 3.5—but don't worry, Silverlight is still completely separate from the

.NET Framework) in the code-behind, as well as support for both reading and writing XML files and serialization to and from objects. This chapter concludes with a look at how to save state on the client, mainly through the use of isolated storage—a private, secure area on disk for Silverlight applications.

Chapter 6, "Working with Media"

Silverlight makes it easy to create rich user interfaces involving images, audio, and video. This chapter details how to access and utilize these media elements. Silverlight can be used to create sites that manage video—such as YouTube (`www.youtube.com/`)—or sophisticated image-browsing sites like Hard Rock Memorabilia (`http://memorabilia.hardrock.com/`). This chapter details the various media controls, including Image, MediaElement, and Multi-ScaleImage (also known as Deep Zoom, the MultiScaleImage control was used to create the Hard Rock Memorabilia site). The chapter concludes with a look at Silverlight Streaming, a service Microsoft provides to host both Silverlight applications and videos for streaming.

Chapter 7, "Extending the User Interface"

Although Chapter 2 detailed many controls useful for building Silverlight applications, it only showed one aspect of Silverlight's support for building user interfaces. This chapter returns to building user interfaces. Silverlight has support for 2D graphics, such as lines and ellipses, and even complex geometrical shapes. Almost anything that can be drawn on a user interface (such as 2D graphics or controls) can be transformed (e.g., rotated or scaled down). These transforms are discussed along with performing custom transformations by using a transformation matrix. This chapter concludes with a look at the various brushes provided by Silverlight, useful for painting colors, images, video, or even color gradients onto foregrounds or backgrounds of elements in a user interface.

Chapter 8, "Styling and Templating"

Silverlight provides the ability to centrally manage styles that control the appearance of elements on a user interface, such as those for font face, font size, and color. It also supports the ability to completely replace the visual representation of controls using control templates. Both of these mechanisms are explored in this chapter.

Chapter 9, "Animation"

Animation provides the ability to change the properties of user interface elements over time. This chapter discusses the support Silverlight provides for animation, beginning with an explanation of a timeline and continuing with an exploration of storyboards and the different ways to animate elements of a user interface. The chapter concludes with a look at animating using Expression Blend, an invaluable tool for easily developing and previewing animation.

Chapter 10, "Dynamic Languages and the Browser"

A big aspect of Silverlight that is currently not officially available in .NET on Windows is the Dynamic Language Runtime (DLR). This enables the smooth execution of dynamic languages such as IronPython, IronRuby, and Managed JScript within Silverlight. After showing how to utilize dynamic languages in Silverlight applications, this chapter switches gears to the support Silverlight provides for interoperating with the browser. Silverlight provides the ability to send and receive data from the hosting browser, including invoking JScript and accessing the DOM.

Chapter 11, "Security"

Silverlight can interact with the host operating system—for example, isolated storage ultimately writes files to disk. This direct access is impossible from your application code because all application code is considered unsafe. This forms the core of the security model for executable code in Silverlight. Beyond the security of executable code, there are other aspects at an application level that contribute to sound security in Silverlight applications. These aspects include authentication/authorization to control access, communicating over SSL, and using cryptography to protect sensitive data. This chapter explores all of these, along with how to design a Silverlight application with security in mind.

Chapter 12, "Testing and Debugging"

Applications must be tested to prove, as best as possible, that they are bug free and work as designed. This chapter primarily focuses on unit testing—testing Silverlight applications from the perspective of a developer. A strong set of unit tests can prove a useful part of the build and verification process. When bugs are found, during development or from testing, the root cause must be discovered. This is where debugging proves useful. Debugging is more than simply attaching a debugger to a Silverlight application and tracing execution. Both proactive and reactive debugging measures are discussed.

Chapter 13, "Packaging and Deploying Silverlight Applications"

Silverlight is a client-side technology. A Silverlight application can be placed on any web server (e.g., IIS, Apache, etc.); however, there are some benefits to deploying Silverlight on IIS 7 (primarily in the handling of video). This chapter will discuss how Silverlight applications are packaged and deployed on web servers, how they are embedded in HTML/ASPX pages, and also what is necessary to support building Silverlight applications using MSBuild.

Chapter 14, "Advanced Topics"

One of the most frustrating things for users of an application is a frozen user interface. Long-running operations should never occur on the user interface thread, and you should be well aware of this if you've done any Windows Forms development. Silverlight supports several techniques to improve responsiveness of user interfaces, including asynchronous communication and threading. This chapter explores techniques to create responsive user interfaces by looking at both explicit and implicit ways of leveraging multiple threads. Silverlight also provides several timer-related classes useful for certain periodic tasks, such as providing a time signature for a video that is playing.

Chapter 15, "Case Study: Campus Explorer"

The book concludes with the design and development of an example application that uses many aspects of Silverlight. The application provides an interactive map of a university campus and displays images/video linked to buildings on campus to give visitors to the application a good idea of what the campus is like. The key features of this application include images, video, control templating and styling, data binding, and various controls.

Contacting the Author

You can contact the author by visiting his site at www.artofcoding.net/, or via this book's site, at www.acceleratedsilverlight.net/. Comments on this book can be sent directly to the author at feedback@acceleratedsilverlight.net.

CHAPTER 1

∎∎∎

Introducing Silverlight

Silverlight is an exciting new technology from Microsoft for developing rich user experiences that are accessible on a variety of platforms. Stated succinctly, Silverlight is a cross-platform Common Language Runtime (CLR) with a strong presentation framework for compositing user interfaces and displaying images and video, making development of rich user experiences much easier than before. At the core of Silverlight is a new markup language called Extensible Application Markup Language, or XAML (pronounced *zammel*). XAML helps designers and developers work more effectively with each other since it is a declarative language with tools built around it. Silverlight 2.0 is a natural extension to technologies already in existence, specifically .NET and Windows Presentation Foundation (WPF). If you strip out the parts of .NET that just aren't needed or don't easily work across platforms (such as interoperating with COM), add in an implementation of XAML that is close to WPF's, and mix in a few new things such as browser interoperability and ability to execute dynamic languages such as Python (IronPython, as the .NET implementation is called), you end up with Silverlight 2.0.

Developing applications that work on multiple platforms is a difficult problem. What constitutes a platform is an important question, and for the purposes of this book, it is any unique host environment that provides an execution environment for code. If you give it some thought, it is easy to categorize Windows XP, Windows Vista, OS X, and Linux as platforms; but Firefox, Internet Explorer 6, Internet Explorer 7, Opera, and so on also count as platforms. If you've done any web development targeting multiple browsers, you're familiar with the inherent headaches in getting a web site to render and operate the same on Internet Explorer as it does on Firefox and others. Technically, this web site is a cross-platform application. The goal of Silverlight is to create a consistent execution environment across different browsers and operating systems.

There is no magical reason why a cross-platform application is automatically "good." Any responsible software engineering starts with a careful examination of the business reasons for a project. If all users are on a single platform, such as Windows, there is no reason to spend extra development time ensuring that the software also works on other platforms. Also, a significant amount of software that enables business applications (data and business logic layers) has no need to work on multiple platforms (though it can potentially be *consumed* by different platforms), and in fact benefits from platform-specific optimizations.

However, cross-platform applications are definitely important—as is best evidenced by web sites that are usable, generally, on any browser. The ability to develop cross-platform applications is of the most importance when the potential users for an application are on multiple platforms. This is a rather obvious statement, but it is important to note that development of a cross-platform application offers no inherent benefits if all users are on a single platform.

That is, unless the cross-platform aspect is obtained free or near-free (therefore helping to future-proof the application if the user base changes). This concept of "free or near-free" is important—software engineering is already a challenging endeavor, and if making software cross-platform is difficult to implement, it requires either significantly more development time for a single code base, or a second code base for a different platform that replicates the functionality of the first (not to mention a third or fourth code base if other platforms must be supported). Without question, this means more time, more money, and more development resources are needed. Optimally, we want a relatively easy way to create cross-platform applications. Fortunately, a number of frameworks have attempted to make the creation of cross-platform applications free or near-free.

Cross-Platform Frameworks

Frameworks for developing cross-platform applications are not new. Even the C language is arguably cross-platform, since the source can be written once and compiled on each target platform, thus enabling portability of projects written in C. While arguments over what truly constitutes cross-platform can be interesting, they aren't of much practical use for us here, so let's take a brief look at the serious contenders for developing cross-platform applications.

Qt

Qt (pronounced *cute*) is a cross-platform application development toolkit mainly for C++; however, it has support for other languages such as Java. The significant benefit to Qt is that programs execute natively after compilation (i.e., no new virtual machine is needed). The cross-platform nature of Qt is provided at the source level, as long as developers utilize Qt's platform-agnostic API. The major downsides to Qt are the learning curve for developers and the degree to which applications might become intertwined with Qt (though this might be acceptable to many organizations). Visit `www.trolltech.com/products/qt` for more information.

The Java Platform

The Java platform is possibly the closest comparison to Silverlight on the market. Much like .NET, the Java platform is a managed environment. Until Silverlight, though, .NET was only available on Windows. Both platforms provide the ability to compile a program and immediately execute it on multiple platforms. The Java platform and Silverlight approach this similarly: an execution environment (known as a virtual machine) is developed for each platform where programs might be run. Java source code is compiled to Java bytecode, which is then executed by the Java virtual machine. The downsides to this approach are the plethora of virtual machines that can be created, each with potential quirks that sometimes affect existing applications, and the time cost of starting up a Java virtual machine on a web site (you've no doubt seen the gray rectangle and the loading symbol on web pages). Sun also has a more direct competitor to Silverlight called JavaFX, a framework including a scripting language to more easily create Java applications. This framework makes the most sense for institutions and developers already used to working in the Java environment or needing to extend their existing Java applications. Visit `http://java.sun.com/javafx/` if you are curious about learning more.

Flash/Flex

Flash is, by far, the most popular comparison to Silverlight. A browser plug-in that enables execution of rich content for the Web—doesn't that sound familiar? This comparison is made even more explicit with Adobe releasing Flex, an environment for executing rich applications in the browser and on the desktop. While there are some feature differences between Flex and Silverlight that can make one more appealing than the other, Flex is a viable alternative to Silverlight; however, it caters to a different set of developers than Silverlight does. Flex capitalizes on the languages people already know, including JavaScript, HTML, CSS, and ActionScript. Silverlight, however, provides a brand new markup language, but is an incredibly natural platform to develop on if you're already a .NET developer. Visit `www.adobe.com/products/flex/` if you want to learn more about Flex.

Silverlight

This brings us to the subject of this book: Silverlight 2.0. The .NET 3.0 Framework included the first release of WPF, along with other key technologies. With WPF came XAML, essentially a way to create applications in markup (there is an almost one-to-one correspondence between XAML constructs and code). While XAML is not necessarily tied to presentation logic, the two most visible uses of it are in WPF and Silverlight. Silverlight's implementation of XAML is a subset of WPF's—it does not have 3D support, for example. While Silverlight does contain a CLR, it has absolutely no dependence on any of the .NET Framework versions—the Silverlight plug-in brings with it a CLR and a base class library all its own.

If you are already a .NET developer, you will be in familiar territory after learning XAML and its features. The correspondence of XAML to classes in .NET is a major strength, and the tool support built around XAML for designers and developers is strong and growing.

The History of Silverlight

Before the MIX conference in March 2007, Silverlight was known by the relatively boring but descriptive name WPF/E, which stands for Windows Presentation Foundation/Everywhere. While the details were sparse at the time, the rough goal of the technology was clear: a browser-hosted version of WPF. Silverlight 1.0 was unveiled at the conference and would no longer be known as WPF/E. This initial release of Silverlight did not have a CLR or anywhere close to the capabilities provided by 2.0. What it did have, though, is support for a small subset of XAML and a variety of capabilities that foreshadowed the future of Silverlight. Possibly the most obvious aspect of Silverlight 1.0 is that applications are written either completely in XAML or in a mix of XAML and JavaScript. Since there is no CLR, there is no compilation step, and the JavaScript is interpreted on the client. The major features supported by Silverlight 1.0 are

Core architecture: This includes `DependencyObject` at the root, and `UIElement` forming the base of user interface classes (but no `FrameworkElement` class).

Basic layout: The Canvas is the only layout component, so user interface elements can only be placed using absolute positions.

Basic controls: The TextBlock and Run controls are provided to display text. In terms of handling user input, nothing specialized is provided. This limitation extended to Silverlight 1, and the full control architecture debuted when Silverlight 2.0 was first released in beta.

2D graphics: Geometry-based classes (which are flexible but can't be directly placed on a user interface) and Shape-based classes (which can be directly placed on a user interface) provide the ability to draw 2D shapes.

Media: Many early Silverlight applications showcased the image and video support provided by Silverlight. Also included is support for easily downloading media such as images so that bandwidth could be utilized more effectively.

Animation: The Storyboard class known from WPF became part of the XAML implementation in this first release of Silverlight, providing the ability to animate different user interface elements in a variety of ways.

Brushes and transforms: Brushes such as the image brush, video brush, and color brushes (solid colors and gradients) have been in Silverlight since this initial release.

Silverlight 1.0 does require a plug-in on the client side, and in the spirit of Microsoft's commitment to backward compatibility, Silverlight 1.0 applications still work on Silverlight 2.0. Two of the most important parts of the latest release of Silverlight that are not present in Silverlight 1.0 are a rich set of controls and performance advantages due to compiled code.

Soon after Silverlight 1.0 was released, the next version of Silverlight was released in preview form. This preview release was known as Silverlight 1.1, the most significant aspect of which is the cross-platform CLR. While Silverlight 1.0 could be used to develop some impressive media-based applications, the possibilities greatly expand with the ability to target the .NET platform and know that the application will run on multiple host platforms. The biggest missing feature from Silverlight 1.1 was a set of standard controls. This made developing useful user interfaces difficult. Handling input events was also difficult since events could only be captured on the root container. You then had to manually propagate the events to child objects. Input focus was also tricky.

After several months, as it got closer to the MIX08 conference in March 2007, Microsoft revealed that Silverlight 1.1 would actually be released as Silverlight 2.0 since the feature set grew so much. Fortunately, the 2.0 release of Silverlight includes a standard control set (probably everything you would want except for a tree control and a combo box control) and an input event system that saves Silverlight developers the tedium of handling input events manually. Silverlight 2.0 comes with much more than just these important additions. We get strong networking support, even including the ability to communicate over sockets. We get the System.Xml classes, though they are a subset of the same classes in the .NET Framework on Windows. We get the ability to develop in any .NET language we want—including dynamic languages such as compiled JavaScript and IronPython. This book will cover Silverlight 2.0 in detail and help you quickly get up to speed on this new technology.

Creating Your First Application

Since Visual Studio 2008 supports .NET 3.0 and 3.5, WPF application support is already built in. However, since the release of Visual Studio 2008 preceded Silverlight 2.0, Silverlight support is not provided out of the box. After you install the Silverlight 2.0 SDK, Visual Studio 2008 gains support for building Silverlight 2.0 applications and class libraries, and adds a read-only design surface and appropriate IntelliSense in the XAML editor. While Visual Studio is an established tool targeted to developers, tool support for WPF and Silverlight for both designers and developers is necessary. This need is satisfied by the Expression suite of products from Microsoft. Let's install the Silverlight 2.0 SDK and briefly explore it and one of the Expression tools.

Visit `http://silverlight.net/GetStarted/` and download Microsoft Silverlight Tools for Visual Studio 2008. This single download includes the SDK for Visual Studio 2008 (Standard edition and above) and the runtime for Silverlight 2.0.

Two more tools are available at this page: Expression Blend and the Deep Zoom Composer. If you have seen the Hard Rock Memorabilia site, you have seen a product of the Deep Zoom Composer. This technology will be discussed when we take a closer look at media support in Silverlight in Chapter 5. For now, just download and install Expression Blend 2.5 Preview.

When you edit a XAML file in a WPF application using Visual Studio, you have access to a toolbox of controls, a design surface onto which you can drag and drop controls, and a text editor view of the XAML code. When you edit a XAML file in a Silverlight application, you still have these three elements, but the design surface is read-only. This is probably a result of the Silverlight package being an add-on to Visual Studio. One thing you can do, though, is drag and drop controls from the toolbox onto the text editor. This can help a lot when you want to work with XAML exclusively in Visual Studio.

You can use Expression Blend if you want a full drag-and-drop user interface construction tool for Silverlight. It's possible to use Expression Blend simultaneously with Visual Studio. Modifications to both XAML files and the project/solution file are fine, since when you switch from one tool to the other, the tool will reload the updated files.

Start by loading Visual Studio 2008 and creating a new project (see Figure 1-1).

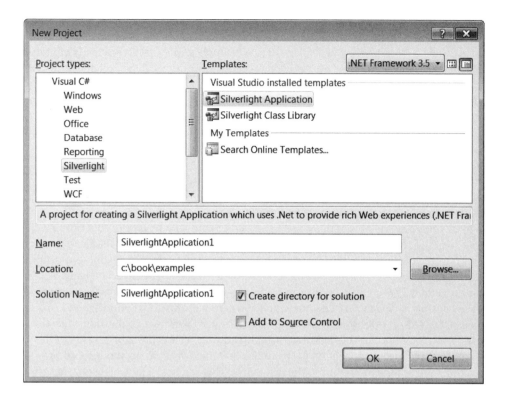

Figure 1-1. *The New Project dialog in Visual Studio 2008*

After you click OK, the next dialog allows you to create a web site/web application project that hosts the Silverlight application (see Figure 1-2).

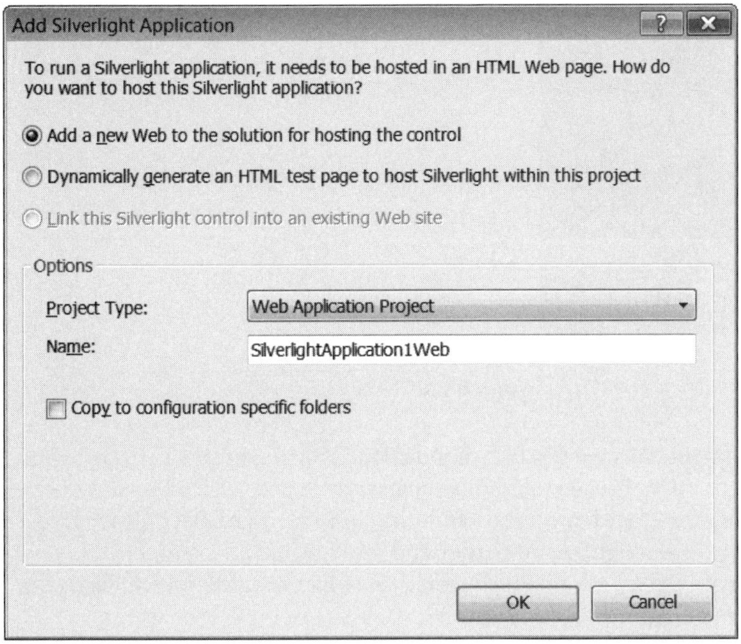

Figure 1-2. *The Add Silverlight Application dialog in Visual Studio 2008*

For the purpose of the examples in this book, it does not matter if you use a web site or a web application project; however, web application projects are better for eventual deployment since they contain a project file suitable for MSBuild.

Click OK, and the Solution Explorer will show two projects: the Silverlight application (SilverlightApplication1) and the web site supporting it (SilverlightApplication1_Web). If you now build the application, the Silverlight application is built to a XAP file that is automatically copied to the ClientBin folder within the web site. This XAP file contains the Silverlight application and will be downloaded by the client when it visits the web site.

If you now start the development server in Visual Studio (by pressing F5 or Ctrl+F5), you will see the Silverlight application start. If, however, you create a new web site in IIS, point the document root to SilverlightApplication1_Web, and navigate to this site, you will get a 404 error when trying to load the Silverlight application in your browser. What's going on? IIS must know about the new file extension .xap. You accomplish this by adding a new MIME type to either the root of IIS or to the specific web site you created. The file extension is .xap and the MIME type is application/x-silverlight-app.

Now let's take a look at Expression Blend, a tool used to lay out user interface controls and create animations in WPF and Silverlight. Without closing Visual Studio, start Blend, go to File ➤ Open ➤ Project/Solution, and navigate to the solution file created in Visual Studio (in C:\book\examples\SilverlightApplication1 if you used the same directory structure).

The top-right portion of Blend is devoted to managing the project files (like the Solution Explorer in Visual Studio); properties for various user interface elements; and resources, which include style templates, and animation storyboards, stored in XAML. Double-click Page.xaml to open this XAML page in the designer (see Figure 1-3).

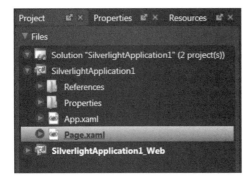

Figure 1-3. *The Project Property pane in Expression Blend*

Along the left side of the Blend screen is the toolbox. This provides access to both layout and input controls, and several tools used to modify the user interface, such as a paint bucket and a transform tool for brushes. Hold down the left mouse button when selecting any icon with a white triangle in the lower-right-hand corner and more tools will expand from it. Figure 1-4 shows an example when clicking the Button icon (which looks like a mouse cursor hovering over a rounded rectangle).

Figure 1-4. *The control toolbox in Expression Blend*

The Objects and Timeline area to the immediate right of the toolbox provides a place to create and manage animation storyboards, but more importantly for us right now, it shows the object hierarchy in XAML. After creating our application, we see [UserControl] and

LayoutRoot. Click [UserControl] to highlight it and then click Properties in the top-right portion of the screen. The control with the gray highlight is the control that shows up in the Properties pane (see Figure 1-5).

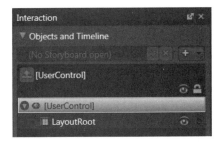

Figure 1-5. *The Objects and Timeline pane in Expression Blend*

Go to the Properties pane and set the width and height of the UserControl to 400 and 100, respectively, as shown in Figure 1-6.

Figure 1-6. *The size properties for a control in Expression Blend*

You can also click XAML or Split along the right side of the design surface and view and edit the XAML directly. However, as interfaces get more complex, Blend becomes an invaluable design tool for working with the XAML indirectly. Hand-editing XAML should generally be used for tweaking some XAML instead of creating full-blown user interfaces.

Next, right-click LayoutRoot in the Objects and Timeline pane and select Delete. This removes the default Grid layout control. While you can go to the toolbox and select the Canvas control (it's in the group four controls up from the bottom), let's view the XAML and create a Canvas control by hand. Click Split alongside the design surface to see the design surface simultaneously with the XAML. Edit the XAML to look like the following (reintroducing the `close` tag to the UserControl and dropping in the `Canvas` tag):

```
<UserControl
    xmlns="http://schemas.microsoft.com/client/2007"
    xmlns:x="http://schemas.microsoft.com/winfx/2006/xaml"
    x:Class="SilverlightApplication1.Page"
    Width="400" Height="100">
    <Canvas Height="Auto" Width="Auto" Background="White"/>
</UserControl>
```

Now go to the toolbox and select the TextBlock control, as shown in Figure 1-7.

Figure 1-7. *Choosing the TextBlock control from the toolbox*

This control is used to place text on a user interface, much like a label in Windows Forms or ASP.NET. Click the design surface and hold the mouse button down, and then drag right and down to create a rectangle describing the area for the TextBlock. Now the TextBlock should appear as a child of the Canvas in the Objects and Timeline pane. Make sure the TextBlock is selected, and go to Properties.

If you've read even just one other programming book, you know what's coming next. Scroll down the properties until you see the Common Properties area, and set the text to "Hello World!" as shown in Figure 1-8.

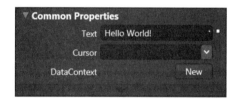

Figure 1-8. *Setting the Text property of a TextBlock in Expression Blend*

If you now switch back to Visual Studio, it will ask to reload Page.xaml. Go ahead and reload. Press F6 to build the application and then Ctrl+F5 to start the application without debugging. You should see something similar to Figure 1-9 in your browser.

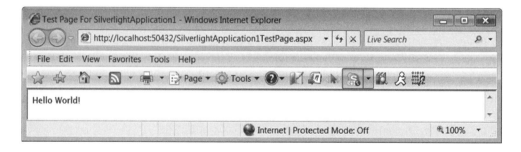

Figure 1-9. *The Hello World application as viewed in Internet Explorer 7*

Congratulations, you have now created your first Silverlight application using both Expression Blend and Visual Studio!

Summary

This chapter began with a discussion of Silverlight and its major competitors. Next, it covered how to create a new Silverlight application in Visual Studio with a supporting web site, how to modify the user interface in Expression Blend, and finally, how to build and execute an application in Visual Studio. The next stop on our journey through practical Silverlight development takes us to XAML. Many of the core concepts needed to understand how Silverlight works are covered in the next chapter, including markup extensions, dependency properties, and previews of features such as data binding and styling applications.

CHAPTER 2

■■■

Getting to Know XAML

Now that you understand what Silverlight is and where it fits in the general technology land-scape, and have installed the tools necessary to develop in Silverlight and created your first Silverlight application, it is time to peel back the layers. This chapter will start by properly introducing Extensible Application Markup Language (XAML), and then exploring its many features, such as the new property and event systems needed to support data binding, animation, and other key parts of Silverlight. The chapter will wrap up with more information on Silverlight applications, such as project structure and connecting XAML to events in code-behind.

Introducing XAML

Let's jump right in and look at a simple Silverlight application. This application will display a basic login screen with a text entry area for username and password, and a button. There is no logic behind this screen—we will only look at the markup for now. Figure 2-1 shows what this application looks like on Windows Vista. Focus on the content on the right—the navigation list on the left provides an easy way to navigate to other examples used in this chapter.

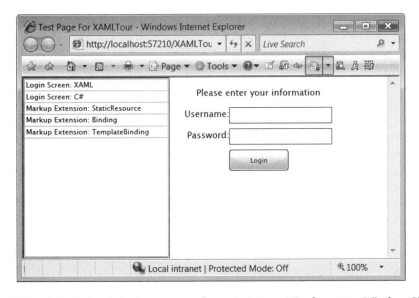

Figure 2-1. *A simple login screen as shown in Internet Explorer 7 on Windows Vista*

Since Silverlight is cross-platform, Figure 2-2 shows you what this application looks like on OS X in Safari.

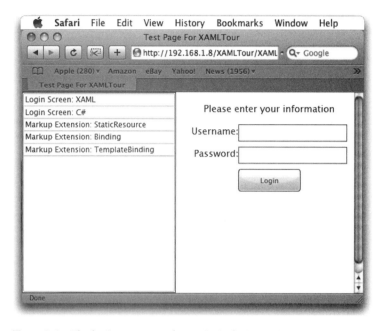

Figure 2-2. *The login screen as shown in Safari on OS X*

Unsurprisingly, it looks the same. As long as this behavior holds true throughout Silverlight applications, it should reinforce the fact that Silverlight provides a viable cross-platform framework, delivering on its promise.

Now let's look at the XAML that describes the login screen. If you create a new Silverlight application, you can paste this code into Page.xaml (make sure project is named XAMLTour, or change the namespace in the x:Class attribute to match the project name). We've placed this code in a XAML file named LoginScreenXAML.xaml. We will circle back at the end of this chapter and see how this file becomes the main user interface for the application. Also, many aspects of this code will be discussed in detail in later chapters, such as how the Grid and Canvas layout controls work.

```
<UserControl
    xmlns="http://schemas.microsoft.com/client/2007"
    xmlns:x="http://schemas.microsoft.com/winfx/2006/xaml"
    x:Class="XAMLTour.LoginScreenXAML">
  <Canvas Background="White">
    <Grid Height="140" Width="250" Canvas.Left="25" Canvas.Top="15">
      <Grid.RowDefinitions>
        <RowDefinition/>
        <RowDefinition/>
        <RowDefinition/>
        <RowDefinition/>
      </Grid.RowDefinitions>
```

```
        <Grid.ColumnDefinitions>
            <ColumnDefinition Width="Auto"/>
             <ColumnDefinition/>
        </Grid.ColumnDefinitions>
        <TextBlock HorizontalAlignment="Center"
                   Text="Please enter your information"
                   Grid.Column="0" Grid.Row="0" Grid.ColumnSpan="2"/>
        <TextBlock Text="Username:" VerticalAlignment="Top"
                   HorizontalAlignment="Right"
                   Grid.Column="0" Grid.Row="1"/>
        <TextBox VerticalAlignment="Top" Grid.Column="1" Grid.Row="1"/>
        <TextBlock HorizontalAlignment="Right" VerticalAlignment="Top"
                   Grid.Column="0" Grid.Row="2">
            Password:
        </TextBlock>
        <TextBox VerticalAlignment="Top" Grid.Column="1" Grid.Row="2"/>
        <Button Content="Login" Grid.Row="3" Width="100" Grid.Column="1"
                HorizontalAlignment="Left"/>
    </Grid>
  </Canvas>
</UserControl>
```

XAML is a markup language that provides mechanisms for constructing and configuring object hierarchies that are traditionally done in code, such as C#. The login screen, constructed in C# instead of XAML, looks like the following:

```
Canvas canvas = new Canvas();
canvas.Background = new SolidColorBrush(Color.FromArgb(255, 255, 255, 255));
Grid grid = new Grid();
grid.Width = 250;
grid.Height = 140;
grid.SetValue(Canvas.LeftProperty, 25);
grid.SetValue(Canvas.TopProperty, 15);
grid.RowDefinitions.Add(new RowDefinition());
grid.RowDefinitions.Add(new RowDefinition());
grid.RowDefinitions.Add(new RowDefinition());
grid.RowDefinitions.Add(new RowDefinition());
ColumnDefinition cd = new ColumnDefinition();
cd.Width = new GridLength(0, GridUnitType.Auto);
grid.ColumnDefinitions.Add(cd);
grid.ColumnDefinitions.Add(new ColumnDefinition());
TextBlock headerText = new TextBlock();
headerText.HorizontalAlignment = HorizontalAlignment.Center;
headerText.Text = "Please enter your information";
headerText.SetValue(Grid.ColumnProperty, 0);
headerText.SetValue(Grid.ColumnSpanProperty, 2);
headerText.SetValue(Grid.RowProperty, 0);
TextBlock usernameText = new TextBlock();
usernameText.Text = "Username:";
```

```
usernameText.HorizontalAlignment = HorizontalAlignment.Right;
usernameText.SetValue(Grid.ColumnProperty, 0);
usernameText.SetValue(Grid.RowProperty, 1);
TextBox usernameInput = new TextBox();
usernameInput.VerticalAlignment = VerticalAlignment.Top;
usernameInput.SetValue(Grid.ColumnProperty, 1);
usernameInput.SetValue(Grid.RowProperty, 1);
TextBlock passwordText = new TextBlock();
passwordText.Text = "Password:";
passwordText.HorizontalAlignment = HorizontalAlignment.Right;
passwordText.SetValue(Grid.ColumnProperty, 0);
passwordText.SetValue(Grid.RowProperty, 2);
TextBox passwordInput = new TextBox();
passwordInput.VerticalAlignment = VerticalAlignment.Top;
passwordInput.SetValue(Grid.ColumnProperty, 1);
passwordInput.SetValue(Grid.RowProperty, 2);
Button loginButton = new Button();
loginButton.Content = "Login";
loginButton.SetValue(Grid.ColumnProperty, 1);
loginButton.SetValue(Grid.RowProperty, 3);
loginButton.HorizontalAlignment = HorizontalAlignment.Left;
loginButton.Width = 100;
grid.Children.Add(headerText);
grid.Children.Add(usernameText);
grid.Children.Add(usernameInput);
grid.Children.Add(passwordText);
grid.Children.Add(passwordInput);
grid.Children.Add(loginButton);
this.Content = canvas;
canvas.Children.Add(grid);
```

The C# code is more verbose and thus more difficult to read and maintain. The C# code also requires a compilation step, though XAML files also have that requirement since they have code-behind and must be packaged as part of a XAP file. C# also requires a software developer to create the user interface, either by hand or by using a designer, as with Windows Forms. XAML provides a way to create user interfaces such as the login screen in a straightforward and (relatively) easy-to-maintain fashion. Markup is easier to read (at least in small doses—complex user interfaces are a different story) and has far better tool support for creating and maintaining. XAML isn't just another markup language—its strength lies in its ability to model object hierarchies and easily configure object state via attributes or child elements. Each element name (e.g., UserControl, Canvas, etc.) directly corresponds to a Silverlight object of the same name.

Let's look closer at the XAML. The root element is UserControl, a container for other controls. A UserControl on its own has no visual representation—layout controls such as Canvas and Grid combined with standard controls such as text input boxes and buttons create the visual representation. User controls provide a way to compose controls into a reusable "master" control, not unlike user controls in ASP.NET. The next chapter will take a closer look at what goes into user controls in Silverlight.

Silverlight has rich support for composing what is ultimately viewed on screen. Many controls can contain arbitrary content, such as a ListBox containing Buttons as items or even other ListBoxes! This makes composing a custom user interface possible using nothing other than markup. Since XAML is a dialect of XML, elements describing content are nested in a tree hierarchy. From the perspective of XAML, this tree is known as a *logical tree*.

■**Caution** XAML is case sensitive. Since XAML is a dialect of XML, it possesses all of the characteristics of XML. Most importantly, all element names, property names, and so on are case sensitive. Button is *not* the same as button. However, this does not necessarily apply to property values, which are handled by Silverlight's XAML parser. In the preceding example, Auto is used in one place and auto in another—this is perfectly valid.

By reading this XAML code closely, you can see that it describes a UserControl that contains a Canvas that contains a Grid that contains the various visual elements of the login screen. You can view the logical tree of these elements in Visual Studio by right-clicking the design surface and choosing Document Outline or, alternately, going to the View menu and choosing Other Windows ➤ Document Outline. This displays a window showing the logical tree of elements describing what's currently on the design surface. The document outline for the login screen is shown in Figure 2-3. This view of the logical tree is slightly different from a similar logical tree in (Windows Presentation Foundation) WPF, as the document outline focuses on what is explicitly found in the XAML. For example, if a ListBoxItem contains a Content attribute, the type-converted string is not shown. However, creating a Button as a child of a ListBoxItem will cause the Button to show up in the document outline.

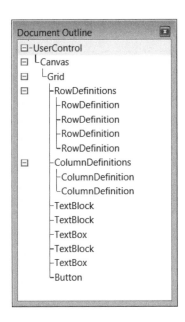

Figure 2-3. *The document outline describing the login screen*

Namespaces

There are two important namespaces that appear in the root element of each XAML file. (Expression Blend adds a couple others, but we'll look at the two most important here.) The first is the default namespace, specified by xmlns="http://schemas.microsoft.com/client/2007". This namespace contains the various elements that correspond to objects in Silverlight, such as UserControl, Canvas, and Grid. If you remove this declaration from a XAML file in Visual Studio, blue squiggly lines will show just how much is defined in this namespace.

The other namespace declaration contains Silverlight-specific extensions. Elements in this namespace are assigned to the x scope. While this is a convention, it is one that Silverlight and all Silverlight documentation follows. The most important aspects of this namespace are shown in Table 2-1.

Table 2-1. *Features of the x: Namespace*

Feature	Description
x:Class	Used to join different pieces of a partial class together. Valid syntax for this is x:Class="namespace.classname" and x:Class="namespace.classname; assembly=assemblyname". The XAML page causes generation of code to a piece of the class that combines with the code-behind.
x:Key	Provides a unique identifier to resources defined in XAML, vital for referencing resources via a markup extension. Identifiers must begin with a letter or an underscore, and can only contain letters, digits, and the underscore.
x:Name	Provides a way to give an identifier to an object element in XAML for accessing via the code-behind. This is not appropriate for use with resources (instead use x:Key). Many elements have a Name property, and while Name and x:Name can be used interchangeably, only one should be set. Identifiers must begin with a letter or an underscore, and can only contain letters, digits, and the underscore.
x:Null	Corresponds to null in C# (or Nothing in VB .NET). Can be used via a markup extension ({x:Null}) or through a property element (<x:Null/>).

Dependency Property System

The dependency property system is a significant aspect of Silverlight. It provides a way for multiple discrete sources, such as animation and data binding, to gain access to object properties. Silverlight contains approximately 50 classes that directly relate to constructing user interfaces. You can see the top classes in this hierarchy in Figure 2-4. Notice that the root of the hierarchy is DependencyObject. This root object provides much of the infrastructure needed to support the dependency property system, though it has only a few public methods. Let's look closer at what dependency properties are and then highlight a few aspects of DependencyObject that will make more sense in light of dependency properties.

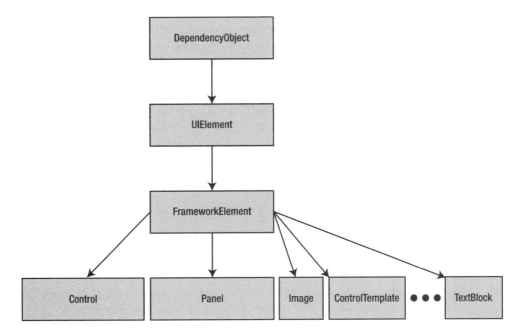

Figure 2-4. *Top portion of object hierarchy relating to visual elements*

Dependency Properties

A dependency property is a special type of property that backs a .NET property. The importance of dependency properties lies in the fact that the value depends on multiple sources (hence the name *dependency property*) and therefore, a standard .NET property is not enough. The value of a dependency property might come from data binding, animation, template resources specified in the XAML, styles, or local values. The precedence of these sources is shown in Figure 2-5.

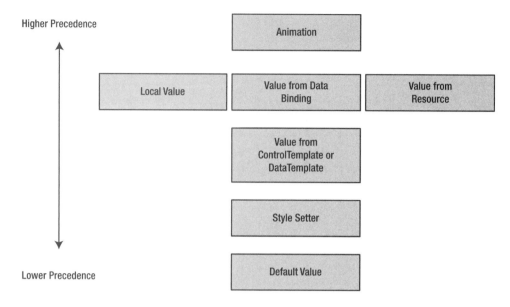

Figure 2-5. *Precedence for sources of dependency property values*

Animation has the highest precedence. Property values influenced by animation must be the values that take effect or the user will never see the animation, since a different source would trump the animation values. Local values are those set via an attribute or property element. Local values can also be set via data binding or a static resource, so these are effectively local values—thus, at equal precedence. Next lowest are values from a data template or a control template, which take effect if a local value does not override them. Styles defined in the page/application are next lowest, and if absolutely nothing is set, the dependency property takes on its default value.

■**Caution** The base value for a property is not the same as its default value. A property's base value is determined by applying the sources in the preceding precedence chart, but stopping before getting to animation. A property's default value is its value when no other sources provide a value (e.g., a layout container's constructor may establish a default value for a size property, and if this is not modified anywhere else, its value remains untouched).

Let's examine an actual dependency property, one that we have already used. The Width property, defined in the FrameworkElement class, is first defined as a dependency property, and then wrapped by a .NET property. This provides all the capability of a dependency property while providing a traditional approach to getting and setting its value. Let's examine how this particular dependency property is defined.

```
public static readonly DependencyProperty WidthProperty;
```

By convention, dependency properties end with the word `Property`, and this is adhered to throughout Silverlight. Notice that it is marked `public`—while this is also a convention, there is no compelling reason to not expose it publicly. The dependency property should be just as visible as the .NET property wrapper. The .NET property provides a shortcut, hiding the fact that there is an underlying dependency property, since it wraps the calls to `GetValue` and `SetValue`.

```
public double Width
{
   get {
      return (double) this.GetValue(WidthProperty);
   }
   set {
      base.SetValue(WidthProperty, value);
   }
}
```

Simply declaring the dependency property is not enough—it must be registered with the dependency property system using the `DependencyProperty.Register` static method. The `Register` method takes the following parameters:

```
public static DependencyProperty Register(
    string name,
    Type propertyType,
    Type ownerType,
    PropertyMetadata typeMetadata)
```

Although we won't do much with it for now, let's create a new dependency property named `TextSize` in the `LoginScreenCS.xaml.cs` file. We can add the following code to the class:

```
public static readonly DependencyProperty TextSizeProperty =
    DependencyProperty.Register("TextSize",
                                typeof(double),
                                typeof(LoginScreenCS),
                                null);
    public double TextSize
    {
        get { return ((double)this.GetValue(TextSizeProperty)); }
        set { this.SetValue(TextSizeProperty, value); }
    }
```

The name of the dependency property (passed as the first parameter to `Register`) does not need to have Property appended to it—this convention only holds for the actual field name in the class. Now you have a new dependency property that can be used for data binding or any of the other various sources that can modify dependency property values.

There is one other useful aspect to dependency properties: property change notifications. This ability to capture property changes is vital for validating a property value at the last possible moment. This is useful for scenarios such as a progress bar, where there is a clear minimum and maximum value, and values below or above these should be constrained to their respective endpoints. The final parameter to the `Register` method is where you specify a handler for the property change notification. Here's a handler for constraining the `TextSizeProperty` to no larger than 36:

```
private static void onTextSizeChanged(DependencyObject source,
                                      DependencyPropertyChangedEventArgs e)
{
    if (((double)source.GetValue(e.Property)) > 36)
    {
        source.SetValue(e.Property, 36.0);
    }
}
```

■**Note** A callback for property changes is the perfect place to validate and constrain dependency property values. It is also a great place to hold logic for modifying dependent properties, so when one changes, it affects other dependency property values of the DependencyObject that contains the properties.

The first parameter is the instance of DependencyObject—this is what you use to retrieve and set the value for the property. The Property member of the EventArgs class for this handler is then used as a parameter to GetValue and SetValue. If you try setting the value of the TextSize property to higher than 36 and then display its value, you will see it goes no higher than 36.

Attached Properties

An attached property is a special type of dependency property. Attached properties provide a way to assign values to properties on objects that do not actually have the property—the attached property values are generally used by parent objects in the element hierarchy. You have already seen several attached properties. Let's look again at the XAML code used to create header text for the login screen:

```
<TextBlock HorizontalAlignment="Center"
           Text="Please enter your information"
           Grid.Column="0" Grid.Row="0" Grid.ColumnSpan="2"/>
```

The Grid class defines several attached properties, including Column, Row, and ColumnSpan, which are used by the TextBlock object. If you look up the TextBlock object on MSDN, you won't find anything close to Grid.Row or Grid.Column properties. This is because Column, Row, and ColumnSpan are defined as attached properties on the Grid class. The Grid class defines a total of four attached properties: Column, Row, ColumnSpan, and RowSpan. The dotted syntax is used to specify the class that *does* provide these dependency properties. By using this syntax, it is possible to attach arbitrary properties to objects that do not have them. The attached properties for the Grid layout control provide a way for child elements to specify where they should be located in the grid. You can identify the attached properties by looking for an "Attached Properties" section in the MSDN documentation for a particular class. If you attempt to use a random dependency property as an attached property, the parser will throw an exception. Registering an attached property is accomplished in a similar fashion to normal dependency properties, but uses RegisterAttached instead of Register.

Dependency properties are important to many aspects of Silverlight and will be used often, generally transparently, throughout the rest of this book.

The Root of Visual Elements: DependencyObject

Any class inheriting from DependencyObject, directly or indirectly, gains the ability to interact with dependency properties. You have already seen the GetValue and SetValue methods, probably the two most important methods of DependencyObject. This root object also provides the ability to obtain the value of the property (its base value) as if no animation occurred.

Type Converters

XAML introduces type converters in order to easily support setting of complicated property values. A type converter simply converts a string representation of an object to the actual object, but allows for complex handling, such as wrapping a value in several objects. While not explicitly tied to Silverlight (or WPF or XAML), type converters are heavily used when parsing XAML. Let's take a look at the definition of the Canvas layout control in the login screen's XAML.

```
<Canvas Background="White" Width="300" Height="Auto">
```

The Background and Height properties are type-converted from a string to their actual type (so is Width—however, it's a more trivial conversion since Width is of type double and 300 is a simple parsing). If you were to create this Canvas in C#, the code would look like the following:

```
Canvas canvas = new Canvas();
canvas.Background = new SolidColorBrush(Color.FromArgb(255, 255, 255, 255));
canvas.SetValue(Canvas.WidthProperty, 300);
canvas.SetValue(Canvas.HeightProperty, Double.NaN);
```

If you had to take a guess, you might think that the Background property is backed by the Color type; however, it is actually backed by a Brush. Using a Brush for the background provides the ability to easily display solid colors, gradients, and other fancy backgrounds, thus providing much more flexibility for creating backgrounds. Brushes will be discussed in more detail in Chapter 7. Specifying the Canvas's background as an attribute in XAML is the quickest way to provide a background, and is known as *property attribute* syntax. XAML also supports *property element* syntax, which makes the fact that the Background is a Brush explicit.

```
<Canvas Width="300" Height="Auto">
    <Canvas.Background>
        <SolidColorBrush Color="White"/>
    </Canvas.Background>
</Canvas>
```

When the property appears as an element, it must take the form of object name, followed by a dot and then the property name, as in the case of Canvas.Background.

In many cases, content can also be provided via an attribute or inside an element's opening tag. Each approach is illustrated in the text labels for the username and password entry boxes. The username label uses the content attribute Text.

```
<TextBlock Text="Username:"/>
```

The password label, however, is specified as a child of the TextBox element.

```
<TextBox VerticalAlignment="Top" Grid.Column="1" Grid.Row="2">
Password:
</TextBox>
```

The content attribute syntax, much like the property attribute syntax, is a useful shorthand, both in markup and when working with the code-behind. The content element syntax, however, is required when specifying more complex content than what can be captured by a simple attribute. Also note that content might be restricted based on which control you use—for example, a TextBox cannot contain a Button as content.

Markup Extensions

A markup extension is a special syntax used to specify property values that require interpretation. This interpretation is based on which markup extension is used. A markup extension takes the format of a { followed by the markup extension name, optionally followed by parameters to the markup extension, and ending with a }. These are required to support some of the key features of Silverlight, including resources, data binding, and template binding. Each of these features will be briefly discussed here to highlight the syntax and usage of markup extensions.

■**Note** What's with the funny syntax? Markup extensions may seem strange at first, and might leave you wondering why context can't dictate how a property value is interpreted (e.g., by utilizing a type converter). Markup extensions provide a mechanism to specify more than a simple value—they stand in for more complicated processing, such as completely changing the appearance of a user interface element via a style. If you want to explicitly show something in curly braces, such as a label, you must escape it by placing an empty set of curly braces in front—for example, {}{text here}.

Static Resources

If we want to define a color object in C# once and reuse it in multiple places, we can create an instance of Color and reference it many times. XAML supports this approach via *resource dictionaries*—special sections we can add to many content elements. Any object that contains a Resources member can contain resources. Resource dictionaries are used to hold styles, templates, animation storyboards, and other useful resources. Let's revise the login screen to use a resource dictionary to specify font style information. This screen will look slightly different since the fonts are configured with different values. You can see the result in Figure 2-6. This will make it easy to change the appearance of the header and labels. Only the germane parts of the login screen code are shown here, with the new additions bolded.

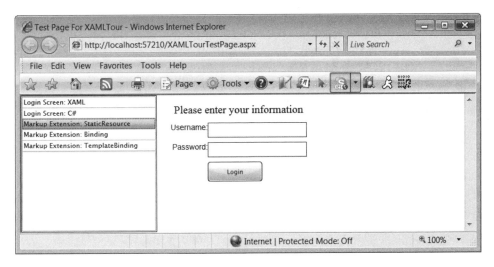

Figure 2-6. *The login screen with font properties specified by a style resource*

```
<Canvas Width="300" Height="Auto" x:Name="canvasTag">
  <Canvas.Resources>
    <Style x:Key="LoginHeaderFontStyle" TargetType="TextBlock">
      <Setter Property="FontFamily" Value="Times New Roman"/>
      <Setter Property="FontSize" Value="20"/>
    </Style>
    <Style x:Key="LoginLabelFontStyle" TargetType="TextBlock">
      <Setter Property="FontFamily" Value="Arial"/>
      <Setter Property="FontSize" Value="14"/>
    </Style>
</Canvas.Resources>
...
<TextBlock HorizontalAlignment="Center"
    Text="Please enter your information"
    Grid.Column="0" Grid.Row="0" Grid.ColumnSpan="2"
    Style="{StaticResource LoginHeaderFontStyle}"/>
...
<TextBlock HorizontalAlignment="Right" VerticalAlignment="Top"
    Text="Username:" TextWrapping="Wrap"
    Grid.Column="0" Grid.Row="1"
    Style="{StaticResource LoginLabelFontStyle}"/>
<TextBox VerticalAlignment="Top" Grid.Column="1" Grid.Row="1" x:Name="userNameTB"/>
<TextBlock HorizontalAlignment="Right" VerticalAlignment="Top"
    TextWrapping="Wrap"
    Grid.Column="0" Grid.Row="2"
    Style="{StaticResource LoginLabelFontStyle}">
  Password:
</TextBlock>
<TextBox VerticalAlignment="Top" Grid.Column="1" Grid.Row="2"/>
```

In order to reference static resources, we need a way to tell the XAML parser that we want to use a resource and which resource to use. The markup extension name for referencing a static resource is simply `StaticResource`, and it appears after the open curly brace. The `StaticResource` markup extension takes a single parameter: the name of the resource to reference.

The `x:Key` property is used to give each style a name for referencing in the markup extension. While styles will be discussed in Chapter 8, what's going on here isn't a big mystery. The `TargetType` property of the `Style` element is used to specify the object type the style is meant for, and the `Setter` elements are used to specify values for properties on this target type. In this case, we are defining two styles: one for the header text (the "Please enter your information") and the other for the labels next to the text input boxes. By changing the `LoginLabelFontStyle`, we affect both the username and password labels at the same time. This is good—it makes styling applications significantly easier both because the style information is stored in a central place and because the specific styles only need a single definition to affect potentially many elements of a user interface.

Data Binding

Data binding is a way to connect data between the user interface and a data source. It is possible to transfer data from a data source to the user interface once or each time the data changes, or to constantly keep the data source synchronized with the user interface. The markup extension controlling data binding is named `Binding` and has four possible syntaxes. Let's imagine the login screen authorizes access to an online bank. After a customer logs in, they are able to select one of their accounts to manage (and also instantly see their balance for each account), as shown in Figure 2-7.

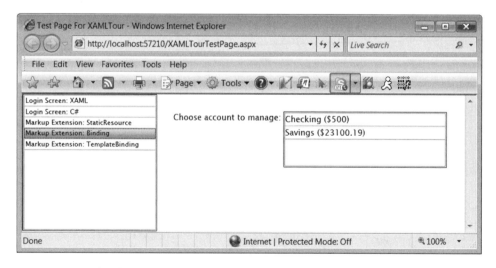

Figure 2-7. *Results of data binding Account objects to a ListBox*

Here's what a simplistic business object for account information looks like:

```
public class Account
{
    public string AccountName { get; set; }
    public double AccountBalance { get; set; }
    public Account(string n, double b)
    {
        this.AccountName = n;
        this.AccountBalance = b;
    }
}
```

Let's create a new UserControl in Visual Studio and call it ChooseAccount. You can do this by right-clicking the project in the top right and clicking Add ➤ New Item ➤ Silverlight User Control. Give it the name ChooseAccount.xaml and click OK. Edit the ChooseAccount.xaml.cs file, create a generic List containing the account type, and add a couple accounts. This will serve as a data source for the data binding.

```
private List<Account> accountList;
public ChooseAccount()
{
    // Required to initialize variables
    InitializeComponent();
    accountList = new List<Account>();
    accountList.Add(new Account("Checking", 500.00));
    accountList.Add(new Account("Savings", 23100.19));
    accountListBox.DataContext = accountList;
}
```

Notice the final line in the constructor—this is where the data source (accountList) is connected to the ListBox. The ListBox, named accountListBox, is our display control that we add to the XAML shown here. The markup extensions for data binding are bolded.

```
<UserControl
    xmlns="http://schemas.microsoft.com/client/2007"
    xmlns:x="http://schemas.microsoft.com/winfx/2006/xaml"
    x:Class="XAMLTour.ChooseAccount">
    <StackPanel Orientation="Horizontal" Margin="30 30 0 0">
        <TextBlock Text="Choose account to manage: "></TextBlock>
        <ListBox x:Name="accountListBox" Height="100" Width="300"
                    VerticalAlignment="Top" ItemsSource="{Binding Mode=OneWay}">
            <ListBox.ItemTemplate>
                <DataTemplate>
                    <StackPanel Orientation="Horizontal">
                        <TextBlock Text="{Binding AccountName}" />
                        <TextBlock Text=" ($"></TextBlock>
                        <TextBlock Text="{Binding AccountBalance}" />
                        <TextBlock Text=")"></TextBlock>
```

```
              </StackPanel>
            </DataTemplate>
          </ListBox.ItemTemplate>
        </ListBox>
      </StackPanel>
</UserControl>
```

The `Binding` markup extension used in the `ItemsSource` property specifies that the items in the ListBox are data bound, and here you can specify how the data binding works (in this case, `OneWay`, which causes data to flow only from the data source to the user interface). A `DataTemplate` is used to format the data coming from the data source, in this case by using the `Binding` markup extension to access properties on the data source (accountList). The `Binding` markup extensions used to bind to `AccountName` and `AccountBalance` treat the parent object (Account) implicitly. This is described in Table 2-2.

Table 2-2. *Data Binding Markup Extensions*

Syntax	Description
{Binding}	This signals data binding, configured with default properties (such as `OneWay` for Mode). See Chapter 5 for specific property values.
{Binding *path*}	This is used to specify specific object properties to pull data from. A dotted syntax is valid here, allowing you to drill down inside the objects from the data source.
{Binding *properties*}	This is used to set properties affecting data binding, following a *name=value* syntax. Specific properties affecting data binding will be discussed later.
{Binding *path, properties*}	The properties affect the data specified by the path. For example, a converter might be used to format data. The path must come first.

We will delve deeper into data templates and data binding in Chapter 5.

Template Binding

Using something called a *control template* along with styles provides a mechanism to completely redefine how a control appears. This is one scenario where designers and developers can work independently—the designer fleshes out how the user interface looks while the developer focuses on handling events and other logic related to the control. The `TemplateBinding` markup extension is used to connect the template to properties of the control that uses the template. Let's look at a brief example of utilizing control templates to enforce a consistent label on all buttons that use this template. Here's what the XAML looks like:

```
<UserControl
  xmlns="http://schemas.microsoft.com/client/2007"
  xmlns:x="http://schemas.microsoft.com/winfx/2006/xaml"
  x:Class="XAMLTour.TemplateBindingExample">
  <Canvas Background="White">
    <Canvas.Resources>
```

```xml
            <Style x:Key="ButtonStyle" TargetType="Button">
                <Setter Property="Template">
                    <Setter.Value>
                        <ControlTemplate TargetType="Button">
                            <StackPanel Orientation="Horizontal"
                                                   Background="Gainsboro">
                                <TextBlock Text="Label from Template: "
                                                   FontSize="16"/>
                                <ContentPresenter
                                           Content="{TemplateBinding Content}"/>
                            </StackPanel>
                        </ControlTemplate>
                    </Setter.Value>
                </Setter>
            </Style>
        </Canvas.Resources>
        <Button Style="{StaticResource ButtonStyle}" Content="I'm a Button"/>
    </Canvas>
</UserControl>
```

The template is created as a style that the button references using the StaticResource markup extension. The first TextBlock contains the label that never changes, and the ContentPresenter is used to display any content the button specifies. In this case, the content is a simple string. The TemplateBinding is used to connect a property of a control in the template to a property on the control utilizing the template. The resulting user interface for this XAML is shown in Figure 2-8.

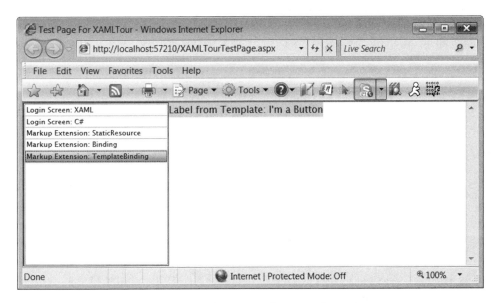

Figure 2-8. *What a Button looks like when using the ControlTemplate*

The bad news about this approach is also the good news: the Button's visual implementation is completely overridden, so if you try to click it, nothing will happen visually. Using a control template, though, provides a way to create any visual representation you want for when the mouse hovers over the button and when the mouse clicks the button. The button is still a button—it can just look drastically different from the default Silverlight button through the control template mechanism.

More About Silverlight Applications

Now that you should be comfortable with many of the new concepts Silverlight introduces, let's take a closer look at the Silverlight application that gets created. If you reveal the referenced assemblies in the Solution Explorer, you will see eight assemblies listed. These assemblies provide the majority of what you need when writing applications. Briefly, here are the important namespaces/classes in each assembly:

mscorlib: Provides the core functionality you always need, including collections, input/output, reflection, security, host interoperability, and threading. The important root namespace here is System, which includes System.Collections, System.Security, System.IO, and so on.

system: Supplements classes provided by mscorlib, such as by providing Queue and Stack classes in the System.Collections.Generic namespace.

System.Core: Contains LINQ support (in the System.Linq namespace) and cryptography support (System.Security.Cryptography).

System.Windows: Provides the bulk of what Silverlight uses, such as input-related classes in System.Windows.Input (mouse/keyboard event classes and stylus-related classes), image/video/animation-related classes in System.Windows.Media, the XAML parser in System.Windows.Markup, control classes in System.Windows.Controls, and many others. Chances are high that if you're looking for something, it's in this assembly.

System.Windows.Browser: Support classes for obtaining information about and communicating with the browser (via classes in the System.Windows.Browser namespace) and the managed host environment (via classes in System.Windows.Hosting).

System.Xml: Provides all XML-related classes (e.g., for an XML reader/writer/parser).

System.Windows.Controls: Provides many more useful controls, including Button, CheckBox, and ListBox. The System.Windows assembly has the control framework along with the layout controls and basic controls, and this assembly extends the control set of Silverlight.

System.Windows.Controls.Extended: Supplementary controls, mainly Calendar-related, extending the control set in the System.Windows.Controls namespace.

So far, you have seen several user interfaces created in XAML. Each XAML file has a corresponding code-behind file; however, there is a third file that we have not yet discussed explicitly. If you open the XAMLTour project in Visual Studio, open the LoginScreenXAML.xaml.cs file, right-click the InitializeComponent method call, and choose Go to Definition, you will be taken to the LoginScreenXAML.g.cs file. This is a generated file based on the XAML. Any objects in the XAML that have an x:Name will cause a class member to get placed in this generated file. Partial classes in C# make this assemblage of different pieces easy, as illustrated in Figure 2-9.

■Note The Name property on objects can only be set in XAML. This is most likely because the object is either created in XAML (in which case it needs a corresponding member on the class for manipulation in the code-behind) or created in code (in which case you have a reference to it that you can name and store however you like).

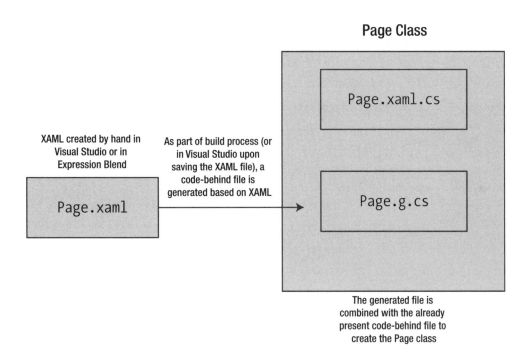

Figure 2-9. *How the full class implementation for XAML comes together*

When you create a new Silverlight application in Visual Studio or Expression Blend, you might notice an App.xaml file along with an App.xaml.cs file. The application is based on the System.Windows.Application class—it supports centralization of resources for the application, it supports several important events, and it provides a direct connection to the browser/host environment.

The code placed in the initial project includes App.xaml and App.xaml.cs files. The App.xaml file doesn't have much in it, but there is one important feature to observe:

```
<Application xmlns="http://schemas.microsoft.com/client/2007"
            xmlns:x="http://schemas.microsoft.com/winfx/2006/xaml"
            x:Class="XAMLTour.App">
    <Application.Resources>
```

```
      </Application.Resources>
</Application>
```

The `Application` class contains a `Resources` element. Any resources specified in the `Application` class can be referenced throughout a Silverlight application. This is the perfect place to put style and template resources that are available to the entire application. The UserControl is actually turned into the main user interface for the application in the code-behind file, `App.xaml.cs`, as follows:

```
public partial class App : Application
{
  public App()
  {
    this.Startup += this.Application_Startup;
    this.Exit += this.Application_Exit;
    this.UnhandledException += this.Application_UnhandledException;
    InitializeComponent();
  }
  private void Application_Startup(object sender, StartupEventArgs e)
  {
    // Load the main control
    this.RootVisual = new MainPage();
  }
  private void Application_Exit(object sender, EventArgs e)
  {
  }
  private void Application_UnhandledException(object sender,
                             ApplicationUnhandledExceptionEventArgs e)
  {
  }
}
```

The `RootVisual` property on the `Application` class specifies what will be shown when the application starts. The generated `App.xaml.cs` file also registers itself for all application-level events. The `Exit` and `UnhandledException` events come already registered with empty handler methods. The `Startup` method comes registered with a method that establishes where the main user interface comes from (`RootVisual`). This `Startup` event handler is where the connection to the `MainPage` class was established in the project code for this chapter.

These application events are the first events you've seen in this chapter. Many of the objects in Silverlight support events that can be hooked up either in the code-behind, as in the `App.xaml.cs` code, or through XAML.

Events in Silverlight

When a user clicks a button, chooses an item in a list box, or uses the cursor keys, the application must be able to respond to these events. These events are *input events*, and are actually forwarded to Silverlight by the browser hosting the Silverlight plug-in. Other events, such as the application events just shown, are defined within Silverlight itself.

Keyboard and mouse events are *routed events*. These events bubble up the tree of objects starting at the first control to receive the input event. Let's revisit the login screen and hook up a few events.

Note If you have any experience with WPF, you should be aware that there is a vital difference between WPF routed events and Silverlight routed events. Silverlight routed events *only* bubble; they do not "tunnel" as they can in WPF. This means that events are only passed up the tree (bubbling); they cannot be passed down the tree (tunneling).

```
<UserControl
    xmlns="http://schemas.microsoft.com/client/2007"
    xmlns:x="http://schemas.microsoft.com/winfx/2006/xaml"
    x:Class="XAMLTour.RoutedEventExample">
    <Canvas Background="White" x:Name="canvas"
            MouseLeftButtonDown="canvas_MouseLeftButtonDown"
            MouseLeftButtonUp="canvas_MouseLeftButtonUp">
        <Grid Height="140" Width="250" Canvas.Left="25" Canvas.Top="15"
                x:Name="grid" MouseLeftButtonDown="grid_MouseLeftButtonDown">
            <Grid.RowDefinitions>
                <RowDefinition/>
                <RowDefinition/>
                <RowDefinition/>
                <RowDefinition/>
                <RowDefinition/>
                <RowDefinition/>
            </Grid.RowDefinitions>
            <Grid.ColumnDefinitions>
                <ColumnDefinition Width="Auto"/>
                <ColumnDefinition/>
            </Grid.ColumnDefinitions>
            <TextBlock HorizontalAlignment="Center"
                    Text="Please enter your information"
                    Grid.Column="0" Grid.Row="0" Grid.ColumnSpan="2"/>
            <TextBlock Text="Username:" VerticalAlignment="Top"
                    HorizontalAlignment="Right"
                    Grid.Column="0" Grid.Row="1"/>
            <TextBox VerticalAlignment="Top" Grid.Column="1" Grid.Row="1"/>
            <TextBlock HorizontalAlignment="Right" VerticalAlignment="Top"
                    Grid.Column="0" Grid.Row="2">
            Password:
            </TextBlock>
            <TextBox VerticalAlignment="Top" Grid.Column="1" Grid.Row="2"/>
            <Button Content="Login" Grid.Row="3" Width="100" Grid.Column="1"
                    x:Name="loginButton"
```

```
              MouseLeftButtonDown="loginButton_MouseLeftButtonDown"
              HorizontalAlignment="Left"/>
      <TextBlock Grid.Row="4" Grid.ColumnSpan="2" Text=""
                                  x:Name="eventTextBlock"/>
    </Grid>
  </Canvas>
</UserControl>
```

When the mouse button is pressed, the click event starts at the lowest control that is aware of the event. For example, when the Login button is pressed, the event starts there. Look at Figure 2-10 to visualize the mouse down event bubbling up the nested controls.

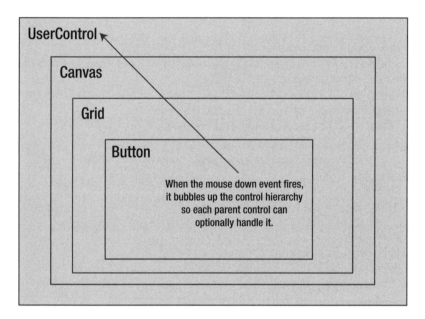

Figure 2-10. *An input event bubbling up nested controls*

The events are wired up to display which controls have received the mouse down event (which occurs when a button is initially pressed). If you hold a mouse button down on the Login button, the event originates at the button, gets sent up the tree to the enclosing Grid control, and then gets sent up again to the enclosing Canvas control. You can see the results of this in Figure 2-11. The controls receiving the event are shown beneath the Login button.

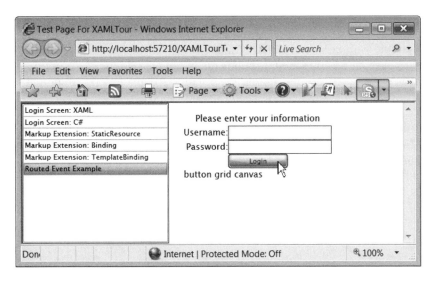

Figure 2-11. *Clicking the Login button causes the event to bubble up to the button's parents.*

If instead the mouse button is held down on one of the text entry boxes, the event originates with the Grid and is passed up to the enclosing Canvas (see Figure 2-12).

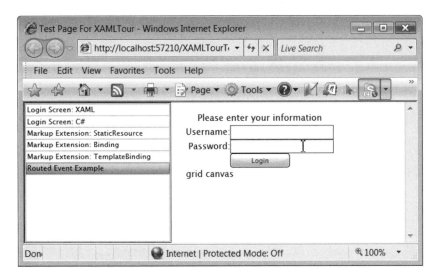

Figure 2-12. *Clicking the grid causes the event to bubble up to the grid's parent.*

If you want to mark an event as handled, you can set the Handled property on the EventArgs class to true. However, just because an event is marked as handled doesn't mean that the bubbling of the event will stop. Any event handlers on parent controls will still receive the event. Therefore, if you want to prevent processing of an event that was handled, you must check this property on the EventArgs parameter.

Summary

This chapter covered the foundations of Silverlight. Before we can explore in detail more advanced topics such as theming, animation, handling media, and data binding, it is important to understand how these core features support the rest of Silverlight. Any exploration of Silverlight starts at understanding XAML and its many features, such as dependency properties, markup extensions, and resources. This chapter also showed how a Silverlight application is structured and how routed events work in Silverlight. You are now prepared to learn more about Silverlight. The next chapter explores creating user interfaces by using the layout controls and other standard controls, some of which you have already briefly seen.

CHAPTER 3

■ ■ ■

Creating User Interfaces

Now that you've seen what XAML is all about, let's look at the basic user interface controls that Silverlight provides. Silverlight supplies *standard controls* such as text boxes for display and for user input, list boxes, check boxes, radio buttons, and others. While a standard set of controls is important for building user interfaces, even more important is how these controls are placed on a user interface. This is handled by Silverlight's *layout controls*: one that enables absolute positioning and two that allow more intelligent layouts of controls relative to each other. This chapter will conclude with some advice and examples on how you can build navigation into a Silverlight application, something not directly supported yet.

Building Blocks

Silverlight provides many useful controls for displaying information and handling data input, but before I get to the specifics of each control, it's important to understand the base functionality Silverlight provides all controls. Figure 3-1 shows an abbreviated class diagram with a subset of Silverlight's controls and panels (used for positioning objects). While there is a `Control` class, not all elements of a user interface are controls, as you can see in Figure 3-1.

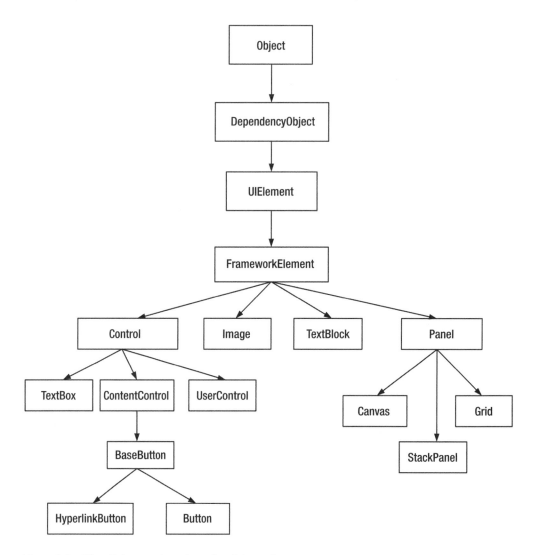

Figure 3-1. *Silverlight user interface class hierarchy*

The DependencyObject class provides the functionality for interacting with the dependency property system. The next class, UIElement, is the sign that a class has a visual appearance. The FrameworkElement class provides some interesting behavior such as data binding, but the only requirement for a visual appearance is a class must inherit (directly or indirectly) from UIElement. Chapter 7 will detail some classes that inherit from UIElement but not FrameworkElement. Let's start at the top of this class hierarchy so you can see just what functionality is provided by each class before getting to panels and controls.

DependencyObject

The DependencyObject class is arguably the most important class in Silverlight. This object enables the dependency property system. In the last chapter, you saw what dependency properties are and how to create them. The piece left out, however, is what enables the setting and reading of these properties. Any class that inherits directly or indirectly from DependencyObject can participate in Silverlight's dependency property system. Its most important features are the methods it provides, shown in Table 3-1.

Table 3-1. *Methods of the System.Windows.DependencyObject Class*

Method	Description
CheckAccess	Returns true if the calling thread has access to this object.
ClearValue	Removes the local value of the specified dependency property. The property might take on its default value or a value from another source.
GetAnimationBaseValue	Gets the value of the specified dependency property as if no animation were applied.
GetValue	Returns the current value of the specified dependency property.
ReadLocalValue	Returns the local value of the specified dependency property or the special value UnsetValue if the property does not have a local value.
SetValue	Sets the value of the specified dependency property.

THREADING AND THE USER INTERFACE

Silverlight is a multithreaded environment. You can't modify elements of a user interface from a non-user interface thread since it can lead to a number of problems. The proper way to modify a user interface from a different thread is by using a dispatcher. The DependencyObject class provides a single property, Dispatcher, which holds a reference to the associated dispatcher. If you want to set the value of a text block from a different thread, you must use Dispatcher.BeginInvoke to queue the modification on the main thread's work items queue like this:

```
Dispatcher.BeginInvoke(delegate() { textBlock.Text = "changed"; });
```

You'll get a closer look at threading in Silverlight in Chapter 14.

UIElement

The UIElement class is the next class you encounter as you walk down the inheritance hierarchy. This class forms the base for all classes that have the ability to draw themselves on a user interface, including input handling, focus support, and basic layout support. Table 3-2 lists the methods of this class.

Table 3-2. *Methods of the System.Windows.UIElement Class*

Method	Description
Arrange	Positions objects contained by this visual element. Invoked by the layout system.
CaptureMouse	Sends mouse input to the object even when the mouse pointer is not within its bounding box. Useful for drag-and-drop scenarios. Only one UIElement can have the mouse captured at a time.
HitTest	Returns an IEnumerable<UIElement> collection of UIElement objects that are considered "hit" by a specified point or rectangle. The enumeration is ordered by descending Z-order, so you generally only need the first object.
InvalidateArrange	Causes UIElement to update its layout.
Measure	Sets the DesiredSize property for layout purposes. Invoked by the layout system.
OnCreateAutomationPeer	Implemented by inheritors that participate in the automation system. Returns an AutomationPeer object.
ReleaseMouseCapture	Removes the mouse capture obtained via CaptureMouse.
TransformToVisual	Returns a GeneralTransform that is used to transform coordinates from this UIElement to the object passed in.
UpdateLayout	Ensures all child objects are updated for layout. Invoked by the layout system.

The properties of UIElement are shown in Table 3-3.

Table 3-3. *Properties of the System.Windows.UIElement Class*

Property	Type	Description
Clip	Geometry	Defines a clipping region to for the UIElement.
DesiredSize	Size	Indicates the size of the UIElement as determined by the measure pass, which is important for layout. RenderSize provides the actual size of the UIElement.
IsHitTestVisible	bool	Gets or sets whether UIElement can participate in hit testing.
Opacity	double	Specifies the opacity/transparency of the UIElement. The default value is 1.0, corresponding to full opacity. Setting this to 0.0 causes the UIElement to disappear visually, but it can still respond to hit testing.
OpacityMask	Brush	Uses a brush to apply opacity to the UIElement. This only uses the alpha component of a brush. Do not use a video brush for this property due to lack of an alpha component.
RenderSize	Size	Indicates the actual size of the UIElement after it has passed through the layout system.
RenderTransform	Transform	Applies a transform to the rendering position of this UIElement. The default rendering offset is (0,0)—the top left of the UIElement.
RenderTransformOrigin	Point	Gets or sets the render transform origin. Defaults to (0,0) if not specified. This can be used to translate the UIElement.

Property	Type	Description
Visibility	Visibility	Gets or sets the visibility state of the UIElement. Set this to Visibility.Collapsed to hide the UIElement (it does not participate in layout, is removed from the tab order, and is not hit testable). Set this to Visibility.Visible to restore the UIElement's position in its container.

UIElement also defines several important events, shown in Table 3-4.

Table 3-4. *Events of the System.Windows.UIElement Class*

Event	Description
GotFocus	Fires when the UIElement gains focus, if it doesn't already have it. Event args class: RoutedEventHandler.
KeyDown	Fires when a key is pressed. This event will bubble up to the root container. Event args class: KeyEventHandler.
KeyUp	Fires when a key is released. This event also bubbles. Event args class: KeyEventHandler.
LostFocus	Fires when the UIElement loses focus. This event bubbles. Event args class: RoutedEventHandler.
MouseEnter	Fires if the mouse pointer is in motion and enters the UIElement's bounding box. A parent UIElement, if it also handles this event, will receive the event before any children. Event args class: MouseEventHandler.
MouseLeave	Fires when the mouse pointer leaves the UIElement's bounding box. Event args class: MouseEventHandler; however, the information provided in the event args is without meaning since the mouse has left the UIElement's bounds.
MouseLeftButtonDown	Fires when the mouse's left button is pressed down while the mouse pointer is within the bounds of the UIElement. Event args class: MouseButtonEventHandler.
MouseLeftButtonUp	Fires when the mouse's left button is released while the mouse pointer is within the bounds of the UIElement. Event args class: MouseButtonEventHandler.
MouseMove	Fires each time the mouse pointer moves within the bounds of the UIElement. This event bubbles. Event args class: MouseEventHandler.

FrameworkElement

The next class, FrameworkElement, adds to the support introduced by UIElement. This class extends the layout support, introduces object lifetime events (such as when a FrameworkElement is loaded), and provides data binding support. This class forms the direct base of Panel and Control, the base classes for object positioning support and most controls. Its methods are shown in Table 3-5.

Table 3-5. *Methods of the System.Windows.FrameworkElement Class*

Method	Description
FindName	Searches the object tree, both up and down relative to the current FrameworkElement, for the object with the specified name (x:Name in XAML). Returns null if the object was not found.
SetBinding	Binds a specified dependency property to a System.Windows.Data.Binding instance.

An abbreviated list of FrameworkElement's properties is shown in Table 3-6.

Table 3-6. *Properties of the System.Windows.FrameworkElement Class*

Property	Type	Description
ActualWidth	double	Indicates the width of the FrameworkElement after rendering.
ActualHeight	double	Indicates the height of the FrameworkElement after rendering.
Cursor	System.Windows. Input.Cursor	Gets/sets the cursor that is shown when mouse hovers over this element. Possible values (from the Cursors type): Arrow, Eraser, Hand, IBeam, None (invisible cursor), SizeNS, SizeWE, Stylus, Wait. Set to null to revert to default behavior.
DataContext	Object	Defines context (source of data) used in data binding.
Height	double	Indicates the asked-for height of the FrameworkElement.
HorizontalAlignment	HorizontalAlignment	Gets/sets the horizontal alignment. Behavior of this property is deferred to the layout control hosting this FrameworkElement. Possible values: Left, Center, Right, Stretch (default: fills the entire layout slot).
Language	System.Windows. Markup.XmlLanguage	Specifies localization/globalization language used by this FrameworkElement. Consult the XmlLanguage class documentation and RFC 3066 for details.
Margin	Thickness	Gets/sets the outer margin of this FrameworkElement.
Name	String	Gets the name of the FrameworkElement. When set in XAML, corresponds to the name of the variable automatically generated.
Resources	ResourceDictionary	Returns the resource dictionary defined on this FrameworkElement.
Style	Style	Gets/sets the style applied during rendering of this FrameworkElement.
Tag	Object	Places arbitrary information on a FrameworkElement. Restricted to the string type, although defined as an object.

Property	Type	Description
VerticalAlignment	VerticalAlignment	Gets/sets the vertical alignment. Behavior is subject to the container that has this control. Possible values: Top, Center, Bottom, Stretch (default).
Width	double	Indicates the asked-for width of the FrameworkElement.

Events of FrameworkElement are shown in Table 3-7.

Table 3-7. *Events of the System.Windows.FrameworkElement Class*

Event	Description
BindingValidationError	Fires when a data validation error occurs as part of data binding. Event args class: ValidationErrorEventArgs.
LayoutUpdated	Fires when the layout of the FrameworkElement is updated. Event args type: EventArgs (this is a CLR event).
Loaded	Fires when the layout is complete and element is ready for interaction. Event args type: RoutedEventHandler.
SizeChanged	Fires when the ActualWidth or ActualHeight properties are updated by the layout system. Event args type: SizeChangedEventHandler.

Positioning Objects on Screen

Having a variety of controls and other visual objects gives us the raw material for user interfaces, but in order to form a full user interface, these objects must be positioned on screen. This is accomplished via the Panel class—the base class of layout containers.

A layout container is used to contain controls and to oversee positioning of these controls on a user interface. In ASP.NET, layout of controls on a web page results from the application of styles to HTML tags that contain ASP.NET controls. In Windows Forms, layout is accomplished via absolute positioning: there is no layout control; instead, controls specify their position and size. Silverlight strikes a balance between these two approaches, providing a layout control that works in conjunction with properties of its children controls (such as size properties). Silverlight provides three layout controls: the Canvas, the Grid, and the StackPanel. The Canvas provides the ability to absolutely position child elements, much like in Windows Forms. The Grid provides support for laying controls out in a tabular configuration with rows and columns. The StackPanel displays its child controls one next to the other, either in a horizontal or vertical orientation. Layout controls can be nested, so by combining multiple controls together you can assemble some sophisticated user interfaces.

Canvas

The Canvas provides the ability to absolutely position elements. Controls that are added directly to a Canvas can use the `Canvas.Left` and `Canvas.Top` attached properties to specify where they should appear on the canvas. Figure 3-2 depicts several controls placed on a canvas, including a nested canvas.

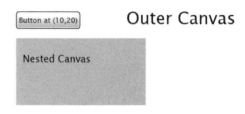

Figure 3-2. *The Canvas panel*

The XAML for this screen looks like this:

```
<UserControl x:Class="chapter3.CanvasPanel"
    xmlns="http://schemas.microsoft.com/winfx/2006/xaml/presentation"
    xmlns:x="http://schemas.microsoft.com/winfx/2006/xaml"
    Width="400" Height="300">
    <Canvas x:Name="LayoutRoot" Background="White">
        <Button Canvas.Left="10" Canvas.Top="20" Content="Button at (10,20)"/>
        <TextBlock Text="Outer Canvas" Canvas.Left="180" Canvas.Top="10"
          FontSize="26"/>
        <Canvas Canvas.Top="60" Canvas.Left="10" Background="LightSkyBlue"
                    Width="200" Height="100">
            <TextBlock Text="Nested Canvas" Canvas.Left="10" Canvas.Top="20"/>
        </Canvas>
    </Canvas>
</UserControl>
```

StackPanel

A StackPanel stacks visual objects next to each other, either horizontally or vertically. The `Orientation` property of the StackPanel can be set to `Vertical` (the default) or `Horizontal`. Figure 3-3 shows stacking a label next to a text entry box in a horizontal orientation.

Enter user id: [   ]

Figure 3-3. *The StackPanel*

Here's the XAML for this control:

```
<StackPanel x:Name="LayoutRoot" Background="White" Orientation="Horizontal">
    <TextBlock Text="Enter user id: "/>
    <TextBox Width="200" Height="20" VerticalAlignment="Top"/>
</StackPanel>
```

Grid

The Grid is the most complicated (relatively) and most capable layout container. It consists of one or more rows and one or more columns. Let's look at the XAML for a simple grid consisting of two rows and two columns:

```
<Grid x:Name="LayoutRoot" Background="White">
    <Grid.ColumnDefinitions>
        <ColumnDefinition/>
        <ColumnDefinition/>
    </Grid.ColumnDefinitions>
    <Grid.RowDefinitions>
        <RowDefinition/>
        <RowDefinition/>
    </Grid.RowDefinitions>
</Grid>
```

Four attached properties control where in the grid content is placed. These attached properties are shown in Table 3-8.

Table 3-8. *Properties of the System.Windows.Controls.Control Class*

Property	Type	Description
Grid.Row	Int32	The row of the grid where content is placed. The first row is index 0. The default value is 0.
Grid.Column	Int32	The column of the grid where content is placed. The first column is 0. The default value is 0.
Grid.RowSpan	Int32	The number of rows the content will occupy. The default value is 1.
Grid.ColumnSpan	Int32	The number of columns the content will occupy. The default value is 1.

Placing content within a grid is a simple matter of creating content and then setting values for the various attached properties. Figure 3-4 shows the result of placing content in each column of the first row and then using RowSpan to cause the content to fill the second row.

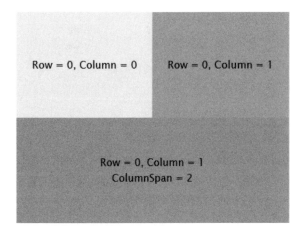

Figure 3-4. *The Grid panel*

■**Note** There is an attribute called ShowGridLines that you can set to true on the Grid element to visibly see where the columns and rows are. This is incredibly useful when designing the Grid; however, the grid lines aren't especially good looking. You should only use this for designing/debugging grids. If you want grid lines, look to the Border control.

Here's what the XAML looks like to create what's shown in Figure 3-4.

```
<Border Grid.Row="0" Grid.Column="0" Background="Beige">
    <TextBlock HorizontalAlignment="Center" VerticalAlignment="Center"
                    Text="Row = 0, Column = 0"/>
</Border>
<Border Grid.Row="0" Grid.Column="1" Background="BurlyWood">
    <TextBlock HorizontalAlignment="Center" VerticalAlignment="Center"
                    Text="Row = 0, Column = 1"/>
</Border>
<Border Grid.Row="1" Grid.Column="0" Grid.ColumnSpan="2" Background="DarkKhaki">
    <StackPanel HorizontalAlignment="Center" VerticalAlignment="Center" >
        <TextBlock Text="Row = 0, Column = 1"/>
        <TextBlock HorizontalAlignment="Center" Text="ColumnSpan = 2"/>
    </StackPanel>
</Border>
```

The ColumnDefinition class has a property named Width that allows you to set the width of the column. Likewise, the RowDefinition class has a property named Height. These properties are of type GridLength, a special class that provides capabilities beyond a simple double value representing size. In XAML, the Width and Height properties can be set to the special value Auto. The Auto value causes the row/column to size automatically to the largest piece of content. More sophisticated control over space is provided by something known as *star sizing*.

The Width and Height properties can be set to the special value * or a "star" with a number in front, such as 2* or 3*. This syntax gives a proportional amount of the available space to a row or a column. Figure 3-5 shows a grid with a single row and two columns given the star sizes * and 2*.

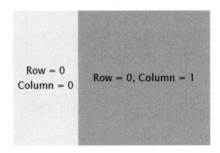

Figure 3-5. *Using star sizing with a Grid*

The XAML to create this grid looks like this:

```xml
<UserControl x:Class="chapter3.BasicStarSizing"
    xmlns="http://schemas.microsoft.com/winfx/2006/xaml/presentation"
    xmlns:x="http://schemas.microsoft.com/winfx/2006/xaml"
    Width="300" Height="200">
    <Grid x:Name="LayoutRoot" Background="White">
        <Grid.ColumnDefinitions>
            <ColumnDefinition Width="*"/>
            <ColumnDefinition Width="2*"/>
        </Grid.ColumnDefinitions>
        <Grid.RowDefinitions>
            <RowDefinition/>
        </Grid.RowDefinitions>
        <Border Grid.Row="0" Grid.Column="0" Background="Beige">
            <StackPanel HorizontalAlignment="Center" VerticalAlignment="Center">
                <TextBlock HorizontalAlignment="Center" Text="Row = 0"/>
                <TextBlock HorizontalAlignment="Center" Text="Column = 0"/>
            </StackPanel>
        </Border>
        <Border Grid.Row="0" Grid.Column="1" Background="BurlyWood">
            <TextBlock HorizontalAlignment="Center"
                    VerticalAlignment="Center" Text="Row = 0, Column = 1"/>
        </Border>
    </Grid>
</UserControl>
```

The total width of the grid is 300. The second column is twice as big as the first, specified by the 2* property value for the width. If no number is specified before the star, it is treated the same as if the value were 1*. In this case, the first column is 100 since the second column is twice as big, and 200 added to 100 gives the total width of the grid, 300. If you combine the other sizing methods with star sizing, the value of 1* will equal whatever space is available.

Customizing Silverlight Controls

The System.Windows.Controls.Control class forms the base of many controls in the complete Silverlight control set. This class provides properties for setting the background and foreground of a control, configuring the appearance of text within the control, and enabling control templating (something we will look at in Chapter 8). The specific properties the Control class introduces are shown in Table 3-9.

Table 3-9. *Properties of the System.Windows.Controls.Control Class*

Property	Type	Description
Background	Brush	Gets/sets the current brush used to paint the background of the control.
BorderBrush	Brush	Gets/sets the brush used to draw the border of the control.
BorderThickness	Thickness	Gets/sets the thickness of the control's border.
FontFamily	FontFamily	Indicates the font used for the text shown in the control.
FontSize	double	Gets/sets font size of the text shown in control. Defaults to 11 pt.
FontStretch	FontStretch	Gets/sets font compression/expansion for fonts that support it.
FontStyle	FontStyle	Gets/sets the font style. Possible values: Normal (default) and Italic.
FontWeight	FontWeight	Gets/sets thickness of font. Possible values range from Thin (100) to ExtraBlack (950). The default is Normal (400).
Foreground	Brush	Gets/sets the brush used to draw the foreground of the control.
IsTabStop	bool	Gets/sets whether control participates in tab order.
Padding	Thickness	Gets/sets the space between the content of the control and its border or margin (if no border).
TabIndex	Int32	Gets/sets the position of the control in the tab order. Lower numbers are encountered first in the tab order.
TabNavigation	KeyboardNavigationMode	Controls how tabbing with this control works. Possible values: Local (default), None, Cycle.
Template	Template	Gets/sets the control template used for the visual appearance of this control.

ContentControl

Many controls can define their content by using other controls. This provides an amazing degree of flexibility over how you construct user interfaces. One place where this is useful is in the ListBox control, where the items of the list box can be anything you can construct in XAML using controls. The controls that support this capability inherit from System.Windows.Controls. ContentControl. You can tell immediately that a specific control inherits from ContentControl by noticing it has a Content property in the IntelliSense window. The properties of ContentControl are shown in Table 3-10.

Table 3-10. *Properties of the System.Windows.Controls.Primitives.ContentControl Class*

Property	Type	Description
Content	Object	Gets/sets the content control. This is generally set to a Panel-based class, though can be set to any UIElement-based class.
ContentTemplate	DateTemplate	Gets/sets the data template for this content control, used for data binding.
TextAlignment	TextAlignment	Gets/sets the text alignment used for this control. Possible values: Left (default), Center, Right.
TextDecorations	TextDecorationCollection	Gets/sets the decorations applied to text for this control. Possible values: Underline or null (default; corresponds to no decorations).
TextWrapping	TextWrapping	Gets/sets how text wraps when it reaches the width of the control. Possible values: NoWrap (default), Wrap.

The controls that inherit from ContentControl are ListBoxItem, ButtonBase, ScrollViewer, TabItem, DataGridCell, DataGridColumnHeader, and DataGridRowHeader.

Border

The Border control is used to surround content with a border. It also provides the ability to easily add a background to a smaller part of a user interface. Its properties are shown in Table 3-11.

Table 3-11. *Properties of the System.Windows.Controls.Primitives.ButtonBase Class*

Property	Type	Description
Background	Brush	Gets/sets the brush used to paint the background.
BorderBrush	Brush	Gets/sets the brush used to paint the border.
BorderThickness	Thickness	Gets/sets the thickness of the border.
Child	UIElement	Indicates the single child that the border is drawn around.
CornerRadius	CornerRadius	Gets/sets the degree of rounding used for each corner. Set to a single value to apply a uniform rounding for all corners.
Padding	Thickness	Defines the space between the child content and the border.

Figure 3-6 shows the Border control used in various ways.

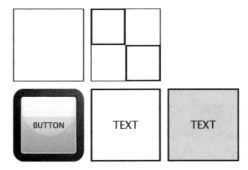

Figure 3-6. *The Border control*

The fanciest border uses a gradient brush and contains a button. We'll take a closer look at brushes in a later chapter. Here's what the XAML looks like. The Border control can contain a single child element that forms the child content of the control, and in this case it is a button.

```
<Border BorderThickness="10" Width="100" Height="100" CornerRadius="10">
    <Border.BorderBrush>
        <LinearGradientBrush StartPoint="0,1" EndPoint="1,0">
            <GradientStop Color="#FF000000" Offset="0"/>
            <GradientStop Color="#FFFFF0000" Offset="1"/>
        </LinearGradientBrush>
    </Border.BorderBrush>
    <Button Content="BUTTON"></Button>
</Border>
```

The Button Controls

Many specialized versions of buttons exist, all inheriting directly or indirectly from the ButtonBase class (in the System.Windows.Controls.Primitives namespace). The ButtonBase class provides the basic pressing behavior that is common to all buttons. Its properties are shown in Table 3-12.

Table 3-12. *Properties of the System.Windows.Controls.Primitives.ButtonBase Class*

Property	Type	Description
ClickMode	ClickMode	Controls how the mouse triggers the Click event. Possible values: Hover (when the mouse moves over the button); Press (the left mouse button is pressed down); Release (the left mouse button is released while over the button). Defaults to Release.
IsFocused	bool	True if this button has focus, false otherwise.
IsMouseOver	bool	True if the mouse pointer is hovering over this button, false otherwise.
IsPressed	bool	True if the button is in a pressed state, false otherwise.

The ButtonBase class provides a single event, Click (event args class: RoutedEventHandler). Figure 3-7 shows what various buttons look like by default.

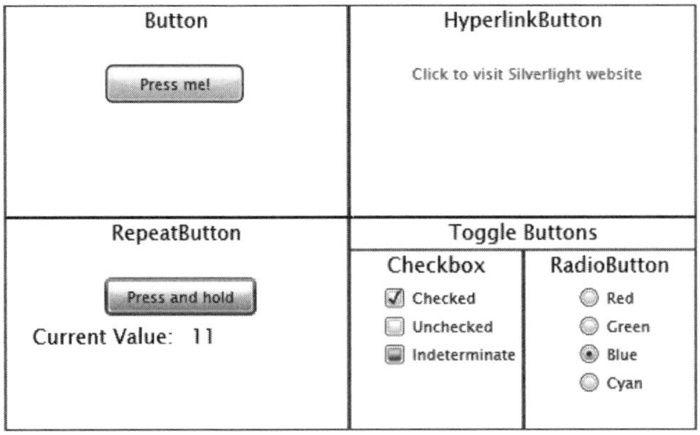

Figure 3-7. *Collection of different button controls*

Button

The Button control provides basic button functionality. Its implementation is completely supplied by the base class, BaseButton. Here's a basic button in XAML where the content is set to text:

```
<Button Canvas.Left="74" Canvas.Top="20" Width="100"
              Content="Press me!" x:Name="button" Click="button_Click" />
```

HyperlinkButton

The HyperlinkButton control introduces the capability to cause the browser to navigate to a specific web site when it is clicked. The new properties provided by the HyperlinkButton class are shown in Table 3-13.

Table 3-13. *Properties of the System.Windows.Controls.HyperlinkButton Class*

Property	Type	Description
NavigateUri	Uri	Gets/sets the URI to navigate to
TargetName	String	Gets/sets the name of target window/frame where navigation happens

Here's the XAML for the hyperlink button shown in Figure 3-7:

```
<HyperlinkButton x:Name="hyperlinkButton" Canvas.Left="45" Canvas.Top="20"
                     Width="200" Content="Click to visit Silverlight website"
                     NavigateUri="http://www.silverlight.net"
                     TargetName="_new"/>
```

RepeatButton

The functionality introduced by a RepeatButton is the repeated firing of the Click event for as long as the button is clicked. You can set several properties to control how the Click event fires, and these are shown in Table 3-14.

Table 3-14. *Properties of the System.Windows.Controls.Primitives.RepeatButton Class*

Property	Type	Description
Delay	Int32	Number of milliseconds before the click action repeats, after the button is initially pressed. The default is 250.
Interval	Int32	Number of milliseconds between repeated Click events, after repeating starts. The default is 250.

Here's the XAML for the repeat button shown in Figure 3-7:

```
<RepeatButton Canvas.Left="73" Canvas.Top="20" Width="110"
                       Content="Press and hold" Click="RepeatButton_Click"/>
```

An event handler shows the current value increment as the button is held down.

```
private int currentValue = 0;
private void RepeatButton_Click(object sender, RoutedEventArgs e)
{
    currentValue++;
    repeatButtonValue.Text = currentValue.ToString();
}
```

Toggle Buttons: CheckBox and RadioButton

The ToggleButton provides the base functionality for both radio buttons and check boxes, controls that can switch states. Its properties are shown in Table 3-15.

Table 3-15. *Properties of the System.Windows.Controls.Primitives.ToggleButton Class*

Property	Type	Description
IsChecked	Nullable<bool>	Indicates true if checked, false if not, and null if in an indeterminate state. If IsThreeState is set to true, the user can cause this property's value to cycle between true/false/null.
IsThreeState	bool	Gets/sets whether the control supports three states. If false, the button supports only two states.

The ToggleButton class introduces three new events, Checked, Unchecked, and Indeterminate. These events use RoutedEventArgs as the event argument type and capture the various states a ToggleButton can switch into. The two classes that inherit from ToggleButton are CheckBox and RadioButton. The main distinguishing factor between check boxes and radio buttons is that radio buttons can be grouped, so only one specific radio button within a group can be selected at any given moment. The properties of RadioButton are shown in Table 3-16. If no group is specified, all ungrouped radio buttons within a single parent control become part of the same group.

Table 3-16. *Properties of the System.Windows.Controls.Primitives.RadioButton Class*

Property	Type	Description
GroupName	string	Gets/sets the name of the group this radio button belongs to

Here's the XAML for the check boxes shown in Figure 3-7:

```
<CheckBox x:Name="checkBox" Canvas.Left="25" Canvas.Top="20"
                IsChecked="True" Content="Checked"/>
<CheckBox x:Name="checkBox2" Canvas.Left="25" Canvas.Top="40"
                IsChecked="False"  Content="Unchecked"/>
<CheckBox x:Name="checkBox3" Canvas.Left="25" Canvas.Top="60"
                IsChecked="" IsThreeState="True" Content="Indeterminate"/>
```

The radio buttons are given unique names, but they share the group name to ensure the mutual exclusion functionality.

```
<RadioButton x:Name="radioButton1" GroupName="group1"
                Canvas.Left="40" Canvas.Top="20" Content="Red"/>
<RadioButton x:Name="radioButton2" GroupName="group1"
                Canvas.Left="40" Canvas.Top="40" Content="Green"/>
<RadioButton x:Name="radioButton3" GroupName="group1"
                Canvas.Left="40" Canvas.Top="60" Content="Blue"/>
<RadioButton x:Name="radioButton4" GroupName="group1"
                Canvas.Left="40" Canvas.Top="80" Content="Cyan"/>
```

TextBlock

The TextBlock control is used to display text on a user interface. This directly compares to the label controls in both Windows Forms and ASP.NET. Its properties are shown in Table 3-17.

Table 3-17. *Properties of the System.Windows.Controls.TextBlock Class*

Property	Type	Description
FontFamily	FontFamily	Gets/sets the set of font families. Each specified after the first is a fallback font in case a previous font is not available. Defaults to "Portable User Interface," which encompasses several fonts in order to render the range of international language possibilities.
FontSize	double	Gets/sets the desired font size in pixels. Defaults to 14.666 (11 pt).
FontSource	FontSource	Gets/sets the font used to render text.
FontStretch	FontStretch	Gets/sets the degree to which a font is stretched. Possible values are from the usWidthClass definition in the OpenType specification.

Continued

Table 3-17. *Continued*

Property	Type	Description
FontStyle	FontStyle	Gets/sets the font style used for rendering text. Possible values: Normal (default) and Italic.
FontWeight	FontWeight	Gets/sets the desired font weight. Possible values are from the usWeightClass definition in the OpenType specification.
Foreground	Brush	Gets/sets the brush to apply to the text.
Inlines	InlineCollection	Gets/sets the collection of inline elements, such as Run and LineBreak, to render.
LineHeight	double	Specifies the height of a line of text in pixels. This property is only used when the LineStackingStrategy is set to BlockLineHeight.
LineStackingStrategy	LineStackingStrategy	Specifies how each line of text is stacked. Possible values: MaxHeight (maximum height of an element within the line dictates height of line) and BlockLineHeight (maximum height controlled by the LineHeight property).
Padding	Thickness	Gets/sets the amount of space between the border of the content area and the text.
Text	string	Gets/sets the text to display.
TextAlignment	TextAlignment	Gets/sets horizontal alignment of text. Possible values: Left, Center, Right.
TextDecorations	TextDecorationCollection	Gets/sets the set of decorations to apply to the text. Currently the only decoration available is Underline.
TextWrapping	TextWrapping	Controls how text wraps when it reaches the edge of its content area. Possible values: Wrap and NoWrap.

The TextBlock control can contain inline elements, providing an alternative way to piece text together. This approach is most useful when you want to apply specific font styles, such as different colors or sizes, to elements of a larger set of text. Figure 3-8 shows several uses of the TextBlock control.

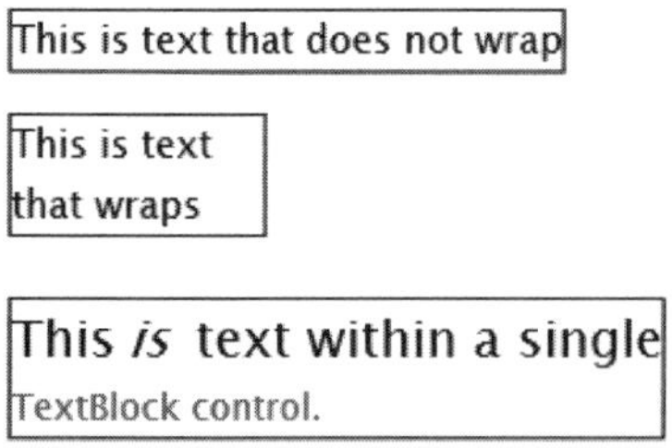

Figure 3-8. *The TextBlock control*

Here's the XAML used for each of the TextBlock controls shown in Figure 3-8, including one where the TextBlock contains multiple inline elements:

```
<Border BorderBrush="Black" BorderThickness="1" Canvas.Left="20" Canvas.Top="20">
    <TextBlock Text="This is text that does not wrap"/>
</Border>
<Border BorderBrush="Black" BorderThickness="1" Canvas.Left="20" Canvas.Top="60">
    <TextBlock Text="This is text that wraps" TextWrapping="Wrap" Width="100"/>
</Border>
<Border BorderBrush="Black" BorderThickness="1" Canvas.Left="20" Canvas.Top="130">
    <TextBlock>
        <Run FontSize="20" Text="This"/>
        <Run FontSize="20" FontStyle="Italic" Text="is "/>
        <Run FontSize="20" Text="text within a single"/>
        <LineBreak/>
        <Run Foreground="Red" FontSize="14" Text="TextBlock control."/>
    </TextBlock>
</Border>
```

TextBox

The TextBox control is used to get free-form text-based information from a user. It provides single line and multiline input and the ability to let the user select text. Its properties are shown in Table 3-18.

Table 3-18. *Properties of the System.Windows.Controls.TextBox Class*

Property	Type	Description
AcceptsReturn	bool	Indicates true if text box accepts/interprets newline characters. False otherwise.
FontSource	FontSource	Defines the font used for text within the text box.
HorizontalScrollBarVisibility	ScrollBarVisibility	Controls how/when the horizontal scrollbar is displayed. Possible values: Disabled (scrollbar never appears); Auto (scrollbar appears when content cannot fully be displayed within the bounds); Hidden (like Disabled, but the dimension of the content is not set to the viewport's size); and Visible (scrollbar is always visible).
IsReadOnly	bool	Indicates no edits from the user are allowed if true. Defaults to false.
MaxLength	Int32	Defines the maximum number of characters that can be entered into a text box. The default is 0 (no restriction).

Continued

Table 3-18. *Continued*

Property	Type	Description
SelectedText	string	Gets the currently highlighted text. If set, the highlighted text is replaced with the new string. Any change (including programmatic) causes the SelectionChanged event to fire.
SelectionBackground	Brush	Specifies the brush used to paint background of selected text.
SelectionForeground	Brush	Specifies the brush used to paint the text within the selection.
SelectionLength	Int32	Defines the number of characters currently selected, or zero if there is no selection.
SelectionStart	Int32	Specifies the index where the selected text begins within the text of the text box.
Text	string	Defines the text currently stored in the text box.
TextAlignment	TextAlignment	Gets/sets alignment of text within a text box. Possible values: Left, Center, Right.
TextWrapping	TextWrapping	Controls whether text wraps when it reaches the edge of the text box. Possible values: Wrap, NoWrap.
VerticalScrollBarVisibility	ScrollBarVisibility	Controls how/when a vertical scrollbar is displayed. See HorizontalScrollBarVisibility for possible values.

A single line and multiline TextBox control with scrollbars is shown in Figure 3-9. Note that for scrollbars to appear on a TextBox, the AcceptsReturn property must be set to true.

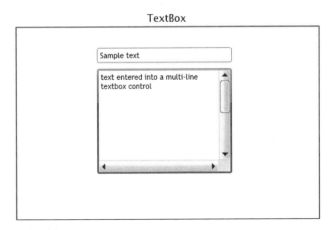

Figure 3-9. *The TextBox control*

Here's the corresponding XAML:

```
<TextBox Canvas.Top="30" Canvas.Left="120" Width="200"/>
<TextBox Canvas.Top="60" Canvas.Left="120" Height="150" Width="200"
                AcceptsReturn="True" HorizontalScrollBarVisibility="Visible"
                VerticalScrollBarVisibility="Visible"/>
```

ItemsControl

Certain controls provide the ability to present a set of content as individual items. Currently, these controls are the ListBox and TabControl. The base class that provides the item handling behavior is ItemsControl. Its properties are shown in Table 3-19.

Table 3-19. *Properties of the System.Windows.Controls.ItemsControl Class*

Property	Type	Description
DisplayMemberPath	string	Gets/sets the path to the property on the source object to display.
Items	ItemCollection	Defines a collection of items to display if this is nonnull.
ItemsPanel	ItemsPanelTemplate	Specifies the panel to use for displaying items. Defaults to an ItemsPanelTemplate that uses a StackPanel.
ItemsSource	IEnumerable	Similar to Items, provides the set of items to display, but provides more flexibility since any IEnumerable can be used.
ItemTemplate	DataTemplate	Specifies the data template used to display items. Used with data binding.

ListBox

The ListBox control provides a way to display one or more items and allows the user to select among them. Its properties are shown in Table 3-20.

Table 3-20. *Properties of the System.Windows.Controls.ListBox Class*

Property	Type	Description
ItemContainerStyle	Style	Gets/sets the style applied to the container for the list box's items
SelectedIndex	Int32	Indicates the index of first selected item, or -1 if no items are selected
SelectedItem selected	Object	Indicates the first selected item, or null if no items are

It exposes one event—SelectionChanged (event args: SelectionChangedEventArgs).

The ListBoxItem class represents a ListBox's individual item. This class inherits from ContentControl and so can contain a wide variety of content. It exposes a single property of type bool, IsSelected, that is true when the item is selected. The appearance of the list box items can be controlled by setting the DataTemplate property of the ListBox control. As implied by the properties shown in Table 3-20, the ListBox control only supports single selection. You can include a check box in the content for each item or create a custom list control (inherit from ListControl or combine a ScrollViewer with a StackPanel).

A ListBox containing several simple items (text blocks) is shown in Figure 3-10.

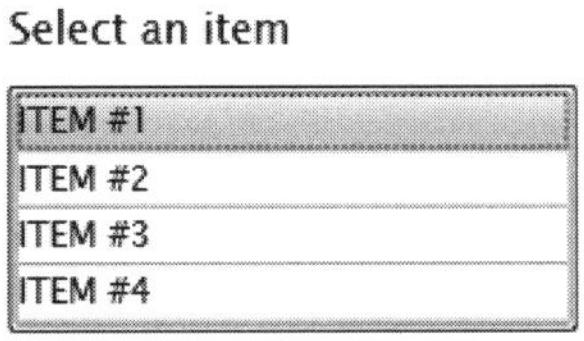

Select an item

ITEM #1
ITEM #2
ITEM #3
ITEM #4

Figure 3-10. *The ListBox control*

The corresponding XAML looks like this:

```
<ListBox Canvas.Top="50" Canvas.Left="40" Width="200">
    <ListBox.Items>
        <ListBoxItem>
            <TextBlock Text="ITEM #1"/>
        </ListBoxItem>
        <ListBoxItem>
            <TextBlock Text="ITEM #2"/>
        </ListBoxItem>
        <ListBoxItem>
            <TextBlock Text="ITEM #3"/>
        </ListBoxItem>
        <ListBoxItem>
            <TextBlock Text="ITEM #4"/>
        </ListBoxItem>
    </ListBox.Items>
</ListBox>
```

We'll take a look at displaying more complex items in a ListBox by using data templates in Chapter 5.

Popup

The Popup control is used to display content over the existing user interface, for example, showing a tool tip. Its properties are shown in Table 3-21.

Table 3-21. *Properties of the System.Windows.Controls.Primitives.Popup Class*

Property	Type	Description
Child	UIElement	Gets/sets the content to display.
HorizontalOffset	double	Defines the horizontal offset used in displaying the pop-up. Defaults to 0 (left side).
IsOpen	bool	Gets/sets whether the pop-up is open.
VerticalOffset	double	Vertical offset used in displaying the pop-up. Defaults to 0 (top).

The Popup class provides two events: Opened and Closed. These events fire when the pop-up is opened or closed via setting of the IsOpen property. Figure 3-11 shows a button and the pop-up that opens when the button is clicked.

Figure 3-11. *The Popup control*

The XAML for the pop-up looks like this:

```
<Popup x:Name="xamlPopup" VerticalOffset="40"
           HorizontalOffset="270" IsOpen="False">
    <Border BorderBrush="Black" BorderThickness="5" CornerRadius="3">
        <Button Content="Click to close" Click="button_Click"/>
    </Border>
</Popup>
```

The showing and hiding of the pop-up is done programmatically by simply setting the IsOpen property of the Popup control to the correct value to show or hide the pop-up.

```
void button_Click(object sender, RoutedEventArgs e)
{
    xamlPopup.IsOpen = false;
}
private void showPopup_Click(object sender, RoutedEventArgs e)
{
    xamlPopup.IsOpen = true;
}
```

ToolTipService

The ToolTipService class is used to programmatically associate a UIElement describing content of the tool tip with the control. It provides an attached property (ToolTip) that is used in the XAML to create a tool tip without having to go to the code-behind. Figure 3-12 shows two buttons, the first with a tool tip already attached, and the second that gets a tool tip after the first button is clicked. Figure 3-12 includes the tool tip for the first button.

Figure 3-12. *The tool tip control*

The XAML for the first button looks like this:

```
<Button Canvas.Left="20" Canvas.Top="40"
        ToolTipService.ToolTip="Click button to add a tooltip to the other button"
        Content="I have a tooltip!"   Click="Button_Click"/>
```

The click handler programmatically adds the second button's tool tip via the SetTooltip method.

```
private void Button_Click(object sender, RoutedEventArgs e)
{
    Border b = new Border();
    b.BorderBrush = new SolidColorBrush(Color.FromArgb(255, 128, 128, 128));
    b.BorderThickness = new Thickness(5);
    TextBlock t = new TextBlock();
    t.Margin = new Thickness(5);
    t.Text = "I am another tool tip";
    b.Child = t;
    ToolTipService.SetToolTip(secondButton, b);
}
```

RangeBase

The RangeBase class provides behavior to handle a range of values and a selected value within this range. It is the base class of the ScrollBar control and the Slider control that comes with the Silverlight SDK. The RangeBase class uses value coercion in order to ensure the current value is within the range. An ArgumentException will be raised if any of the properties defining the end points of the range are set to a value that does not make sense, such as setting Minimum to NaN or SmallChange to a value less than zero. The properties of RangeBase are shown in Table 3-22.

Table 3-22. *Properties of the System.Windows.Controls.Primitives.RangeBase Class*

Property	Type	Description
LargeChange	double	Specifies the value to add/subtract from the current value. Defaults to 1. Exact behavior is specified by the inheritor.
Maximum	double	Defines the highest value possible for this range.
Minimum	double	Defines the lowest value possible for this range.
SmallChange	double	Specifies the value to add/subtract from the current value. Defaults to 0.1. Exact behavior is specified by the inheritor.
Value	double	Gets/sets the current value. This property is subjected to value coercion to ensure it stays within range.

The RangeBase provides one event: ValueChanged.

ScrollBar

The ScrollBar class is visually represented by two repeat buttons and a Thumb control that corresponds to the currently selected value within the range. You can see what a horizontal and vertical scrollbar on their own look like in Figure 3-13.

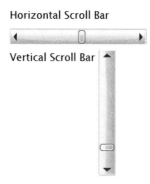

Figure 3-13. *ScrollBar controls*

ScrollBar's properties are shown in Table 3-23.

Table 3-23. *Properties of the System.Windows.Controls.Primitives.ScrollBar Class*

Property	Type	Description
IsEnabled	bool	Gets/sets whether the scrollbar currently responds to user interaction.
Orientation	Orientation	Gets/sets the orientation of the scrollbar. Possible values: Horizontal, Vertical.
ViewportSize	double	Specifies the amount of content that is currently visible according to the position of the thumb within the scrollbar. Defaults to 0.

The ScrollBar class provides one event: Scroll (event args class: ScrollEventArgs). This event fires only when the user changes the position of the thumb, not when the Value property is changed in the code-behind.

The XAML for the scrollbars shown in Figure 3-13 looks like this:

```
<Canvas x:Name="LayoutRoot" Background="White">
    <TextBlock Text="Horizontal Scroll Bar" Canvas.Left="20" Canvas.Top="40"/>
    <ScrollBar Orientation="Horizontal" Canvas.Left="20" Canvas.Top="70" Width="200"
               Minimum="0" Maximum="100"
               SmallChange="1" LargeChange="10" Value="50"/>
    <TextBlock Text="Vertical Scroll Bar" Canvas.Left="20" Canvas.Top="100"/>
    <ScrollBar Orientation="Vertical" Canvas.Left="150" Canvas.Top="100"
        Width="25"/>
</Canvas>
```

Slider

The Slider control is essentially a scrollbar, but it provides the capability to select a value from within a range. It inherits from `RangeBase`. Its properties are shown in Table 3-24.

Table 3-24. *Properties of the System.Windows.Controls.Slider Class*

Property	Type	Description
IsDirectionReversed	bool	Reverses the direction of increasing values if true: down for vertical sliders and left for horizontal sliders.
IsEnabled	bool	Returns true if the slider can respond to user interaction, false otherwise.
IsFocused	bool	Returns true if the slider currently has input focus.
Orientation	Orientation	Gets/sets the orientation of slider. Possible values: Vertical, Horizontal.

Figure 3-14 shows what a horizontal and vertical slider look like.

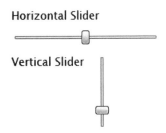

Figure 3-14. *Slider controls*

Here's the XAML used to create those sliders:

```
<Canvas x:Name="LayoutRoot" Background="White">
    <TextBlock Text="Horizontal Slider" Canvas.Left="20" Canvas.Top="40"/>
    <Slider Orientation="Horizontal" Canvas.Left="20" Canvas.Top="70" Width="200"
            Minimum="0" Maximum="100" SmallChange="1" LargeChange="10"
                Value="50"/>
    <TextBlock Text="Vertical Slider" Canvas.Left="20" Canvas.Top="100"/>
    <Slider Orientation="Vertical" Canvas.Left="130" Canvas.Top="100"
            Width="25" Height="100"/>
</Canvas>
```

ScrollViewer

The ScrollViewer control is used to display content that is possibly larger than the allotted space, so scrollbars are used to let the user scroll to different sections of the content. It exposes a large set of properties that control the presentation of content, shown in Table 3-25.

Table 3-25. *Properties of the System.Windows.Controls.GridSplitter Class*

Property	Type	Description
ComputedHorizontalScrollBarVisibility	Visibility	Gets/sets whether the horizontal scrollbar is currently visible
ComputedVerticalScrollBarVisibility	Visibility	Gets/sets whether the vertical scrollbar is currently visible
HorizontalOffset	double	Gets/sets the current horizontal offset of the content
HorizontalScrollBarVisibility	Visibility	Gets/sets whether the horizontal scrollbar should be displayed
ScrollableHeight	double	Defines the total vertical size of the content
ScrollableWidth	double	Defines the total horizontal size of the content
VerticalOffset	double	Gets/sets the current vertical offset of the content
VerticalScrollBarVisibility	Visibility	Gets/sets whether the vertical scrollbar should be displayed
ViewportHeight	double	Gets/sets the height of the viewport (the window into the content that is on screen)
ViewportWidth	double	Gets/sets the width of the viewport

Figure 3-15 shows a grid with a checkerboard pattern contained in a ScrollView control. The content is too large to display completely, so the vertical scrollbar is added automatically (the horizontal scrollbar is added automatically but must be set to Auto first).

Scroll Viewer: width=250, height=200
Inner Grid: width=400, height=300

Figure 3-15. *The ScrollViewer control*

Here's the XAML to create the grid inside the scroll viewer:

```
<Canvas x:Name="LayoutRoot" Background="White">
    <ScrollViewer Canvas.Left="60" Canvas.Top="70" Width="250"
                  Height="200" HorizontalScrollBarVisibility="Auto">
        <Grid Background="White" Height="300" Width="400">
            <!-- 3 rows, 3 columns -->
            <!-- Border controls to draw a different background in each cell -->
        </Grid>
    </ScrollViewer>
</Canvas>
```

Incorporating SDK Controls

Several useful controls are provided with the Silverlight SDK. In order to gain access to these controls in XAML, you must add a reference to the System.Windows.Controls assembly and add the following to the UserControl element in XAML. Note that using these controls means an extra assembly will be added to the XAP file, thus making a slightly larger file for users to download.

```
xmlns:swc=
"clr-namespace:System.Windows.Controls;assembly=System.Windows.Controls"
```

GridSplitter

The GridSplitter control is used to provide the user with the capability of changing sizes of rows and columns in a grid. It exposes three properties, shown in Table 3-26.

Table 3-26. *Properties of the System.Windows.Controls.GridSplitter Class*

Property	Type	Description
IsEnabled	bool	Gets/sets whether the grid splitter responds to user interaction
PreviewStyle	Style	Gets/sets the style used for previewing changes
ShowsPreview	bool	Gets/sets whether the preview is shown before changes from the grid splitter are applied

Figure 3-16 shows a checkboard pattern with a grid splitter between the first and second column, spanning all three rows.

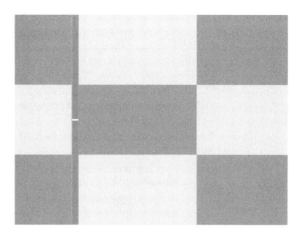

Figure 3-16. *The GridSplitter control*

The XAML for this grid splitter looks like this:

```
<Grid x:Name="LayoutRoot" Background="White">
    <!-- 3 rows, 3 columns -->
    <!-- Border controls to draw a different background in each cell -->
    <swcx:GridSplitter Grid.Row="0" Grid.Column="1" Width="10" Grid.RowSpan="3"
                       HorizontalAlignment="Left" VerticalAlignment="Stretch"/>
</Grid>
```

Calendar and DatePicker

The Calendar control provides a full calendar on screen that the user can use to navigate to a month and select a date. It supports forbidding certain dates from being selected and constraining itself to a given date range. The properties for the Calendar control are shown in Table 3-27.

Table 3-27. *Properties of the System.Windows.Controls.Calendar Class*

Property	Type	Description
BlackoutDates	CalendarDateRangeCollection	Contains a set of dates that are blacked out and thus cannot be selected by a user.
DisplayDate	DateTime	Specifies the date to display in the calendar.
DisplayDateStart	Nullable<DateTime>	Specifies the first date to display.
DisplayDateEnd	Nullable<DateTime>	Specifies the last date to display.
DisplayMode	CalendarMode	Controls how the calendar presents itself. Possible values: Month (displays a full month at a time), Year (displays a full year at a time), and Decade (displays a decade at a time).

Continued

Table 3-27. *Continued*

Property	Type	Description
FirstDayOfWeek	DayOfWeek	Specifies the day that marks the beginning of the week. Defaults to DayOfWeek.Sunday.
IsEnabled	bool	Gets/sets whether the control responds to user interaction.
IsTodayHighlighted	bool	Returns true if today's date is selected in the calendar.
SelectedDate	Nullable<DateTime>	Indicates null if no date is selected, otherwise the selected date.
SelectedDates	SelectedDatesCollection	Contains one or more selected dates, unless selection mode is None.
SelectionMode	CalendarSelectionMode	Gets/sets how the selection works in the calendar. Possible values: None (no selections are allowed), SingleDate (only one date can be selected), SingleRange (only one consecutive range of dates can be selected), MultipleRange (different, disconnected ranges of dates can be selected).

The Calendar control provides three events: DisplayDateChanged, DisplayModeChanged, and SelectedDatesChanged. There is another control, the DatePicker, that is made up of a text box, a button, and a Calendar control. The Calendar control only appears when the button is clicked. Figure 3-17 shows what the Calendar and DatePicker controls look like.

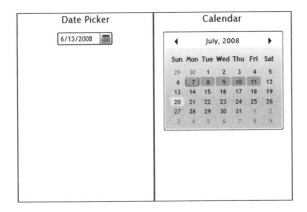

Figure 3-17. *The Calendar and DatePicker controls*

The XAML for these controls looks like this:

```
<Border Grid.Column="0" Grid.Row="0" Grid.RowSpan="2"
          BorderBrush="Black" BorderThickness="1">
    <Canvas>
```

```
            <swcx:DatePicker x:Name="datePicker" Canvas.Top="30" Canvas.Left="65"/>
        </Canvas>
    </Border>
    <Border Grid.Column="1" Grid.Row="0" Grid.RowSpan="2"
                BorderBrush="Black" BorderThickness="1">
        <Canvas>
            <swcx:Calendar x:Name="calendar" Canvas.Top="30" Canvas.Left="15"
                                    SelectionMode="SingleRange"/>
        </Canvas>
    </Border>
```

TabControl

The TabControl is used to host content within a set of pages, each page accessible via a tab. Its properties are shown in Table 3-28.

Table 3-28. *Properties of the System.Windows.Controls.TabControl Class*

Property	Type	Description
IsEnabled	bool	Returns true if the TabControl currently responds to user interface interaction, false otherwise.
SelectedContent	Object	Specifies the content of the currently active TabItem.
SelectedIndex	Int32	Gets/sets the index of the currently active TabItem, or -1 if none are active.
SelectedItem	Object	Specifies the currently active TabItem, or null if none are active.
TabStripPlacement	Dock	Gets/sets where tabs are placed within the TabControl. Possible values: Left, Top (default), Right, Bottom.

The TabControl provides one event, SelectionChanged (event args class: SelectionChangedEventArgs). The TabControl consists of TabItems, each with a Header property that is used to set the tab label and a Content property used to set the contents of the specific tab page. Figure 3-18 shows a tab control with three tabs.

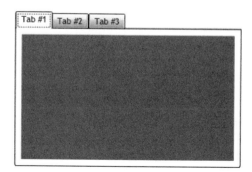

Figure 3-18. *The TabControl*

Here's the XAML for this control:

```
<Canvas x:Name="LayoutRoot" Background="White">
    <swcx:TabControl Canvas.Left="20" Canvas.Top="40" Width="300" Height="200">
        <swcx:TabItem Header="Tab #1">
            <Canvas Background="Red"></Canvas>
        </swcx:TabItem>
        <swcx:TabItem Header="Tab #2">
            <Canvas Background="Green"></Canvas>
        </swcx:TabItem>
        <swcx:TabItem Header="Tab #3">
            <Canvas Background="Blue"></Canvas>
        </swcx:TabItem>
    </swcx:TabControl>
</Canvas>
```

Implementing Navigation

You have an application designed that involves multiple user interface screens, each corresponding to a different XAML page, but now what? How do you change from one XAML page to another? Unfortunately, Silverlight does not directly provide any navigation functionality. The good news is this is fairly straightforward to implement in your application, though there are a few caveats related to some of the ways you could implement navigation.

There are roughly two types of Silverlight applications that can be developed. The first operates like a desktop application where all navigation is built into the application via menus and smaller windows that might dock within the larger user interface. The other type of application more closely mimics the behavior of web sites. An online store where a user can browse items might naturally fit navigation using the back/forward buttons of the browser.

One problem with this second type of application, however, is that Silverlight doesn't directly support navigation, let alone navigation tied to the browser. Another problem: how does a user bookmark a page? If a user uses his or her browser's bookmarking functionality, all the bookmark will do is take that user back to the the Silverlight application—not a specific part of the application. You should make an attempt to use the first type of application as a model—viewing Silverlight as an application in and of itself, not tied to the browser it is hosted in. If browser navigation and/or bookmarking make good sense in the design of your application, however, there are ways to go about adding this support to a Silverlight application.

One approach is to use isolated storage (covered in Chapter 5) and build bookmarking and forward/backward navigation into the application itself, much like HTML help files do (each stores its own private bookmarks since the bookmarks make no sense outside the help file). The downside of this is additional design and development effort. A second approach is to split the various aspects of a Silverlight application that need bookmarking into different applications, each on their own HTML or ASPX page, which can then be bookmarked. This isn't a great approach because of the extra development, maintenance, and deployment effort required, and it loses consistency if the smaller Silverlight applications are parts of a larger whole that should contain them.

If you really need to use the browser's navigation and bookmarking, you can use browser interoperability to, for example, save a custom bookmark with state information that can be read by the Silverlight application from the query string. Working with the browser is covered in Chapter 10. Internet Explorer 8 will introduce better capability for Silverlight applications to respond to the browser's back and forward buttons.

Creating navigation within the application is mandatory for anything except the simplest applications. By navigation, I am specifically talking about representing and selectively display-ing two or more XAML pages. You might conceive of three main approaches if you sit down and think about building your own navigation support.

The first is by making a specific UserControl fully opaque by setting its Opacity property to #00xxxxxx (where xxxxxx does not matter since a 00 opacity value makes the page disappear). This is the worst approach because the UserControl is still there—it still responds to input (technically, it is still hit testable), it still handles events, and so forth.

If Opacity isn't the right property to use, the next most logical one is the Visibility prop-erty. By setting a UserControl's Visibility property to Collapsed, the page disappears. This gets you closer to what you want—hide one page, show another. This in fact might be a work-able solution for your application; however, UserControls with their Visibility property set to Collapsed still handle events (but they are not hit testable). This may or may not be what you want, depending on which events are implemented.

The third approach is to completely disconnect a UserControl from its visual tree. This can be accomplished by either setting the application's RootVisual to a completely different XAML page or using a parent XAML page's Children.Remove to remove a specific page and then add another one. This requires a bit more work, but it ensures *only* the visible page receives event notifications and also ensures the Loaded event does not happen until the page is requested by the user (provided page construction is deferred until the page is needed).

Each chapter's code in this book uses a class called XAML_Viewer. This class associates a friendly name with an instance of a XAML page and then presents the pages in a list box along the left-hand side. When a user clicks a name in the list box on the left-hand side, the content on the right changes to the specific XAML page associated with the friendly name. You've seen screenshots of only the content side in the examples in this chapter; however, you can see what the entire application for this chapter looks like in Figure 3-19.

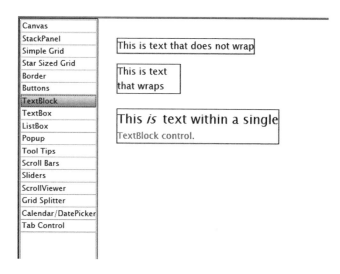

Figure 3-19. *Full view of the XAML_Viewer*

The XAML_Viewer class works by associating the instance of a UserControl with its friendly name (a string) in an instance of a Dictionary<string,UserControl>. When an item is clicked in the list box, the currently displayed XAML page's Visibility property is set to Collapsed and the selected UserControl's Visibility property is set to Visible. This is a simple and effective way to showcase examples for each chapter.

While it is unlikely your application will have precisely this list box/content visual split, the mechanism used is something you might well find useful. Let's briefly consider some other types of navigation.

First, if you have a backward/current/forward navigation (much like a web browser, but also like you might see in a slide deck), the UserControl containing other XAML pages must store the sequence in an ordered list. You could use a List<UserControl> for this purpose and store the index to the currently displayed page in a member variable.

Second, a ListBox control could be used as a simple menu, either at the top of the application or alongside the left side. Using data templates, styles, and possibly even control templates, the appearance of the list box can be completely changed. The list-box-as-menu can be placed within a grid containing other content providing for more sophisticated placement.

Summary

This chapter introduced the classes that enable the dependency property system and enable the visual dimension of Silverlight: DependencyObject, UIElement, and FrameworkElement. After going over these important classes, you were exposed to many of the controls that come with Silverlight. Finally, you were introduced to approaches to adding navigation and bookmarking of Silverlight applications.

CHAPTER 4

■■■

Network Communication

So far, you have explored Silverlight via XAML and seen how to create basic user interfaces. The next piece of the Silverlight picture is the support it provides for communication with network services. The network communication classes in Silverlight provide the capability to send/receive data over either HTTP or raw sockets. This chapter and the next two (on data and media) are closely related. The next chapter, which covers consuming data, will utilize communication techniques to retrieve data before consuming it, such as using web service calls to retrieve data from a database or direct download over HTTP to get syndication feeds and other XML documents. In Chapter 6, you'll utilize techniques from this chapter to retrieve video and other media from a server, and then show how to utilize the media. This chapter lays the groundwork for the coming chapters, so let's jump right in!

Enabling Cross-Domain Communication

Silverlight can communicate over the network via sockets or HTTP, but if a Silverlight application could communicate to any arbitrary host, then it could be leveraged for hacking into a network or participating in a denial-of-service attack. Therefore, network communication in Silverlight must be controlled. A simplistic approach is to restrict communication between a Silverlight application and the server that serves it (known as the application's site of origin), as shown in Figure 4-1.

Figure 4-1. *Communication with site of origin*

Fortunately, Silverlight provides support for cross-domain access via a special property file that controls network access in specific ways. Nothing special must be done if the application is communicating with its site of origin, but since the cross-domain request requires permission, Silverlight must first determine that a network request is cross-domain. Three conditions must be met to identify a request as a site of origin, and if any of these conditions aren't met, the request is viewed as cross-domain and triggers downloading of the cross-domain policy file. These conditions are as follows:

- The protocol must be the same. If the application was served over HTTP, it can only communicate over HTTP; likewise for HTTPS.

- The port must be the same. Again, the port must match the original URL the application was downloaded from.

- The domain and path in the URL must match exactly. If the Silverlight application was downloaded from `http://www.fabrikam.com/app` and the request is made to `http://fabrikam.com/app`, the domains don't match.

Caution There are restrictions placed on what characters are considered valid in a request's URI to help prevent canonicalization attacks. The valid characters are all lowercase and uppercase letters (*A* through *Z* and *a* through *z*), all digits (0 through 9), the comma (,), the forward slash (/), the tilde (~), the semicolon (;), and the period (.), as long as there aren't two consecutive periods.

What if Silverlight determines that a particular request is cross-domain? Before deeming the request invalid, Silverlight checks permissions on the remote server. A server that wishes to provide cross-domain permissions to Silverlight applications hosts a cross-domain policy file. There are actually two cross-domain policy files usable by Silverlight: `crossdomain.xml`, introduced by Flash; and `clientaccesspolicy.xml`, introduced with Silverlight.

Note During the lifetime of a Silverlight application, only a single request is made to a cross-domain policy file per server. This means it is safe (and suggested) to mark the cross-domain policy files as no-cache. This prevents the browser from caching the file while offering no performance penalty to Silverlight, since Silverlight will cache the file itself.

The `crossdomain.xml` file is the most straightforward since it is used to opt in the entire domain. No other capabilities from this file are supported by Silverlight.

```
<?xml version="1.0"?>
<!DOCTYPE cross-domain-policy
        SYSTEM
        "http://www.macromedia.com/xml/dtds/cross-domain-policy.dtd">
<cross-domain-policy>
    <allow-access-from domain="*"/>
</cross-domain-policy>
```

■**Caution** The cross-domain policy files must be located in the root of the server. If you are trying to enable cross-domain communication and it isn't working, ensure the file is located in the server root, not in a sub-path such as www.fabrikam.com/services. You can use a tool such as Fiddler (www.fiddlertool.com), an HTTP traffic sniffer, to see the requests your Silverlight application is making. If this file is present and being downloaded successfully, check the contents of the cross-domain policy file.

If you want more granular control over the allowed domains, you must use the clientaccesspolicy.xml. This file provides the capability to restrict which domains are allowed and which paths on the local server can be accessed. The domains correspond to where the Silverlight application is served, not any host information based on the client computer. Let's take a look at the structure of this clientaccesspolicy.xml file:

```xml
<?xml version="1.0" encoding="utf-8"?>
<access-policy>
  <cross-domain-access>
    <policy>
      <allow-from http-request-headers="CustomHeader,Mail-*">
        <domain uri="*"/>
        <domain uri="http://www.fabrikam.com"/>
        <domain uri="https://www.fabrikam.com"/>
      </allow-from>
      <grant-to>
        <resource path="/services" include-subpaths="false"/>
      </grant-to>
    </policy>
  </cross-domain-access>
</access-policy>
```

The root element must only appear once; however, multiple cross-domain-access elements can be specified in order to link different sets of allowed domains with paths on the server.

The allow-from element is the parent element for the list of domains access is being granted to. Access is granted to all Silverlight applications if you use the value * for the domain element. The http-request-headers attribute is optional, but must be specified in order to allow the sending of HTTP headers with requests from the client. It takes the form of a comma-separated list of header names, and the wildcard character (*) can be used in a part of the header or to allow all headers (when http-request-headers is set to *).

The grant-to element is the parent of resources (paths) local to the server that the set of domains are allowed to access. Each resource element has a path attribute used to specify the path (relative to root of server) to grant access to. The include-subpaths attribute is optional. Setting this to true is an easy way to grant access to an entire hierarchy of paths by specifying the base path in the path attribute. The default value for this attribute is false.

This file is also used to grant access to Silverlight applications communicating over sockets. The format is basically the same, but instead of using resource in the grant-to section, socket-resource is used.

```
<?xml version="1.0" encoding="utf-8"?>
<access-policy>
  <cross-domain-access>
    <policy>
      <allow-from>
        <domain uri="*"/>
      </allow-from>
      <grant-to>
        <socket-resource port="4502-4534" protocol="tcp"/>
      </grant-to>
    </policy>
  </cross-domain-access>
</access-policy>
```

The port attribute can be a range of ports or a single port. Currently, the only supported protocol is TCP and thus the protocol attribute must be set to tcp.

The need for this policy file is placed on all communication, including client proxies generated for services, the System.Net.WebClient class, and the System.Net.HttpWebRequest class. Now that we've gone over the network security restrictions placed on communication in Silverlight, let's take a closer look at the communication classes.

Using Services

Silverlight uses an implementation of Windows Communication Foundation (WCF) to manage its network communication. The service implementation used by Silverlight is a subset of WCF. The only binding that can be used is the classic web service binding. This means that when it comes to web services, Silverlight can only communicate with classic ASMX web services or WCF services that expose an endpoint with the basicHttpBinding.

■**Note** WCF is a communication stack introduced in .NET 3.0. Its aim is to separate the nature of communication from the service implementations. It uses communication endpoints that can be defined and utilized outside the actual service. An endpoint consists of an *address*, a *binding*, and a *contract* (commonly known as the ABCs of WCF). The address is an URI, such as www.fabrikam.com. The binding specifies the nature of the communication, such as communicating over HTTP or TCP. The contract is typically an interface defined in a language such as C#, and includes the service contract (what operations are exposed by the service) and possibly a data contract (how data represented by objects appears).

Let's start by creating a simple web service the traditional way (as an ASMX file). This service provides a simple way to obtain a book in a hypothetical online bookstore. The Book class only contains a few members: the book's title, ISBN, authors, and price.

```
public class Book
{
    public string title, isbn, authors;
    public double price;
}
```

The web service provides a method, getBookCount, to retrieve the count of books available, and a method to retrieve a book by its identifier, which we'll specify as an index.

```
[WebMethod]
public int getBookCount()
{
    return (2);
}
[WebMethod]
public Book getBook(int bookId)
{
    // ...
}
```

While we can use a classic web service, it is also possible to construct WCF services for consumption by Silverlight applications. In both approaches to developing a service, the visibility keyword of a data member specifies whether it is serialized or not. We don't have to specify any attributes on the Book class or its members to make them visible to Silverlight. If there is a public member that you do not want serialized, mark it with the IgnoreDataMemberAttribute. While public types are serialized by default, using the DataContractAttribute and the DataMemberAttribute to specify the data contract does no harm, and is a good idea if the service will be consumed by more than just Silverlight.

Either the Book class, configured for use by a WCF service, can be left as is, or the data contract can be specified as shown here:

```
[DataContract]
public class Book
{
    [DataMember]
    public string title, isbn, authors;
    [DataMember]
    public double price;
}
```

The implementation of WCF used by Silverlight shares a lot with the full WCF implementation in .NET 3.5; however, there are restrictions. Since Silverlight is limited to using SOAP 1.1 (which the basic HTTP binding provides), the various web service protocols cannot be used. One-way operations are not supported—either avoid using one-way operations in your WCF service or provide a counterpart suitable for use by Silverlight. Service methods cannot have as a parameter or a return type the Stream type. Also, you cannot have as part of a data contract or operation contracts the types ISerializable or XmlElement, or arrays of XmlNode or IXmlSerializable. Custom SOAP headers are also unsupported.

Creating and Using a Client Service Proxy

After deploying this web service and creating a new Silverlight application in Visual Studio, the easiest way to connect to the web service is by adding a service reference. Right-click the Silverlight application in Solution Explorer and select Add Service Reference, as shown in Figure 4-2. This will create a client proxy and add it to the project. The client proxy class is based on the `System.ServiceModel.ClientBase` class, and for each operation in the service, there is a class based on `System.ComponentModel.AsyncCompletedEventArgs`.

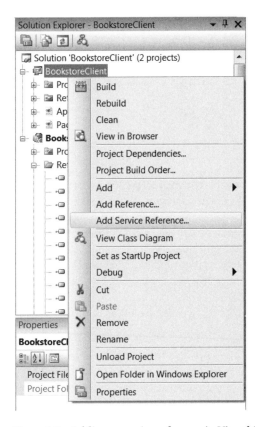

Figure 4-2. *Adding a service reference in Visual Studio 2008*

Type in the address to the web service and click Go, and the services and service methods will be discovered, just like you've seen when adding a web service reference in Visual Studio 2008 (see Figure 4-3).

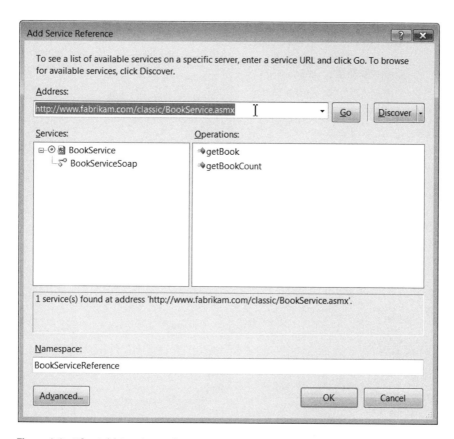

Figure 4-3. *The Add Service Reference dialog in Visual Studio 2008*

Along with the files that are created to support the new service reference, a `ServiceReferences.`
`ClientConfig` file is created (if it doesn't already exist) and added to the project. This file must
have that name and be packaged in the XAP file for deployment. Silverlight consults this file at
runtime to determine the address of the service along with any configuration options provided
for the binding or the endpoint. For the `BookServiceReference` just added, this file contains the
following:

```
<configuration>
    <system.serviceModel>
        <bindings>
            <basicHttpBinding>
                <binding name="BookServiceSoap"
                        maxBufferSize="65536"
                        maxReceivedMessageSize="65536">
                    <security mode="None" />
                </binding>
            </basicHttpBinding>
        </bindings>
        <client>
            <endpoint address="http://www.fabrikam.com/classic/BookService.asmx"
```

```
                binding="basicHttpBinding"
                bindingConfiguration="BookServiceSoap"
                contract="chapter4.BookServiceReference.BookServiceSoap"
                name="BookServiceSoap" />
    </client>
  </system.serviceModel>
</configuration>
```

The security mode is set to None for HTTP communication, but you can set this to Transport for HTTPS communication. Although this file represents a subset of the capability provided by WCF, it still has a range of configuration options available, such as buffer size restrictions and timeout parameters for send/receive operations. Consult the MSDN documentation for a full list.

We'll create a simple interface to connect to the web service. It will provide the ability to input a book's ID and retrieve information about the book (see Figure 4-4).

Book Store Service Client
   Enter book ID: 1
   [Get Book]

Results
   Title:A Wind in the Door
   Author:Madeleine L'Engle
   Price:6.99

Figure 4-4. *The client interface to the Book service*

In the code-behind, we'll add the service client as a private member on the class:

```
private BookServiceReference.BookServiceSoapClient serviceClient;
```

If you create an instance of this class and bring up IntelliSense, you'll see something interesting. Look at Figure 4-5. There are no getBook or getBookCount methods, meaning that there is no support for synchronous service calls.

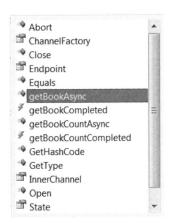

```
Abort
ChannelFactory
Close
Endpoint
Equals
getBookAsync
getBookCompleted
getBookCountAsync
getBookCountCompleted
GetHashCode
GetType
InnerChannel
Open
State
```

Figure 4-5. *Methods on the client service proxy as shown in IntelliSense*

Synchronous communication, as shown in Figure 4-6, follows the standard request-response pattern. A service method is invoked and then the application waits for the response from the service.

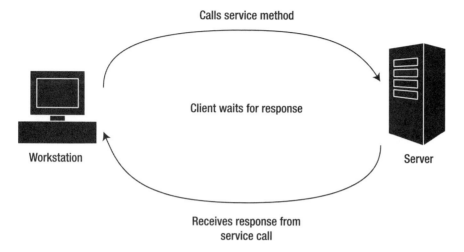

Figure 4-6. *Synchronous communication: The client sends requests and waits for a response*

The disadvantage to synchronous communication is that the client application must wait for a response before doing something else. In Silverlight, service calls are done on the user interface thread—which means that any synchronous invocation of a service will cause the user interface to block (i.e., it becomes unresponsive and appears frozen to the user). Due to how networking works in the browser, Silverlight does not directly support synchronous communication. This isn't necessarily a bad thing, since it's better for developers to utilize asynchronous communication. This will contribute to more responsive user interfaces, even if it adds a small learning curve for developers unfamiliar with asynchronous communication. Figure 4-7 shows a diagram of asynchronous communication—here, the request/response is not a cycle; instead, the response is disconnected from the request.

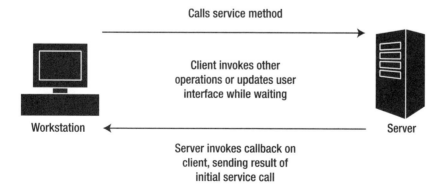

Figure 4-7. *Asynchronous communication: The client sends requests and eventually gets a response*

Each asynchronous service operation is made up of an asynchronous method (the name of the operation with `Async` appended) and an `EventArgs` subclass that contains a `Result` property matching the return type of the service operation. The `EventArgs` subclass also contains an additional property, `UserState`, which is an optional final parameter to the asynchronous method. This parameter is used to pass arbitrary data from the invocation of the service to the method that handles the completion of the operation.

The bookstore client example first invokes the service to obtain the number of books in its database. This code is located in the constructor of the `Page` class.

```
public Page()
{
    InitializeComponent();
    BookServiceSoapClient serviceClient;
    serviceClient = new BookServiceSoapClient();
    serviceClient.getBookCountCompleted +=
                        new EventHandler<getBookCountCompletedEventArgs>
                                    (serviceClient_getBookCountCompleted);
    serviceClient.getBookCountAsync();
}
```

There is an alternate constructor for the client proxy that accepts the name of an endpoint. This is useful if the service exposes multiple endpoints and you want to use an endpoint other than the default.

Now we need the `serviceClient_getBookCountCompleted` method to handle the completion of the asynchronous operation. If you type the code up to and including the +=, you can press Tab twice to automatically generate the event handler.

```
void serviceClient_getBookCountCompleted(
                            object sender, getBookCountCompletedEventArgs e)
{
    if (e.Cancelled == false && e.Error == null)
    {
        bookCount = e.Result;
        getButton.IsEnabled = true;
    }
}
```

The `getBookCountCompletedEventArgs` contains the `Result` property that matches the return type of `getBookCount`, so no cast is necessary when assigning to the `bookCount` integer class member.

Along with `Result` and `UserState`, there are two other important properties on the specific `EventArgs` subclasses: `Cancelled` and `Error`. The `Cancelled` property is a `boolean` that indicates whether the operation was cancelled (such as via the `Abort` method on the service client object). The `Error` is of type `Exception` and communicates an exception that occurs on the service side to the client. If all goes well with the service call, `Cancelled` is `false` and `Error` is `null`. You should always check these properties in the asynchronous event handler in case something went wrong.

Generating and using a proxy to invoke a service is rather straightforward after you understand the asynchronous nature of operations. Silverlight also contains two classes for direct HTTP communication, which we'll look at next.

Communicating Over HTTP Directly

Two classes are provided to support direct communication over HTTP: System.Net.WebClient and System.Net.HttpWebRequest. WebClient is simpler but only exposes simplified access to the GET and POST methods of HTTP. WebClient is most useful for easily downloading resources. The HttpWebRequest class provides greater control over HTTP communication.

The WebClient Class

The WebClient class provides simplified access to communicating over HTTP (it is located in the System.Net assembly). Its most important members are listed in Table 4-1.

Table 4-1. *Members of the System.Net.WebClient Class*

Name	Type	Description
DownloadStringAsync	Method	Asynchronously downloads data and returns it as a string.
DownloadStringCompleted	Event	Occurs when DownloadStringAsync is complete.
UploadStringAsync	Method	Uploads a string to a specified URI.
OpenReadAsync	Method	Asynchronously downloads data and returns it as a Stream.
OpenReadCompleted	Event	Occurs when OpenReadAsync is complete.
DownloadProgressChanged	Event	Occurs when some/all data is transferred. This is useful for building a status indicator such as a download progress bar.
CancelAsync	Method	Used to cancel an already issued asynchronous operation.
BaseAddress	Property (URI)	Gets/sets base address. This is useful for using relative addresses in multiple operations with a single WebClient.
IsBusy	Property (bool)	Indicates whether an asynchronous operation is in progress.

One aspect of Silverlight that is really useful is its support of archived media. You can store images, audio, and video in a ZIP file, download it to the client via WebClient, and then use MediaElement's or BitmapImage's SetSource method to connect the visual element to the media content within the archive. Let's take a look at a simple Silverlight application to download and display images. We'll also implement the DownloadProgressChanged event for showing a simple progress indicator. We need a System.Windows.Resources.StreamResourceInfo object in the code-behind to store the result of the download (i.e., the archive of images).

```
private StreamResourceInfo imageArchive;
```

Next, we'll implement the click event on the button to initiate the download. We are using the OpenReadAsync method to download a stream of data and thus implement an OpenReadCompleted event handler to handle the data when it is finished downloading.

```
private void downloadButton_Click(object sender, RoutedEventArgs e)
{
    WebClient wc = new WebClient();
    wc.OpenReadCompleted +=
            new OpenReadCompletedEventHandler(wc_OpenReadCompleted);
    wc.DownloadProgressChanged +=
            new DownloadProgressChangedEventHandler(wc_DownloadProgressChanged);
    wc.OpenReadAsync(new Uri("/ImageBrowser/renaissance.zip", UriKind.Relative));
}
```

The OpenReadCompleted event handler is straightforward: we'll check for an error or cancel and make our list box of image names visible (we're cheating here—the image names are hard-coded in a string array). We could add a metadata file to the ZIP archive that the Silverlight application can access and then cache the downloaded image archive for later use.

```
private void wc_OpenReadCompleted(object sender, OpenReadCompletedEventArgs e)
{
    if ((e.Error == null) && (e.Cancelled == false))
    {
        imageListBox.Visibility = Visibility.Visible;
        imageArchive = new StreamResourceInfo(e.Result, null);
    }
}
```

The download progress indicator is simply a percentage value displayed in a TextBlock. The DownloadProgressChangedEventArgs contains several useful properties (listed in Table 4-2), including the percentage progress, so we don't have to calculate percentage completion.

```
private void wc_DownloadProgressChanged(object sender,
                                        DownloadProgressChangedEventArgs e)
{
    progressTextBox.Text = e.ProgressPercentage + "%";
}
```

Table 4-2. *Members of the DownloadProgresschangedEventArgs Class*

Name	Type	Description
Address	URI	The URI to the file currently downloading
BytesReceived	long	A count of the bytes received so far
ProgressPercentage	int	A number from 0 to 100 representing percentage of bytes downloaded; equates to the formula (BytesReceived / TotalBytesToReceive) * 100
TotalBytesToReceive	long	Corresponds to the file size of the file requested
UserState	object	Corresponds to the optional data passed to the OpenReadAsync or DownloadStringAsync methods

Now that we have the image archive cached in the class, we can access an image inside when the user selects a different image in the ListBox.

```
private void imageListBox_SelectionChanged(object sender,
                                           SelectionChangedEventArgs e)
{
    BitmapImage bitmapImageSource = new BitmapImage();
    StreamResourceInfo imageResourceInfo =
        Application.GetResourceStream(imageArchive, new
                               Uri(imageListBox.SelectedItem.ToString(),
                               UriKind.Relative));
    bitmapImageSource.SetSource(imageResourceInfo.Stream);
    image.Source = bitmapImageSource;
}
```

First, we need to get access to the specific image inside the archive. We use the `Application.GetResourceStream` to access the specific image we want. `GetResourceStream` has two overloads: one to access resources stored in the application, and the other to access resources within an arbitrary ZIP stream. The resource to access is specified by a `Uri` object. The images in the ZIP archive are referenced relative to the path within the ZIP—the path to the Silverlight application has no relation to the paths of images inside the archive. The only other remarkable thing about this piece of code is that the `BitmapImage` class is needed to get a source for the `Image` object.

The `DownloadStringAsync` method works just like the `OpenReadAsync` method does. The only difference is the `Result` property of the `DownloadStringCompletedEventArgs` class is of type `String` instead of `Stream`. This method makes it easy to download content such as XML documents for parsing by the XML classes. We will be utilizing `DownloadStringAsync` in the next chapter.

The `WebClient` class provides only basic communication support. Downloading files, either as a `String` or a `Stream`, is done via the `GET` method of HTTP. The HTTP `POST` method is supported via the `UploadStringAsync` method. There are three overloads of this method. One version takes a `Uri` and the string to upload. A second version takes the `Uri`, a string specifying the HTTP method (it defaults to `POST` if this parameter is `null`) to use, and the string to upload. The final variant includes a user token that is passed to the asynchronous response handler.

If we want to utilize HTTP in more complex ways, manipulate cookies, or communicate securely, we need something more powerful. This power is provided by the `System.Net.HttpWebRequest` class.

The HttpWebRequest Class

The `HttpWebRequest` is a specialization of the `WebRequest` class designed to communicate over the HTTP and HTTPS protocols. It also supports the `POST` method along with `GET`, whereas `WebClient` only supports `GET`. Generally, if the host browser can do it, the `HttpWebRequest` can do it too, since this class leverages the host browser's networking. To use this class, you must first add a reference to the `System.Net` assembly since Silverlight projects do not include this by default.

An instance of `HttpWebRequest` cannot be created directly. The `WebRequest` class contains a factory method named `Create` that returns an appropriate instance of a `WebRequest` inheritor, based on protocol specified in the URI. As of Silverlight 2.0, the only protocols supported are HTTP and HTTPS, and both cause `Create` to return an instance of `HttpWebRequest` (actually, since HttpWebRequest is also abstract, a concrete implementation of HttpWebRequest is created; however, for all intents and purposes, it is an HttpWebRequest).

The HttpWebRequest class works in concert with HttpWebResponse to handle the data sent back from the server. The nature of communication using HttpWebRequest is also asynchronous; however, it utilizes the Begin*XXX*/End*XXX* pattern that you may be familiar with from .NET. Tables 4-3 and 4-4 describe the methods and properties of this class, respectively.

Table 4-3. *Methods of the System.Net.HttpWebRequest Class*

Name	Description
BeginGetRequestStream	Begins an asynchronous request to obtain a Stream to write data
EndGetRequestStream	Returns a Stream. Use this in the asynchronous callback method passed to BeginGetRequestStream to get the Stream to write your request to
BeginGetResponse	Begins an asynchronous request to communicate with a server
EndGetResponse	Returns a WebResponse; provides access to a Stream containing the data downloaded from the server
Abort	Cancels an executing asynchronous operation

Table 4-4. *Properties of the System.Net.HttpWebRequest Class*

Name	Description
ContentType	Corresponds to the Content-Type HTTP header.
HaveResponse	true if a response has been received; false otherwise.
Headers	A collection containing the HTTP headers.
Method	Corresponds to the method used in the request. Currently, it can only be GET or POST.
RequestUri	The URI of the request.

The EndGetResponse of the HttpWebRequest class returns a WebResponse. Much like the WebRequest, the WebResponse is abstract and actually requires us to look one level deeper in the hierarchy, so let's take a look at the HttpWebResponse class.

The HttpWebResponse class provides access to the data sent by the server to Silverlight. Its most important method is GetResponseStream, inherited from the WebResponse class. This method gives you a Stream containing the data sent by the server. When you are done with the response, make sure you call its Close method since the connection to the server remains open in the meantime. Tables 4-5 and 4-6 describe the methods and properties of this class.

Table 4-5. *Methods of the System.Net.HttpWebResponse Class*

Name	Description
Close	Closes the stream and releases the connection to the server.
GetResponseStream	Returns a Stream. Use this to access the data sent by the server to Silverlight.

Table 4-6. *Properties of the System.Net.HttpWebResponse Class*

Name	Description
ContentLength	Length of the data sent to Silverlight
ContentType	MIME type of the content sent, if available
ResponseUri	URI of the server that sent the response

One way to use the HttpWebRequest class is to retrieve data from a server. In this case, we can go straight to using the BeginGetResponse method, since all we care about is retrieving data from a server, not sending data. This code uses an address we enter in a user interface to connect to, such as downloading an HTML file from our site of origin.

```
HttpWebRequest request = (HttpWebRequest)HttpWebRequest.Create(
                                            new Uri(addressTB.Text));
request.BeginGetResponse(new AsyncCallback(responseHandler), request);
```

The implementation of the response handler is where we read the response from the server.

```
void responseHandler(IAsyncResult asyncResult)
{
   try
   {
      HttpWebRequest request = (HttpWebRequest)asyncResult.AsyncState;
      HttpWebResponse response =
                         (HttpWebResponse)request.EndGetResponse(asyncResult);
      StreamReader reader = new StreamReader(response.GetResponseStream());
      string line;
      outputTB.Text = "";
      while ((line = reader.ReadLine()) != null)
      {
         outputTB.Text += line;
      }
   }
   catch (Exception ex)
   {
      outputTB.Text = ex.Message;
   }
}
```

In the response handler, we grab the request object via the AsyncState parameter, and then get the Stream from EndGetResponse. This is the equivalent of the GET HTTP method.

Sending data to a server is similar to initiating an asynchronous operation for retrieving the response. BeginGetRequestStream starts the operation, and then EndGetRequestStream gives us the Stream in the asynchronous callback method passed to BeginGetRequestStream. This is equivalent to the HTTP POST method.

Raw Network Communication

While most applications will use either the service proxy or one of the classes for downloading via HTTP/HTTPS, some applications will need a raw communication channel. Severe restrictions are placed on Silverlight when communicating over sockets, so for advanced scenarios, you'll want to create a proxy service on your server for Silverlight to utilize to talk to a wider range of network services (unless, of course, your system design can completely account for the restrictions placed on Silverlight). Silverlight can only communicate over ports ranging from 4502 to 4532 (inclusive), and requires a special policy server to deliver the `clientaccessproxy.xml` file for all socket communication, either with the application's site of origin or a cross-domain server.

There are several key classes used in the course of communicating over sockets. The `Socket` class contains the core functionality for socket communication. The `SocketAsyncEventArgs` class is used to pass parameters to a socket operation and also handle the result of a socket operation, such as data received. The `DnsEndPoint` class specifies an endpoint as a combination of a hostname and port number, while `IPEndPoint` specifies the endpoint as an IP address and port number. An endpoint must be specified when executing a socket operation.

The Socket Class

The `Socket` class has three socket operations: connecting (`ConnectAsync`), sending data (`SendAsync`), and receiving data (`ReceiveAsync`). The socket must first connect to a remote endpoint, described by either the `IPEndPoint` class or `DnsEndPoint` class. The former is used to connect to an IP address, and the latter is used to connect to a hostname. Tables 4-7 and 4-8 display the methods and properties of the `Socket` class. You should always call the `Shutdown` method before `Close` to ensure that data is finished sending/receiving on the open socket.

Table 4-7. *Methods of the System.Net.Socket Class*

Name	Description
ConnectAsync	Initiates a connection to a remote host. A nonstatic version takes only a `SocketAsyncEventArgs`, while a static version takes a `SocketType`, a `ProtocolType`, and a `SocketAsyncEventArgs`. It returns `true` if the operation is pending, and `false` if the operation has completed.
CancelConnectAsync	Used to cancel a pending connection. It must pass the `SocketAsyncEventArgs` used in the `ConnectAsync` method.
SendAsync	Sends data specified in a `SocketAsyncEventArgs`. It returns `true` if the operation is pending, and `false` if the operation has completed.
ReceiveAsync	Receives data from the open socket. It returns `true` if the operation is pending, and `false` if the operation has completed.
Shutdown	Shuts down sending, receiving, or both on the socket. It ensures that pending data is sent/received before shutting down a channel, so you should call this before you call `Close`.
Close	Closes the socket, releasing all resources.

Table 4-8. *Properties of the System.Net.Socket Class*

Name	Description
AddressFamily	Addressing scheme used to resolve addresses. Valid values from the AddressFamily enumeration are Unknown, Unspecified, InterNetwork (for IPv4), and InterNetworkV6 (for IPv6). AddressFamily is initially specified when a socket is created.
Connected	Used to cancel a pending connection. It must pass the SocketAsyncEventArgs used in the ConnectAsync method.
NoDelay	Sends data specified in a SocketAsyncEventArgs.
OSSupportsIPv4	Static property; indicates whether IPv4 addressing is supported or not.
OSSupportsIPv6	Static property; indicates whether IPv6 addressing is supported or not.
ReceiveBufferSize	The size of the socket's receive buffer.
RemoteEndPoint	The endpoint of the remote server.
SendBufferSize	The size of the socket's send buffer.
Ttl	The time-to-live value for IP packets.

The SocketAsyncEventArgs Class

The SocketAsyncEventArgs class is possibly the most important class for socket communication, since it is used as a way to both pass data/configuration to the three socket operation methods and pass access status information/data after an asynchronous call completes. Table 4-9 lists its members.

Table 4-9. *Members of the System.Net.SocketAsyncEventArgs Class*

Name	Type	Description
SetBuffer	Method	Initializes the data buffer for an asynchronous operation. One overload sets only the Count and Offset properties (Buffer is set to null) while the other also sets the Buffer property to an array of bytes.
Buffer	Property (byte[])	Accesses the data buffer. This property is read-only—use the SetBuffer method to initialize and possibly place data into this buffer.
BufferList	Property (IList<ArraySegment<byte>>)	Specifies an array of data buffers for use by ReceiveAsync and SendAsync. This property has precedence over the Buffer property.
BytesTransferred	Property (int)	Number of bytes transferred in socket operation. After a read operation, if this property is 0, it indicates that the remote service has closed the connection.
ConnectSocket	Property (Socket)	Socket related to this operation.
Count	Property (int)	Maximum number of bytes to send/receive. It is set via SetBuffer.

Continued

Table 4-9. *Continued*

Name	Type	Description
LastOperation	Property (SocketAsyncOperation)	Valid values from SocketAsyncOperation enumeration are None, Connect, Receive, and Send. This is set to None before one of the asynchronous methods is invoked, and then it is set to the value corresponding to the asynchronous operation.
Offset	Property (int)	The offset, in bytes, into the Buffer property. This is set via the SetBuffer method.
RemoteEndPoint	Property (EndPoint)	Specifies remote endpoint used for the ConnectAsync method. This can be IPEndPoint or DNSEndPoint. It supports both IPv4 and IPv6 addressing.
SocketError	Property (SocketError)	Corresponds to a socket error from the most recent socket operation (Connect, Send, or Receive). There are a large number of error codes; however, SocketError.Success is the only code representing success. Check against this to ensure that the most recent operation succeeded.
UserToken	Property (object)	Arbitrary object used to pass data from the invocation of an asynchronous method to the Completed event handler.
Completed	Event	Used to specify an event handler that is invoked when the asynchronous operation is complete.

Using the Socket Class

You generally want to use asynchronous communication as much as possible. Sometimes, though, you might want to handle a send-and-receive cycle despite an impact to the user interface, so a synchronous approach might prove useful. Let's look at how to develop a class to layer synchronous semantics onto the Socket class. In the course of this discussion, you will see how to utilize the Socket class asynchronously. Since the Socket class already contains asynchronous semantics, you won't need a wrapper class for that approach.

```
public class SynchronousSocket : IDisposable
{
    public Exception Error { get; set; }
    private Socket _socket;
    private EndPoint _endPoint;
    public SynchronousSocket(string hostName, int port)
    {
        if (port < 4502 || port > 4532)
        {
            throw new ArgumentException(
                "TCP port must be between 4502 and 4532, inclusive");
        }
```

```
            _endPoint = new DnsEndPoint(hostName, port);
            _socket = new Socket(AddressFamily.InterNetwork,
                                        SocketType.Stream, ProtocolType.Tcp);
    }
    // ...
}
```

Since we are implementing a wrapper for the socket, we might as well add a check for the port range. We first create an endpoint based on the DnsEndPoint class since we expect a host name as a parameter to the constructor, and then we configure the socket for IPv4 communication (using AddressFamily.InterNetwork) and the only currently valid options for SocketType and ProtocolType.

Before looking at the connect, send, and receive implementations, let's implement the Completed event handler:

```
protected void SocketOperationCompleted(object sender, SocketAsyncEventArgs e)
{
    if (e.SocketError != SocketError.Success)
    {
        this.Error = new SocketException((int)e.SocketError);
    }
    ((AutoResetEvent)e.UserToken).Set();
}
```

This handler exists to signal the end of the operation via an AutoResetEvent. This is the mechanism by which we enforce the synchronous semantics. When connecting, sending, or receiving, we clear the AutoResetEvent, and then wait for it to get signaled. Notice that the AutoResetEvent is passed via the UserToken property of the SocketAsyncEventArgs class. The AutoResetEvent class is located in the System.Threading namespace, which will be covered in more detail later in this book.

While this particular implementation performs the same actions for all socket operations, the LastOperation property of SocketAsyncEventArgs could be used here in order to create a single event handler for all socket operations. You could utilize the following switch statement inside the event handler:

```
switch (e.LastOperation)
{
    case SocketAsyncOperation.Connect:
        break;
    case SocketAsyncOperation.Receive:
        break;
    case SocketAsyncOperation.Send:
        break;
}
```

Now let's move on to the implementations of the socket operations. First, we'll take a look at the Connect method. The SocketAsyncEventArgs class is instantiated in this method. There is no need to hold onto this reference, so we aren't storing it at the class level. In fact, after a socket operation is initiated, the particular instance of SocketAsyncEventArgs can be reused.

If you are making a large number of SendAsync/ReceiveAsync calls, you could create a pool of SocketAsyncEventArgs objects and store these at the class level. Although this requires more management, it can cut down on object creation and disposal if your application performance is negatively impacted.

```
public void Connect()
{
    SocketAsyncEventArgs asyncEventArgs = new SocketAsyncEventArgs();
    asyncEventArgs.RemoteEndPoint = _endPoint;
    asyncEventArgs.Completed +=
                new EventHandler<SocketAsyncEventArgs>(SocketOperationCompleted);
    AutoResetEvent connectEvent = new AutoResetEvent(false);
    asyncEventArgs.UserToken = connectEvent;
    bool completedSynchronously = _socket.ConnectAsync(asyncEventArgs);
    if (!completedSynchronously)
    {
        connectEvent.WaitOne();
    }
    connectEvent.Close();
    if (asyncEventArgs.SocketError != SocketError.Success)
    {
        throw this.Error;
    }
}
```

The ConnectAsync operation is the only socket operation that requires the RemoteEndPoint to be set. The rest of this method consists of creating the AutoResetEvent, invoking ConnectAsync, and then waiting for the signaling of the AutoResetEvent before completing. One important aspect to notice is the return value from ConnectAsync: the asynchronous handler will *not* be called if the connect operation finishes synchronously. Since we are treating Connect as a logical synchronous connection, it will throw the exception if an error occurs during the connect attempt.

Since it goes along with the Connect method, let's look at the Disconnect method:

```
public void Disconnect()
{
    if (_socket.Connected)
    {
        _socket.Shutdown(SocketShutdown.Both);
        _socket.Close();
    }
}
```

Before closing the socket, we call Shutdown to ensure that all data is sent/received, in case any data is currently in the buffer. The Shutdown method can also selectively shut down the sending or receiving channels, specified by SocketShutdown.Send or SocketShutdown.Receive. No further operations are allowed after the socket is closed.

We'll create a simple Send method that matches the signature of Socket's Send method, specifying a byte buffer containing the data to send, an offset marking the beginning of the data in the buffer, and the length of the data to send. The offset and length parameters are useful for sending data that is larger than the SendBufferSize of the socket. In this method, we use the SetBuffer method of the SocketAsyncEventArgs class to initialize and set the data we're about to send over the socket:

```
public void Send(byte[] data, int offset, int length)
{
    if (!this.Connected)
    {
        throw new Exception("Not connected.");
    }
    SocketAsyncEventArgs asyncEventArgs = new SocketAsyncEventArgs();
    asyncEventArgs.SetBuffer(data, offset, length);
    asyncEventArgs.Completed += new
                    EventHandler<SocketAsyncEventArgs>(SocketOperationCompleted);
    AutoResetEvent sendEvent = new AutoResetEvent(false);
    asyncEventArgs.UserToken = sendEvent;
    _socket.SendAsync(asyncEventArgs);
    sendEvent.WaitOne();
    sendEvent.Close();
    if (asyncEventArgs.SocketError != SocketError.Success)
    {
        this.Error = new SocketException((int)asyncEventArgs.SocketError);
        throw this.Error;
    }
}
```

Again, we wait for the event to get signaled. The Receive is similar to what we've seen so far; however, after the operation is complete, we have a result—this is what we wait on so that we have data to return from the method. The Receive here will return the data received as a string.

```
public string ReceiveAsString()
{
    if (!this.Connected)
    {
        throw new Exception("Not connected.");
    }
    SocketAsyncEventArgs asyncEventArgs = new SocketAsyncEventArgs();
    byte[] response = new byte[1024];
    asyncEventArgs.SetBuffer(response, 0, response.Length);
    asyncEventArgs.Completed +=
                new EventHandler<SocketAsyncEventArgs>(SocketOperationCompleted);
    AutoResetEvent receiveEvent = new AutoResetEvent(false);
    asyncEventArgs.UserToken = receiveEvent;
    _socket.ReceiveAsync(asyncEventArgs);
    receiveEvent.WaitOne();
    receiveEvent.Close();
```

```
    if (asyncEventArgs.SocketError == SocketError.Success)
    {
        return (Encoding.UTF8.GetString(asyncEventArgs.Buffer,
                    asyncEventArgs.Offset, asyncEventArgs.BytesTransferred));
    }
    else
    {
        throw this.Error;
    }
}
```

This method wraps the ReceiveAsync, waits for it to complete, and returns the data encoded as a string. This is a rather simple receive method, since we're not taking into account the possibility that the data is larger than can be received in a single ReceiveAsync. Figures 4-8 and 4-9 show a Silverlight application that uses the SynchronousSocket class to implement a simple chat application. Before Silverlight can communicate over sockets, however, it needs to download the cross-domain policy file. In order for this to happen, a policy server must be running on the same machine as the service that your Silverlight wants to communicate with. The requirements for this policy server are fairly straightforward: it must listen on port 943, and it must send the policy file to the requesting client after receiving the special request <policy-file-request/>. Here's the main implementation of a very stripped-down policy server, sufficient to work but not suitable for production:

```
byte[] policyFileBytes;
FileStream fileStream = new FileStream("clientaccesspolicy.xml", FileMode.Open);
policyFileBytes = new byte[fileStream.Length];
fileStream.Read(policyFileBytes, 0, policyFileBytes.Length);
fileStream.Close();
TcpListener listener = new TcpListener(IPAddress.Parse("127.0.0.1"), 943);
listener.Start();
Console.WriteLine("Waiting for connection...");
TcpClient client = listener.AcceptTcpClient();
Console.WriteLine("Connection accepted from " +
                                        client.Client.RemoteEndPoint.ToString());
NetworkStream ns = client.GetStream();
byte[] buf = new byte[1024];
int bytesRead = ns.Read(buf, 0, 1024);
string msg = System.Text.Encoding.UTF8.GetString(buf, 0, bytesRead);
if(msg.Equals("<policy-file-request/>")) {
    ns.Write(policyFileBytes, 0, policyFileBytes.Length);
} else {
    Console.WriteLine("Unrecognized request from client: [" + msg + "]");
}
ns.Close();
client.Close();
Console.WriteLine("Sent policy file to client");
```

Silverlight Chat Client
Enter Message:
Connect
Send Message

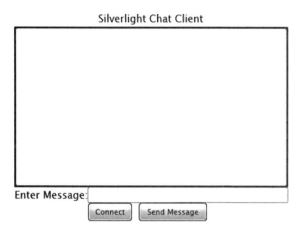

Figure 4-8. *Socket client example before connecting to a remote service*

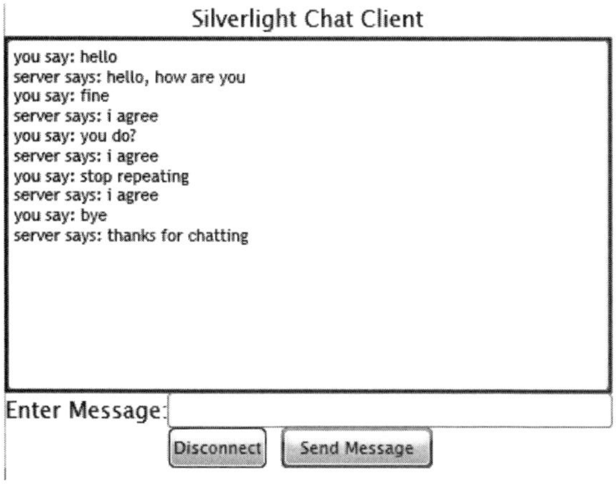

Silverlight Chat Client
you say: hello
server says: hello, how are you
you say: fine
server says: i agree
you say: you do?
server says: i agree
you say: stop repeating
server says: i agree
you say: bye
server says: thanks for chatting
Enter Message:
Disconnect
Send Message

Figure 4-9. *Socket client example after connecting and sending data*

The code connects directly to the host that served the application. This is accomplished by the following code:

```
socket = new SynchronousSocket(App.Current.Host.Source.DnsSafeHost, 4502);
```

Connecting to the remote server is done via the following code:

```
socket.Connect();
```

The send button performs the send and receive and then appends the response to the main text box that shows the chat conversation.

```
private void sendButton_Click(object sender, RoutedEventArgs e)
{
    if (socket != null && socket.Connected)
    {
        try
        {
            outputTextBox.Text += "you say: " + inputTextBox.Text + "\r\n";
            socket.Send(inputTextBox.Text);
            outputTextBox.Text += "server says: "
                            + socket.ReceiveAsString() + "\r\n";
            inputTextBox.Text = "";
        }
        catch (Exception ex)
        {
            outputTextBox.Text = ex.Message;
        }
    }
}
```

Considerations for Using Networking

So far, you have seen three ways to communicate over HTTP and one way to communicate over sockets in Silverlight. Some great question to ask at this point are "How do these approaches compare to each other?" and "When should you use which?"

Generating a client proxy for a service is the easiest from a development standpoint. It's also easy to use a different endpoint when constructing an instance of the client proxy. Using a generated proxy is the easiest, best way to call services exposed on the World Wide Web. If the service changes, you can simply update the proxy. If there are multiple endpoints exposed, you will see these in the ClientConfig and can choose which to use. It is also important to note that this approach uses SOAP 1.1 as a way to communicate with objects over HTTP.

The easiest way to download a resource from a site is to use the System.Net.WebClient class. The two biggest resources are files (e.g., the archived media in the example earlier in this chapter) and text files (such as syndication feeds in XML format). The WebClient class provides a way to download data via a Stream or as a String, making the access of resources quite easy.

Although the WebClient class provides both the HTTP GET and POST methods, it is impossible to send more complicated requests to a server. The System.Net.HttpWebRequest class supports both GET and POST, and also supports both the HTTP and HTTPS protocols. The other major benefit of the HttpWebRequest class is that capabilities provided by the browser, such as authentication and cookies, are supported.

Finally, the socket support exists to directly communicate with an exposed TCP service. Whereas HTTP is an application layer protocol, socket communication has no application layer protocol. A communication protocol must be previously agreed on between a service and the Silverlight application. The major benefit to socket communication is performance—a well-designed TCP service can have less overhead than communication directly over HTTP/SOAP.

Summary

Silverlight exists in a connected world. Its network support is primarily focused on communication over HTTP(S), which enables it to easily invoke services on the World Wide Web and download documents such as syndication feeds. In this chapter, you've seen the support for HTTP(S) communication provided by the `WebClient` and `HttpWebRequest` classes. Silverlight also supports raw socket communication, albeit with severe restrictions. The next two chapters will utilize the networking support built into Silverlight to retrieve data for consumption by Silverlight.

CHAPTER 5

■ ■ ■

Working with Data

Data can take many forms, from simple types passed back from web services to complex formats such as XML. In the previous chapter, you saw how to consume web services from Silverlight and connect to various servers, including ones that live outside your application's host domain and others that communicate over sockets. Once you have data, though, you must process it and/or display it to users. Silverlight provides a DataGrid control, a data binding architecture to connect data to user interface elements, and even item templates for controls like the ListBox to specifically define how each item should appear. On the data-processing side, Silverlight provides a number of classes for working with XML, including LINQ, which was introduced in .NET 3.5 on Windows (but remember, while Silverlight is based on .NET 3.5, it has no dependence on the .NET 3.5 Framework!). Another important aspect to data is how to save data on the client. While you can use cookies, Silverlight provides something called *isolated storage* that provides file system semantics for saving and loading data. Let's dig into all this support Silverlight provides for working with data.

Displaying Data

In Chapter 3, you were introduced to a number of controls, including the ListBox. Data templates and the `Binding` markup extension were previewed in Chapter 2. Controls such as the ListBox enable you to connect a user interface element to a data source and automatically display data. One control that wasn't discussed in Chapter 2 is the DataGrid—a control specifically designed for displaying data in rows and columns. It provides a lot of flexibility for displaying the data and the column headers and footers. We'll take a brief look at this control in this section.

Data Binding

Data binding is the connection of a data source to a user interface element such as a text block, text box, or list box. It is possible to do one-way data binding where data is simply displayed in the user interface, and two-way data binding where any changes a user makes within the user interface elements gets reflected in the underlying data source. Data sources in Silverlight are generally objects or collections of objects with properties that can be accessed.

Before we can take a closer look at data binding, we need to examine what makes it happen: the `Binding` markup extension. This can be used either in XAML or in the code-behind. It's not possible to bind directly to basic data types such as `Int32` and `string`, so we need at least one containing class, such as `AccountSettings` shown here:

```
public class AccountSettings
{
    public string Name { get; set; }
    public string EmailAddress { get; set; }
    public string SignatureLine { get; set; }
    public bool HideEmailAddress { get; set; }
}
```

This class contains several properties that will be used in the data binding. If we have a TextBlock and want to display the Name property, we first bind the Text property of the TextBlock to the Name property:

```
<TextBlock x:Name="nameTextBlock" Text="{Binding Name}"/>
```

This gets us halfway there. The other step is to set the DataContext property of the TextBlock to the AccountSettings object. This step is only necessary when it isn't possible to set the data context in XAML, and a simple object like this is one of those cases. The Binding markup extension provides support for three modes of operation: OneTime, OneWay, and TwoWay. These modes of operation control how data is bound and controls the flow between data source and user interface elements. The following list describes each of these modes:

OneTime: The data binding happens exactly once, meaning that any changes to the data source after the initial binding will not be reflected in the user interface.

OneWay: The data flows only from the data source to the user interface. Any time the data source is updated, the user interface will reflect the changes.

TwoWay: The data flows from the data source to the user interface and also from the user interface to the data source. Any changes on either side will automatically be reflected in the other side.

Table 5-1 displays the various valid XAML syntax for the Binding markup extension.

Table 5-1. *Valid Syntax for the Binding Markup Extension*

Syntax	Description
{Binding}	This signals data binding. The mode of operation is OneWay. This is most commonly used with item templates for controls such as the ListBox.
{Binding *path*}	This signals data binding and specifies which property will supply the data. The path takes the form of object properties separated by dots, allowing you to drill down into an object.
{Binding *properties*}	This signals data binding but provides the ability to set data binding configuration properties using a *name=value* syntax.
{Binding *path, properties*}	This combines the previous two formats, allowing you to specify which object property supplies the data and also configure the data binding.

There are a number of properties that help control how data binding behaves, such as controlling how errors during data binding are handled. The full list of properties is shown in Table 5-2.

Table 5-2. *System.Windows.Data.Binding Properties*

Name	Type	Description
Converter	IValueConverter	This is used to easily perform a custom conversion of the data on its way to or from the data source. This is useful for changing how data appears in the user interface while still maintaining proper data format for the data source.
ConverterCulture	CultureInfo	This is used to specify the culture the converter uses.
ConverterParameter	object	This is a custom parameter for use in the converter.
Mode	BindingMode	The binding mode specifies how and where data flows between the data source and user interface. The valid modes are OneWay, OneTime, and TwoWay.
NotifyOnValidatonError	bool	When set to true, the data binding system will raise a BindingValidationError event if validation fails when committing changes to the data source in TwoWay data binding. If false, validation errors will be ignored.
Path	string	This specifies the property path to the binding data source.
Source	object	This specifies the source object for data binding. This overrides the DataContext set on containing elements within the visual tree.
ValidatesOnExceptions	bool	When this and NotifyOnValidationError are true, any exceptions generated from the source object's setters or the binding engine's type converters will be reported by raising BindingValidationError. If this is false, or if it's true and NotifyOnValidationError is false, your application will not be aware of exceptions generated by the binding system. This only applies in TwoWay binding when the data source is updated.

Now let's take a closer look at data binding an AccountSettings object. This will be a TwoWay data binding scenario, where changes done to the user interface will be reflected in the data source and vice versa. Figure 5-1 shows an interface where the same data is shown twice.

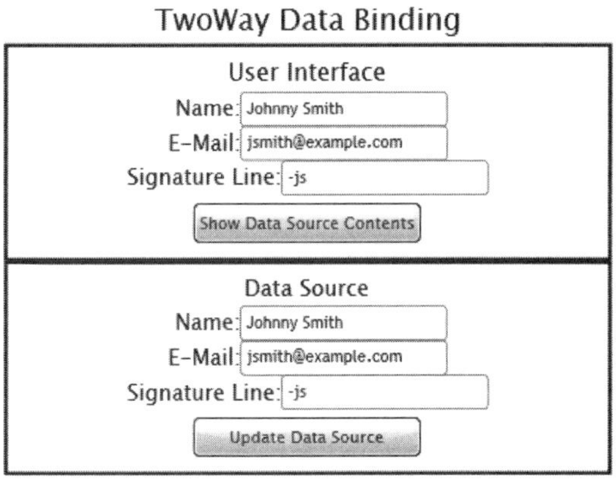

TwoWay Data Binding

User Interface

Name: Johnny Smith

E-Mail: jsmith@example.com

Signature Line: -js

Show Data Source Contents

Data Source

Name: Johnny Smith

E-Mail: jsmith@example.com

Signature Line: -js

Update Data Source

Figure 5-1. *TwoWay data binding example*

In the top half, the user interface elements (in this case, text boxes) are bound to the data source. Any changes made to these text boxes are reflected in the data source. You can verify this by clicking Show Data Source Contents after modifying a value. The lower half lets you change the data source directly. When you click Update Data Source, the values in the data source will be updated directly and the corresponding fields in the top half will automatically change. The following XAML shows how this user interface is put together and how the Binding markup extension is used on several of the user interface elements.

```
<Border BorderBrush="Black" BorderThickness="2" Grid.Row="1">
    <StackPanel Orientation="Vertical">
        <TextBlock Text="User Interface" FontSize="16"
                            HorizontalAlignment="Center"/>
        <StackPanel Orientation="Horizontal" HorizontalAlignment="Center">
            <TextBlock Text=" Name:"/>
            <TextBox x:Name="nameTextBox"
                            Text="{Binding Name, Mode=TwoWay}" Width="140"/>
        </StackPanel>
        <StackPanel Orientation="Horizontal" HorizontalAlignment="Center">
            <TextBlock Text="E-Mail:"/>
            <TextBox x:Name="emailTextBox" Width="140"
                            Text="{Binding EmailAddress, Mode=TwoWay}"/>
        </StackPanel>
        <StackPanel Orientation="Horizontal" HorizontalAlignment="Center">
            <TextBlock Text="Signature Line:"/>
            <TextBox x:Name="signatureTextBox" Width="140" />
        </StackPanel>
        <Button x:Name="viewDataSourceButton" Margin="5" Width="155"
                Content="Show Data Source Contents"
                Click="viewDataSourceButton_Click"/>
    </StackPanel>
</Border>
```

The lower half of the user interface is similar but uses no data binding. An instance of AccountSettings is created in the constructor of this page and then connected when the page loads via the Loaded event handler:

```
private void UserControl_Loaded(object sender, RoutedEventArgs e)
{
    dsNameTextBox.Text = settings.Name;
    dsEmailTextBox.Text = settings.EmailAddress;
    dsSignatureTextBox.Text = settings.SignatureLine;
    nameTextBox.DataContext = settings;
    emailTextBox.DataContext = settings;
    Binding dataBinding = new Binding("SignatureLine");
    dataBinding.Source = settings;
    dataBinding.Mode = BindingMode.TwoWay;
    signatureTextBox.SetBinding(TextBox.TextProperty, dataBinding);
}
```

There are two things of note in this event handler. First, the DataContext property for two of the text boxes must be set. Between the DataContext and the Binding markup extension, the data source is fully linked to the user interface element. The second thing of note is how to create this linkage completely in the code-behind. If you look at the XAML again, you'll see that the SignatureLine doesn't use the Binding markup extension. Instead, the property name is set in the Binding constructor, the data source is linked, and then the data is bound by setting the TextProperty dependency property to the Binding instance. This is almost everything we need to completely enable TwoWay data binding.

Enabling Data Change Notification

If you assemble the code as is, you'll discover that direct changes to the data source are not reflected immediately in the user interface. This is because the data binding system isn't aware that the data source changed. In order to provide this notification, the object being used as the data source must implement the INotifyPropertyChanged interface. This interface defines a single event, PropertyChanged, that must be provided. Let's modify the AccountSettings class to implement this interface:

```
public class AccountSettings : INotifyPropertyChanged
{
    public event PropertyChangedEventHandler PropertyChanged;
    protected void OnPropertyChanged(string propertyName)
    {
        PropertyChangedEventHandler handler = PropertyChanged;
        if (handler != null)
        {
            handler(this, new PropertyChangedEventArgs(propertyName));
        }
    }
    private string _name;
    public string Name
    {
```

```
        get { return (_name); }
        set
        {
            _name = value;
            OnPropertyChanged("Name");
        }
    }
    // other properties; each setter must invoke OnPropertyChanged
}
```

Each time the Name property is updated, the PropertyChanged event will be raised and the data binding system will be notified. This is the mechanism that will cause the user interface elements (the top half of our demonstration interface) to change immediately after clicking the button to update the data source directly.

Next, let's take a look at using data binding to supply the items for a ListBox. This is accomplished by combining two concepts: item templates and data templates. *Item templates* are specifically related to various controls that can contain items, such as the ListBox. They are used to define the appearance of each item within the control. *Data templates* define, using user interface elements, how a single data object within an items control uses properties from the each item stored in a data source such as a collection. Figure 5-2 shows a ListBox used to display a customer's bank accounts. A customer can have one or more bank accounts. These are stored within a collection and the collection is set as the data source for the ListBox.

Figure 5-2. *A data template used to connect data to items within a ListBox*

Let's use the following BankAccount class to hold details about a customer's bank account:

```
public class BankAccount
{
    public string AccountNumber { get; set; }
    public double Balance { get; set; }
    public string AccountName { get; set; }
}
```

Here's what the ListBox looks like in the XAML:

```
<ListBox Grid.Row="2" x:Name="accountsListBox">
    <ListBox.ItemTemplate>
        <DataTemplate>
            <StackPanel Orientation="Vertical">
                <StackPanel Orientation="Horizontal">
                    <TextBlock FontSize="16" Text="Account #"/>
                    <TextBlock FontSize="16" Text="{Binding AccountNumber}"/>
                </StackPanel>
                <StackPanel Orientation="Horizontal">
                    <TextBlock FontSize="12" Text="Account Type: "/>
                    <TextBlock FontSize="12" Text="{Binding AccountName}"/>
                </StackPanel>
                <StackPanel Orientation="Horizontal">
                    <TextBlock FontSize="12" Text="Current Balance: "/>
                    <TextBlock FontSize="12" Text="{Binding Balance}"/>
                </StackPanel>
            </StackPanel>
        </DataTemplate>
    </ListBox.ItemTemplate>
</ListBox>
```

In the code-behind, we create a `List<BankAccount>` collection to hold the bank accounts, create a couple dummy accounts, and then set the `ItemsSource` property of the ListBox to the collection.

```
List<BankAccount> accounts = new List<BankAccount>();
BankAccount ba1 = new BankAccount();
ba1.AccountName = "Checking";
ba1.AccountNumber = "9048120948109185";
ba1.Balance = 2300.17;
accounts.Add(ba1);
BankAccount ba2 = new BankAccount();
ba2.AccountName = "Savings";
ba2.AccountNumber = "9128059128590812";
ba2.Balance = 18964.00;
accounts.Add(ba2);
accountsListBox.ItemsSource = accounts;
```

The rest happens automatically. Between the item template and the data template, each item within the data source is queried for the property specified in the `Binding` markup extension in the XAML. This makes it easy to display a set of objects within a data source.

Type Converters

This is basically all there is to combining data binding with an items control such as a ListBox for displaying data from a data source. Actually, wouldn't it be nice to have a better formatting for the balance amount than what is shown in Figure 5-2? Silverlight provides something called a type converter that can be used by the data binding system to conduct custom conversion as the data flows from the data source to the user interface or vice versa. A custom type converter implements the IValueConverter interface, providing Convert and ConvertBack methods for handling the conversion. Here's the implementation of a type converter used for formatting the currency. Just in case this type converter is used in a TwoWay data binding scenario, the ConvertBack method is also implemented.

```
public class BalanceConverter : IValueConverter
{
    public object Convert(object value, Type targetType,
                          object parameter,
                          System.Globalization.CultureInfo culture)
    {
        return (String.Format("{0:C}", (double)value));
    }
    public object ConvertBack(object value, Type targetType,
                          object parameter,
                          System.Globalization.CultureInfo culture)
    {
        string balance = (string)value;
        return(System.Convert.ToDouble(balance.Replace("$", "").Replace(",", "")));
    }
}
```

The type converter must be registered as a resource and assigned an x:Key value before it can be used in the XAML. Here's what this registration looks like in the BankAccountsPage.xaml page:

```
<UserControl x:Class="chapter5.BankAccountsPage"
             xmlns="http://schemas.microsoft.com/winfx/2006/xaml/presentation"
             xmlns:x="http://schemas.microsoft.com/winfx/2006/xaml"
             xmlns:u="clr-namespace:chapter5"
             Width="400" Height="300" Margin="10">
    <UserControl.Resources>
        <u:BalanceConverter x:Key="BalanceConverter"/>
    </UserControl.Resources>
```

Next, the TextBlock used to show the balance for an account is modified to include the type converter in the Binding markup extension:

```
<TextBlock FontSize="12"
           Text="{Binding Balance, Converter={StaticResource BalanceConverter}}"/>
```

Now this gives us a nicely formatted balance without having to exert too much effort. You can see the result in Figure 5-3.

Your Bank Accounts

Account #9048120948109185

Account Type: Checking
Current Balance: $2,300.17

Account #9128059128590812

Account Type: Savings
Current Balance: $18,964.00

Figure 5-3. *Using a type converter to format data for the user interface*

Introducing the DataGrid

The DataGrid control is useful for displaying data in tabular format with rows and columns. It isn't part of the core Silverlight installation, so you must download the Silverlight SDK and distribute the System.Windows.Controls.Data assembly with your application. In order to use the DataGrid in XAML, you must make its namespace visible.

```
<UserControl x:Class="chapter5.DataGridDemo"
    xmlns="http://schemas.microsoft.com/winfx/2006/xaml/presentation"
    xmlns:x="http://schemas.microsoft.com/winfx/2006/xaml"
    xmlns:c="clr-namespace:System.Windows.Controls;
                assembly=System.Windows.Controls.Data"
    Width="400" Height="300" Margin="10">
    <Grid x:Name="LayoutRoot" Background="White">
        <c:DataGrid x:Name="accountsDataGrid"/>
    </Grid>
</UserControl>
```

You then connect the DataGrid to a data source using the ItemsSource property. By default, the DataGrid automatically generates column headings. The appearance of the default DataGrid is shown in Figure 5-4 after connecting it to the collection of bank accounts used previously.

Figure 5-4. *The default DataGrid control*

The DataGrid provides a lot of functionality. You can change the style of rows, alternate rows, and change column/row headers. The DataGrid can be configured to permit or prevent the reordering of columns, enable row selection, and enable in-place editing of data. It also provides a number of events to give you plenty of opportunity to transform or otherwise handle data.

Processing Data

You've seen how to connect data directly to the user interface. This data can be retrieved in a number of ways, including directly downloading it via WebClient or HttpWebRequest/Response, and having it returned from a web service call. The sample code for this chapter has a simple implementation of a web search utilizing Microsoft's Live Search web service. The ListBox is configured with bindings to properties in the result set from Live Search.

```
<ListBox Grid.Row="3" x:Name="resultsListBox">
    <ListBox.ItemTemplate>
        <DataTemplate>
            <StackPanel Orientation="Vertical">
                <TextBlock FontFamily="Arial" Text="{Binding Title}"/>
                <TextBlock FontSize="10" Text="{Binding Url}"/>
                <TextBlock Text="{Binding Description}" FontSize="10" />
            </StackPanel>
        </DataTemplate>
    </ListBox.ItemTemplate>
</ListBox>
```

Invoking the web service is done according to the Live API documentation available on MSDN, the code for which is shown here:

```
MSNSearchPortTypeClient client = new MSNSearchPortTypeClient();
client.SearchCompleted += new
                EventHandler<SearchCompletedEventArgs>
```

```
                                              (client_SearchCompleted);
SearchRequest req = new SearchRequest();
SourceRequest[] sourceReq = new SourceRequest[1];
sourceReq[0] = new SourceRequest();
sourceReq[0].Source = SourceType.Web;
req.Query = searchTerms.Text;
req.Requests = sourceReq;
req.AppID = /* enter your AppID here!! */
req.CultureInfo = "en-US";
client.SearchAsync(req);
```

The asynchronous callback simply sets ItemsSource to the data source, provided no error has occurred:

```
resultsListBox.ItemsSource = e.Result.Responses[0].Results;
```

This demonstrates how easy it can be to hook up data returned from web services to the user interface. The services infrastructure within Silverlight handles the serialization/deserialization of data for communication purposes, so your application can focus on the objects that can serve as data sources. Of course, sometimes you'll retrieve data directly; for example, by downloading XML data files specific to your application. Silverlight provides a rich set of XML classes for reading/writing/processing XML files. And since Silverlight is based on the .NET 3.5 Framework, it also provides support for LINQ (Language Integrated Query), a new technology that provides syntax roughly similar to SQL for working with data directly within C# or VB .NET.

Parsing XML

The System.Xml.XmlReader class provides the ability to parse XML documents from a variety of sources, such as a stream or a string. It also provides the ability to directly access an XML file contained in the XAP file. These various approaches to handling an XML file are accessed through the many overloads of the XmlReader.Create method. Let's use the BankAccount class again, this time stored in an XML file:

```xml
<?xml version="1.0" encoding="utf-8"?>
<ArrayOfBankAccount xmlns:xsi="http://www.w3.org/2001/XMLSchema-instance"
                                    xmlns:xsd="http://www.w3.org/2001/XMLSchema">
  <BankAccount>
    <AccountNumber>8203598230958</AccountNumber>
    <Balance>1100.27</Balance>
    <AccountName>Checking</AccountName>
  </BankAccount>
  <BankAccount>
    <AccountNumber>8293852952359</AccountNumber>
    <Balance>91824.00</Balance>
    <AccountName>Savings</AccountName>
  </BankAccount>
</ArrayOfBankAccount>
```

You use XmlReaderSettings to configure the behavior of XmlReader. In this case, we'll instruct XmlReader to ignore whitespace. If we didn't do this, it would take more code to advance to the correct nodes within the XML file.

```
List<BankAccount> bankAccounts = new List<BankAccount>();
XmlReaderSettings settings = new XmlReaderSettings();
settings.IgnoreWhitespace = true;
XmlReader xmlReader = XmlReader.Create("BankAccountData.xml", settings);
while (xmlReader.ReadToFollowing("BankAccount"))
{
    BankAccount account = new BankAccount();
    xmlReader.ReadToDescendant("AccountNumber");
    account.AccountNumber =
                xmlReader.ReadElementContentAsString("AccountNumber","");
    account.Balance = xmlReader.ReadElementContentAsDouble("Balance","");
    account.AccountName = xmlReader.ReadElementContentAsString("AccountName","");
    bankAccounts.Add(account);
}
```

Silverlight also provides an XmlWriter class that you can use to write data to isolated storage—essentially a secure, private file system for your Silverlight applications.

Serializing XML

Sometimes you'll need to use XmlReader to parse XML files directly, such as when you want to extract only certain details. If you're saving/loading business objects manually (i.e., not leveraging the automatic serialization provided by web services), then you can use serialization directly. The System.Xml.Serialization namespace provides the XmlSerializer class that you can use to easily save and load objects to any stream. XmlSerializer also supports working directly with XmlReader and TextReader.

After creating a couple more fake bank accounts, this is how you can serialize the List<BankAccount> collection to isolated storage. Using serialization with isolated storage is an easy way to save a collection of objects to a special permanent storage area on the client.

```
XmlSerializer ser = new XmlSerializer(typeof(List<BankAccount>));
using (IsolatedStorageFile rootStore =
                        IsolatedStorageFile.GetUserStoreForApplication())
{
    using (IsolatedStorageFileStream fs =
                new IsolatedStorageFileStream("accounts.xml",
                                    FileMode.Create, rootStore))
    {
        ser.Serialize(writer, accounts);
    }
}
```

After serializing the list to isolated storage, you can verify that the file is created and even view its contents. When you want to turn the file within isolated storage back into objects, you follow a similar pattern, but invoke Deserialize.

```
List<BankAccount> bankAccounts = new List<BankAccount>();
XmlSerializer ser = new XmlSerializer(typeof(List<BankAccount>));
using (IsolatedStorageFile rootStore =
                        IsolatedStorageFile.GetUserStoreForApplication())
{
    using (IsolatedStorageFileStream fs =
                    new IsolatedStorageFileStream("accounts.xml",
                                    FileMode.Open, rootStore))
    {
        bankAccounts = (List<BankAccount>)ser.Deserialize(fs);
    }
}
```

Serialization is by far the easiest way to save business objects to XML files and load them from sources such as isolated storage, or download them via the Web using a class like WebClient.

Using LINQ

LINQ is a language-level technology that makes working with data such as collections of objects and XML documents much easier. While it looks like SQL in some regards, and uses relational model thinking, it has many differences. One similarity, though, is that you can use LINQ to query databases. Revisiting the bank accounts, this time we'll download the accounts.xml file (containing the bank account data) packaged in the XAP file. Then we can use LINQ to easily process the data and load it into an array.

```
void wc_DownloadStringCompleted(object sender, DownloadStringCompletedEventArgs e)
{
    XDocument xmlDocument = XDocument.Parse(e.Result);
    var bankAccountData = from b in xmlDocument.Descendants("BankAccount")
                        select new BankAccount
                        {
                            AccountName = b.Element("AccountName").Value,
                            AccountNumber = b.Element("AccountNumber").Value,
                            Balance = Convert.ToDouble(b.Element("Balance").Value)
                        };
    outputTextBox.Text = "";
    int count = 1;
    foreach (BankAccount ba in bankAccountData)
    {
        outputTextBox.Text += "Record #" + count + "\r\n";
        outputTextBox.Text += "----------\r\n";
        outputTextBox.Text += "Account Number: " + ba.AccountNumber + "\r\n";
        outputTextBox.Text += "Account Name: " + ba.AccountName + "\r\n";
        outputTextBox.Text += "Account Balance: " +
                            string.Format("{0:C}", ba.Balance) +"\r\n";
        outputTextBox.Text += "\r\n";
        count++;
    }
}
```

The var keyword is a LINQ-ism that can be viewed as a way to hold a reference to an unknown type. It provides an easy way to obtain an `IEnumerable` from the LINQ query— in this case, the `BankAccount` objects. The `var` keyword here could easily be replaced with `IEnumerable<BankAccount>` since we know the query will return a collection of `BankAccount` objects. The call to `Descendents` is used to get ahold of all the `BankAccount` nodes. Next, `new BankAccount` is used to signal the creation of new `BankAccount` objects, which the data we "`select`" will fill. The compound statement specifies exactly where the properties of `BankAccount` get their values from—specifically the values of the three elements within each `BankAccount` element. Since the `Value` property is of type `string`, it must be converted to a `double` value, which is accomplished how it normally is in C#. LINQ is a huge topic that can't satisfactorily be covered in this chapter. If you want to learn more about LINQ, consult *Pro LINQ: Language Integrated Query in C# 2008*, by Joseph C. Rattz, Jr. (Apress, 2007); and if you want to learn more about the differences between LINQ in .NET 3.5 and Silverlight, consult the MSDN online documentation.

Saving State on the Client

There are two ways to store data on the client: through cookies and through isolated storage. The most direct method to save and access cookies is through the `HtmlPage.Document` class:

```
HtmlPage.Document.Cookies = "name=value; expires=Saturday, 1-Nov-2008 12:00:00 GMT";
```

I won't go into too much detail on working with cookies, since the important thing is how to access them from Silverlight. Isolated storage, however, is much more interesting. It is a mechanism provided by Silverlight to cache data or store user-specific data on the client. The isolated storage support in Silverlight is based on the isolated storage support in .NET, so you may already be familiar with this topic. Besides granting the ability to persist information on the client, the two biggest advantages to isolated storage are safety and ease of use. Each Silverlight application has its own dedicated storage area on disk, but the application isn't aware of the actual disk usage since it is managed by the runtime. This ensures safety because each application can only use its own dedicated storage area, and there is isolation between the application and the actual disk, mediated by the runtime. Different users on the same computer using the same Silverlight application will each have their own isolated store for the application, ensuring any data stored for one user is safe from other users since each user's store is private and isolated.

The other advantage is ease of use—while access to the underlying disk is prevented, nonetheless, file/directory semantics are used for saving and accessing data in isolated storage. The runtime transparently handles the translation of isolated storage paths to physical paths on the computer.

In Silverlight, the isolated storage area is linked to a Silverlight application via the application's address—including its full path. For example, if you use a Silverlight application at `http://www.fabrikam.com/productbrowser`, each time you visit this address, the application served will access the same isolated storage area. By default, each application is limited to 1MB of storage. This limit can be increased; however, it requires the user to explicitly grant permission. When a Silverlight application attempts to grow its reserved space in isolated storage, a pop-up like the one shown in Figure 5-5 will ask the user for permission.

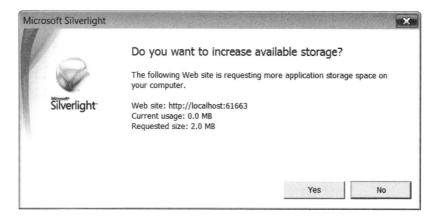

Figure 5-5. *Confirmation dialog shown when application attempts to increase space*

The two significant classes used when working with isolated storage are IsolatedStorageFile and IsolatedStorageFileStream. These can be found in the mscorlib assembly in the System.IO.IsolatedStorage namespace. The IsolatedStorageFile class contains methods for working with directories and files, and querying and increasing allocated space. It has 2 properties (listed in Table 5-3) and 16 methods (listed in Table 5-4). All methods will throw an IsolatedStorageException if the store has been removed (through IsolatedStorageFile.Remove) or if there's an isolated storage–related error. They also will throw an ObjectDisposedException if you attempt an operation on an IsolatedStorageFile instance that has been disposed.

Table 5-3. *System.IO.IsolatedStorageFile Properties*

Name	Type	Description
AvailableFreeSpace	long	The free space, in bytes, for the current application; read-only
Quota	long	The maximum space allocated, in bytes, for current application; read-only

Table 5-4. *System.IO.IsolatedStorageFile Methods*

Name	Description
CreateDirectory	Attempts to create a directory based on the string path passed in. It can create a tree of directories by passing in a path such as \root\data.
CreateFile	Attempts to create a file at the specified string path. If successful, it returns an instance of the IsolatedStorageFileStream class.
DeleteDirectory	Attempts to remove a directory from isolated storage. The directory must be empty for the delete to succeed.
DeleteFile	Attempts to delete a specific file from isolated storage.
DirectoryExists	Returns true if the specified directory exists, and false otherwise.

Continued

Table 5-4. *Continued*

Name	Description
FileExists	Returns true if the specified file exists, and false otherwise.
GetDirectoryNames	Overloaded. The parameterless version returns a string array of directory names from the root of the store. The overload accepts a string search expression to search subdirectories and also use wildcards: the ? matches a single character and the * matches multiple. If no results are found, the Length property of the returned array will be 0.
GetFileNames	Overloaded. The parameterless version returns a string array of files in the root of the store. The overload accepts a string search expression to search subdirectories and also use wildcards: the ? matches a single character and the * matches multiple. If no results are found, the Length property of the returned array will be 0.
GetUserStoreForApplication	Static method. Used to get a reference to the isolated storage for the current user and application.
OpenFile	Overloaded. Opens a specified file from the store using the requested FileMode and, optionally, FileAccess and FileShare options.
Remove	Removes all contents from the isolated storage and the store itself.
TryIncreaseQuotaTo	Attempts to increase the quota to a certain size, specified in bytes. Expanding the size of an isolated store causes a confirmation dialog to appear for user confirmation. It returns true if successful, and false otherwise.

The System.IO.FileMode enumeration contains the following options. This enumeration is the type for the only parameter used in all of the OpenFile overloads.

Append: Appends to an existing file or creates the file if it does not exist.

Create: Creates a file if one doesn't exist. If a file does exist, OpenFile will fail.

CreateNew: Creates a file if one doesn't exist, and re-creates it if it does exist (use with caution).

Open: Opens a file. Unless Append is specified, it also sets the file pointer at the beginning of the file.

OpenOrCreate: Opens the file if it exists, and creates it otherwise.

Truncate: Removes all contents from the file.

The System.IO.FileAccess enumeration contains the following options. This is used to specify the type of access requested to the file.

Read: Only allows reading from the file

ReadWrite: Allows reading and writing to and from the file

Write: Only allows writing to the file

The System.IO.FileShare enumeration contains the following options. This is used to specify the type of access concurrently granted to other FileStream objects.

Delete: Allows the file to be deleted by others

Inheritable: Allows the file handle to be inherited by others

None: Disallows shared access

Read: Allows others to read from but not write to the file

ReadWrite: Allows others to read and write to and from the file

Write: Allows others to write to the file but not read from it

The code for this chapter has an isolated storage explorer. It provides functionality to view contents of the store, create and delete files and directories, and expand the size of the store. Let's take a look at the code for these operations.

First, we need to get an IsolatedStoreFile object to work with isolated storage. This is accomplished using the IsolatedStoreFile.GetUserStoreForApplication static method. Following best practices in .NET, it's a good idea to always wrap this in a using statement so that Dispose is automatically called:

```
using (IsolatedStorageFile rootStore =
                IsolatedStorageFile.GetUserStoreForApplication())
{
    // can now interact with isolated storage files/directories/etc.
}
```

The XmlReader example uses isolated storage to store an object in XML format. The IsolatedStorageFileStream inherits from System.IO.FileStream, so we can use it directly with the Serialize method since it can write to any Stream.

```
XmlSerializer ser = new XmlSerializer(typeof(List<BankAccount>));
using (IsolatedStorageFile rootStore =
                IsolatedStorageFile.GetUserStoreForApplication())
{
    using (IsolatedStorageFileStream fs =
                new IsolatedStorageFileStream("accounts.xml",
                                FileMode.Create, rootStore))
    {
        ser.Serialize(fs, accounts);
    }
}
```

Once we have an instance of IsolatedStorageFile to work with, we can do things like create files. We could use the CreateFile method of IsolatedStorageFileStream; however, the Stream class also offers the ability to create files. It has three constructors that mirror the parameters of IsolatedStorageFile's OpenFile method, but each constructor takes IsolatedStorageFile as a final parameter. Its public properties are listed in Table 5-5 and its public methods are listed in Table 5-6.

Table 5-5. *System.IO.IsolatedStorageFileStream Properties*

Name	Type	Description
CanRead	bool	Returns true if reading from the file is allowed, and false otherwise; read-only
CanSeek	bool	Returns true if the position of the file pointer can be changed, and false otherwise; read-only
CanWrite	bool	Returns true if writing is allowed, and false otherwise; read-only
Length	long	Specifies the length of the file, in bytes; read-only
Position	long	Specifies the current position of the file pointer

Table 5-6. *System.IO.IsolatedStorageFileStream Methods*

Name	Description
BeginRead	Asynchronous method to begin a read operation. Accepts a byte array buffer along with an offset into the array to start writing to, and the maximum number of bytes to read.
BeginWrite	Asynchronous method to begin a write operation. Accepts a byte array buffer along with an offset into the array to start reading, and the number of bytes to write.
EndRead	Used when the read operation ends. Returns an int specifying the number of bytes read.
EndWrite	Used when the write operation ends.
Flush	Flushes any pending data from the internal buffer to disk.
Read	Synchronous read operation. Accepts a byte array buffer along with an offset into the array to start writing to, and the maximum number of bytes to read. Returns the number of bytes actually read.
ReadByte	Synchronously reads a single byte from the stream and returns it.
Seek	Moves the stream pointer to the specified offset, modified by the SeekOrigin option specified. SeekOrigin.Begin treats the offset as an absolute offset from the beginning of the file. SeekOrigin.Current treats the offset as a relative offset from the current position. SeekOrigin.End treats the offset as relative from the end of the file.
SetLength	Attempts to set the length of the file to the passed-in value.
Write	Synchronous write operation. Accepts a byte array buffer along with an offset into the array to start reading, and the number of bytes to write.
WriteByte	Synchronously writes a single byte to the stream.

The sample code for this chapter provides an interface for experimenting with an isolated store, including listing its contents. Figure 5-6 shows what the interface looks like.

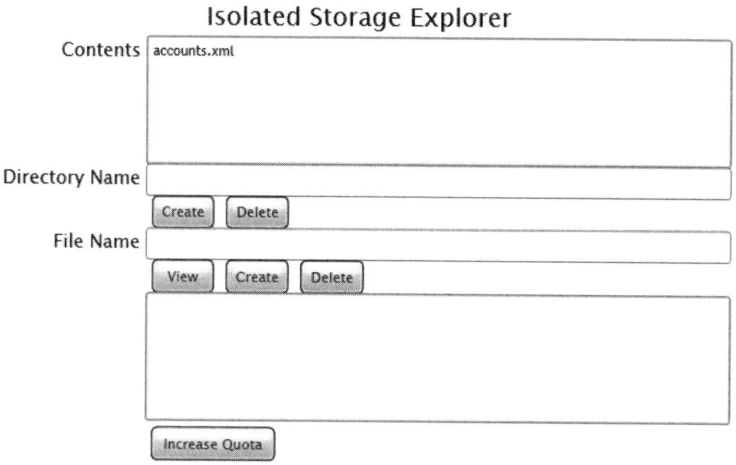

Isolated Storage Explorer

Figure 5-6. *Interface to experiment with and explore an isolated store*

Summary

This chapter discussed connecting data to the user interface and synchronizing the interface with data sources. It also covered support for working with XML documents, including the System.Xml classes and LINQ. It closed with a discussion of how to save state on the client using isolated storage. The next chapter will demonstrate how to work with media, including images, video, and audio. You are now close to having all the pieces to start putting together sophisticated data-connected user interfaces in Silverlight.

CHAPTER 6

■■■

Working with Media

Now that you've seen the support Silverlight provides for communicating with other systems and retrieving, saving, displaying, and manipulating data, it's time to focus again on building user interfaces with Silverlight. Ever since the debut of Silverlight 1.0 under its code name WPF/E, Silverlight has provided support for working with images and video. A significant amount of Silverlight 1.0 applications featured video. Silverlight 2.0 provides the benefits of a managed environment and brings with it rich support for working with images, audio, and video. As you've seen in previous chapters, it isn't too difficult to connect an Image control with an image file on a server. However, it's also possible to package images along with other media, including video files, and work with them on the client side. Microsoft has also introduced two interesting technologies to help enable rich Silverlight applications. The first, Silverlight Streaming, is an environment to host and stream video to Silverlight applications. The second, Deep Zoom, is way to efficiently handle the presentation and network transfer of a large collection of high-quality images. I'll detail these technologies in this chapter.

Images

We have already utilized the Image control in several previous examples, but we haven't delved into the specifics. Silverlight currently supports only PNG and JPEG formats. There are restrictions placed on the PNG formats used, though. The only indexed color depths supported are 1 bit, 4 bits, and 8 bits per channel. The truecolor color depths supported are 24 and 32 bits per channel (for truecolor plus alpha). The simplest way to place an image on a user interface is by using the Image control and setting its `Source` property:

```
<Image Source="sunny.png"/>
```

The Image control inherits from `FrameworkElement`, so it inherits the bits from `FrameworkElement` and `UIElement`. The new properties and event introduced by the `Image` class are listed in Tables 6-1 and 6-2.

Table 6-1. *Properties of the Image Class*

Property	Type	Description
DownloadProgress	double	Holds a value between 0 and 100 representing the percentage of the image downloaded.
Source	ImageSource	Gets or sets the image source. Currently, only the BitmapImage class can be an image source. From XAML, you can specify a relative or absolute URI.
Stretch	Stretch	Gets or sets how the image is sized within the width/height set on the Image control.

Table 6-2. *Event of the Image Class*

Event	Description
ImageFailed	Fires if there's a problem downloading or rendering an image. Possible causes are the image not being found at the specified address and the image format not being supported. The EventArgs class is ExceptionRoutedEventArgs and provides ErrorException (the thrown Exception) and ErrorMessage properties.

The specific image to display is set via the Source property. In XAML, you can specify the Source using a relative or absolute address.

```
<Image Source="../Images/10062506.jpg"/>
```

The Source property is being type-converted to a BitmapImage that inherits from ImageSource. BitmapImage has two events, shown in Table 6-3. The specific image that BitmapImage represents can be a Uri set via a constructor or via the UriSource property after object creation.

■**Tip** Images (and media) can have their Build Action set to Resource within Visual Studio in order for them to be exposed via a relative path. If you can't or don't want to do this, you can make things easy on yourself by utilizing the Application.Current.Host.Source property to retrieve the path to where the Silverlight application is served. This can be useful when constructing image/media sources in the code-behind without needing to know the full path at compile time, such as when things change between development and production. If you specify a relative path in the XAML, however, it's relative to the XAP location, such as the ClientBin folder in this chapter's example code.

You can also download an image and pass the Stream object to the SetSource method. Currently, this is the only ImageSource inheritor, so this class handles both PNG and JPEG images.

Table 6-3. *Events of BitmapImage*

Event	Type
DownloadProgress	Reports the progress of the image download. The EventArgs class is DownloadProgressEventArgs and contains a Progress property that either reports a 0 (indicating that the image is possibly in the process of downloading) or 1 (indicating that the image has finished downloading).
ImageFailed	Fires when the image cannot be downloaded or the image format is invalid. The event handler is passed an ExceptionRoutedEventArgs instance, which has ErrorException (the thrown Exception) and ErrorMessage properties.

If you don't specify a width or height for an image, it will display without any modifications to the image's natural width and height. The Image control has a property named Stretch (it is also a dependency property) that controls how an image conforms to a container. The Stretch property can be one of four possible values:

None: The image maintains its original size.

Fill: The image completely fills the output area, both vertically and horizontally. The image might appear distorted because the aspect ratio is not preserved.

Uniform: The image fills the output area, both vertically and horizontally, but maintains its aspect ratio. This is the default value.

UniformToFill: The image is scaled to completely fill the output area, but its aspect ratio is maintained.

You can see the result of the various Stretch values in Figure 6-1. Reading left to right and top to bottom, Stretch takes on the values None, Fill, Uniform, and UniformToFill.

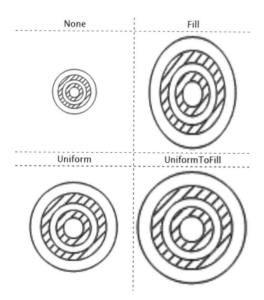

Figure 6-1. *A visual demonstration of each Stretch value*

The image is 100×80, so we can see how the image is treated in a 200×200 square area. The bounding box for the image is defined on the Image control.

```
<Image Source="target.png" Stretch="None" Height="200" Width="200"/>
```

The image is left completely unaltered when Stretch is set to None—it maintains its size of 100×80. When Stretch is set to Fill, the image appears distorted because it is taller than it is wide. For Uniform, the image now almost doubles in size. It doesn't quite fill its bounding box because it is maintaining its aspect ratio. Finally, UniformToFill is similar to Uniform but the image is scaled to the full size of the bounding box—while this specific image can still be completely seen, it is possible that the image will be cut off either horizontally or vertically in order to simultaneously fill its bounding box and maintain its aspect ratio.

You've seen some simple implementations of using images with list boxes in previous chapters. Let's take a closer look at an implementation of an image viewer. A ListBox will contain several ListBoxItem instances, each containing an image scaled down by setting its width/height (we're only using one source image, but for a serious image browser, you might want to store thumbnails separately due to image file size). When a specific image is clicked, the image is shown at full size. The resulting user interface is shown in Figure 6-2.

Figure 6-2. *User interface for an image browser using a ListBox*

```
<ListBox x:Name="thumbnailList" Width="100" Grid.Column="0"
        SelectionChanged="thumbnailList_SelectionChanged">
    <ListBox.Items>
        <ListBoxItem>
            <Image Source="/SpaceImages/10062506.jpg" Width="75" Height="50"/>
        </ListBoxItem>
        <ListBoxItem>
            <Image Source="/SpaceImages/10063680.jpg" Width="75" Height="50"/>
        </ListBoxItem>
    </ListBox.Items>
</ListBox>
```

The full-size image is represented by the following Image control in the XAML:

```
<Image Grid.Column="1" Width="250" x:Name="fullImage"/>
```

The following code is used to display the full-size image. Note that we can't set the source of the `fullImage` to the same source; it instead must reference a new `BitmapImage` instance.

```
private void thumbnailList_SelectionChanged(object sender,
                              SelectionChangedEventArgs e)
{
    ListBox lb = (ListBox)sender;
    ListBoxItem item = (ListBoxItem)lb.SelectedItem;
    Image img = (Image)item.Content;
    fullImage.Source = new BitmapImage(((BitmapImage)img.Source).UriSource);
}
```

Multiscale Images (Deep Zoom)

Deep Zoom first debuted as SeaDragon at the TED technology conference. The various Silverlight announcements at MIX08 included the revelation that SeaDragon is now called Deep Zoom and is a standard feature in Silverlight 2.0. The MultiScaleImage control is used to provide the deep zoom functionality in a Silverlight user interface.

Just what is Deep Zoom? It is technology that makes it easy to develop applications that can display a set of high-quality images (imagine 20MB per image, or more) in a grid-style layout, allowing a user to explore the images at different zoom levels. When the user is zoomed out, the quality is not as high as when they are zoomed in. Because of this, the full source images don't need to get downloaded by the client. Instead, lower-quality images are sent. As the user zooms in, images closer to the quality level of the original are sent, but only pieces of the images the user can see. This provides a highly optimized way to explore a collection of high-quality images. Since the images are laid out in a grid, the MultiScaleImage control also provides the ability to pan around the image collection.

You can get the gist of what Deep Zoom does to an image by consulting Figure 6-3.

25%   50%   100%

Figure 6-3. *The bull's-eye graphic at different zoom levels*

In this figure, we revisit the image of a bull's-eye used earlier. The image stored at 100% has full detail. When we zoom out, we lose detail, but this also gains us an important advantage—less data has to be sent from the server to the client. This means that if we have a large collection of images and we're zoomed out, Silverlight won't immediately request a 100% zoom level for all the images. Instead, it will request a 50% zoom level, or 25%, or something even lower. As the user zooms into specific images, most of the images around it disappear from view, so these don't need to be downloaded. The images still in view, however, do get sent to the client—but now Silverlight requests a 50% zoom, or perhaps a 100% zoom when the user zooms all the way in. Feel free to use images with the highest resolutions you can get—the higher the resolution, the more detail there is for users to zoom in to.

The Deep Zoom Composer tool is used to create a package usable by Silverlight's MultiScaleImage control. You can obtain this tool at `http://silverlight.net/GetStarted`. This generated package contains versions of the images (stored at a possibly large number of different zoom levels, along with certain slices of images used to optimize partial image display) and information describing the layout as designed in the composing tool. The MultiScaleImage control is pointed to this package and then handles all the logic on the client side, such as displaying the images and downloading the right images at the right time to maintain a smooth user experience.

The MultiScaleImage control exposes some useful properties, methods, and events; these are shown respectively in Tables 6-4, 6-5, and 6-6.

Table 6-4. *Properties of MultiScaleImage*

Property	Type	Description
AspectRatio	double	Current aspect ratio of the images; read-only.
Source	Uri	The URI to the Deep Zoom package containing the images, metadata, and so forth.
SubImages	ReadOnlyCollection <MultiScaleSubImage>	Read-only collection of the subimages used by the control. A MultiScaleSubImage exposes a read-only AspectRatio property along with Opacity, ViewportOrigin, ViewportWidth, and ZIndex properties that can be used to set or discover which set of images and which layer of images is currently exposed.
UseSprings	bool	Controls spring motion of the control. Can be set to false and later reset to true to block initial animation when the control loads.
ViewportOrigin	Point	The top-left corner of the current view as an (x,y) coordinate.
ViewportWidth	double	The width of the current viewport.

Table 6-5. *Methods of MultiScaleImage*

Method	Description
ElementToLogicalPoint	Translates a physical point (the screen) to a point located within the image currently visible beneath the physical point.
LogicalToElementPoint	Translates a point within a currently visible image to a physical point (the screen).
ZoomAboutLogicalPoint	Accepts a zoom increment factor and a center (x,y) point about which to zoom. All parameters are of type double.

Table 6-6. *Events of MultiScaleImage*

Events	Description
ImageFailed	Fires when the image cannot be downloaded or the image format is invalid. The event handler method is passed ExceptionRoutedEventArgs, which provides ErrorException (the thrown Exception) and ErrorMessage properties.
ImageOpenFailed	Fires when an image cannot be opened.
ImageOpenSucceeded	Fires when an image is successfully opened.
MotionFinished	Fires when the currently ongoing motion is complete.

The Deep Zoom Composer is a development tool that allows you to aggregate and package images for a Deep Zoom implementation.

When you start the Deep Zoom Composer, you'll see a screen similar to the Expression products (Figure 6-4). Unsurprisingly, this tool is clearly part of the Microsoft Expression family, which supports WPF and Silverlight applications.

Figure 6-4. *The Deep Zoom Composer's start screen*

There are three steps to creating a new Deep Zoom package, and these are clearly defined at the top of the Deep Zoom Composer interface after you create a new project. These steps are also listed at the top of the Deep Zoom Composer interface, clearly showing the workflow in this tool.

1. Import: This is where you add the images you want to include to the project. Information about the type, dimensions, and file size of each image appear in the lower left, and the full list of added images appears to the right. You can right-click an image to remove it from the project.

2. Compose: The second step is where you define how the images are oriented for display, including setting their initial size and position relative to each other.

3. Export: The final step allows you to create a package suitable for use by the Multi-ScaleImage control. You can export in one of two formats: as a composition or as a collection. Optionally, you can create a new Silverlight application as a wrapper.

The example code with this chapter features a Deep Zoom example with several space shuttle pictures. Two of the pictures have other pictures, initially tiny (they're zoomed way out), but increasing in detail as you zoom into them. Figure 6-5 shows what the shuttle images look like zoomed out.

Figure 6-5. *Zoomed-out view of the space shuttles*

By zooming in to the image on the bottom right, four other images in the sky become visible, as shown in Figure 6-6.

Figure 6-6. *Zooming in to the sky of one of the shuttle pictures*

After zooming in to the tiny image on the left (in the sky), you can see the detail of this new image (see Figure 6-7).

Figure 6-7. *Zooming in to one of the initially tiny images in the sky*

This entire Deep Zoom example was built in the Deep Zoom Composer in a matter of a few minutes. After I exported it to its own Silverlight application, I brought it into this chapter's Silverlight application by first copying the GeneratedImages folder into the chapter6Web folder. This folder contains all of the images and metadata required by the MultiScaleImage control. The XAML for this example is rather bare:

```
<MultiScaleImage Height="600" x:Name="msi" Width="800"/>
```

As part of the generated Silverlight application, the Page.xaml.cs file contains the code to connect the MultiScaleImage control to the GeneratedImages folder stored in the web site:

```
this.msi.Source = new DeepZoomImageTileSource(
            new Uri("GeneratedImages/dzc_output.xml", UriKind.Relative));
```

The Deep Zoom Composer also includes, as part of the generation, all the code necessary to hook the MultiScaleImage control up to user input. Between the MouseWheelHelper.cs class and the event handlers in Page.xaml.cs (in the generated application), users can click to zoom, use the mouse wheel to zoom, and also click and drag to pan around the scene.

Media (Video and Audio)

Silverlight 1.0 did not have a managed execution engine, but it did have great support for media. Many early Silverlight applications featured video in a variety of presentations and interfaces. The System.Windows.Controls.MediaElement control provides media playback capability in Silverlight 2. It can handle both audio and video in a variety of formats. These are the supported video formats:

WMV1: Windows Media Video 7

WMV2: Windows Media Video 8

WMV3: Windows Media Video 9

WMVA: Windows Media Video Advanced Profile (non-VC-1)

WMVC1: Windows Media Video Advanced Profile (VC-1)

ASX: Advanced Stream Redirector files; extension might be `.asx`, `.wax`, `.wvx`, `.wmx`, or `.wpl`

And here are the supported audio formats:

WMA 7: Windows Media Audio 7

WMA 8: Windows Media Audio 8

WMA 9: Windows Media Audio 9

MP3: ISO/MPEG Layer-3; 8 to 320Kbps and variable bit rate; 8 to 48KHz sampling frequencies

You can reference a media file using either the HTTP or HTTPS protocols; or using MMS, RTSP, or RTSPT. The latter three will fall back to HTTP. Using the MMS protocol causes Silverlight to attempt to stream the media first; if that fails, it will attempt to download the media progressively. Other protocols work in reverse—Silverlight attempts to progressively download the media first, and if that fails, the media is streamed. The properties, methods, and events of `MediaElement` are shown in Tables 6-7, 6-8, and 6-9, respectively.

Table 6-7. *Properties of MediaElement*

Property	Type	Description
Attributes	Dictionary<string,string>	A collection of attributes; read-only.
AudioStreamCount	int	The number of audio streams in the current media file; read-only.
AudioStreamIndex	int?	The index of the audio stream that is currently playing with a video.
AutoPlay	bool	If true, the media will begin playing immediately after Source is set (i.e., it will transition into the Buffering state and then into the Playing state automatically). If false, the media will start in the Stopped state.
Balance	double	The ratio of volume across stereo speakers.
BufferingProgress	double	The current buffering progress, between 0 and 1. Multiply by 100 to get a percentage value; read-only.
BufferingTime	TimeSpan	The amount of time to buffer; the default is 5 seconds.
CanPause	bool	Returns true if the media can be paused via the Pause method; read-only.
CanSeek	bool	Returns true if the current position in the media can be set via the Seek method; read-only.

Property	Type	Description
CurrentState	MediaElementState	The current state of the media. Possible states include Closed, Opening, Individualizing, AcquiringLicense, Buffering, Playing, Paused, and Stopped. It is possible for several state transitions to happen in quick succession, so you may not witness every state transition happen; read-only.
DownloadProgress	double	The current download progress, between 0 and 1. Multiply by 100 to get a percentage value; read-only.
DownloadProgressOffset	double	The offset in the media where the current downloaded started. Used when media is progressively downloaded; read-only.
IsMuted	bool	Used to set or determine whether audio is currently muted.
Markers	TimelineMarkerCollection	Accesses the collection of timeline markers. Although the collection itself is read-only, it is possible to dynamically add timeline markers. These are temporary since they are not saved to the media and are reset if the Source property is changed.
NaturalDuration	Duration	Duration of the currently loaded media; read-only.
NaturalVideoHeight	int	The height of the video based on what the video file itself reports; read-only.
NaturalVideoWidth	int	The width of the video based on what the video file itself reports; read-only.
Position	TimeSpan	The current position in the media file.
Source	Uri	Sets or retrieves the source of the current media file.
Stretch	Stretch	Gets or sets how the media fills its bounding rectangle. See the "Images" section of this chapter for a discussion of this property.
Volume	double	Gets or sets the volume of the media based on a linear scale. Value can be between 0 and 1; the default is 0.5.

Table 6-8. *Methods of MediaElement*

Method	Description
Pause	Pauses the media at current position if it is possible to pause. If the media cannot be paused, this method does nothing.
Play	Plays the media from the current position if the media can be played.
SetSource	Used when you want to set the source of the media to a Stream object. Use the Source property to set the URI of the media file.
Stop	Stops the media from playing, and sets the current position to 0.

Table 6-9. *Events of MediaElement*

Event	Description
BufferingProgressChanged	Fires each time BufferingProgress changes by at least 0.05 or when it reaches 1.0.
CurrentStateChanged	Fires when the state of the media changes. If states transition quickly (such as bouncing between buffering and playing), some transitions can be lost.
DownloadProgressChanged	Fires when the progress of the downloading media changes. Use the DownloadProgress property to discover the current progress.
MarkerReached	Fires when a timeline marker is reached. The event handler method is passed a TimelineMarkerRoutedEventArgs instance, which exposes a Marker property of type TimelineMarker.
MediaEnded	Fires when the media is done playing.
MediaFailed	Fires when there is a problem with the media source (e.g., when the media can't be found or when the format is incorrect).
MediaOpened	Fires after media file is opened and validated, and the headers are read.

Since a variety of state changes can happen to media, such as a video switching from playing to buffering when it needs to load more of the file, in most applications you will want to implement an event handler for CurrentStateChanged. The states and state transitions are shown in Figure 6-8. The one transition left out of this diagram is to the Opening state. This can happen any time a new source is set for MediaElement.

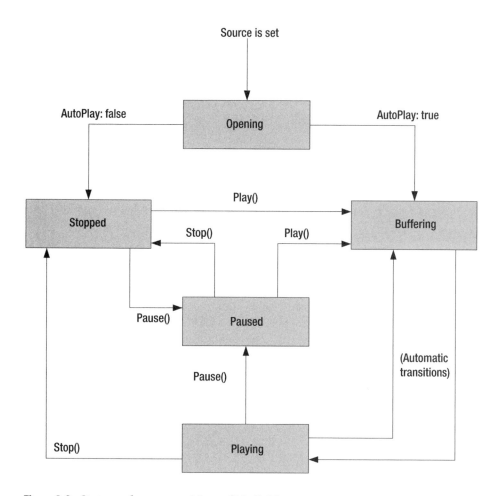

Figure 6-8. *States and state transitions of MediaElement*

While it's fairly simple to specify a source for MediaElement, set AutoPlay to true and let it just go, you probably want to build something with more control for the user. Figure 6-9 shows a simple video player.

Figure 6-9. *Simple video player with position indicator*

Implementing the Start/Stop and Pause/Resume buttons is straightforward. The start/stop event handler checks the media's current state and acts accordingly. This gives you the basic play/stop functionality. Pause and resume are implemented similarly by checking for those states.

```
if (mainVideo.CurrentState == MediaElementState.Stopped ||
    mainVideo.CurrentState == MediaElementState.Paused)
{
    startStopButton.Content = "Stop";
    mainVideo.Play();
    pauseResumeButton.IsEnabled = true;
}
else
{
    startStopButton.Content = "Play";
    mainVideo.Stop();
    pauseResumeButton.IsEnabled = false;
}
```

There's another aspect to media players that is common for users to see: a time signature displaying the length of the video and the current position as it plays. The best approach to adding the current media position to a user interface is by using a timer to poll the `Position` property of `MediaElement` and then displaying it. The best timer to use is `DispatcherTimer` since it works on the user interface thread, allowing you to modify user interface elements directly. (We'll take a closer look at threading and `DispatcherTimer` in Chapter 14.) The following code creates an instance of the timer and sets it to raise the `Tick` event every quarter of a second:

```
timer = new DispatcherTimer();
timer.Interval = new TimeSpan(0, 0, 0, 0, 250);
timer.Tick += new EventHandler(timer_Tick);
```

The Tick event handler calls showCurrentPosition to update the user interface, and the CurrentStateChanged event of MediaElement is handled in order to start/stop the timer:

```
void timer_Tick(object sender, EventArgs e)
{
    showCurrentPosition();
}
private void showCurrentPosition()
{
    currentPositionText.Text = string.Format("{0:00}:{1:00}",
        mainVideo.Position.Minutes,
        mainVideo.Position.Seconds);
}
private void mainVideo_CurrentStateChanged(object sender, RoutedEventArgs e)
{
    MediaElementState currentState = ((MediaElement)sender).CurrentState;
    currentStateTextBlock.Text = currentState.ToString();
    if (currentState == MediaElementState.Paused ||
            currentState == MediaElementState.Stopped)
        timer.Stop();
    else
        timer.Start();
}
```

Timeline Markers

A timeline marker is a point of time in a media file that has some data associated with it. A specific timeline marker (of the System.Windows.Media.Animation.TimelineMarker class) contains three members: Text and Type, both of type String; and Time, of type TimeSpan. Both Text and Type are arbitrary, so you can configure these however you want. Timeline markers can either be embedded in the video file using an editor such as Microsoft Expression Media Encoder or dynamically during program execution. Figure 6-10 shows the Markers pane in Expression Media Encoder. I added one timeline marker to the bear.wmv video to mark when the bird starts flying away. If this were a full-length nature documentary, the timeline markers could be used to initiate different audio files in sync with events happening in the video.

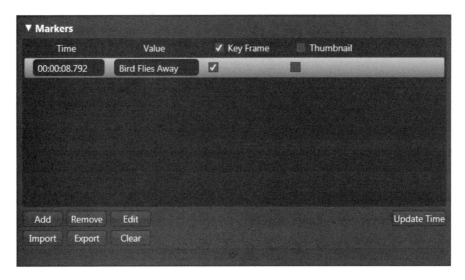

Figure 6-10. *Editing the interface for timeline markers in Expression Media Encoder*

If you define these dynamically, they are good only as long as a particular MediaElement exists and references the same video file. If you load a new video file into a MediaElement control, the timeline marker collection is reset.

The Markers property of MediaElement acts much like a regular collection since it implements the IList interface. Here's an example of creating a new TimelineMarker and adding it to a particular MediaElement:

```
TimelineMarker mark = new TimelineMarker();
mark.Type = "Commercial Cue";
mark.Text = "First Commercial";
mark.Time = new TimeSpan(0, 5, 11);
mainVideo.Markers.Add(mark);
```

Regardless of whether markers are defined in the media file itself or during program execution, you can use the MarkerReached event to perform custom processing when a specific marker is reached. The TimelineMarkerRoutedEventArgs class provides a Marker member to access the specific marker that was reached from the event handler.

Silverlight Streaming

Silverlight Streaming is a service Microsoft provides to host and stream videos to Silverlight applications. It is currently in beta and provides 10GB of storage space free, provided each video is no longer than 10 minutes (or 105MB) and is encoded at a bit rate of no more than 1.4Mbps. Before you can use Silverlight Streaming, you must first have a Live account and a Silverlight Streaming account.

1. Create a Live account: if you don't already have a Microsoft Live account, go to http://login.live.com/ to create one. This account will be associated with your Silverlight Streaming account.

2. Create a Silverlight Streaming account: visit `http://silverlight.live.com/` and click Get It Free. This will lead you to a page where you can create a Silverlight Streaming account. You will need the API key in order for a Silverlight application to use this service.

Before you can use Silverlight Streaming, you must ensure source videos are in the correct format. All video formats supported by Silverlight (as listed earlier in this chapter) are suitable for use by Silverlight Streaming. We'll take a brief look at using Expression Media Encoder to prepare videos; however, you can also use Windows Media Encoder or other tools as long as the encoded format is correct.

■**Tip** If you use Windows Media Encoder, you can download a set of profiles from `http://dev.live.com/silverlight/downloads/profiles.zip`. These provide preset configurations for properly encoding videos for use with Silverlight and Silverlight Streaming.

After you have created your account, you need to generate an account key. Figure 6-11 shows the Manage Account screen with an account key already generated. The account ID is public. The account key, however, is confidential, so it is blurred out in this screenshot. It will not, however, be blurred out when you access your account through Silverlight Streaming.

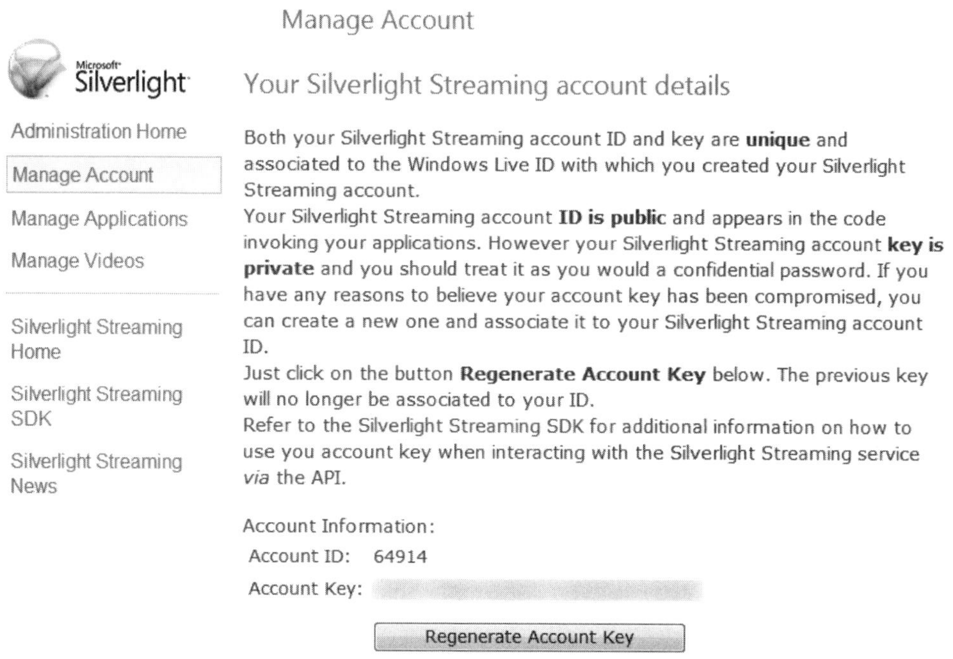

Figure 6-11. *The Manage Account screen on the Silverlight Streaming site*

Preparing an Application

The Silverlight Streaming servers host the Silverlight applications that use Silverlight Streaming. This means there are cross-domain considerations, since the application is embedded in a web page on a server different from the Silverlight Streaming server. In order to upload a Silverlight application to Silverlight Streaming, it must have a manifest file, `manifest.xml`, placed in the root of the archive. Parameters passed to the `Silverlight.createObject` function should be moved to this manifest file. Most child elements are optional—the one that is mandatory is `source`, so Silverlight Streaming knows which file in the uploaded archive to use to start the application. Here's a manifest file with text describing the purpose of each element. All paths are relative to the root of the archive.

```
<SilverlightApp>
    <source>Path to main XAML or XAP file</source>
    <version>Minimum Silverlight runtime version
            (1.0 or 2.0) or latest if this is not specified</version>
    <width>percentage or value</width>
    <height>percentage or value</height>
    <background>
        Named color, 8-bit or 16-bit color value,
        optionally with alpha transparency
    </background>
    <backgroundImage>
        Path to background image to show while application is initializing
    </backgroundImage>
    <isWindowless>
        Set to "True" or "False", specifies whether
        Silverlight control is in windowless mode
    </isWindowless>
    <framerate>Maximum number of frames to render per second</framerate>
    <inPlaceInstallPrompt>
        Specifies whether to display install prompt
        in case Silverlight version is out of date
    </inPlaceInstallPrompt>
    <onLoad>
        JScript function to run when application's content is done rendering
        (not same as Silverlight's onLoad event)
    </onLoad>
    <onError>JScript function called to handle errors</onError>
    <jsOrder>
        <js>Path to first .js file to load</js>
        <js>Path to second .js file to load</js>
        <js>... etc ...</js>
    </jsOrder>
</SilverlightApp>
```

There is a limit on the file types you can place within an archive you upload to Silverlight Streaming. You can include text/XML formats (`.js`, `.xaml`, `.xml`, `.txt`, `.sdx`, and `.bin`), image files (`.gif`, `.jpg`, and `.png`), media files (`.wma`, `.wmv`, and `.mp3`), and certain binary formats (`.ttf`, `.odttf`, `.dll`, `.zip`, and `.xap`). If there are any unrecognized file types within the archive, upload to Silverlight Streaming will fail.

Once you have the Silverlight application created and packaged with a `manifest.xml` file, it's time to upload it to the Silverlight Streaming servers. You can do this by clicking Manage Applications and then "Upload an application" on the administration site, as shown in Figure 6-12.

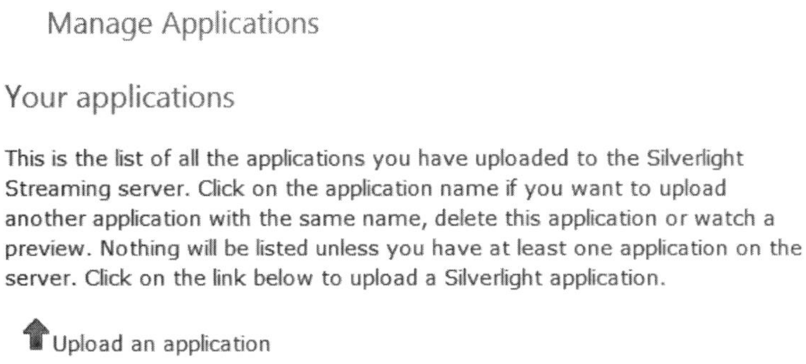

Manage Applications

Your applications

This is the list of all the applications you have uploaded to the Silverlight Streaming server. Click on the application name if you want to upload another application with the same name, delete this application or watch a preview. Nothing will be listed unless you have at least one application on the server. Click on the link below to upload a Silverlight application.

⬆ Upload an application

Figure 6-12. *Creating a new application in Silverlight Streaming*

The first step is to name the application and click Create. Next, you select an archive containing the Silverlight application and, optionally, videos to upload (although videos are typically uploaded via Manage Videos), as shown in Figure 6-13.

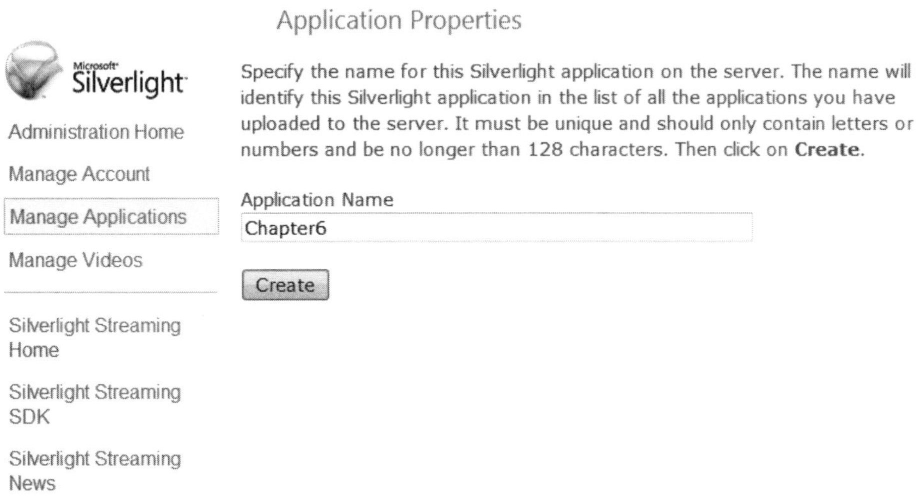

Microsoft® Silverlight

Administration Home

Manage Account

Manage Applications

Manage Videos

Silverlight Streaming Home

Silverlight Streaming SDK

Silverlight Streaming News

Application Properties

Specify the name for this Silverlight application on the server. The name will identify this Silverlight application in the list of all the applications you have uploaded to the server. It must be unique and should only contain letters or numbers and be no longer than 128 characters. Then click on **Create**.

Application Name

Chapter6

Create

Figure 6-13. *Uploading a packaged archive*

Once the Silverlight application is uploaded, the easiest way to reference the Silverlight application in your own web site is by using an IFrame. You do this by using an `iframe` tag with the `src` attribute pointing to the Silverlight application you uploaded:

```
<iframe src="..." frameborder="0" width="200" height="300" scrolling="no"></iframe>
```

The value for `src` takes the following format:

```
http://silverlight.services.live.com/invoke/ [account ID] / [App. name]/iframe.html
```

The [account ID] is replaced with your account ID, which you see when you log in to your Silverlight Streaming account (shown earlier in Figure 6-11). The [App. name] is replaced with the application name you specified when creating an application.

You can include videos as part of the application upload you archive (these videos are still limited in size, bit rate, etc.), or you can upload videos directly to Silverlight Streaming using the Manage Videos link on the administration site. After the video is done uploading, the server processes it to ensure it is encoded properly and meets the restrictions. After this validation is done, an Acknowledge button will appear. Click this button and the video will be properly migrated to your account. Figure 6-14 shows the result of uploading the `bear.wmv` video that comes with Windows Vista.

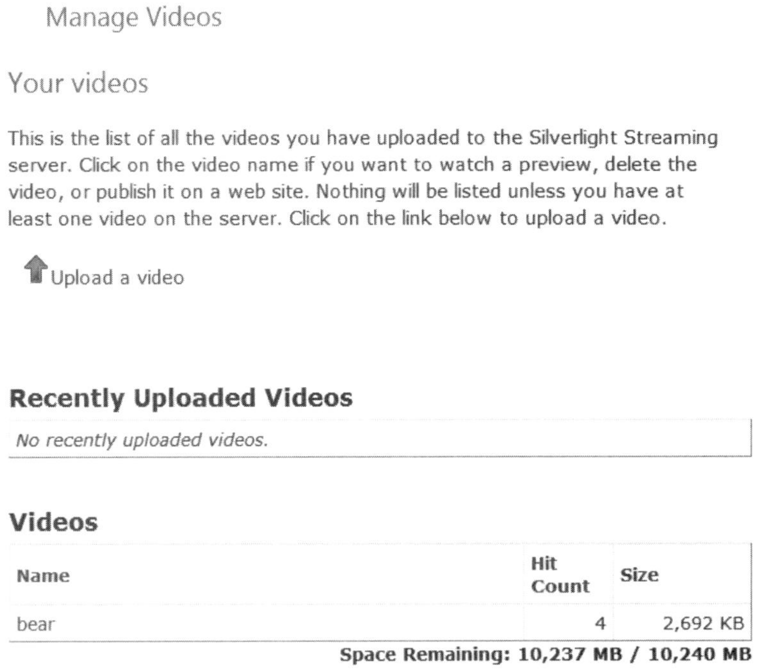

Manage Videos

Your videos

This is the list of all the videos you have uploaded to the Silverlight Streaming server. Click on the video name if you want to watch a preview, delete the video, or publish it on a web site. Nothing will be listed unless you have at least one video on the server. Click on the link below to upload a video.

Upload a video

Recently Uploaded Videos

No recently uploaded videos.

Videos

Name	Hit Count	Size
bear	4	2,692 KB

Space Remaining: 10,237 MB / 10,240 MB

Figure 6-14. *Administrative interface after uploaded video is done processing*

Now that you have all the pieces, the rest is putting together an actual application. Let's take the simple video player used earlier and use it with Silverlight Streaming. The good news is that the only thing you really have to change within the application is the source URI for the video.

```
<MediaElement
    x:Name="mainVideo"
    AutoPlay="False"
    CurrentStateChanged="mainVideo_CurrentStateChanged"
    VerticalAlignment="Stretch"
    Source="http://silverlight.services.live.com/64914/bear/video.wmv"
    Stretch="Fill" />
```

When you click Manage Videos, and then click a specific video you've uploaded, the Silverlight Streaming web site will give you the exact code to drop in to your web site or Silverlight application, as shown in Figure 6-15.

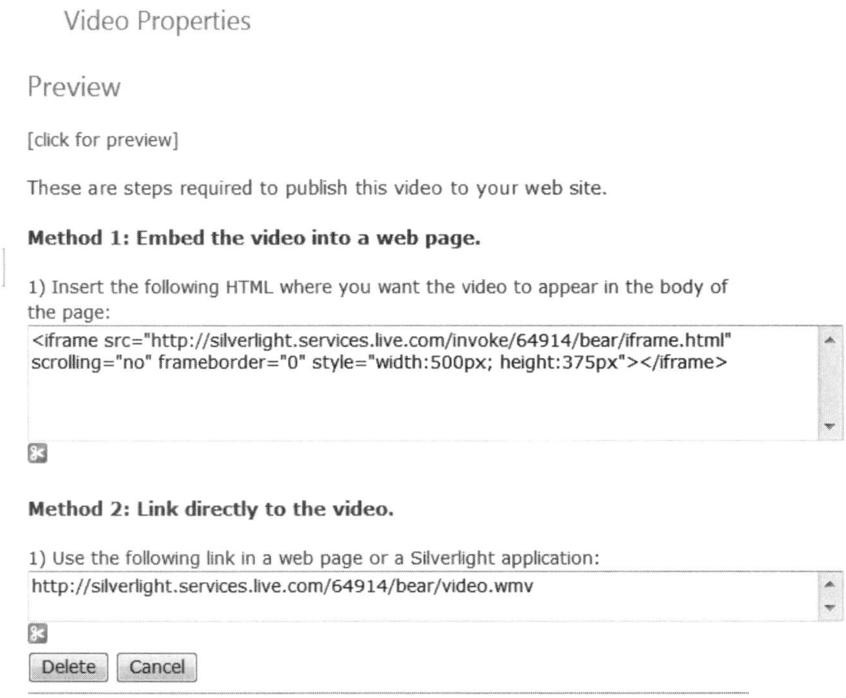

Video Properties

Preview

[click for preview]

These are steps required to publish this video to your web site.

Method 1: Embed the video into a web page.

1) Insert the following HTML where you want the video to appear in the body of the page:

```
<iframe src="http://silverlight.services.live.com/invoke/64914/bear/iframe.html"
scrolling="no" frameborder="0" style="width:500px; height:375px"></iframe>
```

Method 2: Link directly to the video.

1) Use the following link in a web page or a Silverlight application:

```
http://silverlight.services.live.com/64914/bear/video.wmv
```

[Delete]   [Cancel]

Figure 6-15. *Links to the video provided by the administrative interface*

Before the application can be uploaded to Silverlight Streaming, it must have a manifest, and the XAP file and manifest file must be packaged into a ZIP file. The manifest for this application supplies just a few parameters:

```
<SilverlightApp>
    <source>chapter6_streaming.xap</source>
    <width>400</width>
```

```
    <height>350</height>
    <background>white</background>
    <isWindowless>false</isWindowless>
</SilverlightApp>
```

The rest is a simple matter of uploading the ZIP archive and then clicking the link to preview it. The video player, as served by Silverlight Streaming, is shown in Figure 6-16.

Application Test Page - Chapter6

Silverlight Streaming Demo

Figure 6-16. *The video player, as shown from Silverlight Streaming*

Packaging Images and Media

While you can download images and media file by file, sometimes an application requires a collection of related images or other media before it can start. One example of this is a game that might need a number of images to display scenes, characters, and the background. You can package these resources into a single ZIP archive and download it. After downloading the ZIP file, using the WebClient class perhaps, you can save its stream. Let's revisit the image browser from earlier in the chapter and alter it to download the images stored in a ZIP file. The image-browsing interface is essentially the same, but there's a download button that initiates the download of the image archive.

```
private StreamResourceInfo imageArchiveStream;
private void downloadButton_Click(object sender, RoutedEventArgs e)
{
    WebClient wc = new WebClient();
    wc.OpenReadCompleted +=
        new OpenReadCompletedEventHandler(wc_OpenReadCompleted);
    wc.OpenReadAsync(
        new Uri("/chapter6Web/HubbleImageArchive.zip",
            UriKind.Relative));
}
```

The `OpenReadCompleted` event handler is where the ZIP archive is processed. First, the stream is saved, and then we get a reference to a custom XML file stored within the archive.

```
void wc_OpenReadCompleted(object sender, OpenReadCompletedEventArgs e)
{
    imageArchiveStream = new StreamResourceInfo(e.Result, null);
    StreamResourceInfo manifestStream =
                Application.GetResourceStream(imageArchiveStream,
                            new Uri("manifest.xml", UriKind.Relative));
    // ...
}
```

The `manifest.xml` file exists to specify where files such as images are stored within the archive. The `manifest.xml` file is stored at the root of the archive and the images are stored in a directory named images. Here's the `manifest.xml` file:

```
<?xml version="1.0" encoding="utf-8" ?>
<contents>
   <images>
      <image label="Hubble Picture 1" path="images/gpn-2000-000876.jpg"/>
      <image label="Hubble Picture 2" path="images/gpn-2000-000877.jpg"/>
      <image label="Hubble Picture 3" path="images/gpn-2000-000880.jpg"/>
      <image label="Hubble Picture 4" path="images/gpn-2000-000891.jpg"/>
      <image label="Hubble Picture 5" path="images/gpn-2000-000938.jpg"/>
   </images>
</contents>
```

The code that fills in the ... in the `OpenReadCompleted` event handler processes the manifest file and adds thumbnails of the images to the ListBox:

```
XmlReaderSettings settings = new XmlReaderSettings();
settings.IgnoreWhitespace = true;
XmlReader reader = XmlReader.Create(manifestStream.Stream, settings);
reader.ReadToDescendant("image");
do
{
    string path = reader.GetAttribute("path");
    StreamResourceInfo imageStream =
                Application.GetResourceStream(
                            imageArchiveStream,
                            new Uri(path, UriKind.Relative));
    ListBoxItem item = new ListBoxItem();
    Image thumb = new Image();
    BitmapImage imgSource = new BitmapImage();
    imgSource.SetSource(imageStream.Stream);
    thumb.Source = imgSource;
    item.Content = thumb;
    thumb.Width = 75;
    thumb.Height = 50;
```

```
    thumb.Tag = path;
    thumbnailList.Items.Add(item);
} while (reader.ReadToNextSibling("image"));
reader.Close();
```

You can use this approach to store references to other media files (video/audio) and even any arbitrary data you might need to download on demand.

Summary

So far, we've been laying the groundwork to build a Silverlight application. This chapter covered the pieces most popularly associated with Silverlight since its 1.0 days: displaying images and media. You saw how to manage and manipulate images, including exploring the MultiScaleImage control, which provides the Deep Zoom user experience. Next, we examined video and audio via the MediaElement control and explored the Silverlight Streaming technology. The media support is a rich and deep topic that cannot fully be explored in a single chapter, but you should have a good grasp of the possibilities when using Silverlight. The next chapter will explore more aspects of building user interfaces, such as the 2D drawing and brush support in Silverlight. We'll look at the ImageBrush and VideoBrush, which provide the ability to use images and videos in even more interesting ways than described in this chapter.

CHAPTER 7

■■■

Extending the User Interface

We've covered a lot of ground so far, but now it's time to pull our focus back from the details of the supporting infrastructure and revisit building user interfaces in Silverlight. Silverlight provides a rich set of classes to perform 2D drawing, including lines, Bezier curves, and various geometrical figures such as ellipses and rectangles. Next, we'll take a look at transformations and brushes, both of which provide a great deal of control in how elements are presented on an interface. Any element inheriting from UIElement can have a transform applied to it—you can create some interesting video presentations, for example, by skewing or growing/shrinking a video. We'll also take a look at the support for brushes in Silverlight. You can use specific brushes to fill surfaces with images or video and other effects such as gradients.

2D Graphics

Silverlight provides two categories of classes for two dimensional graphics: shapes and geometries. The System.Windows.Shapes.Shape class forms the base for all shape-related classes. The Shape class inherits directly from FrameworkElement, so it gains all that is provided by the UIElement and FrameworkElement classes. The System.Windows.Media.Geometry class, however, inherits directly from DependencyObject, not from UIElement or FrameworkElement. There are similarities between the two categories, but the difference is what they are designed for. The Geometry-based classes provide more flexibility and focus more on the behavior of the geometric shapes (and are actually used by some of the Shape-based classes). The Shape-derived classes, however, are meant for easily adding 2D shapes to a Silverlight user interface. The hierarchy of 2D classes we will look at are shown in Figure 7-1.

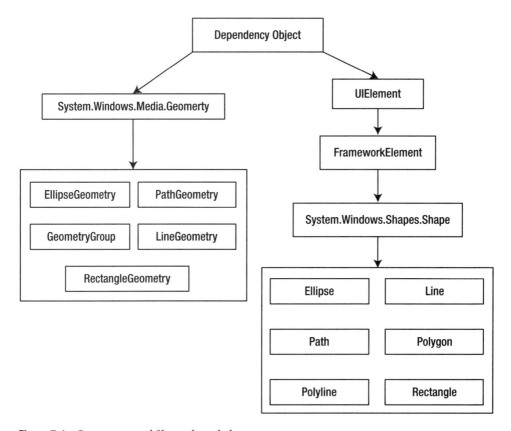

Figure 7-1. *Geometry- and Shape-based classes*

Using Geometries

We'll take a look at the Geometry-based classes first since these provide more versatility. The UIElement class uses a Geometry object to define a region used to clip what's shown, and the Path Shape–derived class uses a Geometry object to know what to draw. The Shapes.Path class is the mechanism to use if you want to draw a Geometry-derived class on a user interface, since the Geometry classes on their own can't do this.

Simple Geometries

The LineGeometry, RectangleGeometry, and EllipseGeometry classes represent basic geometrical figures. These classes cover the basic shapes, including lines, rectangles, and ellipses. These geometries are shown in Figure 7-2.

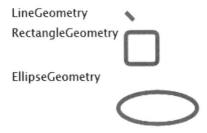

Figure 7-2. *Line, rectangle, and ellipse geometries*

LineGeometry

The LineGeometry class represents a single line with a start point and endpoint. Its two properties are shown in Table 7-1.

Table 7-1. *Properties of the System.Windows.Media.LineGeometry Class*

Property	Type	Description
StartPoint	Point	The (x,y) point of the start of the line
EndPoint	Point	The (x,y) point of the end of the line

Since the Geometry-based classes can't be shown directly, they must be shown using the Path class. Let's draw a line using the LineGeometry class in XAML:

```
<Path Stroke="Red" StrokeThickness="5">
   <Path.Data>
      <LineGeometry StartPoint="10,10" EndPoint="20,20"/>
   </Path.Data>
</Path>
```

RectangleGeometry

The RectangleGeomtery class is used for representing rectangles (and squares, of course). Its properties are shown in Table 7-2. The RadiusX and RadiusY properties are used to round the corners. Combined, these properties represent an ellipse that is used to control the degree to which the corners are rounded. If you set these sufficiently high, the rectangle will not disappear, but instead will render as an ellipse or a circle.

Table 7-2. *Properties of the System.Windows.Media.RectangleGeometry Class*

Property	Type	Description
RadiusX	double	Gets or sets the x radius of the ellipse used for rounding the rectangle's corners.
RadiusY	double	Gets or sets the y radius of the ellipse used for rounding the rectangle's corners.
Rect	System.Windows.Rect	Gets or sets the rectangle's dimensions. The Rect class has x, y and width, height properties, each of type double.

Let's draw a rectangle on the screen again using the Path class:

```
<Path Stroke="Red" StrokeThickness="5">
  <Path.Data>
    <RectangleGeometry Rect="10,10,40,40" RadiusX="5" RadiusY="5"/>
  </Path.Data>
</Path>
```

EllipseGeometry

The EllipseGeometry class represents an ellipse defined by a center point and two radii, one for the top and bottom of the ellipse and the other for the sides. Its properties are shown in Table 7-3.

Table 7-3. *Properties of the System.Windows.Media.EllipseGeometry Class*

Property	Type	Description
RadiusX	double	Gets or sets the x radius of the ellipse used for defining the ellipse's sides.
RadiusY	double	Gets or sets the y radius of the ellipse used for defining the ellipse's top and bottom.
Center	Point	Gets or sets the center point of the ellipse.

Yet again, we use the Path class to display EllipseGeometry on the screen:

```
<Path Stroke="Red" StrokeThickness="5">
  <Path.Data>
    <EllipseGeometry Center="50,50" RadiusX="50" RadiusY="20"/>
  </Path.Data>
</Path>
```

Path Geometries

The PathGeometry class is where the geometries get interesting. The PathGeometry class is used to represent an arbitrary geometrical shape made up of lines and/or curves. PathGeometry contains one or more PathFigure objects. Each PathFigure object contains one or more PathSegment objects. The various segments are connected automatically within each PathFigure object by each segment's start point, starting at the previous segment's endpoint. There are seven segment classes you can use to construct figures, as shown in Table 7-4. Since using these segments to construct geometrical shapes can be unwieldy, there is a special syntax used with the Path class for drawing multiple segments. We'll take a closer look at this in the next section when we look at the various Shape-related classes.

Table 7-4. *Segment Classes Used in a PathFigure*

Class	Description
ArcSegment	Elliptical arc between two points
BezierSegment	Cubic Bezier curve between two points
LineSegment	Straight line between two points
PolyBezierSegment	Represents a series of cubic Bezier curves
PolyLineSegment	Represents a series of lines
PolyQuadraticBezierSegment	Represents a series of quadratic Bezier curves
QuadraticBezierSegment	Quadratic Bezier curve between two points

Before we go over the specific properties of each segment, let's take a look at piecing together a rectangle. You can see what the rectangle looks like in Figure 7-3; its XAML code is shown following.

■**Caution** If you use a StrokeThickness larger than 1, the final segment will leave a gap. Keep this in mind when manually piecing together segments. The final segment might need an adjustment to go far enough to fill in the visual gap left by the difference between the endpoint and the stroke thickness.

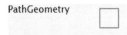

Figure 7-3. *Rectangle drawn using PathGeometry*

```
<Path Stroke="Red" StrokeThickness="1">
   <Path.Data>
      <PathGeometry>
         <PathGeometry.Figures>
            <PathFigure StartPoint="10,10">
               <PathFigure.Segments>
                  <LineSegment Point="10,40"/>
                  <LineSegment Point="40,40"/>
                  <LineSegment Point="40,10"/>
                  <LineSegment Point="10,10"/>
               </PathFigure.Segments>
            </PathFigure>
         </PathGeometry.Figures>
      </PathGeometry>
   </Path.Data>
</Path>
```

Let's take a look at what each segment describes and its properties.

ArcSegment

This segment draws an elliptical segment between the end of the previous segment (or the figure's start point) and the specified destination point. Since the elliptical segment only has two points, there must be a way to define how the arc is drawn since there are multiple candidate arcs. The IsLargeArc and SweepDirection properties exist for this purpose. Table 7-5 shows the properties of ArcSegment.

Table 7-5. *Properties of the System.Windows.Media.ArcSegment Class*

Property	Type	Description
isLargeArc	bool	If true, the arc drawn is greater than 180 degrees. This is one of the two properties required to define how arc is drawn.
Point	System.Windows.Point	This defines the endpoint of the arc.
RotationAngle	double	This specifies the rotation angle (in degrees) of the arc around the x axis. It defaults to 0.
Size	System.Windows.Size	This specifies the x and y radii of the arc.
SweepDirection	System.Windows.Media.SweepDirection	This defines which direction the arc is drawn in. It can be set to Clockwise or Counterclockwise. The use of this property with IsLargeArc fully specifies the type of arc drawn.

BezierSegment

This segment represents a Bezier curve, which is a curve defined by a start point, an endpoint, and two control points. The line is bent toward each control point, so if the control points are placed on opposite sides of the line, the line appears to have a hill and a valley along its length. This class provides three properties, all of type System.Windows.Point, used to specify the Bezier segment's control points and ending point.

- Point1: Defines the first control point

- Point2: Defines the second control point

- Point3: Defines the endpoint of the curve

LineSegment

This segment represents a straight line. It has a single property, Point, which defines the endpoint of the line.

QuadraticBezierSegment

A quadratic Bezier segment is a Bezier curve with only a single control point. It defines a single control point and an endpoint.

- `Point1`: Defines the control point

- `Point2`: Defines the endpoint of the curve

PolyBezierSegment

This segment is similar to `BezierSegment` but provides an easy way to combine multiple Bezier curves. Each curve is defined by three points and automatically connects to the endpoint of the previous line (or previous segment if it's the first line in the series). This class contains one property, `Points`, of type `System.Windows.Media.PointCollection`.

PolyLineSegment

Similar in spirit to `PolyBezierSegment`, this segment allows you to easily combine multiple straight lines in a series. It also exposes a property, `Points`, of type `System.Windows.Media.PointCollection`. Each line is automatically connected to the endpoint of the previous line/segment, so for each new line, all you need to do is add one new point.

PolyQuadraticBezierSegment

This segment combines multiple quadratic Bezier segments together. Each segment is defined by two points: the control point and the endpoint. These are stored in the `Points` property just like the other poly segments.

Grouping Geometries

The `GeometryGroup` class is used to group multiple geometries together. Since it is possible for multiple geometrical shapes to intersect, the `GeometryGroup` class exposes a `FillRule` property to specify how the intersections of geometries are treated to judge whether points within the intersection are in the combined geometry or not. The `FillRule` property can take on one of two possible values:

- `EvenOdd`: A point is judged within the fill region if the number of path segment rays drawn in every direction away from the point ultimately cross an odd number of segments. This is the default value.

- `Nonzero`: A point is judged within the fill region if the number of crossings of segments across rays drawn from a point is greater than zero.

Using Shapes

The `System.Windows.Shapes.Shape` class forms the base for classes that represent geometrical figures that have the ability to draw themselves on the screen. There are classes for drawing lines, rectangles, ellipses, and polygons, all deriving from `Shape`. The most interesting `Shape`-derived class is `Path`. The `Path` class is what we used in the previous section—it has the ability to draw `Geometry`-based objects on the screen, and it can also process a specialized syntax for piecing together `Path`-based geometries. Some of the most useful properties of the `Shape` class are shown in Table 7-6.

Table 7-6. *Properties of the System.Windows.Shapes.Shape Class*

Property	Type	Description
Fill	Brush	The brush used to fill the interior of the shape
Stretch	Stretch	The value from the Stretch enumeration; controls how the shape fills its bounding space
Stroke	Brush	The brush used to paint the outline of the shape
StrokeDashArray	DoubleCollection	Collection of double values specifying the dash pattern to use in outlining the shape
StrokeThickness	double	The thickness of the outline of the shape

Let's briefly look at some of the simple Shape-based classes before moving on to the more complicated Path class. The results of the XAML for each of these shapes are shown in Figure 7-4.

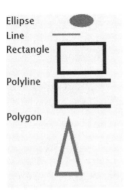

Figure 7-4. *Appearance of the Shape-based classes*

Ellipse

The Ellipse class exposes Height and Width properties that define what the ellipse looks like. Unlike the Geometry class, where you specify a center point and x and y radius values, the Ellipse class only needs to know its bounding box as defined by its Height and Width properties. This provides more flexibility in visual presentation since a Shape can have different stretch behaviors and can be affected by the width of its outline and other properties. You can specify an ellipse in XAML by using the following:

```
<Ellipse Fill="Red" Height="20" Width="40"/>
```

Line

The Line class has two properties to define the start point of the line: X1 and Y1. The X2 and Y2 properties are used to define the endpoint of the line. Drawing a line is accomplished using the following XAML:

```
<Line X1="5" Y1="10" X2="50" Y2="10" Stroke="Red" StrokeThickness="2" />
```

Rectangle

The Rectangle class defines Width and Height properties specifying the dimensions of the rectangle. The following XAML draws a rectangle:

```
<Rectangle Width="80" Height="50" Fill="White" Stroke="Black" StrokeThickness="5" />
```

Polyline

The Polyline class is used to draw multiple connected lines. The Points property contains the set of points defining the lines. The following XAML draws the letter *C*:

```
<Polyline Points="100,10 10,10 10,50 100,50" Stroke="Black" StrokeThickness="5" />
```

Polygon

A polygon is a set of two or more points that form a filled shape. If two points are specified and StrokeThickness and Stroke are defined, a line will be drawn. A set of points is specified in the Polygon's Points property. The following XAML draws a red triangle on the screen. Four points are specified in order to connect the edges back to the triangle's starting point. The shape formed must be a closed shape.

```
<Polygon Points="30,20 50,100 10,100 30,20" Stroke="Red" StrokeThickness="5" />
```

Path

The Path class is by far the most versatile Shape-based class. This class can display any Geometry object by setting its Data property to the object. While this can be used to show complex Path-based geometries using PathGeometry, there is also a special syntax supported in XAML to specify Path-based geometries in a more terse string form. This syntax is utilized by Expression Media when constructing Path-based geometries. This syntax is used when specifying the value for the Data property of the Path class.

The string starts with specifying the fill rule, which is optional. If you want to specify a fill rule it must come first. You can use the string F0 to specify EvenOdd (the default value) or F1 to specify Nonzero for the fill rule.

After the fill rule (if you specify one) comes one or more figure descriptions. A figure description is made up of a move command, a draw command, and optionally a close command. Each point in this string can take the form *x* *y* or *x,y*, and whitespace is ignored.

The move command is marked by either a capital M or a lowercase m, and then one or more points. The capital M represents a move to an absolute position, and the lowercase m means that the point specified is relative to the previous point. Generally, only one point will be specified, since if multiple points are specified, move operations will be combined with draw operations to draw lines. If only a single point is specified, the behavior of the move command is less ambiguous.

The draw command can be used to draw eight possible shapes. Each command is either a capital letter (for absolute positioning) or a lowercase letter (for relative positioning). Table 7-7 lists the possible draw commands. For simplicity each command is shown only in its capital letter form.

Table 7-7. *Valid Draw Commands*

Command	Description
`L endPoint`	Draws a line starting at the current point and ending at `endPoint`.
`H x`	Draws a horizontal line from the current point to the specified x coordinate.
`V y`	Draws a vertical line from the current point to the specified y coordinate.
`C point1 point2 endPoint`	Draws a cubic Bezier curve, with `point1` and `point2` representing the control points and `endPoint` representing the endpoint of the curve.
`Q point1 endPoint`	Draws a quadratic Bezier curve using `point1` as the control point and ending at the point specified by `endPoint`.
`S point2 endPoint`	Draws a smooth cubic Bezier curve. The first control point is a reflection of `point2` relative to the current point. The curve ends at `endPoint`.
`T point1 endPoint`	Draws a smooth quadratic Bezier curve.
`A size rotationAngle isLargeArcFlag sweepDirectionFlag endPoint`	Draws an elliptical arc. See the "EllipseGeometry" section earlier in the chapter for a description of each parameter. You can set the flag to 0 to turn it off and 1 to turn it on.

The close command is optional. If specified, the current figure is automatically closed by connecting the current point to the starting point of the figure using a line. The close command is specified using a capital or lowercase Z.

The star shape shown in Figure 7-5 is drawn using a `Path` with a solid fill.

Figure 7-5. *Star shape drawn using a Path*

The `Path` in XAML used to make the star looks like this:

```
<Path Stretch="Fill"
        StrokeThickness="2"
        StrokeLineJoin="Round"
        Stroke="Blue"
        Data="F1 M 0,100 L 150,100 L 200,0 L 250,100 L 400,100
```

```
                        L 266, 150 L 300,300 L 200,170 L 110,300 L 133,150 Z ">
    <Path.Fill>
        <SolidColorBrush Color="#FFAACCEE"/>
    </Path.Fill>
</Path>
```

Transforms

Transforms are used to alter an element's coordinate system, so applying a transform to a root element causes it and all child content to uniformly alter in appearance. The benefit of a transform is that the underlying elements need no knowledge of the transform—they act as if the coordinate system is unaltered. Silverlight supports transforms for scaling, skewing, and rotating. Scaling makes it easy to shrink or grow an element; skewing can rotate x and y coordinates independently; and rotating causes the entire element to rotate around a center, defaulting to the element's top-left corner. Silverlight also supports a matrix transform, which provides more flexibility in transforms in case you want to do something that isn't a scale, skew, or rotation. Technically, there is one more transform, TransformGroup. This is used to group multiple transformations together and is in itself a Transform.

Many visual elements in Silverlight are eligible for transforming. The Geometry base class has a Transform property that can be set to any of the Transform inheritors. The Brush base class has both a Transform property and a RelativeTransform property. A relative transform is most useful when you don't know the size of the element being transformed—we'll briefly look at this in the next section when we discuss brushes. The UIElement base class has a RenderTransform property that can also be set to any of the Transform inheritors (hopefully, this will be renamed Transform before Silverlight comes out of beta for consistency's sake). Let's take a closer look at the transforms represented by classes in Silverlight.

Translation

A translation transform changes the position of an element. This is a simple operation of moving the top left of the element horizontally and/or vertically. A constant value is added to the x and/or y coordinates to reposition the entire element. These values are specified in the X and Y properties of the TranslateTransform class. The following XAML is used to translate a rectangle. Figure 7-6 shows the rectangle translated in both a positive and a negative direction. Translating an element, such as this rectangle, in XAML is a simple matter of specifying its RenderTransform.

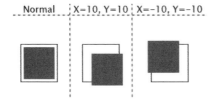

Figure 7-6. *Translating a rectangle diagonally down and up*

```
<Rectangle Stroke="Black" Width="60" Height="60"/>
   <Rectangle Stroke="Crimson" Fill="Crimson" Width="50" Height="50">
      <Rectangle.RenderTransform>
         <TranslateTransform X="10" Y="10"/>
      </Rectangle.RenderTransform>
   </Rectangle>
</Rectangle>
```

Rotation

The RotateTransform class is used to rotate the entire element undergoing transformation. This transform has three important properties for specifying how the rotation is performed: Angle, CenterX, and CenterY. The CenterX and CenterY properties specify which point the rotation is done around. The top left of an element is (0,0), as illustrated in Figure 7-7, and it is around this point that rotation is done by default.

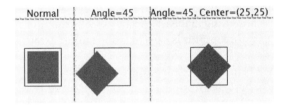

Figure 7-7. *Rotating a rectangle about its default center and true center*

You can rotate in a clockwise direction by using a positive angle (in degrees) between 0 and 360. If you want to rotate counterclockwise, you can specify a negative angle. Angles greater than 360 or less than –360 are valid, but they wrap around the circle. For example, a rotation by 405 degrees has the same result as rotating by 45 degrees, since 405 is equal to 360 (one full rotation) plus 45.

Again, we specify the rectangle's RenderTransform. We will rotate the rectangle on the screen by 45 degrees.

```
<Rectangle Height="50" Width="50" Fill="Crimson">
   <Rectangle.RenderTransform>
      <RotateTransform CenterX="0" CenterY="0" Angle="45"/>
   </Rectangle.RenderTransform>
</Rectangle>
```

Since our center point is at (0,0), the rotation is done around the top-left corner of the rectangle. If you want to rotate the rectangle around its true center, make sure you set CenterX and CenterY appropriately. In this case, we'd set the center to the point (25,25). From left to right, Figure 7-7 shows what our rectangle looks like normally, rotated by 45 degrees around its top-left corner, (0,0), and rotated 45 degrees around its true center, (25,25).

Skewing

A skew transformation stretches the coordinate space in either the x or y direction (or both). This is sometimes called a shear transformation. The angle controls how the corresponding coordinate plane is stretched. For example, if you specify an AngleX of 45 degrees, the x and y planes will form a 45 degree angle with each other. You can see this in Figure 7-8 (first row, second column). As the y values increase (remember, top left of the rectangle is 0,0), the x values are shifted over until the bottom of the rectangle is reached, forming the 45 degree angle at the bottom. The third column shows a skewing transformation done using the AngleY property. Similar to rotation, you can control the center point at which skewing is performed around. The second row of Figure 7-8 shows the same skewing transformations, but with the center of the rectangle, (25,25), as the center point.

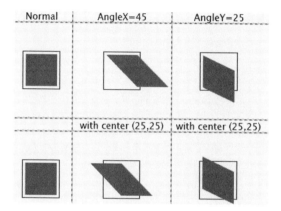

Figure 7-8. *Skewing a rectangle about its default center and true center*

```
<Rectangle Stroke="Crimson" Fill="Crimson" Width="50" Height="50">
    <Rectangle.RenderTransform>
        <SkewTransform AngleX="45"/>
    </Rectangle.RenderTransform>
</Rectangle>
```

Scaling

A scaling transformation uniformly increases or decreases the size of an element. You can zoom into an element by scaling it up, and zoom out (e.g., as a cheap way to show thumbnails) by scaling the element down. The ScaleX and ScaleY properties are used to specify how much to scale the element by. This transformation also has a CenterX and CenterY point. This point specifies which point will stay constant in the scaling. Figure 7-9 shows our normal rectangle again in the top left, and the first row shows a scale up and a scale down using the default,

(0,0), as the center point. Notice how the top-left corner is unmoved. If we specify (25,25) as the center point, as is done in the second row, the rectangle completely overtakes its bounding box when scaled up and is centered within its bounding box when scaled down. This behavior is important to note when you utilize the scaling transformation. If you think about how some menu animation has the menu expanding while its top-left corner stays intact, you can see how using the top-left corner as the anchor point could prove useful. If this were a button, though, and you wanted its size to change when a user hovers over it, it would be better to scale the button up with its true center as the anchor so that it would grow/shrink in a more expected manner for the user.

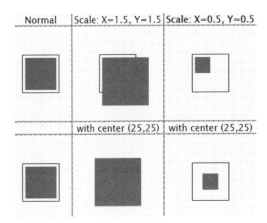

Figure 7-9. *Scaling a rectangle up and down based on its default center and true center*

Here's the XAML used for scaling the rectangle up and down in the second row of Figure 7-9.

```
<Rectangle Stroke="Crimson" Fill="Crimson" Width="50" Height="50">
   <Rectangle.RenderTransform>
      <ScaleTransform ScaleX="1.5" ScaleY="1.5"/>
   </Rectangle.RenderTransform>
</Rectangle>
```

Arbitrary Linear Transforms

The final transformation class that Silverlight provides is the matrix transformation. This can be used when the other transformations don't give you what you want, or when you want to combine multiple transformations into a single transformation (although you could also use TransformGroup to group several). Each of the other transformations can be represented by a 3×3 matrix. Let's dust off our linear algebra textbooks and revisit the basics of matrix math to see how a matrix can give us the other transformations, and even combine multiple transformations into a single operation.

The 3×3 matrix that Silverlight uses looks like Figure 7-10.

M11	M12	0
M21	M22	0
offestX	offsetY	1

Figure 7-10. *The transformation matrix used by Silverlight*

The final column will always be (0,0,1) because Silverlight only supports affine transformations. In reality, the transformation matrix is 2×2, but it includes within its structure translation values for the x and y coordinates (in the third row). An affine transformation is essentially a linear transformation. Any three points that were on a line before the transformation continue to be on a line after the transformation. We won't trouble ourselves with proving this, since this isn't a math textbook, but if you look at a side of a rectangle in the preceding rotation and skewing figures, you'll see that three arbitrary points along this line are still on a line after the transformation (not the same line obviously, but *a* line nonetheless).

The bottom row of the 3×3 matrix contains values for the x and y offsets. These offsets are used for translation. The M11, M12, M21, and M22 properties of the MatrixTransform class are used to specify the custom transformation. Projection and reflection are two examples of affine transformations not supported directly by Silverlight with a class of their own.

The simplest transformation is the translation. By setting M11 and M22 to 1, M12 and M21 to 0, the offsetX property to 10, and the offsetY property to 0, the transformation will shift the entire element being transformed 10 units to the right. The transformed points are calculated by multiplying each point (x,y) in the element being transformed by the matrix shown in Figure 7-11.

0	0	0
0	0	0
10	0	1

Figure 7-11. *Transformation matrix to translate 10 units to the right*

In general, the result of multiplying a point (technically a vector) by the matrix is (x * M11 + y * M12 + offsetX), (x * M21 + y * M22 + offsetY). There is a special matrix, known as the *identity matrix*, where M11 = 1, M12 = 0, M21 = 0, and M22 = 1. If you multiply any (x,y) point by the identity matrix, you'll get the same point again, provided that offsetX and offsetY are 0. (Go ahead and try this on a piece of paper.) This identity matrix is important because it is the default configuration of the matrix. It allows you to specify only offsetX and/or offsetY to perform a translation without having to worry about an unexpected transformation happening if the

M values are all 0 (actually, if they are all 0, the element undergoing transformation might disappear!)

We can skew both coordinates and translate the element at the same time by specifying OffsetX and the M12 and M21 properties, as follows:

```
<Rectangle Stroke="Crimson" Fill="Crimson" Width="50" Height="50">
    <Rectangle.RenderTransform>
        <MatrixTransform>
            <MatrixTransform.Matrix>
                <Matrix OffsetX="-10" M12="0.5" M21="0.5"/>
            </MatrixTransform.Matrix>
        </MatrixTransform>
    </Rectangle.RenderTransform>
</Rectangle>
```

From left to right, Figure 7-12 shows our normal rectangle, the rectangle translated right using a matrix, and the rectangle skewed and translated at the same time.

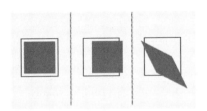

Figure 7-12. *Using MatrixTransform to translate and skew/translate*

Combining Multiple Transformations

While you could use the MatrixTransform class to combine multiple transformations into a single transformation, if you want to combine two or more of the directly supported transformations (such as a rotation and a scale), you can use the TransformGroup transform. Figure 7-13 shows the result of combining a ScaleTransform and a RotateTransform together inside a TransformGroup.

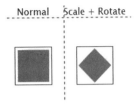

Figure 7-13. *Combining transforms using TransformGroup*

```
<Rectangle Stroke="Crimson" Fill="Crimson" Width="50" Height="50">
  <Rectangle.RenderTransform>
    <TransformGroup>
      <ScaleTransform ScaleX="0.75" ScaleY="0.75" CenterX="25" CenterY="25"/>
      <RotateTransform Angle="45" CenterX="25" CenterY="25"/>
    </TransformGroup>
  </Rectangle.RenderTransform>
</Rectangle>
```

The code download for this chapter provides an interface for exploring the various transforms and brushes (which we will discuss next), and shows how to use the transform classes in C#. The TransformGroup class is used in this code to apply multiple transformations simultaneously.

Brushes

Throughout this book, brushes have been applied several times (generally, any time an element has been filled with a solid color). For filling with a solid color, the SolidColorBrush class is used. Silverlight also provides several other brushes, including an image brush, a video brush, and several gradient brushes. As you can probably surmise, combining a video brush with a geometric shape such as an ellipse or polygon (and perhaps even a transform) provides a staggering degree of flexibility in how content is presented in Silverlight. The hierarchy of brushes is shown in Figure 7-14.

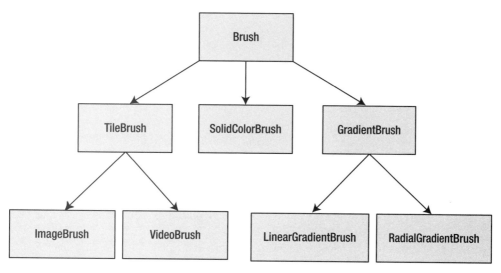

Figure 7-14. *Inheritance hierarchy of Brush-related classes*

The System.Windows.Media.Brush class forms the base of all the brushes in Silverlight. This class inherits directly from DependencyObject. Its properties are listed in Table 7-8.

Table 7-8. *Properties of the System.Windows.Media.Brush Class*

Property	Type	Description
Opacity	double	Gets or sets the opacity of the brush. A value of 0 specifies a fully transparent brush, and a value of 1 specifies a fully opaque brush.
RelativeTransform	Transform	Applies a transform using relative coordinates. This is useful for applying a transform when the size of the surface being filled isn't known.
Transform	Transform	Applies a transform using absolute coordinates.

The SolidColorBrush

The simplest brush you can use is the solid color brush. This inherits directly from Brush and thus does not share functionality with other brush types. The solid color brush has a single property, Color. In XAML, this can be set to the name of a color (see the Brushes class in the MSDN documentation online for a full list of the colors, or use IntelliSense while editing the XAML in Visual Studio) or an ARGB value by using the #FFFF0000 syntax (this example sets the color to full red, no transparency). Filling a rectangle with a solid color can be accomplished with the following XAML:

```
<Rectangle Width="50" Height="50">
    <Rectangle.Fill>
        <SolidColorBrush Color="Crimson"/>
    </Rectangle.Fill>
</Rectangle>
```

The Tile Brushes

The parent of both ImageBrush and VideoBrush is TileBrush. This class cannot be instantiated on its own—it exists to provide tiling behavior to inheriting classes. There are four properties supported by the TileBrush class, listed in Table 7-9. Each is also a dependency property.

Table 7-9. *Properties of the System.Windows.Media.TileBrush Class*

Property	Type	Description
AlignmentX	AlignmentX	Horizontal alignment used for positioning. This can be set to Left, Center, or Right.
AlignmentY	AlignmentY	Vertical alignment used for positioning. This can be set to Top, Center, or Bottom.
Stretch	Stretch	Specifies how the contents of brush fill the bounding space. See Chapter 6 for a discussion of this property.
TileMode	TileMode	Specifies how content is tiled. See the following discussion for specific value descriptions.

The TileMode enumeration describes five different tiling behaviors:

- None: If the content of the brush does not fill the entire space, it is only painted once. Unfilled space becomes transparent.

- FlipX: The base tile is drawn and repeated. Alternate columns are flipped horizontally. The base tile is not flipped.

- FlipY: The base tile is drawn and repeated. Alternate rows are flipped vertically. The base tile is not flipped.

- FlipXY: This is a combination of FlipX and FlipY. The base tile is not flipped.

- Tile: The base tile is drawn and then repeated. Tiles are stacked immediately next to each other, both horizontally and vertically.

The ImageBrush

Using the Stretch and TileMode properties provides many ways to paint an image onto a surface. Figure 7-15 shows what an image brush looks like for each of the possible Stretch values.

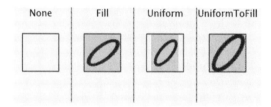

Figure 7-15. *Various stretch configurations of an image brush*

The VideoBrush

The video brush works much like the image brush, but uses a video instead of an image. The VideoBrush class provides methods to play, pause, stop, and seek a different position in the video. The SourceName property of the VideoBrush class must be set to the name of a MediaElement specified in your XAML. The following XAML gives an example:

```
<MediaElement x:Name="videoMediaElement" Source="video.wmv"/>
<Rectangle Width="300" Height="250" Stroke="Red" StrokeThickness="2">
   <Rectangle.Fill>
      <VideoBrush SourceName="videoMediaElement" />
   </Rectangle.Fill>
</Rectangle>
```

The Gradient Brushes

There are two gradient brushes that are used to paint with a gradient of colors. The first is the linear gradient brush, used to paint a gradient along a straight line. The second is the radial gradient brush, used to spread colors across an elliptical surface. Both brushes utilize a gradient specified by one or more gradient stops. What a gradient looks like depends on the values of control parameters and gradient stops. *Gradient stops* specify the color at which a particular gradient ends. It's possible to paint multiple gradients within a surface by using multiple gradient stops. The GradientBrush class forms the base of both the linear and radial gradient brushes. The properties provided by GradientBrush are shown in Table 7-10.

Table 7-10. *Properties of the System.Windows.Media.GradientBrush Class*

Property	Type	Description
ColorInterpolationMode	ColorInterpolationMode	Specifies the color space to use when interpolating colors. Set it to ScRgbLinearInterpolation to use the scRGB space or SRgbLinearInterpolation to use the sRGB space.
GradientStops	GradientStopCollection	The collection of gradient stops defining how colors are spread in the surface being filled.
MappingMode	BrushMappingMode	Gets or sets the coordinate system used by the brush. Set this to Absolute for coordinates to be interpreted in local space, and set it to RelativeToBoundingBox to use coordinates relative to the bounding box (0 corresponds to 0 percent of the box, and 1 corresponds to 100 percent, so 0.5 would be interpreted as the center point). The default value is RelativeToBoundingBox. It does not affect offset values of gradient brushes.
SpreadMethod	GradientSpreadMethod	Gets or sets how the gradient is spread. Valid values are Pad (the default), Reflect, and Repeat.

The LinearGradientBrush

A linear gradient brush spreads a color gradient across a straight line. This straight line can be any straight line through the surface being painted, and is described by the StartPoint and EndPoint properties of the LinearGradientBrush class. The top-left corner is (0,0) and the bottom-right corner is (1,1). Using 0 and 1 for the start point and endpoint of each coordinate plane allows to use this brush without worrying about the actual size of the surface being painted. It is through this line that the gradient spreads by default, starting from the top left and ending at the bottom right. You can see this default behavior in the first column of Figure 7-16.

If you only specify a single gradient stop, the linear gradient brush paints a solid color. If you use two gradient stops—for example, starting at black (#FF000000) and ending in red (#FFFF0000)—the gradient starts at black and the color spreads evenly from black to red along the length of the surface being painted, until the end of the surface is reached. Multiple gradient stops can be specified along a gradient line from 0.0 to 1.0.

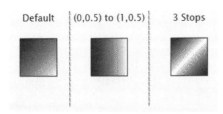

Figure 7-16. *Different configurations of the linear gradient brush*

Figure 7-16 shows the behavior of several different options for the linear gradient brush. The default behavior is shown first, spreading from black to white. Here's the XAML for this gradient:

```
<Rectangle Stroke="Black" Width="60" Height="60">
   <Rectangle.Fill>
      <LinearGradientBrush>
         <GradientStop Color="#FF000000" Offset="0.0"/>
         <GradientStop Color="#FFFFFFFF" Offset="1.0"/>
      </LinearGradientBrush>
   </Rectangle.Fill>
</Rectangle>
```

The following code shows how to spread the gradient horizontally instead of diagonally:

```
<Rectangle Stroke="Black" Width="60" Height="60">
   <Rectangle.Fill>
      <LinearGradientBrush StartPoint="0,0.5" EndPoint="1,0.5">
         <GradientStop Color="#FF000000" Offset="0.0"/>
         <GradientStop Color="#FFFFFFFF" Offset="1.0"/>
      </LinearGradientBrush>
   </Rectangle.Fill>
</Rectangle>
```

The next code block creates a gradient that spreads to the center point of the gradient line and a second gradient that spreads from the center point to fill up the other half of the surface:

```
<Rectangle Stroke="Black" Width="60" Height="60">
   <Rectangle.Fill>
      <LinearGradientBrush>
         <GradientStop Color="#FF000000" Offset="0.0"/>
         <GradientStop Color="#FFFFFFFF" Offset="0.5"/>
         <GradientStop Color="#FF000000" Offset="1.0"/>
      </LinearGradientBrush>
   </Rectangle.Fill>
</Rectangle>
```

The RadialGradientBrush

The radial gradient brush spreads a color gradient from a point outward in an elliptical pattern. The Center property specifies the center of the ellipse, and the RadiusX and RadiusY properties control how the ellipse is shaped. If RadiusX and RadiusY are equal, the resulting ellipse is a circle. The GradientOrigin property specifies the point at which the gradient starts. The gradient spreads outward from this point until it completely fills the bounding ellipse.

Figure 7-17 shows various radial gradients.

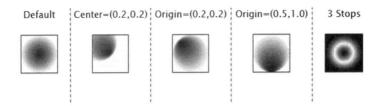

| Default | Center=(0.2,0.2) | Origin=(0.2,0.2) | Origin=(0.5,1.0) | 3 Stops |

Figure 7-17. *Different configurations of the radial gradient brush*

The left-hand image in Figure 7-17 shows the default radial gradient, with the center at (0.5,0.5) and the gradient going from black to white. Here's the XAML for this first radial gradient example:

```
<Rectangle Stroke="Black" Width="60" Height="60">
   <Rectangle.Fill>
      <RadialGradientBrush>
         <GradientStop Color="#FF000000" Offset="0.0"/>
         <GradientStop Color="#FFFFFFFF" Offset="1.0"/>
      </RadialGradientBrush>
   </Rectangle.Fill>
</Rectangle>
```

The next two examples use different gradient origins, and the final one uses three gradient stops.

Summary

This chapter has covered much more of the support Silverlight provides for building user interfaces. First, it covered the support Silverlight provides for 2D drawing, including the Geometry- and Shape-based classes. Then it covered the various transformations used to alter how elements are rendered, such as applying a rotation.

In the coming chapters, we will cover animation, and by combining transformations with animation, you can perform interesting effects such as setting something spinning by continually altering its rotational angle.

Finally, we looked at the various brushes in Silverlight that provide flexibility in how content is drawn within bounding elements. You can achieve some interesting effects when you animate the properties of a brush, which you will also see soon. But before we get to animation, we'll take a look at the support Silverlight provides for styling applications and modifying the visual appearance of controls in the next chapter.

■ ■ ■

CHAPTER 8

Styling and Templating

Silverlight provides the capability to easily style elements of user interfaces and alter the appearance (separate from the behavior) of controls. Styling is similar in spirit to how CSS properties work: user interface elements can reuse fonts, colors, and sizes that are specified as a style by applying a specific style to a `FrameworkElement`. Templating, however, is limited to `Control`-based classes and is used to completely change how controls are rendered visually. This mechanism works because what the control does (its behavior) is separate from how it looks. These two capabilities provide a significant amount of user interface customization to designers and developers when working with Silverlight.

Using Styles

If you're building a simple application that has just a few user interface screens, it probably makes sense to set properties such as `FontSize` and colors on user interface elements themselves. If you're building a larger application, though, you can quickly find yourself replicating the same property values on page after page. A style, in Silverlight, is a group of properties and specific values that you can reuse within a page or even across the whole application. A specific style is given a name and stored within a resource dictionary, so a style can be scoped to the page or application level. It's possible to place a style within any resource dictionary, but in practice, styles are rarely seen outside the page or application level since the benefit of a style is in the reuse of sets of attribute values. Figure 8-1 shows a layout that many web sites follow.

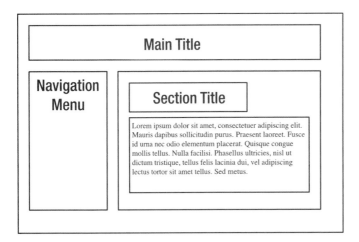

Figure 8-1. *Design layout for a web site*

The main title and the navigation menu are omnipresent as the user navigates from one page to another. The part of the interface that changes, however, features the content from an individual page. In ASP.NET, the navigation menu and main title go into something called a *master page*, which separates the common parts of the site from the page-specific parts. Figure 8-1 shows a section title and some example text that might appear in a specific page of a Silverlight application. The section title and page text will change from one page to the next. In fact, there might be many elements used by different pages, such as hyperlinks and other text. Before you can effectively use styles, you must understand the different user interface elements used throughout your application. Two of these elements are visible in Figure 8-1: the section title and the page-specific text. Some other possible elements are bylines (for blogs or news articles), image captions, and hyperlinks. Once you have a list of the common user interface elements, though, you have to determine exactly which properties you want applied across your application. The properties you choose to group into styles correspond to the properties from various Silverlight controls. Both the section header and the page text from Figure 8-1 could be displayed using a TextBlock. Some useful properties of TextBlock that are great for use in a style are `FontSize`, `Foreground`, `Margin`, and `TextWrapping`. All of these properties control how the text is presented.

■**Caution** The `FontWeight` and `FontFamily` properties of TextBlock are not eligible for use in styles.

Figure 8-2 shows this master page/content page relationship in a theoretical online bookstore. The navigation menu at the left and the title at the top are present regardless of which section of the site a user visits.

Figure 8-2. *User interface for an online bookstore*

Here's the XAML used for the section title (book name) and page content (book description), and the navigation menu without using styles:

```
<StackPanel Grid.Row="1" Grid.Column="0">
    <ListBox>
        <ListBoxItem>
            <Button Content="Home" Width="60" Margin="5"/>
        </ListBoxItem>
        <ListBoxItem>
            <Button Content="DVDs" Width="60" Margin="5"/>
        </ListBoxItem>
        <ListBoxItem>
            <Button Content="Music" Width="60" Margin="5"/>
        </ListBoxItem>
        <ListBoxItem>
            <Button Content="Help" Width="60" Margin="5"/>
        </ListBoxItem>
        <ListBoxItem>
            <Button Content="Sign Out" Width="60" Margin="5"/>
        </ListBoxItem>
    </ListBox>
</StackPanel>
<StackPanel Grid.Row="1" Grid.Column="2" VerticalAlignment="Top">
    <TextBlock FontSize="20">Ulysses by James Joyce</TextBlock>
    <TextBlock FontSize="12" TextWrapping="Wrap">
    The ultimate tale of what it means to be human. Heralded as one
    of the best works of fiction during the 20th century.
    </TextBlock>
</StackPanel>
```

You can see the duplication of the Width and Margin properties in the navigation buttons. Also, the properties used for the content of a page wouldn't necessarily be the same as other content pages (e.g., DVDs and music), since the values must manually be kept consistent. These are two of the biggest issues that styles solve. These properties will be pulled out and grouped into three styles: one for the navigation buttons, one for the page header, and one for the page content.

There are two components to a style: where it is applied and what it does. In order to specify where a style is applied, you must give it a name and a target type. This target type is the name of a class that will use the style. This target type must match directly—the style will not automatically apply to descendents of the specified class. This makes styling a user interface predictable since a derived type won't take on a specific style set for its parent class. Since these user interface elements apply to the entire Silverlight application, the styles will go into the application's resource dictionary in the App.xaml file.

```xml
<Application xmlns="http://schemas.microsoft.com/winfx/2006/xaml/presentation"
            xmlns:x="http://schemas.microsoft.com/winfx/2006/xaml"
            x:Class="chapter8.App">
    <Application.Resources>
        <Style x:Key="ContentHeader" TargetType="TextBlock">
            <Setter Property="FontSize" Value="20"/>
        </Style>
        <Style x:Key="ContentDescription" TargetType="TextBlock">
            <Setter Property="FontSize" Value="12"/>
            <Setter Property="TextWrapping" Value="Wrap"/>
        </Style>
        <Style x:Key="NavigationButton" TargetType="Button">
            <Setter Property="Width" Value="60"/>
            <Setter Property="Margin" Value="5"/>
        </Style>
    </Application.Resources>
</Application>
```

Each style is given an x:Key that serves as the key for the resource dictionary and also the key used when applying a style to a user interface element. The TargetType is set to TextBlock for the page content header and page content, and to Button for the navigation buttons. These properties, grouped in styles and then placed in the application's resource dictionary, provide the consistency and ease of maintenance for your application's look and feel.

Applying the styles is a simple matter of using the StaticResouce markup extension in the Style attribute of a user interface element of the corresponding type. Here's the XAML that makes up the navigation menu and the page content using styles:

```xml
<StackPanel Grid.Row="1" Grid.Column="0">
    <ListBox>
        <ListBoxItem>
            <Button Content="Home" Style="{StaticResource NavigationButton}"/>
        </ListBoxItem>
        <ListBoxItem>
            <Button Content="DVDs" Style="{StaticResource NavigationButton}"/>
        </ListBoxItem>
```

```
            <ListBoxItem>
                <Button Content="Music" Style="{StaticResource NavigationButton}"/>
            </ListBoxItem>
            <ListBoxItem>
                <Button Content="Help" Style="{StaticResource NavigationButton}"/>
            </ListBoxItem>
            <ListBoxItem>
                <Button Content="Sign Out" Style="{StaticResource NavigationButton}"/>
            </ListBoxItem>
        </ListBox>
</StackPanel>
<StackPanel Grid.Row="1" Grid.Column="2" VerticalAlignment="Top">
<TextBlock Style="{StaticResource ContentHeader}">
        Ulysses by James Joyce
    </TextBlock>
    <TextBlock Style="{StaticResource ContentDescription}">
    The ultimate tale of what it means to be human. Heralded as one of
    the best works of fiction during the 20th century.</TextBlock>
</StackPanel>
```

In the style, the setter is used to set a property to a specific value. Property element syntax is also supported when setting the value of a property. One example of using property element syntax is to set a control template, which can completely change the look and feel of a control. We'll examine control templates in more detail in the next section. Setting a control template in a style looks like this:

```
<Style ...>
    <Setter Property="Template">
        <Setter.Value>
            <ControlTemplate ...>
        </Setter.Value>
    </Setter>
</Style>
```

What if a property is defined in a style and also defined locally? If you consult the value precedence diagram shown in Chapter 2 again (see Figure 8-3), you'll see that the style setter actually has rather low precedence. The property values from style setters can be overridden by values from many sources, and as you can see, the local value has a relatively high precedence. If you use a style setter and it doesn't appear to work, look at these other sources for property values since something is most likely overriding the property value.

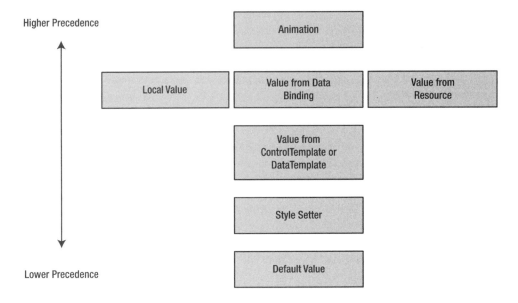

Figure 8-3. *Property value precedence chart*

■**Note** Before the first time a style is applied, the collection of setters in the style can be modified. You can use the x:Name property to make a style easily accessible in the code-behind for modification. After the first time the style is used, however, the style cannot be changed. If you want to test whether a particular style can be modified, check the Style.IsSealed property. This is a bool that is set to true after first application of the style.

There are several significant drawbacks to using styles. Two features supported in WPF but not Silverlight are *conditional styling* (known as property triggers) and *style inheritance*. Conditional styling is useful for applying styles to framework elements based on conditions such as a user hovering over the element. While it would be nice to have this directly supported in the styling system, you can accomplish this behavior using control templates, which we'll look at next.

The other drawback is a lack of style inheritance. Style inheritance is a way for a new style to combine its set of setters with its parent. Since a framework element can only have a single style, it isn't possible to combine multiple styles together at this level. For example, we can't break the previous example into a layout-related style and an appearance-related style. You could potentially implement some custom code that takes multiple styles and programmatically processes the Setter collection to make a new style, but this is more code to maintain and would become useless if Silverlight supports a way to combine or inherit styles in the future.

Using Control Templates

One of the biggest advantages to the control architecture in Silverlight is that the behavior of the standard controls is separated from their visual appearance. A control template is a mechanism used to specify how a control looks but not how it behaves. This core behavior can most simply be viewed as what makes a particular control the control that it is. For example, what is a button? Loosely defined, it is a control that can be pressed. There are specializations of buttons such as repeat buttons—but these specializations provide a different core behavior.

Each control can exist in a number of possible states, such as disabled, having input focus, mouse is hovering over it, and so on. A control template provides the ability to define what the control looks like in each of these states. Sometimes this is referred to as changing the "look and feel" of the control, since changing the visual appearance of each state can alter how a user sees and interacts with a control.

Creating a Control Template

The simplest control template contains a root layout control with a visual representation. Let's take a look at a diamond-shaped button with a gradient to color the top and bottom. You can see the result in Figure 8-4.

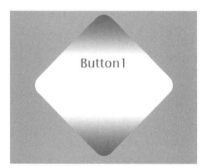

Figure 8-4. *A fancy button using a rotate transform and gradient brush*

The control template is defined as the property value for the `Template` property of the `Control` class. For ease of illustration, the style that contains the control template is stored in the StackPanel's resource dictionary. The button control sets its style and automatically picks up the control template, completely changing its appearance.

```
<StackPanel Background="#FFAAAAAA">
  <StackPanel.Resources>
    <Style  x:Key="buttonStyle" TargetType="Button">
      <Setter Property="Template">
        <Setter.Value>
          <ControlTemplate TargetType="Button">
            <Grid>
              <Rectangle Width="200" Height="200" RadiusX="20" RadiusY="20">
                <Rectangle.Fill>
                  <LinearGradientBrush>
```

```
                        <GradientStop Color="Blue" Offset="0"/>
                        <GradientStop Color="White" Offset="0.3"/>
                        <GradientStop Color="White" Offset="0.7"/>
                        <GradientStop Color="Blue" Offset="1"/>
                      </LinearGradientBrush>
                    </Rectangle.Fill>
                    <Rectangle.RenderTransform>
                      <TransformGroup>
                        <RotateTransform Angle="45"/>
                        <TranslateTransform X="100"/>
                      </TransformGroup>
                    </Rectangle.RenderTransform>
                  </Rectangle>
                  <TextBlock HorizontalAlignment="Center"
                                VerticalAlignment="Center"
                                FontSize="20" Text="BUTTON TEXT"/>
              </Grid>
            </ControlTemplate>
          </Setter.Value>
        </Setter>
    </Style>
  </StackPanel.Resources>
  <Button Content="Button1" FontSize="24" Style="{StaticResource buttonStyle}"/>
</StackPanel>
```

A button that uses this style takes on the diamond shape, but the button's text is forced to display the text "BUTTON TEXT." This isn't useful as a general control template since using this approach requires a new control template defined for each text you would want to display. This problem is solved by the `TemplateBinding` markup extension. This markup extension exists to connect properties used by a control template to properties defined on a specific control, and therefore can only be used in conjunction with control templates. The first revision we will make to the preceding control template is to make `TemplateBinding` use the same content as that specified on a particular button.

■Note The `TemplateBinding` markup extension is one of the few cases where an aspect of XAML does not have a backing class. Since this is a XAML-only construct, there is no way to utilize a `TemplateBinding` in the code-behind. This also means that control templates are XAML-only, since their purpose is to replace the visual appearance of controls. Fortunately, there are tools such as Expression Blend to make working with control templates quite easy.

In order to use the `TemplateBinding` markup extension with a button, a special class called `ContentPresenter` must be used. This class provides the capability to display the wide range of content options possible with Button and other controls' `Content` property. We can revisit the control template included in the preceding style and change the TextBlock that displays "BUTTON TEXT" to the following `ContentPresenter`:

```
<ContentPresenter HorizontalAlignment="Center"
                                VerticalAlignment="Center"
                                Content="{TemplateBinding Content}"/>
```

Using the `ContentPresenter` in this case carries over the `FontSize` and `Content` properties (possibly) defined on a specific Button control. If no `FontSize` property is specified, the default value is used, so while a template might reference several properties, it doesn't mandate that these properties are set in the control utilizing the template.

If you build an application using this control template and attempt to use the button, you will observe that the button doesn't do anything. Actually, it does something—the events still work on the button—but there is no visual feedback communicated to the user reflecting the various states a Button control can have.

Defining different visual appearances based on the different states a control can be in is accomplished using something called the *Visual State Manager (VSM)*. Each control declaratively defines a set of visual state groups and visual states. The states within a group are mutually exclusive, but the control can exist in multiple states if multiple groups are defined. Figure 8-5 shows the two state groups and the valid states within each group for the Button control.

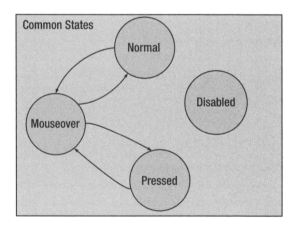

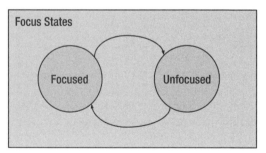

Figure 8-5. *The visual state groups and states of the Button control*

The groups and states are defined declaratively by the control's author. The states and groups shown in Figure 8-5 are defined on the `Button` class using attributes. We'll take a look at these attributes shortly in the context of creating a new control that supports control templates.

The control template must then specify the appearance of the control in each state. Since a control can exist in different states simultaneously (one per visual group), you must be careful to define visual appearances that can be combined. For example, the color of a button's border might change based on whether it has focus, but the contents of the rectangle change based on whether the button is pressed, disabled, moused over, or none of the above (normal). This is the approach that the default Button takes.

Fortunately, Expression Blend makes defining control templates easy. We'll first take a look at defining a new control template for the Button control and then take a closer look at the XAML generated.

Create or open a project in Expression Blend. Drag a new button onto the design surface. Right-click the button and navigate to Edit Control Parts (Template), and you'll see two options. You can edit a copy of the button's current control template or create an empty one by choosing Create Empty. If you were to click Create Empty, the visual appearance of the button would disappear from the design surface, and the generated XAML would be the minimum needed for the button's control template—specifically the list of groups and the states in each group with no state transitions (as shown in the following code). This approach creates a control template resource in the UserControl with the key you specify.

```
<UserControl.Resources>
    <vsm:VisualStateManager.VisualStateGroups>
      <vsm:VisualStateGroup x:Name="FocusStates">
          <vsm:VisualState x:Name="Unfocused"/>
          <vsm:VisualState x:Name="Focused"/>
      </vsm:VisualStateGroup>
      <vsm:VisualStateGroup x:Name="CommonStates">
          <vsm:VisualState x:Name="MouseOver"/>
          <vsm:VisualState x:Name="Pressed"/>
          <vsm:VisualState x:Name="Disabled"/>
          <vsm:VisualState x:Name="Normal"/>
      </vsm:VisualStateGroup>
    </vsm:VisualStateManager.VisualStateGroups>
</UserControl.Resources>
```

When you click Edit a Copy and enter a name for the style in the dialog (as shown in Figure 8-6), the full default control template is placed into the XAML. The default control template for Silverlight's controls are part of a style because other properties of controls are also set, such as padding, content alignment, and cursor appearance. These styled properties apply to every visual state of a control.

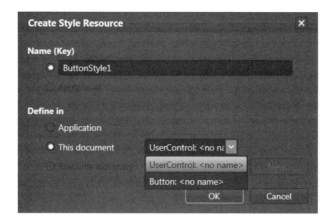

Figure 8-6. *Creating a style resource that contains a control template*

While at this point you could edit the XAML directly to change the appearance of the button in each state, Expression Blend makes it easy to modify each state and state transition without needing to drop down to the XAML. This is facilitated by the States pane in Expression Blend. Figure 8-7 shows what this looks like for the default control template for the Button class.

Figure 8-7. *The States pane for the Button control*

There are several important aspects to this pane. It lists all the states that are defined for the control and also provides capabilities for specifying state transitions. The star on the MouseOver and Pressed states makes it easy to handle specifying transitioning from any state to this state. The state transition duration represents the length of time it takes to transition from one state to another. If you set the MouseOver state duration (currently 0.2) to 5 seconds, the animation to reflect the moused-over state will take a lot longer.

Let's take a closer look at the copy of the default control template for the Button control before replacing it with our own. The style containing the default control template, now located in the XAML file, starts off with 5 simple style property setters:

```
<UserControl.Resources>
    <Style x:Key="ButtonStyle1" TargetType="Button">
        <Setter Property="Background" Value="#FF1F3B53"/>
        <Setter Property="Foreground" Value="#FF000000"/>
        <Setter Property="Padding" Value="3"/>
        <Setter Property="BorderThickness" Value="1"/>
```

The sixth style setter is the control template.

```
<Setter Property="Template">
    <Setter.Value>
        <ControlTemplate TargetType="Button">
            <Grid>
            </Grid>
        </ControlTemplate>
    </Setter.Value>
</Setter>
```

The Grid is the layout container for the various parts of the button. The Grid's resource dictionary includes a number of colors and several brushes that are used by the button. The first child element of the Grid is VisualStateManager:

```
<vsm:VisualStateManager.VisualStateGroups>
    <vsm:VisualStateGroup x:Name="CommonStates">
        <vsm:VisualStateGroup.Transitions>
            <vsm:VisualTransition GeneratedDuration="00:00:00.1" To="MouseOver"/>
            <vsm:VisualTransition GeneratedDuration="00:00:00.1" To="Pressed"/>
        </vsm:VisualStateGroup.Transitions>
        <vsm:VisualState x:Name="Normal"/>
        <vsm:VisualState x:Name="MouseOver">
            <!-- changes background gradient to reflect mouse over state -->
        </vsm:VisualState>
        <vsm:VisualState x:Name="Pressed">
            <!-- changes background gradient to reflect pressed and changes
                 opacity of the DownStroke visual element -->
        </vsm:VisualState>
        <vsm:VisualState x:Name="Disabled">
            <!-- changes opacity of DisabledVisual -->
        </vsm:VisualState>
    </vsm:VisualStateGroup>
    <vsm:VisualStateGroup x:Name="FocusStates">
        <vsm:VisualState x:Name="Focused">
            <!-- makes FocusVisual visible -->
        </vsm:VisualState>
        <vsm:VisualState x:Name="Unfocused">
            <!-- hides FocusVisual -->
```

```
            </vsm:VisualState>
        </vsm:VisualStateGroup>
</vsm:VisualStateManager.VisualStateGroups>
```

The VisualTransition class has four properties that can specify the duration and behavior of state transitions. Its properties are described in Table 8-1.

Table 8-1. *Properties of System.Windows.VisualTransition*

Property	Type	Description
GeneratedDuration	TimeSpan	Gets or sets the length of time the specified state transition takes. This duration will affect the Storyboard specified in the VisualState if none is specified here.
From	string	Gets or sets the starting state. If this property is not specified, the transition will be from any state within the state group to the state specified in the To property.
To	string	Gets or sets the name of the state to transition to.
Storyboard	string	Gets or sets the name of the storyboard that describes the behavior of the state transition. If no storyboard is specified, the Storyboard property of the VisualState class describes the behavior.

The rest of the control template consists of a number of visual elements that, when combined, create the full appearance of a default button. You can edit these visual elements directly using Expression Blend. Figure 8-8 shows each element in the Objects and Timeline pane.

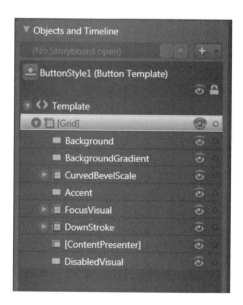

Figure 8-8. *The visual elements that make up the Button control*

These various visual elements are stored next to each other. Each state contains something called a Storyboard, which alters the appearance of different visual elements. We'll take a closer look at what the Storyboard class provides and how to use it in the next chapter. For now, the important thing to note about the Storyboard is that it provides the capability to change the value of any dependency property over a specified length of time.

Let's now create a new button that looks like a jagged-lined bubble you might see in a comic book. This could be useful for a comic-related site, an online store or modeling program, or any site that's on the whimsical side. The outline of the button is created in Expression Design using the PolyLine. Figure 8-9 shows the outline of the button.

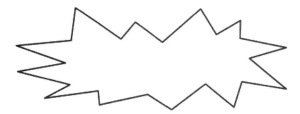

Figure 8-9. *Jagged outline for the new button skin*

The approach we will take for this button is to have separate visual elements for each state. We'll use a thin stroke for the default appearance and the mouseover, but thicken the border when the button is pressed. When the button is hovered over, the fill will change from light blue to light purple. Each visual appearance has a corresponding name that will be used in the storyboards for the state transitions. Figure 8-10 shows a default button in Silverlight, the new button as it appears normally, and the new button as it appears when pressed (from left to right).

Figure 8-10. *A default Silverlight button and the new button in two states*

Here's the corresponding XAML for the normal and pressed versions of the button:

```
<!-- Normal appearance of button -->
<Path x:Name="NormalAppearance"
        Stretch="Fill" StrokeThickness="2"
        StrokeLineJoin="Round" Data="...">
    <Path.Fill>
        <SolidColorBrush Color="#FFAACCEE"/>
    </Path.Fill>
</Path>
<!-- Pressed appearance of button -->
<Path x:Name="PressedAppearance" Visibility="Collapsed"
        Stretch="Fill" StrokeThickness="4"
        StrokeLineJoin="Round" Data="...">
    <Path.Fill>
```

```
        <SolidColorBrush Color="#FFE2CFF6"/>
    </Path.Fill>
</Path>
```

Note that `PressedAppearance` has its `Visibility` initially set to `Collapsed`. This is the approach used to change the appearance of the button: the versions we don't want are hidden, and the visual appearance corresponding to the state being transitioned to is shown. The disabled state of the button still works with how we set the new button up, so we can leave that part of the control template alone. The visual appearance when the button has focus features a black rectangle surrounding the button, as shown on the right in Figure 8-10. The black rectangle is illustrative of two states combined—you might want another visual indication of focus, but this usually depends on the appearance of the other controls in your application, since it's generally good to maintain a degree of consistency.

The entire control template won't be listed, but here's what the transition to the `Pressed` state looks like. A type of animation called *object animation* is used to modify an arbitrary property of an object, in this case the `Visibility` property. The visual appearance of the `MouseOverAppearance` and `NormalAppearance` states is hidden, and `PressedAppearance` is made visible. Again, we'll delve deeper into animation in the next chapter.

```
<vsm:VisualState x:Name="Pressed">
    <Storyboard>
        <ObjectAnimationUsingKeyFrames Duration="0"
                        Storyboard.TargetName="PressedAppearance"
                        Storyboard.TargetProperty="Visibility">
            <DiscreteObjectKeyFrame KeyTime="0">
                <DiscreteObjectKeyFrame.Value>
                    <Visibility>Visible</Visibility>
                </DiscreteObjectKeyFrame.Value>
            </DiscreteObjectKeyFrame>
        </ObjectAnimationUsingKeyFrames>
        <ObjectAnimationUsingKeyFrames Duration="0"
                        Storyboard.TargetName="MouseOverAppearance"
                        Storyboard.TargetProperty="Visibility">
            <DiscreteObjectKeyFrame KeyTime="0">
                <DiscreteObjectKeyFrame.Value>
                    <Visibility>Collapsed</Visibility>
                </DiscreteObjectKeyFrame.Value>
            </DiscreteObjectKeyFrame>
        </ObjectAnimationUsingKeyFrames>
        <ObjectAnimationUsingKeyFrames Duration="0"
                        Storyboard.TargetName="NormalAppearance"
                        Storyboard.TargetProperty="Visibility">
            <DiscreteObjectKeyFrame KeyTime="0">
                <DiscreteObjectKeyFrame.Value>
                    <Visibility>Collapsed</Visibility>
                </DiscreteObjectKeyFrame.Value>
            </DiscreteObjectKeyFrame>
        </ObjectAnimationUsingKeyFrames>
```

```
    </Storyboard>
</vsm:VisualState>
```

Control Templates for Other Controls

There are 16 controls that provide the ability to customize their control template.

Button: The common states are normal, pressed, moused over, and disabled. The focus states are focused and unfocused.

Calendar: The common states are normal and disabled. The Calendar uses the DayButton and MonthButton controls. The DayButton has five state groups: common (normal, disabled, moused over, and pressed); selection (selected and unselected); focus (focused and not focused); active (active and inactive); and day states (regular day and today). The Month-Button shares similar states, but only uses the common, selection, focus, and active state groups.

CheckBox: The common states are normal, moused over, pressed, and disabled. The focus states are focused and unfocused. The check states are checked, unchecked, and indeterminate.

DataGrid: The DataGrid provides normal and unfocused states. There are 11 states defined on each row (for the `DataGridRow` class), 16 states for the `DataGridRowHeader`, 3 for the `DataGridColumnHeader`, and 10 for each cell (for the `DataGridCell` class).

DataPicker: The common states are normal, disabled, moused over, and pressed.

GridSplitter: The common states are normal, moused over, and disabled. The focus states are focused and unfocused.

HyperlinkButton: The common states are normal, moused over, pressed, and disabled. The focus states are focused and unfocused.

ListBox: The ListBox control uses a ScrollViewer and the `ListBoxItem` classes. The `ListBoxItem` defines eight states: common states (normal, moused over, and disabled); focus states (focused and unfocused); and selection states (selected, unselected, and selected, but not focus).

RadioButton: The common states are normal, moused over, disabled, and pressed. The focus states are focused, unfocused, and content focused. The checked states are checked and unchecked.

RepeatButton: The common states are normal, moused over, pressed, and disabled. The focus states are focused and unfocused.

ScrollBar: The ScrollBar itself only has common states (normal, moused over, and disabled). It consists of two sets of a template, two repeat buttons, and a thumb. One set is for vertically oriented scrollbars and the other is for horizontally oriented scrollbars.

ScrollViewer: This has no states, but consists of a horizontal scrollbar, a vertical scrollbar, and a content presenter class (`ScrollContentPresenter`).

Slider: The common states are normal, moused over, and disabled. The focus states are focused and unfocused. Much like the ScrollBar, the Slider consists of two sets of templates (one set for vertical orientation and the other for horizontal). Each set consists of two repeat buttons and a thumb.

TabControl: The common states are normal and disabled. The tab control consists of TabItem instances, each of which has common states (normal, moused over, and disabled); focus states (focused and unfocused); and selection states (selected and unselected).

TextBox: The TextBox includes a normal state, a focused state, and a unfocused state.

ToggleButton: The common states are normal, moused over, pressed, and disabled. The focus states are focused and unfocused. The check states are checked, unchecked, and indeterminate.

Developing a Templated Control

If you want to create your own control, it's a good idea to also make it compatible with control templates. There are really only two things you must do: use the `TemplateVisualState` attribute to specify state groups and states, and use the `VisualStateManager` class within the control's code to handle switching from one state to the next. Since you should be quite familiar with the Button control, let's look at the definition of the `Button` class:

```
[TemplateVisualState(Name = "Normal", GroupName = "CommonStates")]
[TemplateVisualState(Name = "MouseOver", GroupName = "CommonStates")]
[TemplateVisualState(Name = "Pressed", GroupName = "CommonStates")]
[TemplateVisualState(Name = "Disabled", GroupName = "CommonStates")]
[TemplateVisualState(Name = "Unfocused", GroupName = "FocusStates")]
[TemplateVisualState(Name = "Focused", GroupName = "FocusStates")]
public class Button : Control
{
    // class implementation
}
```

The two properties of the `TemplateVisualState` attribute are used here. The groups and states you specify define the behavior of the control. Try to use as few states as possible that still completely define the behavior of your new control. Once these states are defined, the other requirement is for your new control to switch states at the right time.

Some controls consist of other controls, such as the ScrollBar using the RepeatButton control for its increasing/decreasing visual element.

```
[TemplatePart(Name="HorizontalRoot", Type=typeof(FrameworkElement)),
 TemplateVisualState(Name="Normal", GroupName="CommonStates"),
 TemplateVisualState(Name="Disabled", GroupName="CommonStates"),
 TemplatePart(Name="HorizontalLargeIncrease", Type=typeof(RepeatButton)),
 TemplatePart(Name="HorizontalLargeDecrease", Type=typeof(RepeatButton)),
 TemplatePart(Name="HorizontalThumb", Type=typeof(Thumb)),
 TemplatePart(Name="VerticalRoot", Type=typeof(FrameworkElement)),
 TemplatePart(Name="VerticalLargeIncrease", Type=typeof(RepeatButton)),
```

```
 TemplatePart(Name="VerticalLargeDecrease", Type=typeof(RepeatButton)),
 TemplatePart(Name="VerticalThumb", Type=typeof(Thumb)),
 TemplateVisualState(Name="MouseOver", GroupName="CommonStates")]
public sealed class ScrollBar : RangeBase
{
   // ...
}
```

When you edit the control template of a control with template parts in Expression Blend (via Edit a Copy), the control templates for each of the template parts are added as a resource to the root layout container of the main control's control template. The ScrollBar causes the following XAML to be generated (most of the details are left out for brevity). Notice the series of ControlTemplate elements added to the Grid's resource dictionary.

```
<ControlTemplate TargetType="ScrollBar">
    <Grid x:Name="Root">
        <Grid.Resources>
            <ControlTemplate x:Key="RepeatButtonTemplate" TargetType="RepeatButton">
                <Grid x:Name="Root" Background="Transparent">
                    <vsm:VisualStateManager.VisualStateGroups>
                        <vsm:VisualStateGroup x:Name="CommonStates">
                            <vsm:VisualState x:Name="Normal"/>
                        </vsm:VisualStateGroup>
                    </vsm:VisualStateManager.VisualStateGroups>
                </Grid>
            </ControlTemplate>
            <ControlTemplate x:Key="HorizontalIncrementTemplate"
                                            TargetType="RepeatButton">
            </ControlTemplate>
            <ControlTemplate x:Key="HorizontalDecrementTemplate"
                                            TargetType="RepeatButton">
            </ControlTemplate>
            <ControlTemplate x:Key="VerticalIncrementTemplate"
                                            TargetType="RepeatButton">
            </ControlTemplate>
            <ControlTemplate x:Key="VerticalDecrementTemplate"
                                            TargetType="RepeatButton">
            </ControlTemplate>
            <ControlTemplate x:Key="VerticalThumbTemplate" TargetType="Thumb">
            </ControlTemplate>
            <ControlTemplate x:Key="HorizontalThumbTemplate" TargetType="Thumb">
            </ControlTemplate>
        </Grid.Resources>
        <vsm:VisualStateManager.VisualStateGroups>
            <vsm:VisualStateGroup x:Name="CommonStates">
                <vsm:VisualState x:Name="Normal"/>
                <vsm:VisualState x:Name="MouseOver"/>
                <vsm:VisualState x:Name="Disabled">
```

```
            <Storyboard>
              <DoubleAnimationUsingKeyFrames
                          Storyboard.TargetName="Root"
                          Storyboard.TargetProperty="(UIElement.Opacity)">
                  <SplineDoubleKeyFrame KeyTime="00:00:00" Value="0.5"/>
              </DoubleAnimationUsingKeyFrames>
            </Storyboard>
          </vsm:VisualState>
        </vsm:VisualStateGroup>
      </vsm:VisualStateManager.VisualStateGroups>
      <Grid x:Name="HorizontalRoot">
        <!-- Grid definition and main controls -->
        <RepeatButton x:Name="HorizontalSmallDecrease" ...>
        <RepeatButton x:Name="HorizontalLargeDecrease" ...>
        <Thumb MinWidth="10" x:Name="HorizontalThumb" ...>
        <RepeatButton x:Name="HorizontalLargeIncrease" ...>
        <RepeatButton x:Name="HorizontalSmallIncrease" ...>
      </Grid>
      <Grid x:Name="VerticalRoot" Visibility="Collapsed">
        <!-- vertical appearance of ScrollBar -->
      </Grid>
    </Grid>
</ControlTemplate>
```

When you develop a control, the state changes are accomplished using the VisualStateManager's GoToState method. This method takes three parameters: a reference to a control, the name of the state to transition to, and a boolean value specifying whether to use the visual transition specified by the Storyboard in the control template. For example, in the Button control, when the button handles the MouseOver event, it triggers a state transition, accomplished by invoking the VisualStateManager.

```
VisualStateManager.GoToState(this, "MouseOver", true);
```

By using the two attributes, TemplateVisualState and TemplatePart, and handling the state transitions within your custom control via the GoToState method of the VisualStateManager, you can easily create a control that isolates its behavior and allows designers and developers to completely change the look of your control. Of course, if you create a new control that supports control templates, you must create a default control template if you expect others to consume the control.

Summary

This chapter covered styles and control templates. Styles make reusing properties easy, throughout a single page or an entire application, depending on which resource dictionary contains the styles. Control templates are a mechanism to completely change the visual appearance of a control. This chapter also briefly covered developing custom controls to utilize a control template, and using the Storyboard class, a vital part of animation and the topic for the next chapter.

CHAPTER 9

■ ■ ■

Animation

When it comes to making user interfaces that make people go "wow," you have many of the pieces of the puzzle: media (video/audio/images), brushes to easily create interesting surfaces, and a set of controls that can be completely reskinned. There's one final big piece to the user interface support in Silverlight: animation. Silverlight makes it easy to make elements of user interfaces move, and when you put together the various components into a full application, you end up with something quite interesting. Any dependency property can potentially be influenced by animation. If you give some thought to the various properties discussed throughout this book, such as transforms and brushes, it's possible to start coming up with a variety of creative effects to jazz up a user interface. For example, by shifting offsets in gradient stops, a gradient can appear to move from one side of the surface it is filling to the other side, creating a shimmer effect. This chapter will delve into how to use animation and also discuss the support Expression Blend provides for working with animation.

Animation Basics

At its most basic, animation is the modification of a property value over time, usually a property that has a visual effect. If you place a rectangle on a canvas and set its Canvas.Left property to the width of the canvas, and then decrement the Canvas.Left property until it reaches zero, the rectangle will seem like it is moving from off the right side of the canvas to the far left. The animation is made up of one frame per change to the Canvas.Left property, but because the rectangle is repositioned and updated quickly, it seems to the human eye like the rectangle is moving smoothly from one side to the other. This is the illusion of animation that we are witness to on a daily basis when we watch television or movies or play video games.

If we simply specified the starting and ending points for the Canvas.Left property, the rectangle could move at its own merry pace. Perhaps it would take 1 second or 10 minutes. Of course, this isn't suitable, since we want to create predictable animation within user interfaces. This is accomplished using something called a *timeline*, which represents a segment of time (e.g., 10 seconds). Figure 9-1 illustrates a 10-second timeline over which the Canvas.Left property changes from 500 to 0. Notice that at the midway point (5 seconds), Canvas.Left is exactly halfway between its starting value (500) and its ending value (0). For the purpose of this animation, the property value changes in direct relation to time elapsed, which is known as a *linear animation* (technically, it's a linear interpolation of the property value, but we'll get to that in a bit).

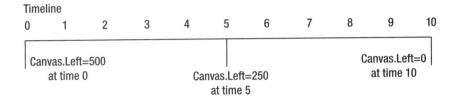

Figure 9-1. *Timeline showing the Canvas.Left animation over 10 seconds*

Timelines

In Silverlight, the `System.Windows.Media.Animation.Timeline` class represents a timeline and forms the base class for the various types of animations (shown in Figure 9-2). The two types of animation Silverlight provides are *from/to/by* and *keyframe*. From/to/by animations make it easy to specify the start and end values for a property. Keyframe animations, however, provide much more control because each keyframe specifies a property's value at a specific time. All animations happens over a length of time. The base `Timeline` class provides time-related behavior to inheritors, featuring a number of properties controlling duration, repeat behavior, and the speed at which time elapses.

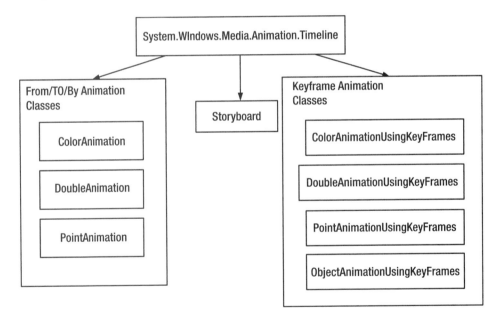

Figure 9-2. *Timeline-related animation classes*

The `Timeline` class defines six properties that influence how time is represented and manipulated. These properties are listed in Table 9-1.

Table 9-1. *Properties of System.Windows.Media.Animation.Timeline*

Property	Type	Description
AutoReverse	bool	If `true`, the animation will happen once and then repeat once in the reverse direction. For more than a single reverse, also use `RepeatBehavior`.
BeginTime	Nullable<TimeSpan>	If this property is `null`, it indicates there is no `BeginTime`. This property can be used to stack animations back to back, so if one animation takes 2 seconds, the `BeginTime` of the second animation can be set to 2s so that it starts immediately after the first.
Duration	Duration	This represents the duration of a single sequence of the animation.
FillBehavior	Animation.FillBehavior	This specifies what happens when an animation hits its end. Set this to `HoldEnd` to make the animation maintain its final value, or to `Stop` to make the animation stop when it reaches its end.
RepeatBehavior	Animation.RepeatBehavior	This specifies how many times the timeline repeats (or if it should repeat forever) and the total length of time.
SpeedRatio	double	This specifies the rate of time the current timeline elapses relative to its parent. The default value is 1, which means, for example, that 5 seconds equates to 5 seconds.

The `Timeline` class also provides a single event, `Completed`, that fires when the timeline has reached its end. `Timeline`'s properties provide a wide range of capabilities in how time is managed and consequently how animation occurs. There are some subtleties in how the properties work together and how a parent timeline can affect a child timeline, so we need to dig deeper into how these properties work.

AutoReverse

The `AutoReverse` property causes the animation to happen in reverse after the animation reaches its end, much like rewinding a tape in a VCR while it is still playing. Figure 9-3 shows what using this property by itself does to a timeline. Note that the forward iteration happens once, the reverse iteration happens once, and then the timeline stops.

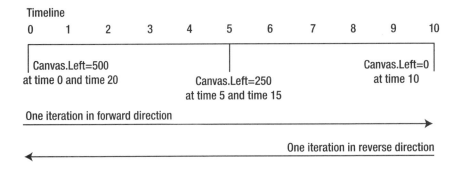

Figure 9-3. *Illustration of the AutoReverse property*

BeginTime

The BeginTime property is used to delay the start of the timeline. When the timeline is started (such as by starting an animation), the current value of this property is used, so this can be changed after a timeline is stopped but before it is restarted. Figure 9-4 illustrates the BeginTime property.

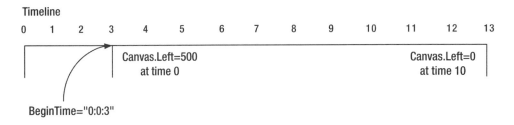

Figure 9-4. *Illustration of BeginTime's effect on a timeline*

■**Note** The BeginTime property is of type TimeSpan. This type specifies a length of time measured in days, hours, minutes, seconds, and fractions of a second. The XAML syntax to specify a TimeSpan takes the form of [*days.*]*hours*:*minutes*:*seconds*[*.fractional seconds*]. The days and fractional seconds are optional and are separated from their nearest neighbor by a period instead of a colon. Hours, minutes, and seconds, however, are mandatory.

Again, we have a 10-second timeline, but there is a 3-second delay. The timeline automatically lengthens by the addition of BeginTime and the timeline's Duration. In this case, a 10-second timeline becomes a 13-second timeline. Since the timeline is used for animation, you can see the begin time as measure of time to delay before the animation starts. This makes it possible to place timelines back to back and cause them to execute in sequence by setting the BeginTime of the next timeline to the length of time it takes for all previous timelines to complete.

It is also possible to specify a negative BeginTime. Doing this provides a way to start the animation at a specified point later in the timeline than its true beginning. For example, a 10-second timeline with a BeginTime of 0:0:-2 starts the timeline at 2 seconds, as if the timeline started at the specified time in the past. This would cause the 10-second timeline to be active only for 8 seconds.

Duration

The Duration property represents the timeline of a single iteration. This property is of the special type System.Windows.Duration. While the Duration type can represent a time span (and uses the same syntax as any property of type TimeSpan when specified in markup), you can also set a property of this type to the special value Automatic. The effects of using Automatic differ depending on whether this property is used on a Storyboard (a Storyboard contains one or more animations, and will be discussed shortly) or on a specific animation. When set on a Storyboard, Automatic causes Duration to be set to the length of time for all the animations it contains put together. For animations, Automatic causes Duration to be set to 1 second (0:0:1). The 1-second default ensures that the animation does something, despite its brevity. You'll rarely if ever use the Automatic value on animations directly. Figure 9-5 highlights the Duration section of the previous timeline.

■**Caution** The value Forever can also be specified for properties of type Duration, but this property value is deprecated; do not use it. See the "RepeatBehavior" section of this chapter for details on how to cause an animation to run continuously.

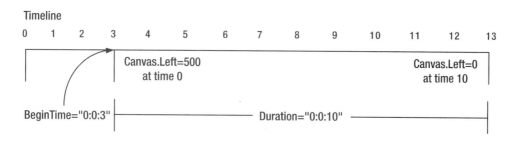

Figure 9-5. *Illustration of Duration combined with BeginTime*

FillBehavior

An animation's *active period*—also known as the animation's *fill period*—is the time during which the animation is happening. The FillBehavior property specifies what happens when the end of the fill period is reached. It can be set to two values: Stop and HoldEnd. When set to HoldEnd, the animation appears to freeze in its final state. For our original moving rectangle example, this means that the rectangle would stop at the left side of the screen, holding its final property value from the animation. The value Stop, however, causes the animation to freeze in its initial state instead of its final state. For our rectangle, this means that after the rectangle reaches the left side, it disappears (since it started completely off the right side of the canvas).

RepeatBehavior

RepeatBehavior, as its name implies, controls how the timeline repeats. It can take one of three forms: a time span, an iteration count, or the special property value Forever (which causes the repetition to happen continuously). The RepeatBehavior property is of the type Animation.RepeatBehavior, which has two properties that specify the exact repeat behavior: Count and Duration. The Count property is of type double and specifies the number of times the timeline should repeat. Since this is a double property, it's possible to repeat a fraction of the timeline by specifying a value (e.g., 1.5). To specify the Count property in XAML, the property value must be followed by x (e.g., 1.5x) to indicate that the timeline repeats a full iteration and a half. There is also a boolean property, HasCount, which is set to true if the RepeatBehavior represents a Count.

The Duration property is the other means used to specify a repeat behavior. This property is of type Duration and is used to specify the total time to run the animation. If the duration of the repeat is longer than the duration of the timeline, the timeline will continue until the length of the repeat behavior's duration. If the repeat's duration is shorter, however, the timeline will stop before reaching its end. For example, if the Duration of the RepeatBehavior property is set to 0:0:5 and the timeline's duration is 0:0:2, the timeline will repeat one and a half times.

There is also a HasDuration property that is set to true when the Duration is specified. It is also possible to set RepeatBehavior to Forever, which represents an animation that continuously repeats.

SpeedRatio

The SpeedRatio property is used to increase or decrease the rate at which time elapses within a timeline. When this value is greater than 1.0 (its default value), the time elapses faster. Likewise, values less than 1.0 cause the timeline to elongate. See Figure 9-6 for a representation of our 10-second timeline sped up and slowed down. The total length of time for a timeline with this property set (and the other properties set to their defaults) is its Duration multiplied by the SpeedRatio.

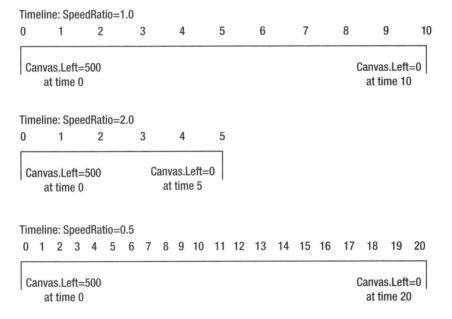

Figure 9-6. *Illustration of different SpeedRatio values*

If we put all these properties together (disregarding a RepeatBehavior set to Forever), the total time it takes for an animation is described by the formula shown in Figure 9-7.

$$\text{Total Timeline Duration} = \text{BeginTime} + \text{RepeatBehavior (as a TimeSpan)}$$

$$\frac{\text{Duration} \times (\text{AutoReverse ? 2 : 1})}{\text{SpeedRatio}} \times \text{RepeatBehavior (as a double)}$$

Figure 9-7. *Formula describing total time span of a timeline*

Now that you're familiar with how timelines can be represented and manipulated, it's time to see exactly what the animation classes bring to the table beyond the inherited timeline support. As mentioned, there are two types of animation: from/to/by and keyframe. From/to/by animations are simpler and are used to alter a single property value over time. They are limited to certain data types, however, which were shown in Figure 9-2. Keyframe animations provide much more capability since you can specify the values you want at different points in time. Also, the values can shift between frames in more than just a linear fashion.

Storyboards and Animation

The Storyboard class also inherits from Timeline. This is a special class used as a container for other animations. Its timeline represents a length of time corresponding to the combination of all the timelines in animations stored in the storyboard (if left unspecified) or a length of time that constrains the total animation runtime. The most important aspects to this class are its methods to begin, stop, pause, and resume the animation. These, along with the other methods of the class, are described in Table 9-2.

Table 9-2. *Methods of System.Windows.Media.Animation.Storyboard*

Method	Description
Begin	Starts the animation with the first timeline in the storyboard.
GetCurrentState	Returns a ClockState enumeration value. Possible states are Active (the animation is active and is changing in direct relation to its parent timeline), Filling (the animation is active but not changing in direct relation to its parent—e.g., it might be paused), and Stopped.
GetCurrentTime	Returns a TimeSpan value corresponding to the current time in the storyboard's timeline.
Pause	Pauses the current storyboard's timeline. Call Resume to unpause the timeline.
Resume	Resumes the current storyboard's timeline.
Seek	Accepts a TimeSpan value corresponding to the time in the storyboard's timeline to move to. This can be done while an animation is active or inactive. The seek operation happens on the next clock tick.

Continued

Table 9-2. *Continued*

Method	Description
SeekAlignedToLastTick	Same as Seek, but the seek operation happens relative to the last clock tick.
SkipToFill	Changes the frame of the animation to the end of the storyboard's active period. If AutoReverse is true, the end of the active period is the initial frame of the animation. If RepeatBehavior is Forever, using this method throws an InvalidOperation exception.
Stop	Stops the animation.

Since the Storyboard class isn't particularly interesting by itself, you'll see it in action when we take a closer look at the animation classes.

From/To/By Animations

The simplest form of animation is generally referred to as from/to/by because of its nature. The "from" and "to" in its name refer to the fact that these animations modify a target property's value starting at the "from" value and ending at the "to" value (not taking into account different configurations of the timeline). The By property provides a relative offset controlling where the animation ends, and is ignored if combined with the To property. Each of these properties can be used by themselves. Table 9-3 describes different configurations of these properties and how they control the timeline.

Table 9-3. *Usages of From/To/By Properties*

Property	Description
From	This specifies the starting value of the property to animate. The animation stops at the base value of the target property or at the final value of the target property from a previous animation.
To	The target property's value starts at its base value or its final value from a previous animation. It finishes at the value specified in the To property.
By	The target property's value starts at its base value or its final value from a previous animation. The final value of the target property is its initial value added to the value specified in the By property.
From/To	This specifies the initial ("from") and final ("to") values of the target property.
From/By	This specifies the initial value of the target property (From) and an offset value used to calculate the target property's final value (From + By).
From/To/By	This is the same as specifying From/To. The value of To overrides By.

Since we've been using it often as an example, let's take a look at how the moving rectangle is animated using XAML. Nothing interesting is going on with the rectangle itself. We give it a name, a position, a size, and a fill:

```
<Rectangle x:Name="rect" Width="25" Height="25" Canvas.Left="370"
                Canvas.Top="270" Fill="Black"/>
```

Then we give the `Storyboard` name so that it can be referenced in the code-behind:

```
<Storyboard x:Name="rectAnimation">
    <DoubleAnimation Storyboard.TargetName="rect" Duration="0:0:2"
                                Storyboard.TargetProperty="(Canvas.Left)"
                                From="370" To="5" />
</Storyboard>
```

`DoubleAnimation` is a type of animation used to modify properties of type `double`. The other two from/to/by animation classes exist to animate points (`PointAnimation`) and colors (`ColorAnimation`). Nothing particularly complicated is going on in this example—`TargetName` refers to the object to animate and `TargetProperty` is the property to animate. You should be familiar with `Duration`, `From`, and `To`.

■Caution If you set a `Duration` on a storyboard that is less than the length of time of the animations the storyboard contains, the animations will not have a chance to run to completion. While this should come as no surprise, it has repercussions when you don't specify the `Duration` on the animations within the storyboard. Individual animations default to 1 second, so a storyboard with a `Duration` of less than 1 second will cause behavior that might be unexpected if you're unprepared.

■Caution Attempting to animate a single target property using multiple animations within a single storyboard will cause the animation to fail (and possibly your application to crash if you don't handle the exception). This happens even if you stagger the animations using the `BeginTime` property. If you want to stagger animations of a specific property, place them in different storyboards and handle the `Completed` event to transition to the next storyboard automatically.

You should take note of how the `TargetProperty` adheres to the property path syntax. The simplest property path is the name of a dependency property on the object specified in `TargetName`. Take, for example, the `Width` property:

```
TargetPropery = "Width"
```

If you want to specify an attached property, however, it must be surrounded by parentheses. This was shown earlier with the `Canvas.Left` property:

```
TargetProperty = "(Canvas.Left)"
```

The object to the left of the dot can be qualified with an XML namespace prefix if the class is not located in the default XML namespace. The property to the right of the dot must be a dependency property. If you want to access a subproperty, you can use the parentheses to surround a *Type.Property* string before accessing the subproperty. For example, if you want to use a `ColorAnimation` to change the background of our moving rectangle, you can specify it using either of the following syntaxes for `TargetProperty`:

```
TargetProperty = "(Rectangle.Fill).Color"
TargetProperty = "(Rectangle.Fill).(SolidColorBrush.Color)"
```

The second syntax simply adds the extra qualification to the `Color` property. This syntax illustrates how to specify other subproperties if they are needed. A final syntax for property paths is required for animating elements such as gradient stops that require indexing:

```
TargetProperty = "GradientStops[0].Offset"
```

As previously shown, the three types of properties you can animate with from/to/by animations are `doubles`, `Points`, and `Colors`. None of these classes provide any specific properties unique to them, and having seen XAML throughout this book, you should be familiar with the property syntaxes for these types. The important thing to keep in mind is that from/to/by animations provide a linear interpolation of values, meaning that the rate at which animation happens is the difference between the initial and final property value during a single iteration, divided by the duration of a single iteration. That is, the rate of change is constant throughout the entire duration of the animation. If you want more control over the animation or the possibility of differing rates of change, Silverlight provides something called a keyframe animation, which will be discussed in the next section.

Let's make the rectangle animation a little more complicated. In the next example, the rectangle will make a circuit around its host canvas and slowly spin as it goes around. While this implies two logical animations, it requires five actual animations (one for each side of the canvas and one for the rotation) and three storyboards (two for the circuit, since we can't animate the same property twice within a storyboard, and one for the rotation).

■**Note** Many of the animation examples use the `Canvas.Left` and `Canvas.Top` attached properties to change an object's position during animation. In more complete applications, this is a poor approach because it assumes the object being animated is within a Canvas and that the position uses absolute coordinates. A much better approach to animating the position and size of objects is to animate the properties of a `TranslateTransform` and a `ScaleTransform` that belong to the object being animated.

```
<Storyboard x:Name="rectAnimBottomLeft"
                 Completed="rectAnimBottomLeft_Completed">
    <DoubleAnimation Storyboard.TargetName="rect"
                 Storyboard.TargetProperty="(Canvas.Left)"
                 From="370" To="5" Duration="0:0:2" />
    <DoubleAnimation Storyboard.TargetName="rect"
                 Storyboard.TargetProperty="(Canvas.Top)"
                 From="270" To="5" Duration="0:0:2" BeginTime="0:0:2"/>
</Storyboard>
<Storyboard x:Name="rectAnimTopRight" Completed="rectAnimTopRight_Completed">
    <DoubleAnimation Storyboard.TargetName="rect"
                 Storyboard.TargetProperty="(Canvas.Left)"
                 From="5" To="370" Duration="0:0:2"/>
    <DoubleAnimation Storyboard.TargetName="rect"
                 Storyboard.TargetProperty="(Canvas.Top)"
                 From="5" To="270" Duration="0:0:2" BeginTime="0:0:2" />
</Storyboard>
```

```xml
<Storyboard x:Name="rectRotationAnim">
    <DoubleAnimation Storyboard.TargetName="rect"
                     Storyboard.TargetProperty="(Rectangle.RenderTransform).Angle"
                     From="0" To="360" RepeatBehavior="Forever" Duration="0:0:4" />
</Storyboard>
```

Each animation is controlled by its own Start/Stop and Pause/Resume button:

```xml
<StackPanel Orientation="Horizontal"
            Grid.Row="0" Grid.Column="0" Background="White">
    <StackPanel Orientation="Vertical">
        <TextBlock FontSize="14">Movement Animation</TextBlock>
        <StackPanel Orientation="Horizontal" Margin="15 0 0 0">
            <Button Content="Start" x:Name="movementStartStopButton"
                    Margin="2" Width="40"
                    Click="movementStartStopButton_Click"/>
            <Button Content="Pause" x:Name="movementPauseResumeButton"
                    Margin="2" Width="60"
                    Click="movementPauseResumeButton_Click"/>
        </StackPanel>
    </StackPanel>
    <StackPanel Orientation="Vertical" Margin="15 0 0 0">
        <TextBlock FontSize="14">Rotation Animation</TextBlock>
        <StackPanel Orientation="Horizontal" Margin="10 0 0 0">
            <Button Content="Start" x:Name="rotationStartStopButton"
                    Margin="2" Width="40"
                    Click="rotationStartStopButton_Click"/>
            <Button Content="Pause" x:Name="rotationPauseResumeButton"
                    Margin="2" Width="60" Click="rotationPauseResumeButton_Click"/>
        </StackPanel>
    </StackPanel>
</StackPanel>
```

We define the Completed event handlers in order to track which of the movement animations is currently executing.

■**Caution** Never invoke the Begin method in a constructor. The animation will not start and you will not get any feedback detailing why. Instead, handle the Loaded event of the UserControl or a layout container, and then invoke Begin.

```csharp
private void rectAnimBottomLeft_Completed(object sender, EventArgs e)
{
    current = rectAnimTopRight;
    rectAnimTopRight.Begin();
}
```

```csharp
private void rectAnimTopRight_Completed(object sender, EventArgs e)
{
    current = rectAnimBottomLeft;
    rectAnimBottomLeft.Begin();
}
```

The start/stop and pause/resume functionality for each animation are similar. Here's the pause/resume button click handler. We need to check whether the animation is running and whether it's paused (in order to build the expected behavior into the buttons).

```csharp
private void movementPauseResumeButton_Click(object sender, RoutedEventArgs e)
{
    if(current.GetCurrentState() != ClockState.Stopped && !movementPaused)
    {
        current.Pause();
        movementPauseResumeButton.Content = "Resume";
        movementPaused = true;
    }
    else
    {
        current.Resume();
        movementPauseResumeButton.Content = "Pause";
        movementPaused = false;
    }
}
```

Animation does not need to always happen in the foreground. We can create a shimmering effect in the background by changing gradient offsets in a linear gradient brush that is used as the background for a Canvas. We also handle the Loaded event of the Canvas in order to start the animation.

```xml
<Canvas x:Name="LayoutRoot" Loaded="LayoutRoot_Loaded">
    <Canvas.Background>
        <LinearGradientBrush x:Name="background" StartPoint="0,1" EndPoint="1,0">
            <GradientStop Color="#FF000000"/>
            <GradientStop Color="#FFAAAAAA"/>
            <GradientStop Color="#FF000000"/>
        </LinearGradientBrush>
    </Canvas.Background>
    <Rectangle Width="350" Height="250" Canvas.Left="25"
                        Canvas.Top="25" Fill="Beige"/>
</Canvas>
```

The animation changes the offsets for each gradient stop evenly over the duration of the animation (1 second). The storyboard's duration is set to 5 seconds so that the shimmering effect doesn't immediately repeat. If it did, it would make the shimmering effect far less effective.

```xml
<Storyboard x:Name="shimmer" Duration="0:0:5" RepeatBehavior="Forever">
    <DoubleAnimation Storyboard.TargetName="background"
                    Storyboard.TargetProperty="GradientStops[0].Offset"
```

```
                      From="-0.2" To="1.0" Duration="0:0:1" />
        <DoubleAnimation Storyboard.TargetName="background"
                      Storyboard.TargetProperty="GradientStops[1].Offset"
                      From="-0.1" To="1.1" Duration="0:0:1" />
        <DoubleAnimation Storyboard.TargetName="background"
                      Storyboard.TargetProperty="GradientStops[2].Offset"
                      From="0" To="1.2" Duration="0:0:1" />
</Storyboard>
```

Let's look at a more complicated example: the classic sliding puzzle game that is commonly given out as children's party favors. Figure 9-8 shows an example.

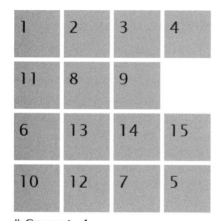

Correct: 4

Figure 9-8. *Sliding puzzle game*

This example uses the By property of the animation to perform relative positional animation:

```
<Storyboard x:Name="horizStoryboard" Completed="horizStoryboard_Completed">
    <DoubleAnimation x:Name="horizAnimation" Duration="0:0:0.5"
                              Storyboard.TargetProperty="(Canvas.Left)"/>
</Storyboard>
<Storyboard x:Name="vertStoryboard" Completed="vertStoryboard_Completed">
    <DoubleAnimation x:Name="vertAnimation" Duration="0:0:0.5"
                              Storyboard.TargetProperty="(Canvas.Top)"/>
</Storyboard>
```

Notice how barren the animations are in this case. Since only one animation can be active at a time, we can take the shortcut of defining only one animation per property: one for the block moving horizontally and the other for it moving vertically. Nothing else related to the sliding blocks in this game is defined in the XAML—the rest is done programmatically to make it easy to track the blocks. Each block is represented by a Canvas with a white background and containing a gray rectangle and a TextBlock to display the number. The Tag property of the Canvas stores an index corresponding to the correct position on the board (the Tag property is set to null for the empty block). You can explore the rest of the game logic in the SlidingGame.xaml.cs file from the code for this chapter. What we are interested in is the actual animation of the blocks. The two animations (horizontal and vertical) use code with similar structure, so we'll just examine the vertical animation:

```
if (emptyCol == col)
{
    if (emptyRow == row - 1 || emptyRow == row + 1)
    {
        Storyboard.SetTarget(vertStoryboard, currentCanvas);
        vertAnimation.By = boardHeight / 4;
        if (emptyRow < row)
            vertAnimation.By *= -1;

        vertInMotion = true;
        vertStoryboard.Begin();
    }
}
```

The first `if` ensures that the animation will be vertical (we know the empty block is above or below since it's the row that differs between the empty block and the block clicked), and the second `if` ensures that the block clicked is only one space away from the empty block. Once we've verified that the move is valid, we set the target of the vertical animation's storyboard. The `Storyboard.SetTarget` method provides an easy way to set the target of an animation to an object. This is a convenient method when working in the code-behind. In XAML, this can only be accomplished by setting the target object's name. After setting the target, we set the `By` property of the animation. It starts out with a positive value, but if the empty space is above the clicked block, the property value must decrease in value, so we multiply by –1 to make the `By` property negative.

There's one tricky aspect of reusing the animations defined in the XAML on different targets: the Storyboard must be stopped before a new target can be set (specifically, setting either TargetName or TargetProperty required a stopped Storyboard). However, if the Storyboard is stopped, the TargetProperty property will revert to its original value (even if FillBehavior is set to HoldEnd). To get everything working, code must be placed in an animation completed event handler to stop the Storyboard and set the target object's property to its correct final value. Here's the event handler for the vertical animation.

```
private void vertStoryboard_Completed(object sender, EventArgs e)
{
    // Get the final value for the Canvas.Top property
    double yPosition = (double)currentCanvas.GetValue(Canvas.TopProperty);

    // Stop the Storyboard
    vertStoryboard.Stop();

    // Set the Canvas.Top property to the final value
    currentCanvas.SetValue(Canvas.TopProperty, yPosition);

    vertInMotion = false;
}
```

Keyframe Animations

Keyframe animations provide significant capabilities over the simpler from/to/by animations. Instead of specifying a starting and ending value and letting the animation smoothly change the target property's value over the animation's duration, keyframe animations instead specify the desired value at two or more points in time. Each specification of a property value is known as a keyframe: a moment in time when you want a property to take on a certain value. The way the value changes during each keyframe is called *interpolation*. Keyframe animation supports interpolations more complicated than the linear interpolations used by from/to/by animations. Keyframe animations also have another important advantage: from/to/by animations can only animate `Points`, `doubles`, and `Colors`, while keyframe animations can animate arbitrary properties using the `ObjectAnimationUsingKeyFrames` class.

A keyframe is a snapshot of a particular property at a specific moment in time. Instead of specifying the starting and ending values of a property using a single animation class, you specify each value of the property you want within a keyframe class. The specific keyframe classes correspond to the property type and interpolation method, which we will discuss shortly. Taking our rectangle from earlier, let's animate it so it moves in a straight line up and down. Figure 9-9 shows what each keyframe looks like.

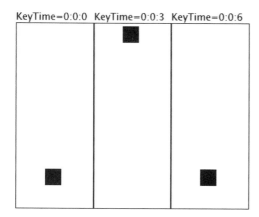

Figure 9-9. *Snapshots of the three keyframes for animating the rectangle*

The `DoubleAnimationUsingKeyFrames` class acts as a container for keyframes. There's one animation class per property type, as shown in Figure 9-2. `LinearDoubleKeyFrame` uses linear interpolation while it is active.

```
<Storyboard x:Name="rectAnimation">
    <DoubleAnimationUsingKeyFrames
            Storyboard.TargetName="rect"
            Storyboard.TargetProperty="(Canvas.Top)"
            RepeatBehavior="Forever">
        <LinearDoubleKeyFrame Value="240" KeyTime="0:0:0"/>
        <LinearDoubleKeyFrame Value="25" KeyTime="0:0:3"/>
        <LinearDoubleKeyFrame Value="240" KeyTime="0:0:6"/>
    </DoubleAnimationUsingKeyFrames>
</Storyboard>
```

Each keyframe specifies the value of the target property at the time specified in the KeyTime property. Since the KeyTime is 0:0:0 in the first keyframe, the target property is set to 240 when the animation begins. If a keyframe is not specified with a KeyTime of 0, the target property uses whatever its current value is, which might be the result of a previous animation or the property's local value.

Interpolation

Interpolation is the process of calculating the set of property values between two known values. As the timeline advances, the property changes to a value within this set. There are three types of interpolation available for use with keyframe animation: *linear, discrete,* and *spline.* The way interpolation works is by using a function that describes a line/curve from (0,0) to (1,1). Linear interpolation uses a diagonal line, as shown in Figure 9-10. If you think back to freshman-level calculus, you'll recall that the derivative of a function describes its rate of change. The linear interpolation function is $y = C \times f(x)$, where C is a constant and the derivative is a horizontal line, also shown in Figure 9-10. Unsurprisingly, this describes a constant rate of change. The coordinate space, although it runs from 0 to 1 in both axes, maps to any timeline/property value range. For example, if a timeline has a duration of 10 seconds, 5 seconds corresponds to x = 0.5 on the graph, and 10 seconds corresponds to 1. This coordinate space will be useful when we look at spline interpolation.

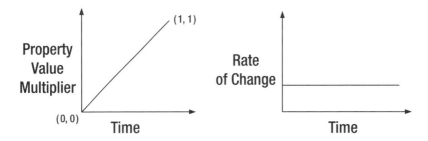

Figure 9-10. *Graph of linear interpolation and its rate of change*

You have already seen linear interpolation in action, since it is the only interpolation supported in from/to/by animations.

Discrete interpolation is even simpler than linear interpolation. The property value can have one of two values: its initial or its final value. As long as the current keyframe is active, the property has its initial value. The target property immediately changes to its final value when the end of the keyframe is reached. This might seem useless at first thought, since if a property can only assume one of two values, where's the animation? However, there are two main advantages to using discrete interpolation: it's a convenient way to hold a specific value for a length of time, and it's the only way to animate properties of types other than Point, double, and Color.

Let's use ObjectAnimationUsingKeyFrames to change an image used in an animation. This will change the Visibility property of two images to only show one image at a time. The two images are animated simultaneously to make it easy to switch between them simply by changing the Visibility.

```
<DoubleAnimationUsingKeyFrames
        Storyboard.TargetName="ballImageUp"
        Storyboard.TargetProperty="(Canvas.Top)">
    <LinearDoubleKeyFrame Value="300" KeyTime="0:0:0"/>
    <LinearDoubleKeyFrame Value="25" KeyTime="0:0:1"/>
    <LinearDoubleKeyFrame Value="300" KeyTime="0:0:2"/>
</DoubleAnimationUsingKeyFrames>
<DoubleAnimationUsingKeyFrames
        Storyboard.TargetName="ballImageDown"
        Storyboard.TargetProperty="(Canvas.Top)">
    <LinearDoubleKeyFrame Value="300" KeyTime="0:0:0"/>
    <LinearDoubleKeyFrame Value="25" KeyTime="0:0:1"/>
    <LinearDoubleKeyFrame Value="300" KeyTime="0:0:2"/>
</DoubleAnimationUsingKeyFrames>
<ObjectAnimationUsingKeyFrames
            Storyboard.TargetName="ballImageUp"
            Storyboard.TargetProperty="Visibility">
    <DiscreteObjectKeyFrame KeyTime="0:0:0">
        <DiscreteObjectKeyFrame.Value>
            <Visibility>Visible</Visibility>
        </DiscreteObjectKeyFrame.Value>
    </DiscreteObjectKeyFrame>
    <DiscreteObjectKeyFrame KeyTime="0:0:1">
        <DiscreteObjectKeyFrame.Value>
            <Visibility>Collapsed</Visibility>
        </DiscreteObjectKeyFrame.Value>
    </DiscreteObjectKeyFrame>
    <DiscreteObjectKeyFrame KeyTime="0:0:2">
        <DiscreteObjectKeyFrame.Value>
            <Visibility>Visible</Visibility>
        </DiscreteObjectKeyFrame.Value>
    </DiscreteObjectKeyFrame>
</ObjectAnimationUsingKeyFrames>
```

The animation for the other image is similar, but the Visibility values are opposite to those used in this XAML. The property element syntax for this keyframe's Value is used to animate different property types.

The final interpolation method is the most complex. Spline interpolation provides a mechanism to alter the rate at which the property value changes at different points during the time a keyframe is active. This means that Silverlight makes it easy to create some sophisticated animations, such as an object that starts out moving slowly and increases its speed over the length of the animation. Let's look at one example of modeling an object that changes its velocity over the course of its total movement. Imagine a single car in motion between two stoplights, as shown in Figure 9-11.

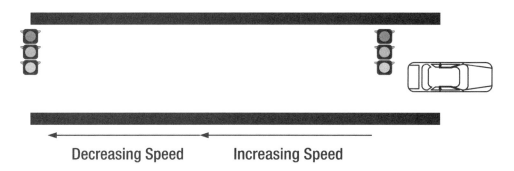

Decreasing Speed   Increasing Speed

Figure 9-11. *Illustration of a car's acceleration and deceleration segments*

The car begins at a full stop and then the first light turns greens. The car's speed increases for a while, but as it approaches the second stoplight, the car must slow down before finally coming to a full stop again. The car's speed can be modeled using the Bezier curve shown in Figure 9-12.

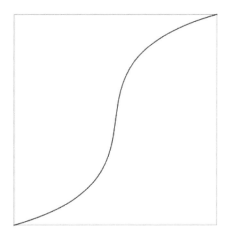

Figure 9-12. *Bezier curve describing the acceleration and deceleration of the car*

A Bezier curve is what the spline interpolation process uses to describe the varying rate of change. Keep in mind this curve describes the values of the property over time. Bezier curves were briefly mentioned in Chapter 7, but let's take a closer look at how they work so it's clear how spline interpolation can be used. The type of Bezier curve used by spline interpolation is a cubic Bezier with two control points, so the cubic Bezier curve is defined by four points, including the endpoints. If P1 and P4 are the endpoints, and P2 and P3 are the control points, the Bezier curve is a line that connects P1 to P4 but is pulled toward P2 and P3 in order to create the curve. The control points are not necessarily touched by the curve. If you set P2 and P3 to points along the line from P1 to P4, such as setting them to (0.25,0.25) and (0.75,0.75), the Bezier curve is a straight line and the animation is effectively using linear interpolation.

The Bezier curve to model the car in Figure 9-12 used the control points (0.9,0.25) (0.1,0.75). The code in this chapter includes a plot of the Bezier curve along with our famous rectangle moving in a straight line (on top of a line that marks the full path of the rectangle). Figure 9-13 shows this curve and the rectangle in its starting position.

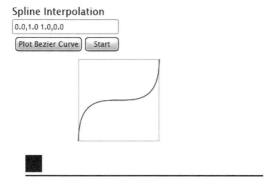

Figure 9-13. *Rectangle animated using spline interpolation, and the curve plotted*

You can divide this Bezier curve into two regions: the first curvy segment (from x = 0 to x = 0.5) and the second curvy segment (from x = 0.5 to x = 1). The first segment starts out with a subtle curve that corresponds to a slowly increasing rate of movement (it's not quite straight along a diagonal, so the rate is not constant). After the bend, the curve is quite steep up to the center point, corresponding to a fast rate of change. The second curvy segment is the mirror opposite of this: the movement continues quickly and suddenly starts slowing down before coming to a complete stop (when the final value of the property is reached).

If you want to figure out the curve that describes the animation you desire, you have several options. There are tools online that can assist, since Bezier curves are a popular approach to modeling animation. You can experiment using the code in this chapter (and possibly extending the code) by plugging in control points and using the Plot Bezier Curve button to preview the animation curve. You can also take out the trusty pen and paper and draw a curve that you think will work, roughly determine the control points, and then experiment. (The derivative for Bezier curves to show the rate of change, while interesting, is left as an exercise for you.)

There's one more way to determine the curve: using Expression Blend's built-in animation editor, which is covered next.

Animating with Expression Blend

Expression Blend makes it easy to create animation using its built-in timeline editor. You may have noticed the Timeline part of the Objects and Timeline section, and now you know exactly what it means.

In Expression Blend, let's animate another rectangle. Create a new UserControl and place a rectangle on the design surface. Next, click the plus sign next to the "(No Storyboard open)" text, as shown in Figure 9-14.

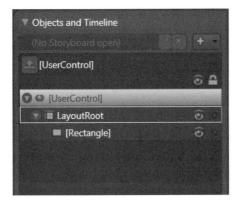

Figure 9-14. *The Objects and Timeline pane in Expression Blend*

Once you click the plus sign, a dialog appears asking for a name for the storyboard. Give it the name rectangleAnimation. The user interface will change in several ways. First, a red outline will surround the design surface and the text "Timeline recording is on" will appear. Next, the timeline editor will open, as shown in Figure 9-15.

Figure 9-15. *The timeline editor in Expression Blend*

The reason the object hierarchy and timeline editing are combined within the same pane is because each object has a corresponding line in the timeline. The control bar at the top of the timeline editor has buttons to change the current frame to the first frame, the previous frame, the next frame, or the last frame. The center button is the play button and runs the animation on the design surface. The only type of animation Expression Blend supports is keyframe, which is reflected in the organization of the timeline editor. The default interpolation used is spline, with the default control points set to effectively create linear interpolation.

Make sure the rectangle object is highlighted in gray in the object hierarchy, and then click the small green plus button next to the time signature. This creates a keyframe with the rectangle in its current position at time 0:0:0. A small white oval appears under the 0-second vertical, showing that a keyframe exists at this time for the corresponding object. Next, click the 1 on top of the timeline's 1-second vertical. This moves the yellow marker to the 1-second line. Next, after ensuring that the rectangle is currently highlighted on the design surface, hold down the Shift key and press the right arrow key to move the rectangle quickly along a straight horizontal line. Stop somewhere close to the right edge of the design surface. As soon as you start moving the rectangle, a new keyframe is created at the 1-second line, shown with another gray oval. The keyframe's target property is set to whatever value corresponds to where you complete the movement. Figure 9-16 shows what the timeline looks after moving the rectangle to a new position at the 1-second mark.

Figure 9-16. *The timeline editor with a keyframe recorded at the 0- and 1-second marks*

Look at the XAML, and notice that the rectangle contains empty versions of the four transforms that Silverlight provides:

```
<Grid x:Name="LayoutRoot" Background="White" >
    <Rectangle Height="80" HorizontalAlignment="Left" Margin="62,0,0,82"
            VerticalAlignment="Bottom" Width="80"
            Fill="#FF000000" Stroke="#FF000000"
            x:Name="rectangle" RenderTransformOrigin="0.5,0.5">
        <Rectangle.RenderTransform>
            <TransformGroup>
                <ScaleTransform/>
                <SkewTransform/>
                <RotateTransform/>
                <TranslateTransform/>
            </TransformGroup>
        </Rectangle.RenderTransform>
    </Rectangle>
</Grid>
```

An empty transform has its default values, which effectively does nothing to the object being transformed. This makes it easy for the animation to affect a specific transform, such as this example does to the X property of the TranslateTransform:

```
<Storyboard x:Name="rectangleAnimation">
    <DoubleAnimationUsingKeyFrames BeginTime="00:00:00"
                            Storyboard.TargetName="rectangle"
                            Storyboard.TargetProperty=
            "(UIElement.RenderTransform).(TransformGroup.Children)[3].
                                        (TranslateTransform.X)">
```

```
        <SplineDoubleKeyFrame KeyTime="00:00:00" Value="0"/>
        <SplineDoubleKeyFrame KeyTime="00:00:01" Value="320"/>
    </DoubleAnimationUsingKeyFrames>
</Storyboard>
```

You can change the interpolation for a specific keyframe in two ways. The first is by right-clicking the gray oval for a keyframe and changing the Ease In or Ease Out value. The ease-in percentage controls how the property value changes as time advances toward the selected keyframe. The higher the ease-in value, the faster this keyframe is approached the closer time gets to it. The ease-out functionality is similar, except it controls how the property value changes as time advances away from the current keyframe. The ease-in and ease-out percentages alter the control points for the KeySpline, for which Expression Blend offers a full-blown editor if you click the Properties tab while a keyframe is selected. The KeySpline editor is shown in Figure 9-17.

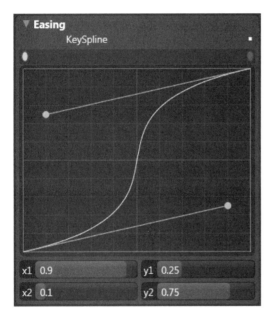

Figure 9-17. *The KeySpline editor in Expression Blend*

The yellow dots correspond to the control points, which are set to the control points used earlier in the car example. You can click and drag these yellow dots, or change the points by using the sliders or entering the numbers by hand after clicking one of the sliders. This editor is likely the best option for exploring KeySplines and discovering which control points will accomplish what you are aiming for.

If you want to change the repeat count of the animation, you need to drill down into the specific target property being animated. You can do this when in timeline recording mode by repeatedly clicking the arrow button on the left of each object until you arrive at a series of highlighted objects, as shown in Figure 9-18.

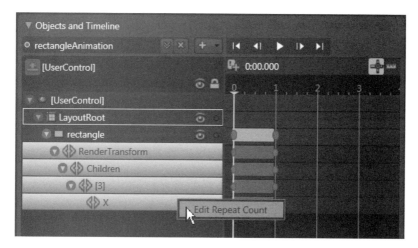

Figure 9-18. *Right-clicking the drilled-down object to modify the repeat count*

Figure 9-18 also shows the context menu when you right-click the target property (X in this case). This context menu also appears if you right-click the time span for the X property. When you select the Edit Repeat Count option, the repeat count dialog appears, as shown in Figure 9-19.

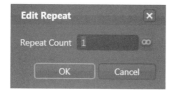

Figure 9-19. *Setting the repeat count using Expression Blend*

You can set a repeat count or click the infinity sign to the right of the text entry to set the repeat count to forever. Expression Blend provides other capabilities as well, such as creating a motion path and converting it to a timeline, and manipulating keyframes in a variety of ways. This section has introduced what Expression Blend can do to make creating animations easier for you.

Summary

This chapter covered the animation support that comes with Silverlight. Timelines are central to the animation support, and the `Timeline` class provides several properties to control how time advances, possibly repeating or even reversing. The simplest form of animation is from/to/by, and several applications of it were demonstrated. Next, you learned about the most powerful animation support in Silverlight: keyframe animation. This provides the capability to alter how property values change by supporting different interpolation methods—specifically linear, discrete, and spline. The keyframe animation also supports modifying properties of types other than `double`, `Point`, and `Color`. Finally, you got a taste of the animation support built into Expression Blend, an invaluable tool for working with animation in both WPF and Silverlight.

CHAPTER 10

■■■

Dynamic Languages and the Browser

One major feature that Silverlight has that .NET doesn't is a second runtime engine designed to execute dynamic languages. A dynamic language is interpreted at runtime, meaning it is possible to add new code while a program is executing. The dynamic language you are likely most familiar with is JScript. Silverlight has direct support for both JScript and Managed JScript— which is JScript executing on the Dynamic Language Runtime (DLR). Two other dynamic languages are supported: Ruby and Python (called IronRuby and IronPython in the Silverlight/ .NET world). This chapter will introduce these dynamic languages, discuss why the DLR is important in the Silverlight picture, and show how to go about using these languages. The latter part of this chapter will discuss the integration of Silverlight with the browser.

Introducing Dynamic Languages

One of the most technically appealing aspects of the .NET platform on Windows is that it supports a wide variety of languages due to how the CLR is designed. Despite the many languages .NET supports, one set of languages that aren't as well supported as they could be are dynamic languages such as Python and Ruby. This lack of support is based largely on the fact that dynamic languages are not compiled, and for a high-level language to execute on the CLR, it must be translated into Intermediate Language (IL). This is a technical hurdle that can be overcome, however. While there is an implementation of Python for .NET, known as IronPython, the most interesting work being done around dynamic languages and .NET is focused on Silverlight.

Dynamic languages are interpreted (eliminating the compilation step) and are usually dynamically typed. What this means, essentially, is you never declare variables of particular types. Everything is handled by the runtime through the context of expressions. The languages you are likely most familiar are C# and VB .NET, which are both statically typed languages. Dynamic languages have many proponents since both development and deployment can be greatly simplified over languages such as C# that require compilation and distribution of output. A certain amount of trust is placed in the runtime that fans of statically typed languages can be resistant to granting. While you do lose type safety with dynamic languages, this can be nearly completely mitigated with a strong set of unit tests.

Both statically typed and dynamic languages have their fans. The great thing about the CLR (and now the DLR, working with the CLR) is that you have a large degree of freedom in language choice when programming on .NET and Silverlight. All the functionality exposed by the various platform assemblies in Silverlight can be accessed from dynamic languages, so you can write Silverlight applications completely in IronRuby, IronPython, or JScript (and potentially others in the future, such as Smalltalk).

One significant feature of most dynamic languages is that functions are first-class citizens. You can create a function and assign it to a variable or pass it as a parameter to another function. This makes things like closures and passing functions as parameters a lot easier. In general, the two defining characteristics of closures are your ability to assign a block of code (a function) to a variable, and this block of code's ability to retain access to variables that were accessible where it was created. If you were to write a method in C# to obtain a subset of a list of words that matches a certain criterion, such as maximum length, the method might look like this:

```
public static List<string> ShortWords(List<string> wordList)
{
    List<string> shortWordList = new List<string>();
    int maximumWordLength = 3;
    foreach(string word in wordList)
    {
        if(word.Length <= maximumWordLength)
        {
            shortWordList.Add(word);
        }
    }
    return(shortWordList);
}
```

Implementing the same method in a dynamic language, such as IronRuby (an implementation of Ruby for the DLR) would be significantly shorter:

```
def ShortWords(wordList)
  maximumWordLength = 3
  return wordList.select {|w| w.Length <= maximumWordLength}
end
```

Just comparing these two implementations of the same algorithm reveals much about IronRuby (and dynamic languages in general, by extension). The IronRuby code is much more concise, and nowhere do you see a data type keyword such as string or int. However, the most interesting aspect of this block of IronRuby code is the closure, located between the curly braces. What's going on here is that the closure, essentially a function, is being passed to the select method. The select method uses a closure to extract a subset of a collection. The code that forms the closure actually executes within the select method (here, the closure extracts strings within the collection wordList that meet the criterion), but it retains access to the variables in its original scope (in this case the maximumWordLength variable). Closures are much more powerful than this simple example illustrates. This is similar to passing a delegate to a method such as Exists or Find in C#, but closures bring the added benefit of retaining access to their original scope.

Dynamic languages in Silverlight are facilitated by the DLR. This runtime is actually just a set of assemblies that creates a bridge between a dynamic language and the CoreCLR in Silverlight. One of the benefits to code running on a managed platform such as Silverlight is that types can typically be discovered at runtime using reflection. The DLR helps facilitate this discovery so that code written in a dynamic language can perform well.

The DynamicApplication Class

The `DynamicApplication` class inherits directly from `System.Windows.Application` and provides the entry point for dynamic language applications. Table 10-1 shows the properties this class provides, extending those already provided by `Application`.

Table 10-1. *Properties of Microsoft.Scripting.Silverlight.DynamicApplication*

Property	Type	Description
Current	static DynamicApplication	The `DynamicApplication` instance for the current application.
Debug	bool	`true` if debugging features are enabled. When debugging is enabled, emitted code is suitable for debugging (it's not optimized) and error reporting is enabled. You can enable debugging by specifying `debug=true` in the `initParams` parameters in the `object` tag for the application in the HTML.
EntryPoint	string	Gets the name of the code file that contains the application's entry point.
Environment	ScriptRuntime	Gets an instance of `ScriptRuntime` that represents the environment the application is executing under.
ErrorTargetID	string	The ID of the HTML element where errors/debugging information will be displayed when `Debug=true` or `ReportUnhandledErrors=true`.
ReportUnhandledErrors	bool	When `true`, unhandled exceptions are displayed in the HTML element specified by `ErrorTargetID`. Otherwise, errors are sent to the JScript function specified in the `onerror` property of the `object` tag for the Silverlight application.

This class operates just like the `Application` class in other Silverlight applications, but provides the extra functionality that dynamic applications need.

Creating a Dynamic Language Application

The best way to get started with dynamic applications and Silverlight is by going to `www.codeplex.com/sdlsdk` and downloading the Silverlight Dynamic Language (SDL) SDK. This SDK contains several important items:

Scripting assemblies: Three assemblies provide the scripting environment that forms the core bridge between Silverlight and dynamic languages in general.

Assemblies specific to a dynamic language: Each dynamic language has assemblies that support the specific language, providing capabilities such as parsing the language and communicating with the host environment.

`Chiron.exe`: This utility serves two main purposes: packaging applications and executing a dynamic language within a development web server.

Application templates: Each dynamic language contained in the SDK (IronPython, Iron-Ruby, and Managed JScript) has a minimal set of files that you can copy and modify to create your own application.

Let's take a look at the application template for IronRuby. After you extract the SDL SDK, the `script\templates\ruby` directory contains the following directories and files:

```
index.html
javascripts\error.js
ruby\app.rb
ruby\app.xaml
ruby\silverlight.rb
stylesheets\error.css
stylesheets\screen.css
```

The `index.html` file contains a large amount of comments that can help guide you (for sake of space, the entire file won't be reproduced here). The `object` tag contains the name of the XAP file for the Silverlight application (the XAP file contains everything in the `ruby` directory from the preceding directory listing). Here's an abbreviated version of the `object` tag from this file:

```
<object data="data:application/x-silverlight,"
            type="application/x-silverlight-2-b2" width="100%" height="100%">
  <param name="initParams" value="debug=true, reportErrors=errorLocation" />
  <param name="onerror" value="onSilverlightError" />
  <param name="background" value="white" />
  <param name="windowless" value="true" />
  <!--
      Shows a "Install Microsoft Silverlight" link if Silverlight is
      not installed
  -->
<a href="http://go.microsoft.com/fwlink/?LinkID=115261"
    style="text-decoration: none;">
      <img src="http://go.microsoft.com/fwlink/?LinkId=108181"
      alt="Get Microsoft Silverlight" style="border-style: none"/>
  </a>
</object>
```

The `reportErrors` parameter (in the `initParams` parameter of the `object` tag) specifies the HTML element to display debugging information and errors. Creating a space for this information is as simple as creating an empty `div`. The error information will be placed into the `innerHTML` property of the HTML element.

```
<div id='errorLocation'></div>
```

If you turn debugging off and don't specify the `reportErrors` parameter, unhandled exceptions will be handled normally and will propagate to the JScript error handler specified in the `onerror` parameter. This handler is located in the `javascripts\error.js` file that is part of the IronRuby template. This handler is essentially the same JScript that is generated when you create a new (nondynamic) Silverlight application in Visual Studio, but you're free to change this to handle errors however you want within the browser.

The two most important files that make up the application are the `app.xaml` and `app.rb` files. The `app.xaml` file that comes with the SDL SDK just contains a TextBox.

```
<UserControl x:Class="System.Windows.Controls.UserControl"
     xmlns="http://schemas.microsoft.com/client/2007"
     xmlns:x="http://schemas.microsoft.com/winfx/2006/xaml">
  <Grid x:Name="layout_root" Background="White">
    <TextBlock x:Name="message" FontSize="30" />
  </Grid>
</UserControl>
```

The `app.rb` file uses code from the `silverlight.rb` file to easily load the XAML stored in `app.xaml`:

```
require "silverlight"
class App < SilverlightApplication
  use_xaml
  def initialize
    message.text = "Welcome to Ruby and Silverlight!"
  end
end
$app = App.new
```

The final line of the `app.rb` file creates the instance of the application and thus the application itself. By going to the `scripts` directory in the SDL SDK, you can execute the `sl.bat` file to copy one of these templates to your own application.

```
C:\book\sdl-sdk\script>sl.bat ruby testapp
7 File(s) copied
Your ruby Silverlight application was created in testapp\.
```

Executing a Dynamic Language Application

Now that you have a starter application, you execute it by making use of the `chiron.exe` tool that comes with the SDL SDK. This tool provides two main functions: it packages a set of files into a XAP and it executes dynamic language applications. One of the interesting features of `chiron.exe` is that any time you modify a file within the application directory, `chiron.exe` will repackage the application into a XAP and reload it. You must still refresh the browser if there is an active browser, though. The full list of command-line options for `chiron.exe` are shown in Table 10-2.

Table 10-2. *Command-Line Options for chiron.exe*

Option	Description
/d:\<path>	Specifies the path for chiron to use; defaults to the current directory.
/x:\<file>	Specifies the file name for the XAP file; cannot be combined with /w or /b.
/n	Does not display the logo banner.
/s	Does not display any output.
/z:\<file>	Similar to /x, but also packages the dynamic language–related files.
/w:[\<port>]	Starts the development web server. If no port is specified, 2060 is used. The XAP file is automatically generated, and is regenerated if any files are changed.
/b:[\<start url>]	Starts the development web server and launches the default browser, optionally to the specified URL; cannot be combined with /x or /z, since XAP generation is handled automatically.
/m	Saves the generated AppManifest.xaml file to disk; can only be combined with /d, /n, or /s.

After creating testapp as shown previously, you can execute it by passing the directory name to chiron.exe and ensuring that a browser automatically opens by using the /b command-line option:

```
C:\book\sdl-sdk_beta2\script>chiron /d:testapp /b
Microsoft(R) Silverlight(TM) Development Utility. Version 1.0.0.0
Copyright (c) Microsoft Corporation.  All rights reserved.
Chiron serving 'C:\book\sdl-sdk\script\testapp' as http://localhost:2060/
00:12:12 200      1,295 /
00:12:12 200        848 /style.css!
00:12:12 200      2,548 /sl.png!
00:12:12 200        698 /slx.png!
00:12:12 404        636 /favicon.ico [Resource not found]
00:12:15 200      5,029 /index.html
00:12:15 200        394 /stylesheets/screen.css
00:12:15 200      2,326 /stylesheets/error.css
00:12:15 200      1,305 /javascripts/error.js
00:12:16 200    925,613 /ruby.xap
```

Notice that the ruby.xap file is rather large. This is because the IronRuby-specific assemblies must be included in the XAP, since they are not part of Silverlight. This is the price you pay for using a dynamic language, since the objective is to keep the Silverlight client installation as small as possible. This also allows dynamic languages to evolve independently from the Silverlight client.

Developing with Dynamic Languages

Each dynamic language has its own syntax. IronPython and IronRuby closely follow their parent language's syntax, and Managed JScript also is close to its parent language, JScript. Each language must support several Silverlight-specific features, such as referencing assemblies.

Several assemblies are automatically available to dynamic languages (i.e., you don't need to add a reference to them). These assemblies are as follows:

- mscorlib.dll

- System.dll

- System.Windows.dll

- System.Windows.Browser.dll

- System.Net.dll

- Microsoft.Scripting.dll

- Microsoft.Scripting.Silverlight.dll

If you want to use classes in any assembly not listed previously, you must first include this assembly in the manifest file (and thus the XAP file) unless it is already part of the Silverlight runtime (in which case, you need only mimic the behavior of the using keyword in C#—which we'll examine next). You can use the /m option of chiron.exe to generate the default manifest and modify it, and then use chiron.exe to repackage it. For example, if you want to add an assembly that contains a service proxy, you can invoke chiron.exe as shown here, combining the /m and /z options, and the /d option with the directory name websearch that contains the dynamic application:

```
C:\book\ dynamic>chiron /m /d:websearch
Microsoft(R) Silverlight(TM) Development Utility. Version 1.0.0.0
Copyright (c) Microsoft Corporation.  All rights reserved.
```

There is no other output to confirm the manifest has been saved to disk, but you should now see an AppManifest.xaml file in the websearch directory. The default manifest file for IronPython applications looks like this:

```
<Deployment xmlns="http://schemas.microsoft.com/client/2007/deployment"
                  xmlns:x="http://schemas.microsoft.com/winfx/2006/xaml"
                  RuntimeVersion="2.0.30523.00"
                  EntryPointAssembly="Microsoft.Scripting.Silverlight"
        EntryPointType="Microsoft.Scripting.Silverlight.DynamicApplication">
  <Deployment.Parts>
    <!-- Add additional assemblies here -->
    <AssemblyPart Name="Microsoft.Scripting.Silverlight"
                          Source="Microsoft.Scripting.Silverlight.dll" />
    <AssemblyPart Source="Microsoft.Scripting.Core.dll" />
    <AssemblyPart Source="Microsoft.Scripting.dll" />
    <AssemblyPart Source="IronPython.dll" />
    <AssemblyPart Source="IronPython.Modules.dll" />
    <AssemblyPart Source="Microsoft.JScript.Runtime.dll" />
    <AssemblyPart Source="Microsoft.JScript.Compiler.dll" />
  </Deployment.Parts>
</Deployment>
```

This manifest file also includes the reference to the DynamicApplication class, specifying the class that serves as the entry point for the dynamic application, much like Application does in the other Silverlight applications. If you add another assembly to this manifest, you then repackage the application with the /z option (to include the dynamic language assemblies in the XAP):

```
C:\book\dynamic>chiron /d:websearch /z:websearch.xap
Microsoft(R) Silverlight(TM) Development Utility. Version 1.0.0.0
Copyright (c) Microsoft Corporation.  All rights reserved.
Generating XAP C:\book\dynamic\websearch.xap from C:\book\dynamic\websearch
```

Once you have a new assembly in the XAP, you must add a reference to it (within a dynamic language source file, since no compilation step is involved with dynamic language applications) and import any classes/namespaces, much like the using keyword in C#. In the three dynamic languages that come with the SDL SDK, this looks like the following.

Here's the IronPython version:

```
import clr
clr.AddReference("Assembly Name, Version=2.0.0.0,
        Culture=neutral, PublicKeyToken=abc012512def25a7")
import System.Windows # this makes the System.Windows namespace visible
# don't need previous line to do the following
from System.Windows.Controls import UserControl
```

This is the IronRuby version:

```
require AssemblyName
include System.Windows.Controls
```

And this is the Managed JScript version:

```
AddReference("Assembly Name, Version=2.0.0.0,
        Culture=neutral, PublicKeyToken=abc012512def25a7")
Import("System.Windows.Controls") // makes namespace visible
// makes the UserControl type available
Import("System.Windows.Controls.UserControl")
```

Let's look briefly at an implementation of a simple dynamic language application. This is an example used in Chapter 9, but with an extra button, as shown in Figure 10-1.

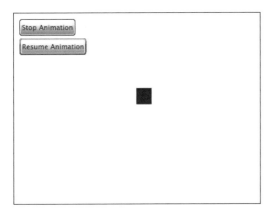

Figure 10-1. *Animation example as implemented in IronPython*

The XAML is exactly the same as is used in any other Silverlight application:

```
<UserControl x:Class="System.Windows.Controls.UserControl"
  xmlns="http://schemas.microsoft.com/client/2007"
  xmlns:x="http://schemas.microsoft.com/winfx/2006/xaml"
      Width="400" Height="300" Margin="10">
  <Canvas x:Name="layout_root" Background="White" Grid.Row="1" Grid.Column="0">
  <Canvas.Resources>
    <Storyboard x:Name="rectAnimation">
      <DoubleAnimationUsingKeyFrames
          Storyboard.TargetName="rect"
          Storyboard.TargetProperty="(Canvas.Top)" RepeatBehavior="Forever">
        <LinearDoubleKeyFrame Value="240" KeyTime="0:0:0"/>
        <LinearDoubleKeyFrame Value="25" KeyTime="0:0:3"/>
        <LinearDoubleKeyFrame Value="240" KeyTime="0:0:6"/>
      </DoubleAnimationUsingKeyFrames>
    </Storyboard>
  </Canvas.Resources>
  <Border BorderThickness="1" BorderBrush="Black" Width="400" Height="300"/>
  <Rectangle x:Name="rect" Width="25" Height="25" Canvas.Left="200"
                  Canvas.Top="240" Fill="Black"/>

  <Button x:Name="animationButton" Canvas.Left="10" Canvas.Top="10"
              Content="Start Animation"/>
  <Button x:Name="pauseButton" Canvas.Left="10" Canvas.Top="40"
              Content="Pause Animation"/>
  </Canvas>
</UserControl>
```

The application file, app.py, connects the events in the __init__ function (essentially a constructor) and defines the event handlers that control the animation:

```
from System.Windows import Application
from System.Windows.Controls import UserControl
from System.Windows.Media.Animation import ClockState
class App:
  def __init__(self):
    self.root = Application.Current.LoadRootVisual(UserControl(), "app.xaml")
    self.root.animationButton.Click += self.startStopAnimation
    self.root.pauseButton.Click += self.pauseAnimation
    self.isPaused = False
  def startStopAnimation(self,s,e):
    if self.root.rectAnimation.GetCurrentState() == ClockState.Stopped:
      self.root.rectAnimation.Begin()
      self.root.animationButton.Content = "Stop Animation"
    else:
      self.root.rectAnimation.Stop()
      self.root.animationButton.Content = "Start Animation"
      self.root.pauseButton.Content = "Pause Animation"
```

```
def pauseAnimation(self,s,e):
  if self.root.rectAnimation.GetCurrentState() ==
                       ClockState.Active and not self.isPaused is True:
    self.root.rectAnimation.Pause()
    self.isPaused = True
    self.root.pauseButton.Content = "Resume Animation"
  else:
    self.root.rectAnimation.Resume()
    self.isPaused = False
    self.root.pauseButton.Content = "Pause Animation"
App()
```

The `App()` at the bottom is what creates an instance of the `App` class defined in this file. There's an additional `from .. import` used to make `ClockState` visible, much like you'd use `using System.Windows.Media.Animation` in C#.

This has been a rather brief overview of the dynamic language support in Silverlight, but it did show you how to go about creating real Silverlight applications using dynamic languages. Visit `http://silverlight.net/learn/dynamiclanguages.aspx` for resources covering dynamic languages in more detail.

Interoperating with the Browser

Along with support for dynamic languages, Silverlight provides libraries to access properties and capabilities of its host environment. Silverlight can access the HTML DOM via the `HtmlDocument` class and can expose classes and data to JScript via attributes and the `HtmlPage` class.

The classes provided for browser interoperability are located in the `System.Windows.Browser` namespace. It provides seven classes related to HTML pages and elements, three classes (two of which are attributes) related to client script, a `BrowserInformation` class to obtain properties about the browser, and an `HttpUtility` class providing encoding/decoding methods for URLs and HTML.

Let's start by taking a closer look at the `BrowserInformation` class. Table 10-3 lists the properties of this class.

Table 10-3. *Properties of BrowserInformation*

Property	Type	Description
BrowserVersion	System.Version	The version number of the browser
CookiesEnabled	bool	true if cookies are enabled; false otherwise
Name	string	String representation of the browser
Platform	string	String representation of the host platform
UserAgent	string	Contains the user agent as communicated from the browser

■**Caution** It is strongly suggested you do not make application decisions based on the UserAgent property. The user agent string is easy to spoof and is not a good way to determine capabilities provided by the browser, since the user may have certain options turned off, or you might block future versions of a browser.

Table 10-4 shows what the BrowserInformation class reports on Internet Explorer 7 running on Microsoft Windows Vista 64-bit.

Table 10-4. *BrowserInformation Properties from Internet Explorer 7 on Windows Vista*

Property	Value
BrowserVersion	4.0
CookiesEnabled	True
Name	Microsoft Internet Explorer
Platform	Win32
UserAgent	Mozilla/4.0 (compatible; MSIE 7.0; Windows NT 6.0; WOW64; SLCC1; .NET CLR 2.0.50727; .NET CLR 1.1.4322; Media Center PC 5.0; .NET CLR 3.0.04506; .NET CLR 3.5.21022; InfoPath.2)

There are ten core classes that support interoperating with the browser. The class hierarchy is shown in Figure 10-2. The HtmlPage class provides several static methods and properties for working with HtmlObject subclasses and other related bits. The methods of HtmlPage are shown in Table 10-5 and the properties are listed in Table 10-6. Note that all the methods and properties are static.

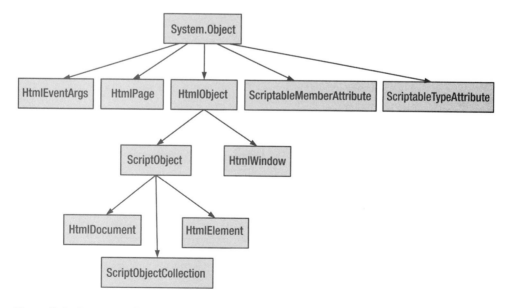

Figure 10-2. *Browser-related class hierarchy*

Table 10-5. *Methods of System.Windows.Browser.HtmlPage*

Method	Description
RegisterCreateableType	Associates a createable type with a string alias. A createable type can be created by using ManagedObject's CreateObject method.
RegisterScriptableObject	Associates an instance of a scriptable object (its class is decorated with ScriptableType) with a string alias.
UnregisterCreateableType	Unregisters a registered createable type (by passing in its alias).
UnregisterScriptableObject	Unregisters a particular scriptable object (by passing in its alias).

Table 10-6. *Properties of System.Windows.Browser.HtmlPage*

Property	Type	Description
BrowserInformation	BrowserInformation	Provides information about the browser
Document	HtmlDocument	Reference to the HTML document displayed in the browser
IsEnabled	bool	Returns true as long as the page is initialized, the enableHtmlAccess hosting option is false, and code isn't executing in a host such as Expression Blend
Plugin	HtmlElement	Provides a reference to the HtmlElement corresponding to the object tag that contains the Silverlight application
Window	HtmlWindow	Returns an instance of the class representing the browser's window; provides access to navigating the browser, ability to change location within the current HTML document, and shortcuts to some client script functions such as alert boxes

The HtmlObject class forms the base for the more interesting classes. It provides functionality to attach and detach events communicated from the browser, such as mouse click events and keyboard events. Table 10-7 lists the methods provided by HtmlObject.

Table 10-7. *Methods of System.Windows.Browser.HtmlObject*

Method	Description
AttachEvent	Overloaded. Registers an EventHandler (optionally parameterized with HtmlEventArgs) for a provided event name.
DetachEvent	Overloaded. Unregisters an EventHandler (optionally parameterized with HtmlEventArgs) for a provided event name. Note that the event handler must still be passed—this makes it possible to unregister only one of possibly many event handlers for a particular event.

The first class we'll look at that descends from HtmlObject is HtmlWindow. The HtmlWindow class provides a direct connection to functionality of the browser, including shortcuts to displaying alert and confirmation dialogs, navigation control, executing arbitrary script code, and accessing bookmarks within the page. Table 10-8 displays the methods of HtmlWindow. This class only has a single property, CurrentBookmark, which can be set or retrieved. Setting CurrentBookmark causes the browser to navigate to the specified bookmark within the current page.

Table 10-8. *Methods of System.Windows.Browser.HtmlWindow*

Method	Description
Alert	Displays an alert dialog containing the text passed in. It's the same as invoking alert(...) from JScript.
Confirm	Displays a confirmation dialog containing the text passed in. If the user clicks yes, this method returns true; otherwise, it returns false.
CreateInstance	Returns an instance of the specified type (can be dotted).
Eval	Directly executes client script contained in a string. It returns an object that contains the result of the executed code, if there is one.
Navigate	Overloaded. Causes the browser to navigate to the URI passed in. It can optionally specify target and targetFeatures to control navigation (such as causing a browser window to contain the content from the URI specified).
NavigateToBookmark	Currently provides the same functionality as setting the CurrentBookmark property directly.
Prompt	Displays a prompt dialog with the text passed in. This is a shortcut to receive user input—the text serves as a label. The input from the user is returned as a string.

The ScriptObject class descends directly from HtmlObject and introduces much useful functionality for its inheritors. It is the abstraction used to uniformly treat client objects. This class handles a lot of the communication with the browser related to client script, such as getting and setting properties of script objects and invoking functions on script objects. Table 10-9 lists its methods.

Table 10-9. *Methods of System.Windows.Browser.ScriptObject*

Method	Description
CheckAccess	Returns true if the thread this is called from is the user interface thread.
GetProperty	Retrieves the value of a named property.
Invoke	Invokes a named function, optionally with arguments (passed in an array of object).
InvokeSelf	Invokes a function on the browser, optionally with arguments (passed in an array of object). The browser function invoked is based on the inheriting class' type.
SetProperty	Sets the named property to an object value.

So far, we've picked up functionality for client-side script events and accessing/executing properties and functions. Beneath ScriptObject are the HtmlDocument, HtmlElement, and ScriptObjectCollection classes. These classes have a one-to-one relationship with aspects of HTML pages.

The HtmlElement class represents an HTML tag. It contains properties for the tag's attributes, styles, name, ID, CSS class, and of course, any children. The ScriptObjectCollection class represents a collection of children (it implements the generic and nongeneric IEnumerable interfaces). The properties of HtmlElement are shown in Table 10-10, and the methods are shown in Table 10-11.

Table 10-10. *Properties of System.Windows.Browser.HtmlElement*

Property	Type	Description
Children	ScriptObjectCollection	Contains a collection of HtmlElement objects, if this tag has any children. Note that this is read-only—use AppendChild and RemoveChild to manipulate this tag's children.
CssClass	string	Gets or sets the CSS class name for this tag.
Id	string	Gets or sets this tag's ID.
Parent	HtmlElement	Gets this tag's parent. This property is read-only.
TagName	string	Gets this tag's name. This property is read-only.

Table 10-11. *Methods of System.Windows.Browser.HtmlElement*

Method	Description
AppendChild	Appends the passed-in HtmlElement to this tag (adds it to the Children collection)
Focus	Sets focus to this tag; most useful for HTML form elements such as input boxes
GetAttribute	Returns the specified attribute's value as a string
GetStyleAttribute	Returns the value of the specified style as applied to this tag
RemoveAttribute	Removes the specified attribute from this tag
RemoveStyleAttribute	Removes the specified named style from this tag
RemoveChild	Removes the specified HtmlElement from this tag's Children collection
SetAttribute	Sets the specified attribute to the specified string value
SetStyleAttribute	Sets the specified style attribute to the specified string value

The HtmlDocument class represents an HTML document—it contains the root HtmlElement of the document, a reference to the body of the HTML document, and methods for retrieving elements on the page by ID. It also has one event, DocumentReady, that fires when the document is finished loading/initializing. If the document finishes loading before Silverlight finishes initializing, this event will *not* fire. The properties of HtmlDocument are shown in Table 10-12, and the methods are shown in Table 10-13.

Table 10-12. *Properties of System.Windows.Browser.HtmlDocument*

Property	Type	Description
Body	HtmlElement	A reference directly to the body of the HTML document; read-only.
Cookies	string	A string containing the cookies associated with this document.
DocumentElement	HtmlElement	A reference to the root of the document; read-only.
DocumentUri	Uri	The URI to this document; read-only.
IsReady	bool	true if the document is done downloading/initializing; read-only.
QueryString	IDictionary<string,string>	A dictionary instance containing name/value pairs corresponding to variables passed in the query string.

Table 10-13. *Methods of System.Windows.Browser.HtmlDocument*

Method	Description
CreateElement	Returns an HtmlElement instance corresponding to the specified tag name.
GetElementById	Returns an HtmlElement corresponding to the specified tag ID, or null if no element was found.
GetElementsByTagName	Returns a ScriptObjectCollection containing all tags that match the specified tag name.
Submit	Causes a postback to the server using the first (or only) form to submit. Via an overload, this can also submit a specific form based on its ID incase there are multiple forms in the document.

The ScriptableMemberAttribute and ScriptableTypeAttribute classes are used to expose classes and class members in the code-behind to client-side script. The ScriptableTypeAttribute class is required in order for JScript to access classes, including granting the ability for managed code in Silverlight to handle DOM events.

Let's create a simple application that shows a drop-down list (the select element) in HTML. This list will be populated by the Silverlight application, and when the user changes the selected value, the background of the Silverlight application will change. You can see what this looks like in Figure 10-3.

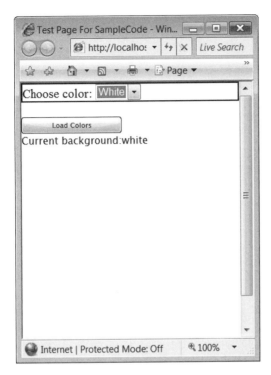

Figure 10-3. *Demonstration of Silverlight influencing and responding to the browser*

The HTML for the list is placed into the ASPX page (or HTML page, if you use that instead):

```
<div id="menu" style="border:solid 2px black">
Choose color:
<select id="colorMenu">
</select>
</div>
```

We can get a reference to the `colorMenu` element by using `GetElementById` from the `HtmlDocument` class:

```
HtmlElement menu = HtmlPage.Document.GetElementById("colorMenu");
```

We need to add `option` tags beneath the `select` element, so we use `HtmlDocument.CreateElement` to create new `option` elements. All HTML tags are treated the same in Silverlight—the `HtmlElement` class provides the functionality needed to work with all the various tags in HTML:

```
HtmlElement option = HtmlPage.Document.CreateElement("option");
```

We now set attributes on the new tag appropriate to the `option` tag and append it to the child collection of the `select` tag:

```
option.SetAttribute("value", "blue");
option.SetAttribute("innerHTML", "Blue");
menu.AppendChild(option);
```

We repeat this sequence for a few more colors, and then we register a method in the code-behind to handle the onchange event of the select tag:

```
menu.AttachEvent("onchange", new EventHandler<HtmlEventArgs>(this.onColorChanged));
```

You will always use HtmlEventArgs when handling DOM events. It contains many properties, including the event name, which keys were pressed (including modifiers such as Ctrl and Alt), mouse information, and a reference to the HtmlObject that generated the event.

The onColorChanged method uses the Source property of HtmlEventArgs to get a reference to the original select tag:

```
public void onColorChanged(object sender, HtmlEventArgs e)
{
    HtmlElement menu = (HtmlElement)e.Source;
    string color = (string)menu.GetProperty("value");
    Color c;
    if (color == "blue")
        c = Color.FromArgb(255, 0, 0, 255);
    else if (color == "red")
        c = Color.FromArgb(255, 255, 0, 0);
    else if (color == "green")
        c = Color.FromArgb(255, 0, 255, 0);
    else
        c = Color.FromArgb(255, 255, 255, 255);
    choiceTB.Text = color;
    LayoutRoot.Background = new SolidColorBrush(c);
}
```

Before this will work, ensure the class containing the managed code for script consumption has the ScriptableType attribute:

```
[ScriptableType]
public partial class Page : UserControl
{
    // code for class here
}
```

We don't need to wait for the user to click the button to populate the drop-down list if we don't want to. However, if the HTML page is big, and the Silverlight application might finish initializing before the entire HTML document is ready, we want to avoid accessing the DOM prematurely. We can account for this case using the DocumentReady event of the HtmlDocument class:

```
HtmlPage.Document.DocumentReady += new EventHandler(Document_DocumentReady);
```

The code from our onClick handler goes into the new Document_DocumentReady method. Remember that if the document finishes loading before the Silverlight application is initialized, this event will not fire.

```
void Document_DocumentReady(object sender, EventArgs e)
{
    // code to manipulate DOM after HTML page is initialized
}
```

The `HtmlWindow` object provides an optimized method to invoke several JScript functions, including `alert`, `confirm`, `eval`, and `prompt`. When working in managed code, it is better to call these JScript functions via the `HtmlWindow` class instead of through the `Eval` method. The `Eval` method is quite useful, as it can call arbitrary JScript code, including functions in JScript. It returns `object`, but the types you can expect back are `bool`, `string`, `double` (for numbers), and `ScriptObject` (for JScript objects).

Let's take a look at calling managed code from JScript. This can be useful for leveraging the speed of managed code from interpreted JScript or for using libraries already written in Silverlight (that hopefully have the correct attributes—but if not, you can write a proxy class that exposes methods to script). To provide an interesting example, we'll use Silverlight to give WCF support to the browser. We'll invoke a service from client-side JScript. Since the generated WCF client is not visible to script by default, we have to build a layer between the JScript and the WCF client in order to expose the latter to the former. You can see what this application looks like in Figure 10-4.

Figure 10-4. *Using Silverlight as a web service proxy to retrieve image data*

This will be a different type of Silverlight application, as we aren't leveraging any of its display capabilities. To ensure the Silverlight application is on the page and doesn't unload at an inopportune time, we'll simply set its width and height to 1:

```
<asp:Silverlight ID="Xaml1" runat="server" Source="~/ClientBin/WebServiceProxy.xap"
                       Version="2.0" Width="1" Height="1" />
```

Since the generated web service client isn't exposed to script by default, we'll create an intermediary type and decorate it with the required attributes:

```
[ScriptableType]
public class ScriptableImageInfo
{
    [ScriptableMember]
    public string name { get; set; }
    [ScriptableMember]
    public string uri { get; set; }
}
```

The ScriptableMember attribute also has a ScriptAlias property that allows you to expose this class member via a different name to client script.

The Silverlight application contains a class decorated with ScriptableType so we can access it from script. This class contains methods for script to invoke the web service. We will maintain the asynchronous approach, so when we create a method to invoke the web service, it will include a string parameter containing a callback function name.

```
[ScriptableMember]
public void getAllImages(string callbackFunc)
{
    // We should move this handler to the class constructor, however it is
    // placed here for demonstration purposes
    _serviceClient.GetAllImagesInformationCompleted += new
                       EventHandler<GetAllImagesInformationCompletedEventArgs>
                                  (_serviceClient_GetAllImagesInformationCompleted);
    _serviceClient.GetAllImagesInformationAsync(callbackFunc);
}
```

This callback function will be invoked via HtmlPage.Eval in the GetAllImagesInformationCompleted event handler:

```
void _serviceClient_GetAllImagesInformationCompleted(object sender,
                       GetAllImagesInformationCompletedEventArgs e)
{
    string callbackFunc = (string)e.UserState;
    imageList = new ScriptableImageInfo[e.Result.Length];
    for (int i = 0; i < e.Result.Length; i++)
    {
        ScriptableImageInfo scInfo = new ScriptableImageInfo();
        scInfo.name = e.Result[i].Name;
        scInfo.uri = e.Result[i].Uri;
        imageList[i] = scInfo;
    }
    HtmlPage.Window.Eval(callbackFunc + "()");
}
```

The callback function, in this case, is used as a signaling mechanism. To get the results of the service call, we need to expose another method for client script:

```
[ScriptableMember]
public ScriptableImageInfo[] getAllImagesResult()
{
    return (imageList);
}
```

Now let's take a look at the JScript side. We'll create a button and a table in the HTML. When the button is clicked, the Silverlight application is invoked and the results are shown in the table.

```
<input type="button" onclick="loadImages()" value="Load Images"/>
<table border="1" id="outputTable">
   <tr>
      <th>Image Name</th>
      <th>Image</th>
   </tr>
</table>
```

The loadImages function caches a reference to the web service class in our Silverlight application and invokes the getAllImages method to retrieve the image data:

```
var imageWebService;
function loadImages()
{
    slPlugin = document.getElementById('Xaml1');
    imageWebService = slPlugin.Content.imageWebService;
    imageWebService.getAllImages("GetAllImagesCompleted");
}
```

The GetAllImagesCompleted function is implemented in JScript. The array from managed code becomes a standard JScript array, so you can use the length property and iterate over it in the expected manner:

```
function GetAllImagesCompleted()
{
    var results = imageWebService.getAllImagesResult();
    for(var i=0; i<results.length; i++)
    {
       var tr = outputTable.insertRow(outputTable.rows.length);
       var td = tr.insertCell(0);
       var text = document.createTextNode(results[i].name);
       td.appendChild(text);
          td = tr.insertCell(1);
          var img = document.createElement('img');
          img.setAttribute('src',results[i].uri);
          img.setAttribute('width','100');
          img.setAttribute('height','100');
```

```
        td.appendChild(img);
    }
}
```

Summary

This chapter introduced the support for dynamic languages that Silverlight provides and showed how to create and deploy dynamic applications. The features of the three supported languages were briefly discussed. Also discussed was the support Silverlight has for interoperating with the host browser, which can be used to greatly expand the capabilities of the browser by using Silverlight as a service provider, and for enabling scenarios where Silverlight and client script communicate.

CHAPTER 11

■■■

Security

The growth of the Internet and the World Wide Web has forever changed the way we use computers. As software engineers, we can no longer ignore security as we did when the average computer wasn't directly connected to a slew of other computers. Silverlight lives online, in users' browsers and other connected devices. No exploration of Silverlight is complete without understanding both the security features it provides and generally how to ensure your Silverlight application has been developed with security in mind. This chapter will go over Silverlight's security model and general techniques for understanding how to design for and evaluate security.

Security in the CoreCLR

While application code executes under the auspices of an environment (the CoreCLR) executing on top of a host operating system, careful thought must still be given to how code is executed. The Silverlight plug-in can interact with the host operating system to communicate over the network, modify files on the file system, and display graphics on screen. Security of the host operating system would be compromised if a Silverlight application were able to make use of these features directly. Therefore, some mechanism must be in place to ensure a division between application code and code that can affect the host operating system.

The managed execution engine that Silverlight provides is based on .NET—specifically the CLR. In .NET, the security model for executable code is called Code Access Security (CAS). There are several important aspects to CAS, including code making requests for specific security permissions (such as asking for the ability to write to files), stack walks to determine the permission levels granted, and the ability for an administrator to control permission levels granted to applications. For example, if your .NET application wants to modify a file stored in a specific location, it must first ensure that it has the rights to access the directory and modify the file. This permission request can be done declaratively by applying a particular permission-related attribute to a method, or imperatively by invoking the Demand method for a specific permission. In C# on the .NET platform, the imperative approach might look like the following.

```
public void saveDataToFile(string outputFilename)
{
    FileIOPermission perm = new FileIOPermission(FileIOPermission.Write,
                                                 outputFilename);
```

```
  try {
    perm.Demand(); // request permission to write to file
                   // throws exception if we don't have permission
    StreamWriter sw = new StreamWriter(outputFilename);
    // write data to sw
    sw.Close();
  } catch(SecurityException ex) {
    // handle security exception
  } catch(Exception generalEx) {
    // handle other exceptions
  }
}
```

It's also possible to make security demands declaratively using a CAS-related attribute:

```
[FileIOPermission(SecurityAction.Demand, Write=@"app.config")]
public void saveDataToFile(string outputFilename)
{
  // method code
}
```

The security model within the CLR ensures that the permission being requested can be granted or the method won't execute. Whether making permission requests imperatively or declaratively, the application code must make specific demands based on what it needs to accomplish. This is a fine-grained approach to ensuring that executable code only has the permissions it needs and works well on the .NET platform.

Silverlight's security model is slightly different. Instead of code asking for permission to accomplish certain tasks, all code in Silverlight is security transparent—that is, it is not trusted. Silverlight applications can still interact with the host operating system (e.g., to save and read files in the file system), but not directly.

Note While there is no CAS available for use by your application, if you explore the online documentation or the assemblies in Reflector, you will come across a namespace related to CAS. This is a holdover from .NET in order to allow the already existing C# compiler to compile Silverlight code, since a CAS-related attribute is emitted by the compiler if the assembly is unverifiable.

Since all application code that you write is security transparent, how is it able to still utilize services offered by the host operating system, such as file system access? There are three categories of code that can execute from the perspective of the Silverlight plug-in. First, there's all the code in a Silverlight application (the code you write and any third-party libraries your application uses). The second and third categories cover code located in the platform assemblies that provide functionality for Silverlight applications, such as isolated storage and network communication. The code in these assemblies either does something high-privilege (e.g., directly modifying a file on disk or invoking a native library on the host operating system) or it calls these high-privilege methods. The code in your application invokes the second category of code. This second category is needed because it serves as the middleman between application code (security-transparent code) and code that is allowed to interact with the host operating system (security-critical code). The relationship between these three categories of executable code is shown in Figure 11-1.

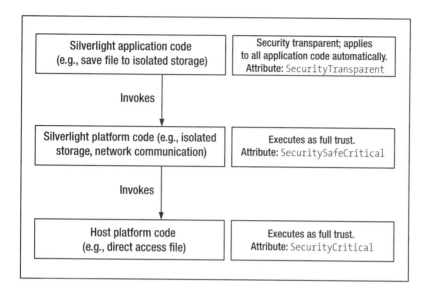

Figure 11-1. *Relationship of executable code and security categories*

Figure 11-1 also shows the attributes that correspond to each category of code. Your application's code cannot use either the SecuritySafeCritical or SecurityCritical attributes—if you attempt to use one, it will be ignored and your code treated as security transparent. Any code decorated with the SecuritySafeCritical attribute can be invoked by security-transparent code. Here are several methods from the System.IO.IsolatedStorage.IsolatedStorageFile class that encompass all three categories of executable code:

```
[SecuritySafeCritical]
public void CreateDirectory(string dir);
public IsolatedStorageFileStream CreateFile(string path);
[SecurityCritical]
private string[] DirectoriesToCreate(string fullPath);
```

Both CreateFile and CreateDirectory can be called from your code. Of course, the private visibility of DirectoriesToCreate hides this method from your code regardless, but the SecurityCritical attribute helps to enforce the fact that only SecuritySafeCritical code is a valid invoker. Your code might call the CreateDirectory method, which then subsequently calls the DirectoriesToCreate method.

This brings about another question, though—why does the platform code get to use the SecuritySafeCritical and SecurityCritical attributes, but your code doesn't? This is enforced by the Silverlight plug-in only granting the ability to run as SecuritySafeCritical or SecurityCritical to code that is signed by Microsoft and downloaded from the Microsoft servers. As shown in Figure 11-1, code marked with SecuritySafeCritical acts as a proxy between code that is security transparent and code that is security critical. Without this intermediate layer, application code could make calls to the security-critical code, giving application code far more privilege than it should have. This security model firmly separates platform code (which might be security critical) from application code (which is always security transparent, no matter what).

Application-Level Security

The security of executable code provided by the CoreCLR is not where the security story ends. While there are guarantees that Silverlight application code cannot gain access to the host operating system, Silverlight applications may still handle confidential information. This information might take the form of a user's credit card data, a user's login credentials, or other information that needs careful handling. This information must be secured in transit, achieved typically via HTTPS, and possibly with a further layer of encryption ensuring that only the intended recipient can decrypt the encrypted information. Secure coding practices combined with the support Silverlight provides can give you confidence that your Silverlight application is secure.

Securing Information in Transit

When a Silverlight application communicates with a server, there is the potential for a third party to listen in on or even tamper with the communication. The established way to secure communication over HTTP is by using the SSL protocol via HTTPS. Silverlight can easily make use of SSL. Both the `WebClient` and `HttpWebRequest` classes support HTTPS, and you can also configure the `ServiceReferences.ClientConfig` to use SSL.

Configuring a service to communicate over HTTPS is accomplished by setting the `mode` attribute of the `security` element to `Transport`, as shown here. Also, make sure the endpoint's address uses the HTTPS protocol.

```
<configuration>
    <system.serviceModel>
        <bindings>
            <basicHttpBinding>
                <binding name="BasicHttpBinding_AuthenticationService"
                        maxBufferSize="65536"
                        maxReceivedMessageSize="65536">
                    <security mode="Transport" />
                </binding>
            </basicHttpBinding>
        </bindings>
        ...
    </system.serviceModel>
</configuration>
```

Securing Information with Cryptography

While communicating over an encrypted channel ensures that information stays secure in transit, the information arrives unencrypted for the application to handle. Regardless of how the application receives information, the information still might need to be decrypted; or if it will be stored locally (such as in isolated storage), it is possible that the information must be encrypted before being written to disk. This is where the System.Security.Cryptography namespace enters the picture. This namespace provides capabilities for encrypting and decrypting data, generating hashes for purposes such as message authentication codes and random number generation suitable for cryptography.

Hash Algorithms and Message Authentication Codes

A hash algorithm transforms a chunk of data into a small, fixed-length set of bytes known as a hash (or hash code). As long as the same chunk of data is processed by the same hash algorithm, the resulting hash code will always be the same. If you've heard of CRC codes or digital signatures, you've heard of the result of hash algorithms. Used as a digital signature, a hash code can prove that the data has not changed, since even a small change in the data will result in a completely different hash code.

The base class of hash classes is HashAlgorithm. This class provides the main features of a hash algorithm, including hash size and hash value properties, and methods for computing a hash value. It provides additional functionality via the KeyedHashAlgorithm—most importantly the addition of a secret password (key) as input to the hash algorithm. This added functionality is important because otherwise, a chunk of data can be tampered with and a recomputed hash code attached to it.

Taking one more step down the hierarchy brings us to the HMAC class. *HMAC* stands for *hash-based message authentication code*. A *message authentication code (MAC)* is another name for a hash value or a digital signature. Changing the data will cause the MAC value to change, thus providing evidence of data tampering. The HMAC class is the one we're most interested in from a class interface perspective since inheritors to HMAC provide specific algorithm implementations. The direct inheritors to HMAC are HMACSHA1 and HMACSHA256, implementations of the SHA-1 and SHA-256 cryptographic algorithms for computing MACs. Table 11-1 shows the properties provided collectively by these three base classes.

Table 11-1. *Properties of System.Cryptography.HMAC*

Property	Type	Description
BlockSizeValue	int	Specifies the size, in number of bits, of the block used by the algorithm
CanReuseTransform	bool	Returns true if you can reuse the current hash transform
CanTransformMultipleBlocks	bool	Returns true if the algorithm can transform multiple blocks
Hash	byte[]	Gets the computed hash value
HashName	string	Gets/sets the name of the algorithm used for hashing
HashSize	int	Specifies the size, in number of bits, of the computed hash value
InputBlockSize	int	Specifies the size, in number of bits, of input blocks
Key	byte[]	Gets/sets the secret key used in the algorithm
OutputBlockSize	int	Specifies the size of the output block

The methods are shown in Table 11-2.

Table 11-2. *Methods of System.Cryptography.HMAC (et al.)*

Method	Description
Clear	Releases all resources used by the algorithm.
ComputeHash	Computes a hash for a byte array (or section thereof) or a Stream. This is the method you use to generate hashes.
Initialize	Initializes an instance of the algorithm.
TransformBlock	Generates a hash value for a section of a byte array and stores it at a specific offset in another byte array.
TransformFinalBlock	Generates a hash value for a section of a byte array.

There are two algorithms that provide the specific implementation for the hash algorithms: SHA-1 and SHA-256. Both algorithms can use a key of any length. The SHA-1 algorithm returns a hash value that is 20 bytes (160 bits), and SHA-256 returns a hash value that is 32 bytes (256 bits). As long as the same input bytes and the same key are used, the specific hash algorithm will always generate the same hash value. Here's a helper method that accepts a message (the input bytes) and the key as strings and will use any specific implementation of the HMAC class that you pass in:

```
byte[] calculateHash(string key, string message, HMAC hashAlgorithm)
{
    UTF8Encoding encoder = new UTF8Encoding();
    hashAlgorithm.Key = encoder.GetBytes(key);
    byte[] hash = hashAlgorithm.ComputeHash(encoder.GetBytes(message));
    return (hash);
}
```

If we pass the string this is a secret message through the HMACSHA1 class, with the secret key p@ssw0rd, and then encode the resulting byte array as a Base64 string, we get the hash value faox88ZBLKYp50KtvKgidtOgRTk=. If we capitalize the first t in the message, the hash value changes to Rs4FcAVPDSFDD+eozXdNcBFHUWw=, which is a significant change. Even changing a single bit in the message or the key will cause a wildly different hash value to be generated.

Encrypting/Decrypting Data

There are two types of encryption algorithms: *symmetric key algorithms* and *asymmetric key algorithms*. A symmetric key algorithm is an algorithm where the key used to encrypt information is the same key used for decryption. An asymmetric key algorithm uses separate keys for encryption and decryption, generally referred to as a *public key* (used for encryption; anyone can obtain the public key to encrypt data for a specific recipient) and a *private key* (this key is kept secret and used to decrypt data encrypted with the public key). Silverlight only supports one encryption algorithm, the symmetric key Advanced Encryption Standard (AES).

The simplest approach to encrypting and decrypting information is by using a single password, as shown in Figure 11-2.

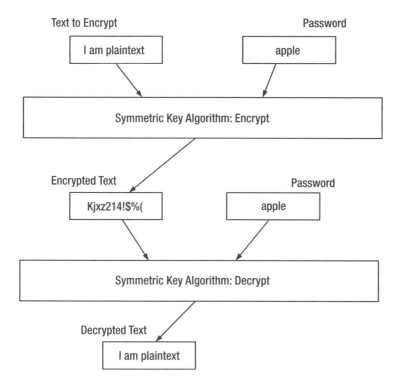

Figure 11-2. *Flow of encryption/decryption using a secret password*

Since the password is used unmodified, an attacker could conceivably launch a dictionary-based attack to find the password by brute force. For example, if an attacker has the encrypted text and has reason to believe a fruit is used for the password, he could try "banana," "orange," "pear," and finally "apple," and suddenly he'll be staring at the original message, successfully decrypted. One way to go about preventing a dictionary-based attack is to use a *salt*. Salts are random data combined with passwords that make dictionary-based attacks much more expensive, since every word in the dictionary must be combined with every possible salt. The salt is stored with the password (usually a password transformed by a hashing algorithm), so decryption is straightforward since the original salt is known and a human-readable password can pass through the same hashing function again. It's possible to make the attacker's job even harder by using a stronger algorithm to transform a password. One such algorithm is the Public-Key Cryptography Standard (PKCS) #5, defined in RFC 2898, which you can find more about at www.ietf.org/.

PKCS #5 actually defines two modes of operation used for deriving a password. The first is Password-Based Key Derivation Function #1 (PBKDF1), and the second is PBKDF2, which you can find in the cryptography namespace in Silverlight. The main advantage to using PBKDF2 is that while the more rudimentary salt-plus-hash approach makes dictionary attacks computationally infeasible, PBKDF2 requires even more computational resources to successfully crack the password. This is accomplished by applying the hash function multiple times. So, instead of an attacker having to try every possible salt with every possible password in a dictionary, he'd also have to try a variety of iteration counts for rehashing along with every possible salt and every password in the dictionary. This means that instead of storing just the salt with a hashed password, you store the salt, the hashed password (the output from the PKCS #5 algorithm), and the iteration count.

The Rfc2898DeriveBytes class provides the implementation of the PBKDF2 algorithm. You pass the password (as a string or a byte array), the salt (as a byte array), and optionally an iteration count to the constructor. Then you invoke the GetBytes member method with the number of bytes you want returned. Here's an example method that does the work of using the Rfc2898DeriveBytes class for you:

```
private byte[] deriveBytes(string input, byte[] salt, int iterations)
{
    Rfc2898DeriveBytes deriver = new Rfc2898DeriveBytes(input, salt, iterations);
    return deriver.GetBytes(16);
}
```

The AesManaged class provides the implementation of the AES algorithm for encrypting/decrypting data. This class inherits from SymmetricAlgorithm. The properties of SymmetricAlgorithm are shown in Table 11-3.

Table 11-3. *Properties of System.Cryptography.SymmetricAlgorithm*

Property	Type	Description
BlockSize	int	Size, in number of bits, of the block used by the algorithm.
IV	byte[]	Initialization vector used by the algorithm; must be BlockSize/8 bytes long.
Key	byte[]	Secret key (e.g., password) used by algorithm.
KeySize	int	Size, in number of bits, of the secret key.
LegalBlockSizes	KeySizes[]	Array of block sizes that are valid for this algorithm. Certain algorithms, such as AES, only support a few different block sizes.
LegalKeySizes	KeySizes[]	Array of key sizes valid for this algorithm.

Used in conjunction with the CryptoStream class, it's straightforward to encrypt data in a stream such as a MemoryStream or a file stream for working with files from isolated storage. Figure 11-3 shows a simple interface for encrypting and decrypting data. The salt must be at least eight characters long. The password entered, combined with the salt, is used for both encrypting and decrypting.

Data Encryption

Password	r@nd0m_p@ssw0rd
Salt	POQWELAKSD
Text to Encrypt	hello world

[Encrypt]

Encrypted Text	DdKYWaNiV3cyiiGnxzpgiw==

[Decrypt]

Decrypted Text	hello world

Figure 11-3. *Demonstration interface for encrypting/decrypting data*

Here's a utility encryption method that takes a key, an initialization vector, and the text to encrypt:

```
private string Encrypt(byte[] key, byte[] iv, string plaintext)
{
    AesManaged aes = new AesManaged();
    aes.Key = key;
    aes.IV = iv;
    using (MemoryStream stream = new MemoryStream())
    {
        using (CryptoStream encrypt = new CryptoStream(stream,
                                     aes.CreateEncryptor(),
                                     CryptoStreamMode.Write))
        {
            byte[] plaintextBytes = UTF8Encoding.UTF8.GetBytes(plaintext);
            encrypt.Write(plaintextBytes, 0, plaintextBytes.Length);
            encrypt.FlushFinalBlock();
            encrypt.Close();
            return Convert.ToBase64String(stream.ToArray());
        }
    }
}
```

The other important aspect to using the AES algorithm is using an initialization vector, as shown in the preceding code in the second parameter. By default, AES uses a 128-bit block size (a block is a fixed length of data used by certain encryption algorithms such as AES), and the initialization vector is used to initialize the block. Since the default block size is 128 bits, the default size of the initialization vector must be 16 bytes (128 bits / 8 bits per byte = 16 bytes). The initialization vector for the encryption must be the same when decrypting data, so if you send encrypted data over the wire, the other side must somehow know which initialization vector to use. This can be something agreed upon by the encryptor and decryptor in the code design phase. Here's what an example initialization vector looks like along with invoking the Encrypt method:

```
byte[] initializationVector = { 0x11, 0xAF, 0x0C, 0x07, 0x17, 0xFC, 0xAA, 0x89,
                                0x09, 0xAE, 0xDA, 0xEA, 0x83, 0x00, 0xC0, 0x90};
encryptedText.Text = Encrypt(deriveBytes(pwText.Text, saltText.Text, 10),
                                        initializationVector, plainText.Text);
```

The Decrypt method is implemented similarly, but uses the decryption functionality of
the AesManaged class:

```
private string Decrypt(byte[] key, byte[] iv, string encryptedText)
{
    AesManaged aes = new AesManaged();
    byte[] encryptedBytes = Convert.FromBase64String(encryptedText);
    aes.Key = key;
    aes.IV = iv;
    using (MemoryStream stream = new MemoryStream())
    {
        using (CryptoStream decrypt =
                       new CryptoStream(stream, aes.CreateDecryptor(),
                                                CryptoStreamMode.Write))
        {
            decrypt.Write(encryptedBytes, 0, encryptedBytes.Length);
            decrypt.Flush();
            decrypt.Close();
            byte[] decryptedBytes = stream.ToArray();
            return UTF8Encoding.UTF8.GetString(
                               decryptedBytes, 0,
                               decryptedBytes.Length);
        }
    }
}
```

User Access Control

ASP.NET 2.0 introduced a membership database that combines database tables with stored
procedures to provide authentication and authorization capabilities. The process of authentication is similar to a guard at a gate, checking identification cards, before allowing access. The
authentication process has a binary answer: either the user has access or she doesn't. Authorization, however, controls the nature of the access once a user is inside the gate. Ushers at
a concert, for example, check concertgoers' tickets to make sure they are permitted access to
the concert. This is an example of authentication. Some concert attendees might have access
to a VIP section or have a backstage pass. These are varying degrees of access, from a regular
concert attendee who can sit and watch, to someone who is allowed to go backstage and meet
the performers. This is an example of authorization—what access does someone have after
they get past the gate that separates insiders from outsiders?

In ASP.NET, authorization is accomplished via roles. A user can be a member of zero or more
roles, and how roles define access is a detail specified in the application design. ASP.NET 3.5
introduces services to provide clients access to the authentication and authorization databases.
Before these services can be used, a web application must be configured to use a membership

database. If you want to install the membership capabilities into a database server, you can use the aspnet_regsql utility that comes with the .NET framework.

Several services are exposed in the System.Web.ApplicationServices namespace. Let's take a look at the services for authentication and authorization. Exposing these services in an ASP.NET application is a simple matter of adding the services and bindings in web.config and enabling the services in the system.web.extensions configuration section. The services must also be referenced in the ServiceHost tag in an SVC file. Let's take a closer look at enabling these services and consuming them from Silverlight.

In web.config, the authentication and roleManager elements within the system.web section are used to configure and enable authentication for the web application.

```
<system.web>
    <authentication mode="Forms" />
    <roleManager enabled="true" />
    <!-- ... -->
</system.web>
```

These services must then be enabled in the system.web.extensions section. The roleService provides web methods for determining whether a user is a member of a particular role.

```
<system.web.extensions>
    <scripting>
      <webServices>
        <authenticationService enabled="true" requireSSL="false"/>
        <roleService enabled="true"/>
      </webServices>
    </scripting>
</system.web.extensions>
```

It is a good idea to enable SSL for authentication. The system.serviceModel section contains the services, bindings, and behaviors related to these services:

```
<system.serviceModel>
  <services>
    <service name="System.Web.ApplicationServices.AuthenticationService"
            behaviorConfiguration="authServiceBehaviors">
      <endpoint contract="System.Web.ApplicationServices.AuthenticationService"
              binding="basicHttpBinding"
              bindingConfiguration="serviceBindingConfig"
              bindingNamespace="http://asp.net/ApplicationServices/v200"/>
    </service>
    <service name="System.Web.ApplicationServices.RoleService"
            behaviorConfiguration="roleServiceBehaviors">
      <endpoint contract="System.Web.ApplicationServices.RoleService"
              binding="basicHttpBinding"
              bindingConfiguration="serviceBindingConfig"
              bindingNamespace="http://asp.net/ApplicationServices/v200"/>
    </service>
  </services>
```

```
<bindings>
  <basicHttpBinding>
    <binding name="serviceBindingConfig">
      <security mode="None"/>
    </binding>
  </basicHttpBinding>
</bindings>
<behaviors>
  <serviceBehaviors>
    <behavior name="authServiceBehaviors">
      <serviceMetadata httpGetEnabled="true"/>
    </behavior>
    <behavior name="roleServiceBehaviors">
      <serviceMetadata httpGetEnabled="true"/>
    </behavior>
  </serviceBehaviors>
</behaviors>
<serviceHostingEnvironment aspNetCompatibilityEnabled="true"/>
</system.serviceModel>
```

Each service has a corresponding SVC file within the web application in order to connect a service host with the service. The following is placed in a file, such as AuthService.svc, for the authentication service:

```
<%@ ServiceHost Language="C#"
                Service="System.Web.ApplicationServices.AuthenticationService" %>
```

The following is for the role service, placed in RoleService.svc:

```
<%@ ServiceHost Language="C#"
                      Service="System.Web.ApplicationServices.RoleService" %>
```

Once you have this configuration done, you can attempt to access a service directly from a browser—for example, by browsing to http://localhost/AuthService.svc.

Using the Authentication Service

The authentication service provides methods to log in and log out, along with checking whether the user is logged in. When a successful login happens, a cookie is set on the client side to store this state. Let's look closer at the methods the authentication service provides.

IsLoggedIn: Returns true if the user is logged in (authentication cookie is present), and false otherwise.

Login: Verifies user's credentials, and if they are validated successfully, the authentication cookie is set. This method takes the username and password, a custom credentials of type string, and a Boolean value specifying whether the authentication cookie persists across sessions.

Logout: Clears the authentication cookie from the browser.

ValidateUser: Verifies a user's credentials. This is similar to Login, but it does not set the authentication cookie if the user's credentials are validated successfully.

Figure 11-4 shows a sample login screen. The login and password shown (testuser/testuser!) are valid with the database distributed with this chapter's code.

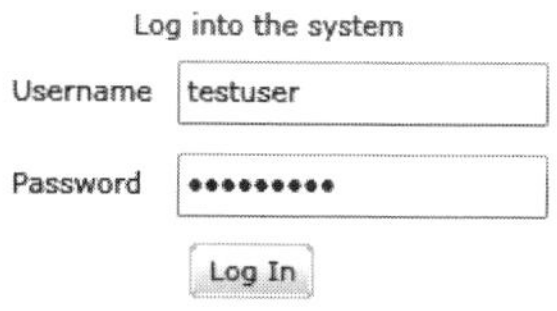

Figure 11-4. *Sample login screen*

In order to transition from a login screen to a screen that represents the main user interface to the application, the XAML that houses the login screen also houses a layout panel that has the main interface. There's a login button on the login screen and a logout button that generally will appear on each screen of the application.

```
<UserControl x:Class="chapter11.LoginScreen"
    xmlns="http://schemas.microsoft.com/winfx/2006/xaml/presentation"
    xmlns:x="http://schemas.microsoft.com/winfx/2006/xaml"
    Width="400" Height="300">
    <Canvas x:Name="LayoutRoot">
        <Grid x:Name="loginScreen" Background="White" Width="400" Height="300">
            ...
            <Button Width="50" Content="Login" x:Name="loginButton"
                    Click="login_clicked" Margin="5"/>
            ...
        </Grid>
        <Canvas x:Name="mainCanvas" Visibility="Collapsed">
            <TextBlock Canvas.Left="25" Canvas.Top="25"
                    Text="You have successfully logged in."/>
            <Button Width="70" Height="50" Content="Logout"
                    Canvas.Left="25" Canvas.Top="75"
                    Click="logoutButton_Click" x:Name="logoutButton"/>
        </Canvas>
    </Canvas>
</UserControl>
```

After adding a service reference to the authentication service, you just need to implement the click event handlers on the buttons for logging in and out:

```
AuthenticationServiceClient client;
public LoginScreen()
{
    InitializeComponent();
    client = new AuthenticationServiceClient();
    client.LoginCompleted +=
            new EventHandler<LoginCompletedEventArgs>(client_LoginCompleted);
    client.LogoutCompleted +=
            new EventHandler<AsyncCompletedEventArgs>(client_LogoutCompleted);
}
```

The login button click handler calls LoginAsync. The third parameter can be custom authentication credentials, but in this case we just pass null. The final parameter is set to true in order to maintain the authentication cookie on the client even after the browser navigates away. This is similar to the "Remember me" check box on the ASP.NET login control.

```
private void login_clicked(object sender, RoutedEventArgs e)
{
    client.LoginAsync(username.Text, password.Password, null, true);
}
```

The LoginCompleted event checks the result of the Login call, and if it indicates that the user successfully logged in, the main user interface is shown. Otherwise, an error message is displayed to the user.

```
void client_LoginCompleted(object sender, LoginCompletedEventArgs e)
{
    if (e.Result)
    {
        loginScreen.Visibility = Visibility.Collapsed;
        mainCanvas.Visibility = Visibility.Visible;
    }
    else
    {
        resultText.Text = "Incorrect username or password";
    }
}
```

The logout button calls the Logout method on the authentication service in order to clear the authentication cookie from the user's browser, and the asynchronous callback handler hides the main user interface and shows the login screen again:

```
private void logoutButton_Click(object sender, RoutedEventArgs e)
{
    client.LogoutAsync();
}
void client_LogoutCompleted(object sender, AsyncCompletedEventArgs e)
{
    loginScreen.Visibility = Visibility.Visible;
    mainCanvas.Visibility = Visibility.Collapsed;
}
```

Since the authentication cookie might be valid when a user first visits the application, your application should call ValidateUser and react accordingly (such as displaying a message that the user is logged in; similar to how web sites display it).

If you don't want to (or can't) use the ASP.NET authentication service, the ASP.NET authentication service serves as a good model for an authentication service you could implement.

Using the RoleService

Once a user is authenticated, the RoleService is used to obtain the roles the user belongs to and to check whether he belongs to a specified role. Let's take a look at the methods the RoleService provides:

GetRolesForCurrentUser: Returns an array of strings containing the roles the currently authenticated user belongs to

IsCurrentUserInRole: Takes a role name and returns true if the user is a member of the role

Once the user is authenticated, you can retrieve the list of roles the user is in using the GetRolesForCurrentUser method. If your application will make a number of role-based decisions, it's better to cache this list of roles locally instead of repeatedly calling the IsCurrentUserInRole service method.

Again, we create an instance of the RoleService client and register the GetRolesForCurrentUser event handler:

```
roleClient = new RoleServiceClient();
roleClient.GetRolesForCurrentUserCompleted +=
    new EventHandler<GetRolesForCurrentUserCompletedEventArgs>
      (roleClient_GetRolesForCurrentUserCompleted);
```

One opportunity to cache the user's roles occurs when the user successfully logs in—although you might want to delay this, since it adds to the amount of time it takes to log the user in. You'd also have to handle loading roles for when the user is already logged in:

```
roleClient.GetRolesForCurrentUserAsync();
```

Once the callback for this web service method occurs, the roles are cached in a List<string>:

```
private List<string> cachedRoles;
private void roleClient_GetRolesForCurrentUserCompleted(object sender,
                          GetRolesForCurrentUserCompletedEventArgs e)
{
    cachedRoles = new List<string>();
    foreach (string role in e.Result)
    {
        cachedRoles.Add(role);
    }
}
public bool isUserInRole(string role)
{
    return(cachedRoles.Contains(role));
}
```

The application can now use the isUserInRole method, instead of the RoleService directly, to make role-based decisions.

Division of Responsibility

You should use a secure communication channel with a server by using HTTPS, and enforce application-level access control (such as using the authentication and authorization services provided by ASP.NET 3.5). This doesn't fully ensure that your application is secure, however. There are several security-related concerns regarding your application's code getting downloaded to the client. These concerns all relate to the possibility that someone can get at the code and resources within a Silverlight application. They can be addressed by application architecture.

The XAP file is just a ZIP archive containing one or more DLL files and resource files. Assume someone wants to take a Silverlight application apart—all they need to do is obtain the XAP file (in the browser's cache or by other means), rename the file extension to zip, and open it in an application that can extract and create ZIP files. The XAP file from this chapter includes chapter11.dll and a manifest file. If you unzip this XAP, someone can now easily get at the DLL.

Once someone has a DLL expanded on disk, it can be disassembled in a utility such as Reflector. Figure 11-5 shows chapter11.dll taken apart in Reflector. It is possible to go a step further and decompile the code, as you can see in Figure 11-6, which shows a method from the LoginScreen class.

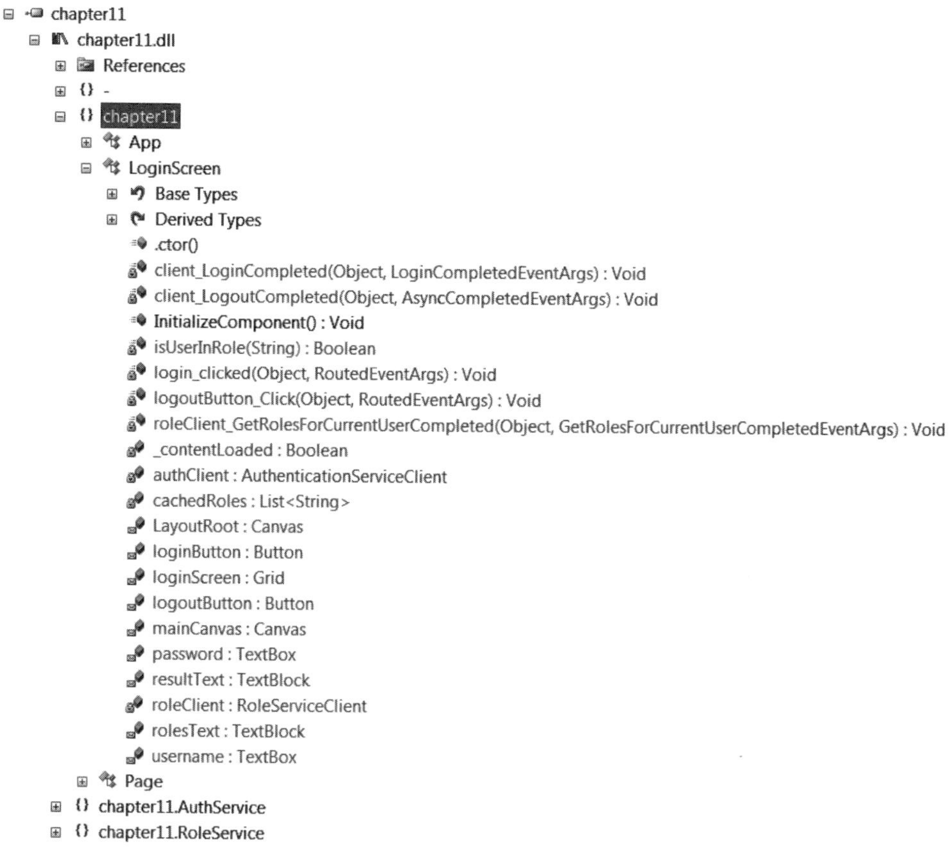

- chapter11
  - chapter11.dll
    - References
    - {} -
    - {} chapter11
      - App
      - LoginScreen
        - Base Types
        - Derived Types
        - .ctor()
        - client_LoginCompleted(Object, LoginCompletedEventArgs) : Void
        - client_LogoutCompleted(Object, AsyncCompletedEventArgs) : Void
        - InitializeComponent() : Void
        - isUserInRole(String) : Boolean
        - login_clicked(Object, RoutedEventArgs) : Void
        - logoutButton_Click(Object, RoutedEventArgs) : Void
        - roleClient_GetRolesForCurrentUserCompleted(Object, GetRolesForCurrentUserCompletedEventArgs) : Void
        - _contentLoaded : Boolean
        - authClient : AuthenticationServiceClient
        - cachedRoles : List<String>
        - LayoutRoot : Canvas
        - loginButton : Button
        - loginScreen : Grid
        - logoutButton : Button
        - mainCanvas : Canvas
        - password : TextBox
        - resultText : TextBlock
        - roleClient : RoleServiceClient
        - rolesText : TextBlock
        - username : TextBox
      - Page
    - {} chapter11.AuthService
    - {} chapter11.RoleService

Figure 11-5. *The methods and classes contained in chapter11.dll as revealed by Reflector*

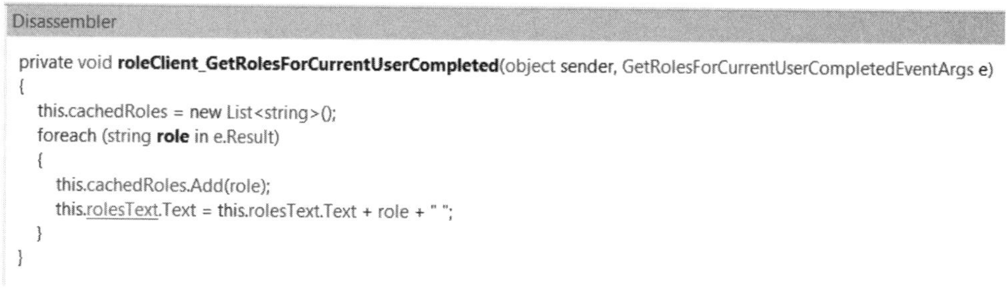

Disassembler

```
private void roleClient_GetRolesForCurrentUserCompleted(object sender, GetRolesForCurrentUserCompletedEventArgs e)
{
    this.cachedRoles = new List<string>();
    foreach (string role in e.Result)
    {
        this.cachedRoles.Add(role);
        this.rolesText.Text = this.rolesText.Text + role + " ";
    }
}
```

Figure 11-6. *The decompiled GetRolesForCurrentUser event callback*

Of course, most users won't have the skill or knowledge to disassemble and decompile a Silverlight application, but an application built with security in mind must pay attention to the people that can. The best solution to the disassembling/decompiling of code is to use an obfuscator, such as Dotfuscator, which is distributed with Visual Studio. After running the DLL for this chapter through Dotfuscator, the identifiers are garbled, and the decompiled methods are a challenge to understand unless you're the CoreCLR. Figure 11-7 shows the obfuscated DLL in Reflector.

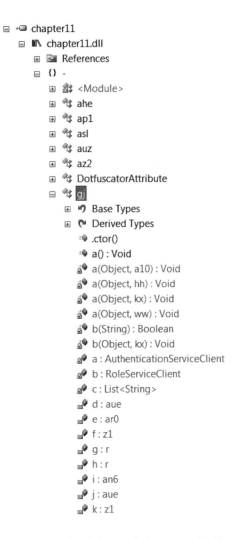

Figure 11-7. *The obfuscated chapter11.dll file*

The method to retrieve and cache roles, after obfuscation, looks like this:

```
private void a(object A_0, hh A_1)
{
    this.c = new List<string>();
    IEnumerator<string> enumerator = A_1.a().l();
    try
    {
        while (enumerator.g())
        {
            string str = enumerator.f();
            this.c.d(str);
            this.k.b(zt.a(this.k.r(), str, " "));
        }
    }
    finally
    {
        if (enumerator != null)
        {
            enumerator.h();
        }
    }
}
```

As you can see, obfuscation is great at making it a challenge to understand the code. But make sure as much code related to the application is obfuscated as possible, since some revealed method names or variable names provide clues to what the code nearby is doing. For example, the decompiled constructor makes the following call, revealing that no matter what type b is, it has an event named `GetRolesForCurrentUserCompleted`:

```
this.b.add_GetRolesForCurrentUserCompleted(new EventHandler<hh>(this.a));
```

Between this and the previously shown obfuscated method (which is the asynchronous callback), it is obvious where code can be modified to alter the roles the user belongs to. So, if it's possible to trick a Silverlight application into believing a user is in roles he doesn't belong to, it demonstrates why you must guard against placing too much functionality within a single Silverlight application.

The simplest application design principle to follow is to place all privileged code on the server side and let the server perform an authentication check before the rest of the method executes. Role-based decisions made on the client side should not create a decision between executing normal-privileged code and high-privileged code. However, you can make role-based decisions on such benign things as the appearance of the user interface.

Another approach to separating different privilege levels of code is to place them behind a traditional web site login screen for user authentication, and then deliver a completely different Silverlight application to the user based on her access level. This is illustrated in Figure 11-8.

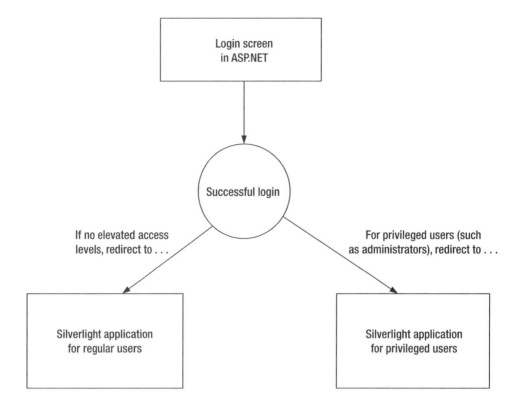

Figure 11-8. *Redirecting to a different Silverlight application based on users' roles*

If you take this approach, make sure any more highly privileged Silverlight applications
are not cached on the client side. This helps makes it tougher to augment an application to
grant a regular user higher privileges. Even if you take this approach, it's wise to place as much
high-privilege code on the server side as possible so you can make sure only users with the right
access level are allowed to run the code.

Another valid concern is the security of resources used by a Silverlight application. As
shown in Figure 11-9, even though the main application assembly has been obfuscated, not only
are resources such as the embedded XAML easily viewable, but they can also be easily extracted.

Disassembler	
Name	Value
page.xaml	ef bb bf 3c 55 73 65 72 ... (1458 bytes)
loginscreen.xaml	ef bb bf 3c 55 73 65 72 ... (2016 bytes)
hmacexample.xaml	ef bb bf 3c 55 73 65 72 ... (2003 bytes)
dataencryption.xaml	ef bb bf 3c 55 73 65 72 ... (2153 bytes)
xaml_viewer.xaml	3c 55 73 65 72 43 6f 6e ... (560 bytes)
app.xaml	ef bb bf 3c 41 70 70 6c ... (292 bytes)

Figure 11-9. *The resources embedded in the application assembly*

One strategy to protect resources is to encrypt them. This is useful for any data files that you want downloaded at same time as the Silverlight application. You can use the `AesManaged` class previously detailed with a secret key that is downloaded as part of the Silverlight application (perhaps an authenticated user's data protection password stored with his profile) to encrypt and decrypt data locally.

Another approach to protecting resources is to avoid packaging them with the Silverlight application. Once a user is authenticated, the application can download the appropriate resources on demand. This applies to both resources stored within the application's DLL and resources stored in the XAP file. Your application design must account for this anywhere a resource (such as an image) differs based on a user's access level.

Summary

Applications must be designed and developed with security in mind. This chapter started off by detailing the security model Silverlight provides for executable code, illustrating how application code cannot directly invoke any code that can interact with the host platform. The rest of this chapter detailed application-level security, such as using HTTPS as a secure channel, encrypting/decrypting information, authenticating and authorizing users, and ensuring your applications are designed well to protect code and resources. Make sure your Silverlight application and surrounding infrastructure (such as an ASP.NET application) are designed and developed with security in mind. Late in development or immediately before deployment are not the times to start thinking about security.

CHAPTER 12

■■■

Testing and Debugging

Testing and debugging are vital activities in building quality software. From a developer's perspective, unit testing ensures small units of code work. By having a suite of tests, it is easy to catch a bug introduced into code that was previously shown to be bug free. Testing helps ensure software quality by catching as many bugs as possible and proactively ensuring bugs aren't introduced. Debugging, however, is generally done after a bug has been found. Debugging involves tools and an effective problem-solving process to find the root cause of a bug in order to apply a fix. You can build defenses into your application to make debugging much easier, such as error logs (to capture errors) and audit logs (to reconstruct what the user of the application did to trigger the bug). This chapter aims to show you how to go about testing Silverlight applications and preparing for and conducting debugging when things do go wrong.

Testing

Testing involves both ensuring applications are error free and verifying applications work according to requirements and design. It is the software developer's job to implement tests, known as *unit tests*, to thoroughly test the code he writes. Other forms of testing include *functional testing* to verify the application corresponds to its specification and *usability testing* to ensure the application is well designed from a user interface perspective. These tests generally belong to a quality assurance department.

Unit Testing

The goal of unit testing is to test the smallest unit of a system as possible. If you're building an airplane, it's impractical to test the smallest pieces, such as verifying that each screw can withstand a certain degree of pressure, or that hoses that pump fluid or oxygen don't disconnect or wear out absurdly fast. These pieces still need testing, however, or the airplane likely won't work. Since the airplane manufacturer can't practically test the tiniest parts, the responsibility of testing lies with the manufacturer of these parts. The screw manufacturer must know how much pressure the screws can withstand and then verify they match the specification. These smallest parts are the units of a system, the building blocks that, when assembled, create something much larger. Just like the screw manufacturer must test his screws, the software developer must test his code at the smallest unit possible—typically methods.

Silverlight provides a unit testing framework very similar to the testing framework used by Visual Studio 2008; however, the testing output is not integrated with Visual Studio. The testing framework takes the form of a Silverlight application, but it isn't distributed as part of

Silverlight or the Silverlight SDK. Instead, you can download the testing assemblies along with the source code of the controls by searching for "source code unit tests silverlight 2" at www.microsoft.com/. Create a new application and add the three testing-related assemblies, as shown in Figure 12-1.

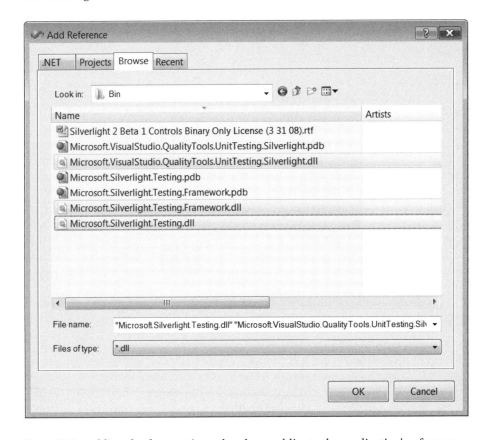

Figure 12-1. *Adding the three testing-related assemblies to the application's references*

You can remove Page.xaml and Page.xaml.cs from the project since these aren't needed. Go to App.xaml.cs and add the following using statement at the top:

```
using Microsoft.Silverlight.Testing;
```

The testing framework provides its own user interface that you can connect to your Silverlight testing application by invoking UnitTestSystem.CreateTestPage, as shown here:

```
private void Application_Startup(object sender, StartupEventArgs e)
{
    this.RootVisual = (UIElement)UnitTestSystem.CreateTestPage(this);
}
```

Now that you have the unit testing framework ready to go, the next step is to add a reference to the application assembly that is the subject of testing. The rest happens automatically after we apply certain test-related attributes to classes that contain tests. Before we look at constructing tests, we need code to test. If you're writing a business application, user input typically must be validated to ensure it meets certain criteria. A validation class might be located in a class library assembly and used by any Silverlight applications developed by a company. Here's a Validators class with a single validation method that verifies a value is within a range:

```
public class Validators
{
    public static bool validateRange(int value, int lowBound, int highBound)
    {
        return (value >= lowBound && value < highBound);
    }
}
```

Even a method this simple may have a bug in it. Bugs aren't only due to poorly written code—bugs can also be due to incorrect assumptions or failure to match requirements. Or a bug can be due to a simple typo. In order to know for sure whether a piece of code contains bugs, a set of unit tests must be written. The Validators class is located in the chapter12 assembly. Let's turn to the application that provides the unit testing framework and implement some tests.

Create a new class (not a user control) and add the following using statements at the top:

```
using Microsoft.Silverlight.Testing;
using Microsoft.VisualStudio.TestTools.UnitTesting;
using chapter12;
```

If you're unfamiliar with unit testing frameworks, they typically work by examining the metadata on classes and methods to get the necessary cues as to what to do. A class that contains test methods is decorated with the TestClass attribute, and individual test methods are decorated with TestMethod, as shown here. Also, the testing class must inherit from SilverlightTest.

```
namespace chapter12test
{
    [TestClass]
    public class ValidatorsTests : SilverlightTest
    {
        [TestMethod]
        public void TestRangeTooLow()
        {
            Assert.IsFalse(Validators.validateRange(0, 10, 20));
        }
        [TestMethod]
        public void TestRangeAtUpperBound()
        {
            Assert.IsTrue(Validators.validateRange(20, 10, 20));
        }
    }
}
```

In the code for this chapter, this class contains other testing methods to test other values inside and outside a range. These two tests, however, represent a test that succeeds (TestRangeTooLow) and one that fails (TestRangeAtUpperBound). The Assert class provides a number of methods to verify conditions to indicate test success. If the conditions are not met, an exception is thrown automatically and is caught by the unit testing framework, informing that the test failed.

When you start the testing application, it immediately executes all tests. Figure 12-2 shows execution of several range validator–related tests, one of which is the failing test, `TestRangeAtUpperBound`.

Figure 12-2. *Unit testing framework output with a failing test*

The reason this test fails is that the requirements for the validator method specify that the lower and upper bounds must both be inclusive. This is easily fixed by changing the < to a <= when testing the value against the upper bound. After making this fix, rerunning the testing application shows all tests succeeding. You can see this in Figure 12-3.

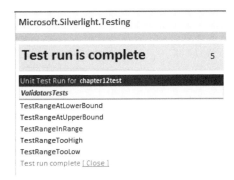

Figure 12-3. *Unit testing framework output with all tests passing*

The Assert class provides a number of useful methods for conveniently verifying test results, and also provides a way to trigger a failure in case the provided methods are not sufficient. Table 12-1 lists the static methods provided by the Assert class. Note that many methods provide a large set of overloads in order to cover a wide variety of data types. These assertion methods also give the ability to pass in a string parameter as a custom message that will be included in the test execution report.

Table 12-1. *Static Methods of Microsoft.VisualStudio.TestTools.UnitTesting.Assert*

Method	Description
AreEqual	Tests whether two values are equal.
AreNotEqual	Tests whether two values are not equal.
AreNotSame	Tests whether two object references point to different objects.
AreSame	Tests whether two object references point to the same objects.
Fail	Causes a test to immediately fail. Use this to fail a test based on custom logic.
Inconclusive	Causes a test to report "inconclusive" in the report. Use this for tests not implemented or for tests where it's impossible to pass or fail the test.
IsFalse	Tests whether the specified Boolean value is false.
IsInstanceOfType	Tests whether an object is an instance of a given type.
IsNotInstanceOfType	Tests whether an object is not an instance of a given type.
IsNotNull	Tests whether a given reference is not null.
IsNull	Tests whether a given reference is null.
IsTrue	Tests whether the specified Boolean value is true.
ReplaceNullChars	Utility method to replace null characters within a string with \0 so that the null characters can be displayed.

The Assert class can throw an AssertFailedException or an AssertInconclusiveException. These exceptions should never be caught by your code since they provide the mechanism for communicating test results to the unit testing framework. There are two other Assert-related classes: StringAssert and CollectionAssert. StringAssert provides a set of methods useful for string-based conditional tests, and CollectionAssert does likewise for collections. Table 12-2 lists the methods of StringAssert and Table 12-3 shows the methods of CollectionAssert.

Table 12-2. *Static Methods of Microsoft.VisualStudio.TestTools.UnitTesting.StringAssert*

Method	Description
Contains	Tests whether one string occurs somewhere within another string
DoesNotMatch	Tests whether two strings do not match
EndsWith	Tests whether one string ends with another string
Matches	Tests whether two strings match
StartsWith	Tests whether one string starts with another string

Table 12-3. *Static Methods of Microsoft.VisualStudio.TestTools.UnitTesting.CollectionAssert*

Method	Description
AllItemsAreInstancesOfType	Tests whether all items in a collection are instances of a specific type
AllItemsAreNotNull	Tests whether all items in a collection are not null
AllItemsAreUnique	Tests whether all items in a collection are different
AreEqual	Tests whether two collections contain the same items (object values are tested, not references) in the same order
AreEquivalent	Similar to AreEqual, but the items can be in any order as long as two collections contain the same items
AreNotEqual	Tests whether two collections contain a different number of items, a different set of items, or the same items in different orders
AreNotEquivalent	Tests whether two collections contain a different number of items or a different set of items
Contains	Tests whether a collection contains a specified item
DoesNotContain	Tests whether a collection does not contain a specified item
IsNotSubsetOf	Tests whether one collection does not contain a subset of items from another collection
IsSubsetOf	Tests whether one collection contains a subset of items from another collection

Besides TestClass and TestMethod, there are many useful attributes for controlling how tests behave. Table 12-4 lists attributes that are useful for initialization and cleanup of resources. All attributes shown in Table 12-4 apply to methods.

Table 12-4. *Testing Framework Attributes Related to Resource Initialization and Cleanup*

Attribute	Description
AssemblyCleanup	Marks the method that executes after all tests within the assembly have completed executing; can only be used on one method within an assembly
AssemblyInitialize	Marks the method that executes before any tests within the assembly have executed; can only be used on one method within an assembly
ClassCleanup	Marks the method that contains the code to execute after all tests within a class containing tests have completed executing; can only apply to a single method within a class
ClassInitialize	Marks the method that contains the code to execute before any tests within a class execute; can only apply to a single method within a class
TestCleanup	Marks the method that contains the code to execute after each test completes executing; can only apply to a single method within a class
TestInitialize	Marks the method that contains the code to execute before each test executes; can only apply to a single method within a class

Note that both TestInitialize and TestCleanup execute once per test, ClassInitialize and ClassCleanup execute once per testing class, and AssemblyInitialize and AssemblyCleanup execute once per testing assembly. These attributes provide for a variety of resource management in a test class.

There are several other useful attributes you might encounter a need for when writing your unit tests. These are shown in Table 12-5.

Table 12-5. *Testing Framework Attributes*

Attribute	Description
Description	Used to provide a description for a test.
ExpectedException	Normally, exceptions indicate the code under test has failed. When a thrown exception indicates success (such as verifying certain methods aren't implemented yet on purpose), this attribute tells the testing framework that the specific exception is expected and avoids failing the test. You can specify this attribute multiple times.
Ignore	Indicates the test should be skipped.
Owner	Provide information on who is responsible for the test.
Priority	Specifies the integer priority of the test.
Timeout	Specifies a timeout in milliseconds for a test. If an operation takes longer than the timeout value specified, the test fails.

The TestContext class is also available for unit test classes; however, the only supported operation for Silverlight testing is the WriteLine method. Before you can use this class, however, you must provide the property in your test class. When the testing framework discovers that your test class provides the following public property, it automatically sets the test context for your class to use:

```
private TestContext testContext;
public TestContext TestContext
{
    get
    {
        return testContext;
    }
    set
    {
        testContext = value;
    }
}
```

There are also just a couple properties in the TestContext class usable in Silverlight testing. These are shown in Table 12-6.

Table 12-6. *Properties of TestContext*

Name	Type	Description
CurrentTestOutcome	UnitTestOutcome	Represents the outcome of the test; possible values are Aborted, Error, Failed, Inconclusive, InProgress, Passed, Timeout, and Unknown
TestName	string	The name of the method containing the test

If you want to save your test results, you can use the properties of TestContext along with a method marked with TestCleanup that saves results to isolated storage or communicates them to a custom web service.

Since the testing application has access to your main application, you can interact with controls on different pages of the application, including calling event handler methods directly to simulate an event firing. While this does work, there are two major drawbacks. The first is that it requires intimate knowledge of the application's code. The second is that it isn't a very flexible approach as an application changes. It's better to make decisions based on the user interface than on the underlying code. It would be nice if it were possible to test an application's user interface from an outsider's perspective, and automate this if possible. Fortunately, Silverlight provides for this automation.

Automated User Interface Testing

Testing must be automated. Software is too complex to reliably test well manually on a consistent basis. Test automation carries over to user interfaces. Manually testing user interfaces is boring, tedious, and highly unreliable since test cases may be skipped or order of operations for tests is violated. Optimally, we want user interface testing to happen automatically, instead of a tester having to manually click every button and explore every screen. Another reason for automated user interface testing is the ability to easily capture test results. Fortunately, Silverlight does indeed provide automation capabilities in the form of a framework for programmatically controlling user interfaces. The main supporting infrastructure for user interface automation is a set of automation peer classes that closely mirror user interface classes in Silverlight.

The UI Automation Library that works for other types of Windows applications can also be used to work with Silverlight applications. Before you can use the automation classes to interact with user interface elements, you must obtain an AutomationElement that serves as a parent element. You can then search for controls that are descendents of the parent. You could use the desktop as the parent, but this would make it slow when searching for controls. Instead, you want to get as close to your Silverlight application as possible. You can use the following code to search the currently running processes for a specific window title:

```
Process process = null;
foreach (Process p in Process.GetProcessesByName("iexplore"))
{
    if (p.MainWindowTitle.Contains("Silverlight (Chapter 12)"))
    {
        process = p;
        break;
    }
}
```

```
if (process != null)
{
    AutomationElement browserInstance  =
        System.Windows.Automation.AutomationElement.FromHandle(
                                        process.MainWindowHandle);
}
```

Once you have an `AutomationElement` that represents a parent to your Silverlight application, you can then search for certain controls of interest. When searching the tree of user interface elements beneath a given `AutomationElement`, you need to define the scope of the search and a condition used to specify what specific elements you want to find. The `AutomationElement` class provides two methods, `FindFirst` and `FindAll`, for finding one or more elements that match the given criteria. The first parameter to these methods is the scope. Table 12-7 shows the different scope values you can use.

Table 12-7. *Enumeration Values from System.Windows.Automation.TreeScope*

Enumeration Value	Description
Element	Search only within the element
Children	Search within the element and its children
Descendents	Search within the element and all its descendents (its children, its children's children, etc.)
Subtree	Search within the root of the search and all descendents

The second parameter to these methods is the condition. A *condition* is essentially a search criterion. The `Condition` class itself provides two shortcuts for making searching easy: `Condition.TrueCondition` and `Condition.FalseCondition`. By combining the first with a search scope, you can obtain all elements within the scope. The latter will return no elements. By combining one of these with one of the `Condition` class's four inheritors, you can create sophisticated search criteria. The `AndCondition`, `OrCondition`, and `NotCondition` classes can be continually nested to support as complicated a search condition as you need. The other inheritor, `PropertyCondition`, is used to find elements with certain properties set to certain values. You can use `PropertyCondition` to search for a value of any of the properties from `AutomationElement`, such as `ClassNameProperty`, `NameProperty`, `AcceleratorKeyProperty`, and many others.

Revisiting the preceding `browserInstance`, which now holds a reference to the Internet Explorer instance that hosts this chapter's Silverlight application, you can search for a specific XAML page within the application like this:

```
AutomationElement loginScreen =
        browserInstance.FindFirst(TreeScope.Descendants,
            new PropertyCondition(AutomationElement.NameProperty,
                                        "Login Screen"));
```

The `AutomationProperties` class provides several useful attached properties you can use to provide cues for the automation system while leaving the rest of your object's properties intact. These attached properties are shown in Table 12-8. When developing an application, you can use the `AutomationId` property to uniquely identify elements throughout your application specifically for use by automation clients.

Table 12-8. *Attached Properties in AutomationProperties*

Name	Type	Description
AcceleratorKey	string	The accelerator key for the element
AccessKey	string	The access key for the element
AutomationId	string	A unique identifier for element; useful as a cue for automation clients in searches
HelpText	string	Help text for the element; generally the associated tool tip text
IsColumnHeader	bool	true if the element is a column header (such as in a data grid)
IsRequiredForForm	bool	true if the element must be filled out for a given form
IsRowHeader	bool	true if the element is a row header (such as in a data grid)
ItemStatus	string	Indicates the status of the item; generally application-specific
ItemType	string	Describes the type of the element
LabeledBy	UIElement	Specifies which UIElement acts as a label for this element
Name	string	The element's name

Once you have a reference to the element of the Silverlight application, you can use other aspects of the UI Automation Library to simulate keyboard and mouse input for the application under test.

Debugging

The debugging process should not begin when a bug is discovered. Instead, it should start during application design. You should include logging functionality in your application, such as error logs and audit logs. An error log is useful for tracking exceptions thrown by an application. Exceptions also come with stack traces that help in identifying the code path that lead to the exception. Audit logs can be used to reconstruct what users were doing within the application leading up to an error. These are important elements that must go into application design and development, but there are also other approaches you can use to make code easier to debug, such as including extra logging or other features in special debug mode builds of an application. Any time you go about debugging, however, you must take a structured approach to hunting bugs down.

The Debugging Process

Debugging may or may not be your favorite activity when developing software, but the same general frame of mind you use for developing code can be applied to debugging. Debugging is just another form of problem solving. Having a plan of attack to discover the source of a bug is invaluable. Here are the steps you should follow when you know of a bug and need to go about fixing it:

1. Get to know the system. If you're unfamiliar with the system you're fixing, you should get enough familiarity to do as good a job as possible at fixing the bug without introducing new bugs. Knowing how the system works, what components it uses, and what technologies are involved (e.g., IIS, ASP.NET, Windows Workflow Foundation) can also possibly give you more clues to narrowing down the bug.

2. Reproduce the bug. You must know what you're fixing in order to fix it. Sometimes you're lucky enough to have a consistent reproduction; sometimes you aren't. The goal here is to have the smallest piece of code or the shortest sequence of actions that reveals the bug.

3. Make a guess. Sometimes by making a guess you can zero-in on the bug right away. This isn't always possible, but when it works, you appear to have special powers. Raymond Chen calls this "psychic debugging." It's really just a matter of having enough experience to know the source of a bug based on symptoms. If you can't solve the bug immediately, sometimes a guess will at least get you closer to the source of it in the code.

4. Gather evidence. Solving a bug isn't the most difficult activity as long as you have a solid plan. Part of this plan is to analyze the evidence at your disposal—usually bug reports, error/audit logs, analysis tools such as file/registry activity monitors, and so on.

5. Conduct heavy debugging. If you haven't discovered the source of the bug yet, then now is likely the time to step through code in a debugger. This can be a slow process, depending on how close you can get to the bug, but it will typically give you a clear view of the system at a line-by-line level.

6. Identify the solution. By now you've found the source of the bug. Sometimes a bug fix is straightforward; other times you must be careful not to affect other parts of the system. A strong set of unit tests is invaluable at this point. If you fix the bug but introduce a new bug, or reintroduce an old bug (a regression), the unit tests can identify this and you can revisit your solution.

7. Apply the fix. You've identified the solution, implemented it, and verified it hasn't broken any existing tests. After applying the fix, you may have to update unit tests or add new unit tests. This is the time to do that.

Let's take a closer look at some tools and techniques that can save you time when you are debugging Silverlight applications.

Conditional Compilation

Much like .NET assemblies, Silverlight assemblies can be compiled in a debug mode configuration or a release mode configuration. The main differences between debug and release mode are which conditional symbols are defined and whether symbols are generated along with the assembly. For debug mode, the preprocessor symbol DEBUG is automatically defined, and for release mode, TRACE is defined.

Sometimes implementing code only for purposes of debugging can be extremely useful. For example, an application might write a significant amount of information to a log file for debugging only. This code can't run in production applications due to performance reasons, and optimally we want to get rid of this code completely. This can be achieved with conditional compilation. The best approach to conditional compilation is to use #if...#endif to isolate blocks of code that must only appear in certain configurations. Generally, these are used to only put debug code in debug builds—for example, writing to a debug trace log.

```
private void login()
{
#if DEBUG
    traceLog.WriteLine("entered login method");
#endif
    authService.Login(usernameTB.Text, passwordTB.Text, null, null);
#if DEBUG
    traceLog.WriteLine("leaving login method");
#endif
}
```

The DEBUG symbol is automatically defined for debug mode configurations and RELEASE is automatically defined for release mode configurations. There is one other approach to conditional compilation that is used to limit the type of code that can call a particular method. This is accomplished using the Conditional attribute on a method, as shown here:

```
[Conditional("DEBUG")]
public void debugWriteLine(string message)
{
    debugLog.WriteLine(message);
}
```

A method like this can be extremely useful when providing a public API to a class library that has its own debug log. Any time client code defines the symbol applied to the method via the Conditional attribute, the code is output with the compiled IL. If the client code does not define this symbol, the code is not included. This means a client can use the following code with the knowledge the debug writes will only happen when their code is in a debug mode configuration.

```
public void doSomething()
{
    library.debugWriteLine("calling doLongOperation");
    library.doLongOperation();
    library.debugWriteLine("doLongOperation finished");
}
```

When you use the Conditional attribute, the method it applies to is always compiled and included in the finished assembly. This is an important difference between the Conditional attribute and preprocessor symbol testing via the #if command. If you're using Conditional to control code within the same assembly (such as making decisions based on symbols other than DEBUG/RELEASE), you can prevent the body of the method from being included in the compilation by combining Conditional with #if:

```
[Conditional("DEBUG")]
public void debugWriteLine(string message)
{
```

```
#if DEBUG
    debugLog.WriteLine(message);
#endif
}
```

Debugging with Visual Studio

The Visual Studio debugger is an invaluable tool for tracing through code. There's little differ-ence between debugging .NET code on Windows and debugging a Silverlight application. The important differences are that the Silverlight plug-in is hosted within a browser (which acts as the host process you debug) and the code on the Silverlight platform runs on the CoreCLR, a runtime completely separate from any other instance of the CLR you have on your system.

Controlling the Debugger

The System.Diagnostics namespace provides a number of attributes that provide cues (such as preventing stepping into certain methods) and more information to the debugger. These attributes are shown in Table 12-9.

Table 12-9. *Attributes in System.Diagnostics That Interact with the Debugger*

Attribute	Description
Debuggable	Used to provide configuration-related cues to the JIT compiler and debugger, such as disabling optimizations.
DebuggerBrowsable	Controls display of a member within the debugger. Valid values are Collapsed, Never (member is never shown), and RootHidden (useful for collections; shows individual items without showing the root).
DebuggerDisplay	Specifies what should be shown in the value column in the debugger for the member this decorates.
DebuggerHidden	Used to hide the member from the debugger.
DebuggerNonUserCode	Indicates that a type/member is not part of the user code and should be hidden from the debugger, not stepped into. This is effectively a combination of DebuggerHidden and DebuggerStepThrough.
DebuggerStepThrough	When applied to a method, causes the debugger to step through the method instead of stepping into it.

If you have long (or long-running) methods that you don't want to consciously step over in the debugger, using the DebuggerStepThrough attribute can save significant time. It is used to avoid stepping through code since it prevents the method from being stepped into. Here's an example usage to mark a validation function that is called often. Make sure you use it in a situation like this when you're sure the method isn't the source of any bugs.

```
[DebuggerStepThrough]
private bool validateIpAddress(string ipAddress)
{
    // parse ipAddress and validate that it's a correct IPv4 address
}
```

The System.Diagnostics.Debug class provides two useful methods: WriteLine, for sending information to the debugger output, and Assert, for testing assumptions. The WriteLine method uses the Windows OutputDebugString under the covers, so unfortunately this only works when the debugger is on Windows. There are no debug listeners/trace listeners in Silverlight as there are in .NET on Windows, so the Debug.WriteLine method is all there really is to writing debug output. Since OutputDebugString is used at its core, you can attach a debugger and see the output in the Output window (in Visual Studio) or through another debug viewer.

The other method, Assert, is used to test certain assumptions in your code. The Assert method (and its overloads) takes a Boolean parameter as a condition to test. When the condition is false, you see either a dialog box when running in release mode or debugger output when in debug mode.

Configuring Startup for Debugging

When you're developing a Silverlight application, you can either use the development web server or another web server such as IIS or Apache. By including a web site or a web application in your solution when you create a Silverlight project, you can point IIS to this and debug a Silverlight application similar to how it will be deployed on a real server. This can help ensure your configuration is correct on the server side, which will mainly consist of ensuring the web server can serve XAP files and possibly PDB files for debugging purposes. Figure 12-4 shows configuring the web project to start up using an external server. You can separate the base URL from specific pages to make it easier to change from one startup page to the next (such as with the switching of the startup to the second Silverlight application in this chapter).

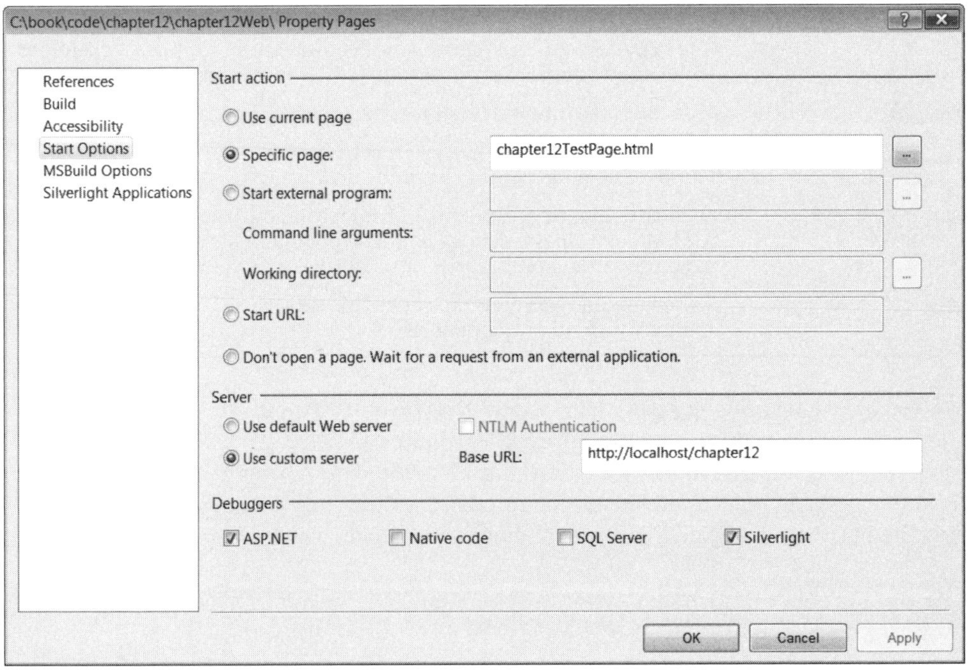

Figure 12-4. *Web site startup properties*

If you create a Silverlight application with no accompanying web site/web application, you can still debug a Silverlight application from Visual Studio. You can accomplish this by going to the property pages for the Silverlight application itself and ensuring "Dynamically generate a test page" is set (or set to a specific page). This page, and the Silverlight application, will then be hosted in the development web server, and you can debug your application. You can see this property page in Figure 12-5.

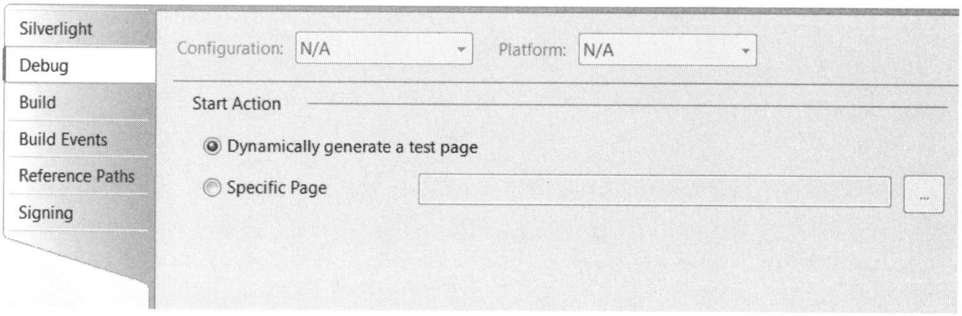

Figure 12-5. *Silverlight application startup properties*

Once you have your startup properly configured, you can set breakpoints and debug your Silverlight application like any other. If you already have a browser running your Silverlight application outside of Visual Studio, you can attach the debugger to the host process (the browser). You can accomplish this by going to the Debug menu in Visual Studio and choosing "Attach to process." If you're debugging ASP.NET, you attach the debugger to the ASP.NET worker process. Similarly, you attach the Visual Studio debugger to the process that hosts the Silverlight plug-in: the browser. On the Attach to Process dialog (shown in Figure 12-6), you can click Select to limit the type of code the debugger focuses on.

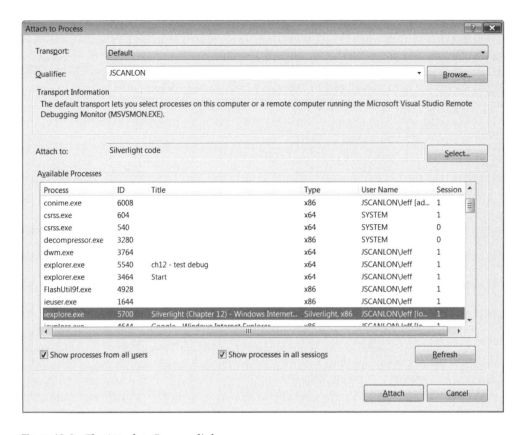

Figure 12-6. *The Attach to Process dialog*

Figure 12-7 shows the Select Code Type dialog. You can leave this on the default to let the debugger automatically determine the code type, or manually override and focus on Silverlight, as shown in Figure 12-7.

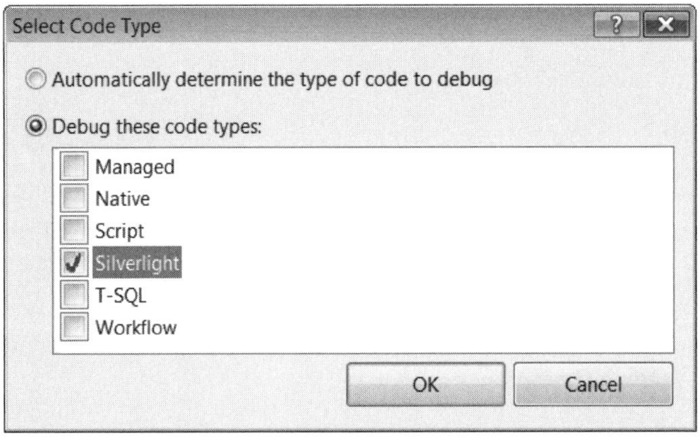

Figure 12-7. *Narrowing the type of code to debug via the Select Code Type dialog*

The easiest way to find the process you want to debug is by the window title. An instance of `iexplore.exe` running this chapter's Silverlight application is highlighted in Figure 12-6. Once you've successfully attached to the correct process, using the debugger is no different from starting the browser within the IDE under the debugger. You can set breakpoints, break into the application, and so on.

Handling Unhandled Exceptions

Exceptions happen. It's your mission as a software developer to handle exceptions, such as using isolated storage and reading from a file that doesn't exist. You must handle these in order to build an application that works well and is resistant to expected problems. Sometimes conditions outside your control or conditions you haven't considered will cause an exception, and the `Application` class provides an unhandled exception handler just for this eventuality. By default (i.e., the default Silverlight application template in Visual Studio), a Silverlight application passes unhandled exceptions on to the browser via the following unhandled exception handler:

```
private void Application_UnhandledException(object sender,
                                    ApplicationUnhandledExceptionEventArgs e)
{
    // If the app is running outside of the debugger then report the exception using
    // the browser's exception mechanism. On IE this will display a yellow alert
    // icon in the status bar and Firefox will display a script error.
    if (!System.Diagnostics.Debugger.IsAttached)
    {
        // NOTE: This will allow the application to continue running after
        //         an exception has been thrown but not handled.
        //         For production applications this error handling should be
        //         replaced with something that will report the error to the
        //         website and stop the application.
        e.Handled = true;
        try
        {
            string errorMsg = e.ExceptionObject.Message +
                                    e.ExceptionObject.StackTrace;
            errorMsg = errorMsg.Replace('"', '\'').Replace("\r\n", @"\n");
            System.Windows.Browser.HtmlPage.Window.Eval
              ("throw new Error(\"Unhandled Error in Silverlight 2 Application " +
                  errorMsg + "\");");
        }
        catch (Exception)
        {
        }
    }
}
```

This is a basic unhandled exception handler. The information provided in the browser's error dialog isn't always especially useful, as you can see in Figure 12-8. The dialog isn't too friendly to users, and you won't know your Silverlight application has problems unless users manually report it.

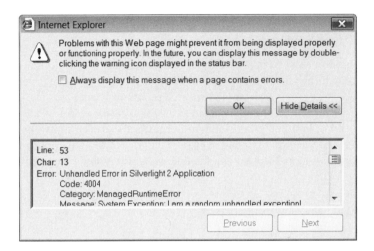

Figure 12-8. *The alert dialog in Internet Explorer displaying the Silverlight exception*

This chapter's code includes a XAML page named ErrorFrame that provides improved handling and display of exceptions. When an exception is thrown and goes unhandled, it gets sent to the unhandled exception handler and then passed to the ErrorFrame. The ErrorFrame then displays a red bar at the top, similar to the information bar in Internet Explorer. This red bar displays the simple feedback to users, "The application has caused an error. Click for details." Clicking this red bar causes a Popup control to appear that contains the exception's message and stack trace, and two buttons: one to report the exception and the other to close the pop-up. You might want to automatically send exception feedback to the server instead of waiting for the user to do so manually, but there are cases where you'll want the user to have a say. Figure 12-9 shows what this exception pop-up looks like.

Figure 12-9. *The exception dialog as implemented within Silverlight*

The ErrorFrame page is made up of three main elements: the red error bar, the pop-up, and an empty canvas that contains your main user interface. The red error bar is a Border control that contains several elements, including a HyperLink button to give it clickability.

```
<Border Background="#FFAA0000" Grid.Row="0"
                x:Name="errorBar" Visibility="Collapsed">
    <StackPanel Orientation="Horizontal">
        <Ellipse Fill="White" Margin="5 0 0 0" Width="10" Height="10"/>
        <HyperlinkButton x:Name="errorDetailsButton"
                                    Click="errorDetailsButton_Click">
            <HyperlinkButton.Content>
                <TextBlock Margin="5" Foreground="White" FontSize="12"
                    Text="The application has caused an error. Click for details."
                    x:Name="errorMesageTB"/>
            </HyperlinkButton.Content>
        </HyperlinkButton>
    </StackPanel>
</Border>
```

The important part of the exception pop-up is the TextBox inside the ScrollViewer:

```
<Popup x:Name="errorPopup" HorizontalOffset="10" VerticalOffset="50">
    <Border>
        ...
        <ScrollViewer Background="LightGray" Grid.Row="0"
                    HorizontalScrollBarVisibility="Auto">
            <TextBox x:Name="exceptionTB" AcceptsReturn="True"/>
        </ScrollViewer>
        ...
    </Border>
</Popup>
```

The final element is simply an empty canvas. This is where your application's user interface will appear.

```
<Canvas x:Name="FrameLayoutRoot" Grid.Row="1">
</Canvas>
```

The most important aspect to the ErrorFrame is a method used to set the exception:

```
public void setException(Exception ex)
{
    exceptionTB.Text = "An unhandled exception has occurred.\n\nMessage: " +
                        ex.Message + "\n\nStack trace:\n" + ex.StackTrace;
    errorBar.Visibility = Visibility.Visible;
}
```

Inside the App.xaml.cs file, the ErrorFrame becomes the root container, instead of the XAML_Viewer, which has been the root throughout this book. The ErrorFrame instance is stored so the unhandled exception handler can communicate the exception to the ErrorFrame.

```
private ErrorFrame errorFrame;
private void Application_Startup(object sender, StartupEventArgs e)
{
    XAML_Viewer viewer = new XAML_Viewer();
    viewer.addXamlPage("Generate Exception", new CreateException());
    errorFrame = new ErrorFrame();
    errorFrame.setLayoutRoot(viewer);
    this.RootVisual = errorFrame;
}
```

The rest is as simple as invoking the `setException` method of the `ErrorFrame` class in the unhandled exception handler.

```
errorFrame.setException(e.ExceptionObject);
```

Now any time your application encounters an exception it can't recover from (otherwise you'd be handling the exception), the user will get immediate feedback and can optionally choose to report the error (if you don't do this automatically or remove this button).

Summary

Testing and debugging are vital activities to develop software effectively. When combined, testing and debugging help form proactive and reactive strategies to reduce the number of defects in software. You saw to how leverage the unit testing libraries and the test harness that you can obtain from Microsoft in order to construct and execute unit tests for Silverlight applications. You also briefly saw how user interface automation is used to interact with Silverlight, and the attached properties you can use to instrument your Silverlight application for user interface automation clients. When it comes to debugging, the class library that comes with Silverlight provides some useful features, such as attributes to control the debugger, and a `Debug` class useful for sending output to the debugger and testing assumptions within debug mode builds of your application. Finally, you saw an approach to catching unhandled exceptions and displaying them to a user within the Silverlight application itself, providing a prime place to also report unhandled exceptions back to your server.

CHAPTER 13

Packaging and Deploying Silverlight Applications

Silverlight is a client-side technology. This means any server can host a Silverlight application since there is no dependence on IIS or ASP.NET. For many applications, the only configuration that must be done on the server for the Silverlight application itself is configuring the MIME type. While server configuration is straightforward, there remain many aspects to creating and deploying Silverlight applications. This chapter will explore in detail the parts of Silverlight applications and will discuss Silverlight class assemblies, as well as issues such as versioning and caching.

Client Considerations

Since the Silverlight plug-in is a self-contained managed environment based on .NET, the plug-in itself must be developed (by Microsoft or a third party, such as the people behind Moonlight, a Silverlight implementation for Linux) for each environment that will host it. The two major aspects of supported platforms are the host operating system and the host browser. The minimum memory requirement for all operating systems is 128 MB, though naturally, the more memory you have, the better Silverlight can perform. The supported operating systems are as follows:

- Windows XP with SP2 or later

- Windows Server 2003

- Windows Vista

- Mac OS X 10.4.8 or higher

The supported browsers on Windows operating systems are as follows:

- Internet Explorer 6 or later

- Mozilla Firefox 1.5.0.8 or later

- Mozilla Firefox 2.0 or later

The supported browsers on OS X are as follows:

- Firefox 1.5.0.8 or later

- Firefox 2.0 or later

- Safari 2.0.4 or later

Once Silverlight is installed, it is possible to temporarily disable the add-on (perhaps for diagnostic purposes). In Microsoft Internet Explorer 7, disabling add-ons is accomplished by going to Tools ➤ Manage Add-Ons ➤ Enable or Disable Add-Ons. You can then disable the add-on by highlighting Microsoft Silverlight and changing the selected radio button, as shown in Figure 13-1.

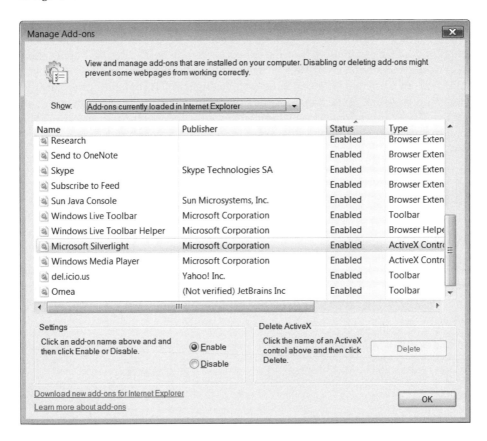

Figure 13-1. *The Manage Add-ons dialog in Microsoft Internet Explorer 7*

Every computer that has the Silverlight plug-in also has a configuration utility (named `Silverlight.Configuration.exe` and located in the Silverlight installation directory) to change options related to the Silverlight plug-in, such as automatic updating. Figure 13-2 shows the configuration utility when it first starts. This is a great place to tell your users to look for the full version number of their Silverlight plug-in if you ever need this information.

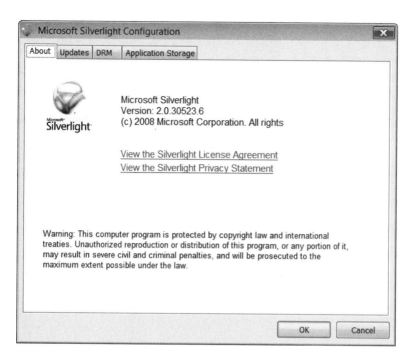

Figure 13-2. *The About tab in the Silverlight configuration utility*

The second tab, Updates (shown in Figure 13-3), provides options to let the user specify how updates to the Silverlight plug-in are handled.

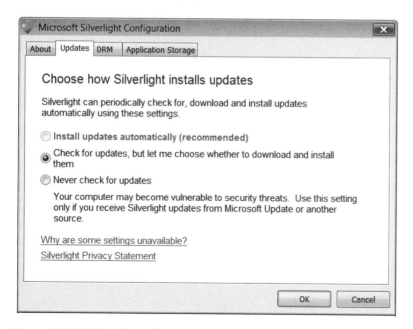

Figure 13-3. *The Updates tab in the Silverlight configuration utility*

The first option, "Install updates automatically," will be disabled on Windows Vista systems that have User Account Control (UAC) enabled. This is because explicit permission from the user is required before an installation can occur, thus making automatic installation of a Silverlight update impossible. If Silverlight is not running on Vista (or UAC is disabled), and this option is still unavailable (or "Check for Updates" is unavailable), it's likely that Windows components needed to enable this functionality are not present or are outdated. Visiting Windows Update should fix this problem.

Then next tab, shown in Figure 13-4, relates to DRM.

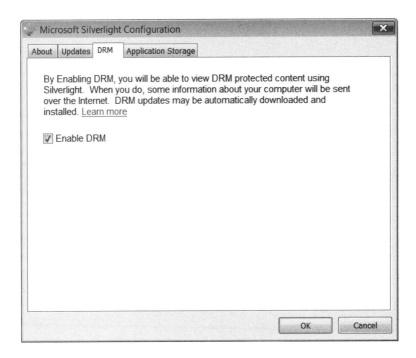

Figure 13-4. *The DRM tab in the Silverlight configuration utility*

Silverlight has the capability of playing media that is protected with DRM, and this provides the user with a mechanism to explicitly forbid the playing of DRM content. The final tab, shown in Figure 13-5, is Application Storage.

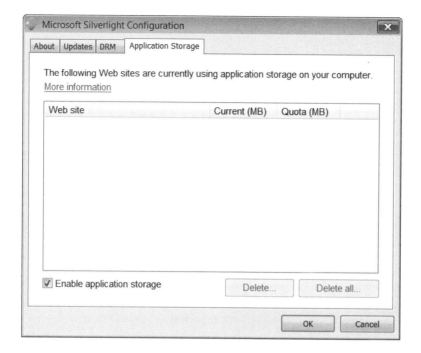

Figure 13-5. *The Application Storage tab in the Silverlight configuration utility*

This tab shows the list of Silverlight applications that utilize isolated storage, as discussed in Chapter 5. This tab provides a way for a user to see how much space is used and by which applications. The user can also selectively delete (by application) or completely delete the contents of isolated storage. Something important to note, however, is the check box at the bottom. A user can completely turn off isolated storage. If you develop a Silverlight application that has issues using isolated storage that you can't track down, this configuration option is a possible cause.

Silverlight Deployment Packages

Silverlight applications are packaged into a file with the .xap extension. This extension stands for XAML Application Package. This file is simply a ZIP archive that stores the main application DLL, auxiliary library DLLs, and resource files. Figure 13-6 shows the components of a XAP file.

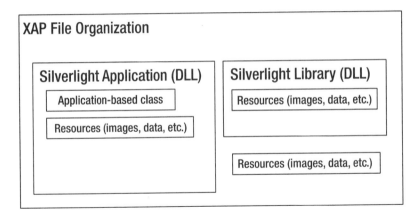

Figure 13-6. *Organization of XAP files*

The defining difference between an application DLL and a library DLL is that the application DLL includes a class that serves as the entry point for the application. If you suspect that this class is called `Application`, you would be correct. You've seen this as part of every application we've developed so far, but I haven't mentioned much about it since the beginning of the book. Your Silverlight application should include both a XAML file and a code-behind file that provide your application with a `System.Windows.Application`-derived class that will conduct the creation of the user interface to show the user. The default application implementation generated by Visual Studio and Expression Blend features the following XAML file:

```
<Application xmlns="http://schemas.microsoft.com/winfx/2006/xaml/presentation"
             xmlns:x="http://schemas.microsoft.com/winfx/2006/xaml"
             x:Class="chapter13.App"
             >
    <Application.Resources>

    </Application.Resources>
</Application>
```

As you can see, this XAML is bare. This is a great place to put application-level resources, such as styles and control templates that you want to use throughout the application. Also generated is the code-behind file:

```
public partial class App : Application
{
    public App()
    {
        this.Startup += this.Application_Startup;
        this.Exit += this.Application_Exit;
        this.UnhandledException += this.Application_UnhandledException;
        InitializeComponent();
    }
    private void Application_Startup(object sender, StartupEventArgs e)
    {
```

```
        this.RootVisual = new Page();
    }
    // ...
}
```

The constructor registers default event handlers for the events defined in the `Application` class. The life cycle of a Silverlight application is shown in Figure 13-7.

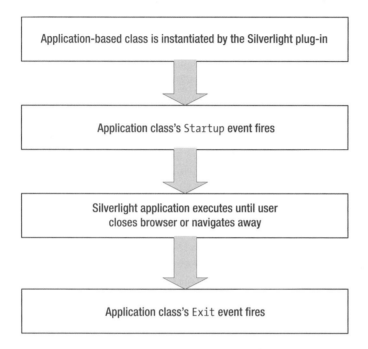

Figure 13-7. *Silverlight application life cycle*

The `Startup` event handler is the place to specify the `UIElement`-based class that provides the main user interface. This is generally a UserControl-based class, such as is generated by default and reflected in setting the `RootVisual` to a new instance of this class (Page). The `Exit` event handler has no implementation, but the method body is there for you to put any code you want executed when the user has exited the Silverlight application (generally by closing the browser or navigating to a different page).

The `Application` class also provides two useful properties. The `Current` property is static and returns the one (and only) instance of the `Application` implementation, making it easy to reference application-level resources from the code-behind. The other property is `Host`, of type `SilverlightHost`; it returns a reference to the environment hosting the Silverlight plug-in.

If you do not include an `Application`-based class, the compiled assembly can be used as a library, either packaged as part of a XAP file containing a Silverlight application or downloaded on demand and loaded via reflection. You can also store other resources, such as data files and media files, outside this XAP file.

Hosting Silverlight on a Web Page

The OBJECT element of HTML is used to place a Silverlight object on a web page. When you create a new application via Visual Studio, you have the option of creating a web site. Part of this web site is an HTML file that features an OBJECT tag to host the Silverlight application. Here's what the generated OBJECT tag looks like:

```
<div id="silverlightControlHost">
    <object data="data:application/x-silverlight,"
            type="application/x-silverlight-2"
            width="100%" height="100%">
        <param name="source" value="ClientBin/chapter13.xap"/>
        <param name="onerror" value="onSilverlightError" />
        <param name="background" value="white" />
        <a href="http://go.microsoft.com/fwlink/?LinkID=115261"
            style="text-decoration: none;">
                <img src="http://go.microsoft.com/fwlink/?LinkId=108181"
                    alt="Get Microsoft Silverlight"
                    style="border-style: none"/>
        </a>
    </object>
    <iframe style='visibility:hidden;height:0;width:0;border:0px'>
    </iframe>
</div>
```

The properties of the OBJECT tag are shown in Table 13-1.

Table 13-1. *Properties of the HTML OBJECT Tag for Hosting Silverlight*

Property	Description
data	Required. Set to the literal data:; followed by the MIME type corresponding to Silverlight.
id	Provides an identifier for this tag within the DOM.
height	Height of the content area devoted to the Silverlight application; can be specified as a number of pixels or a percentage.
type	Required. Set to the MIME type that correlates with the specific version of the Silverlight plug-in the application is built to run on. This controls the specific Silverlight plug-in that loads. See the "Silverlight Versioning" section of the chapter for more information.
width	Width of the content area devoted to the Silverlight application; can be specified as a number of pixels or a percentage.

This particular example of the OBJECT tag includes three parameters. There are actually many parameters that can be specified to control and communicate with the Silverlight plug-in.

background: Defaults to white. Specifies the color used by the Silverlight plug-in to paint its background. Useful when the content of the Silverlight application does not fill up the entire space specified in the OBJECT tag. This parameter uses the same syntax for colors as in XAML.

enableFramerateCounter: Should not be used with production applications! If this is set to true, the current frame rate is displayed in the host browser's status bar. This is only supported on Internet Explorer on Windows.

enableHtmlAccess: Defaults to true. Boolean value that controls whether the Silverlight application can use the HTML DOM bridge classes.

enableRedrawRegions: Should not be used with production applications! If this is set to true, the regions that are being redrawn are specially highlighted.

initParams: Used to communicate initialization parameters to Silverlight that can be accessed from an application. Properties are comma-separated, and the property value is separated by an equal sign from the property's name.

maxFrameRate: Defaults to 60. Integer value specifying an upper limit for the frame rate (the actual frame rate might be lower than what is requested).

onError: Mandatory. Specifies a JavaScript event handler to handle exceptions from the hosted Silverlight application.

onLoad: Specifies a JavaScript event handler invoked when the root XAML file has completed loading.

onResize: Specifies a JavaScript event handler that is invoked when the Silverlight plug-in's ActionWidth or ActualHeight properties are changed.

onSourceDownloadComplete: Invoked when the application specified in the Source parameter has finished downloading.

onSourceDownloadProgressChanged: Invoked periodically while the Silverlight application is downloading in order to report download progress.

Source: Mandatory. Specifies the URI to the XAP file containing the Silverlight application.

splashScreenSource: Specifies the URI to a XAML file to show a splash screen while the Silverlight application is downloading.

windowless: Defaults to false. Only applies to Silverlight running on Windows. Set to true to run Silverlight as a windowless plug-in.

The other important aspects to this specific OBJECT tag are the links that provide direction to a user who does not have the Silverlight plug-in installed. The URLs corresponding to installer packages for each version of Silverlight are shown in Table 13-2.

Table 13-2. *Installer URLs for Silverlight Versions*

Silverlight Version	Installer URL
1.0	http://go2.microsoft.com/fwlink/?LinkId=110408
2.0 Beta 1	http://go2.microsoft.com/fwlink/?LinkId=108182
2.0 Beta 2	http://go2.microsoft.com/fwlink/?LinkID=115261

> **Note** The `iframe` tag is specified in order to prevent the Safari browser from caching the page. If the page is cached, the Silverlight plug-in will fail to reload correctly.

Several of these properties are exposed via the `App.Current.Host.Settings` object (of type `System.Windows.Interop.Settings`). These settings are shown in Table 13-3.

Table 13-3. *Properties of the System.Windows.Interop.Settings Class*

Property	Type	Description
EnableFrameRateCounter	bool	Gets or sets whether the frame rate counter is displayed (Microsoft Internet Explorer only)
EnableHTMLAccess	bool	Gets a value specifying whether HTML DOM access is permitted
EnableRedrawRegions	bool	Gets or sets a value specifying where redraw regions are shown
MaxFrameRate	int	Gets or sets the maximum frame rate per second
Windowless	bool	Gets a value specifying whether the Silverlight plug-in is windowless (only applies to Silverlight running on Windows)

Silverlight Versioning

The `OBJECT` tag provides a way to specify a MIME type that corresponds to the version of the Silverlight plug-in the application targets. Table 13-4 describes the current set of MIME types and the Silverlight versions they correspond to.

Table 13-4. *Silverlight Versions and Their MIME Types*

Silverlight Version	Version Number	MIME Type
1.0	1.0	application/x-silverlight
2.0 Beta 1	2.0.30226	application/x-silverlight-2-b1
2.0 Beta 2	2.0.30523	application/x-silverlight-2-b2
2.0	2.0.30923	application/x-silverlight-2

Table 13-4 also shows the specific version numbers for each release of Silverlight. There is a JavaScript function called `isInstalled` that is located in the `Silverlight.js` file. While you can include the build number and revision number as part of the version string when calling this function, it is suggested you only use the major and minor parts of the version number. This function returns `true` or `false`.

```
var isInstalled = Silverlight.isInstalled(version);
```

ASP.NET provides a server control that handles the generation of the `OBJECT` tag automatically. Along with the HTML page generated with Visual Studio, an ASPX page is generated that uses this server control.

```
<asp:Silverlight ID="Xaml1" runat="server"
                 Source="~/ClientBin/chapter13.xap"
                 MinimumVersion="2.0.30523" Width="100%" Height="100%" />
```

This server control exposes properties that correspond to each of the parameters listed earlier, so there's no need to relist them. Utilize IntelliSense or MSDN if you need more information on the properties this server control supports.

Custom Initialization Parameters

The initParams parameter is used to pass a set of delimited properties with their values to Silverlight, and thus to the Silverlight application. Each property takes the form of *Name=Value*, and the properties are separated by commas. These initialization parameters can be accessed from JScript or from the Silverlight application in the Application class's startup handler. From JScript, you can access the parameters from the onLoaded event handler, or directly via the DOM. Using onLoaded, you just need to get a reference to the plug-in object and then access the initParams string property.

```
function onLoaded(sender, args)
{
   var params = sender.getHost().initParams;

   var paramList = params.split(",");
   for(var i=0; i<paramList.length; i++)
   {
      var propertyName = paramList[i].split("=")[0];
      var propertyValue = paramList[i].split("=")[1];

      // do something with property
   }
}
```

These initialization parameters are accessible via the StartupEventArgs parameter to the Startup event handler in your implementation of the Application class. You can cache these in your App class by handling the Startup event.

```
internal IDictionary<string, string> InitParams;
private void Application_Startup(object sender, StartupEventArgs e)
{
   this.InitParams = e.InitParams;
}
```

Once the parameters are cached in your Application-based class, they can be accessed via the App instance (though you need to cast it to your specific class type in order to access the InitParams member).

```
IDictionary<string,string> initParams = ((App)App.Current).InitParams;
foreach (string key in initParams.Keys)
{
   TextBlock tb = new TextBlock();
```

```
        tb.Text = key + " = " + initParams[key];
        LayoutRoot.Children.Add(tb);
}
```

Resources

There are two main types of resources you can reference from a Silverlight application: *supporting files* (such as images and XML data files) and *class libraries*. Supporting files can be embedded in the application assembly as a resource, packaged as part of the XAP, or downloaded on demand. Class libraries can also be packaged as part of the XAP or downloaded on demand and loaded using reflection.

Supporting Files

Supporting files can be anything the application needs to work, such as media files (images/audio/video), data files, custom configuration files, and so on. These files can be embedded directly in the application assembly. Figure 13-8 shows the Properties pane in Visual Studio 2008 for an image file that was just added to the project.

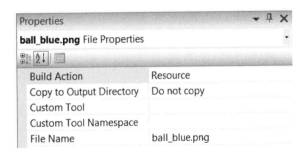

Figure 13-8. *Image resource just added to the Silverlight project*

Any file set with a build action of Resource (set in the file's properties window in Visual Studio) is placed into the application's assembly as a resource. This image file can then be referenced either from the XAML or from the code-behind. In XAML, it's a simple matter of using the image's path and file name.

```
<Image Source="ball_blue.png" Canvas.Left="10" Canvas.Top="10"/>
```

This same image can be set from the code-behind by using a relative URI:

```
Image img = new Image();
img.Source = new BitmapImage(new Uri("ball_blue.png", UriKind.Relative));
```

If you don't want to (or can't) embed resource files in the application assembly, but still want to distribute them with the application, it's possible to put the files into the XAP file. These resource files are known as *content files*. To ensure that they're packaged with the application, you must set their build action to Content in Visual Studio. These files can still be referenced from the XAML; the only change required is to place a forward slash in front of the file name:

```
<Image Source="/ball_red.png" Canvas.Left="10" Canvas.Top="10"/>
```

The forward slash was omitted when referencing the image inside the assembly since the image is part of the application assembly. The forward slash, however, is required to indicate that the relative URI is relative to the root of the XAP file.

One final syntax format is provided to reference resource files. This is useful when you need to access a resource inside a library assembly (not the application assembly).

```
<Image Source="/chapter13library;component/ball_green.png" />
```

The forward slash again corresponds to the root of the XAP file. Next is the name of the assembly, followed by a semicolon and the literal string component, followed by the path to the resource you want to access (in this case an image file).

Libraries

Silverlight class libraries can include both compiled classes and resource files. The library assemblies can be stored within the XAP, or if the application does not need them immediately, can be downloaded on demand. No matter how you deliver the library assemblies to the client, they must be added as references to the Silverlight application within Visual Studio. Two library assemblies are used by the example application for this chapter, named chapter13library and chapter13library2. The first is packaged as part of the XAP and the second isn't. To prevent the second library from being packaged in the XAP, set Copy Local to False in the properties for the assembly, as shown in Figure 13-9.

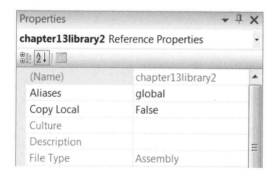

Figure 13-9. *Preventing the library assembly from being packaged in the XAP file*

Using an assembly packaged in the XAP doesn't require anything special. You add a using reference and then use the types from the assembly:

```
using chapter13library;
// ...
private void loadButton_Click(object sender, RoutedEventArgs e)
{
    ImageUtilities iu = new ImageUtilities();
    statusText.Text = "Successfully created instance from class library";
}
```

If you choose not to package the assembly with your application, it must first be downloaded and then loaded into the application domain using the `Load` method of `AssemblyPart`. You can download the assembly using the `WebClient` class.

```
WebClient webClient = new WebClient();
webClient.OpenReadCompleted +=
                 new OpenReadCompletedEventHandler(webClient_OpenReadCompleted);
webClient.OpenReadAsync(new Uri("/chapter13Web/chapter13library2.dll",
                               UriKind.Relative));
```

Once the assembly is finished downloading, you pass the resulting stream to the `Load` method:

```
AssemblyPart part = new AssemblyPart();
Assembly asm = part.Load(e.Result);
Control c = (Control)asm.CreateInstance("chapter13library2.TreeControl");
```

Unfortunately, while you can add a reference to `chapter13library2` and use the types, it does not seem possible to then cast the type created from the dynamically loaded assembly to the types from the same assembly when used in the code. For example, if you add this line below the `CreateInstance` invocation, an exception will be thrown indicating that the assembly was not found:

```
chapter13library2.TreeControl tree = (chapter13library2.TreeControl)c;
```

This will hopefully be fixed in a future release.

Silverlight and the Build Process

An important part of an effective software development process includes a strong build and deployment process. The build process, at a minimum, should leverage scripts to make building software easy and primed for automation (either in the form of scheduled builds or continuous integration). Two of the most popular tools used for building software are NAnt and MSBuild. Both of these tools use XML configuration files that specify a series of tasks, including compiling projects, copying build output to different locations, and packaging applications (such as constructing an install package). Silverlight applications must be compiled (unless they target Silverlight 1.0) and packaged into a XAP for deployment to a web site. MSBuild is the official build tool from Microsoft, and the Silverlight SDK comes with MSBuild-specific tasks related to compiling and packaging Silverlight applications. You must use the version of MSBuild that comes with .NET 3.5 (this version of MSBuild also has the version number 3.5). This section will be most useful to you if you are trying to build Silverlight applications outside the IDE—for example, if you're trying to establish a build process.

One huge advantage to MSBuild is that it can use project files from Visual Studio as build scripts. A Visual Studio CSPROJ file contains a set of properties, many of which are Silverlight-specific. Let's briefly dissect one of these Visual Studio project files to see the Silverlight specific additions:

```
<OutputType>Library</OutputType>
<AppDesignerFolder>Properties</AppDesignerFolder>
<RootNamespace>chapter13</RootNamespace>
```

```
<AssemblyName>chapter13</AssemblyName>
<TargetFrameworkVersion>v3.5</TargetFrameworkVersion>
<SilverlightApplication>true</SilverlightApplication>
<SupportedCultures>
</SupportedCultures>
<XapOutputs>true</XapOutputs>
<GenerateSilverlightManifest>true</GenerateSilverlightManifest>
<XapFilename>chapter13.xap</XapFilename>
<SilverlightManifestTemplate>
      Properties\AppManifest.xml
</SilverlightManifestTemplate>
<SilverlightAppEntry>chapter13.App</SilverlightAppEntry>
<TestPageFileName>TestPage.html</TestPageFileName>
<CreateTestPage>true</CreateTestPage>
<ValidateXaml>true</ValidateXaml>
```

You can see that this project file is configured for Silverlight applications, setting properties related to the XAP file and defining the class that inherits from the IntelliSense class and serves as the entry point to the application. This project file also contains the directive to include the extension for building Silverlight applications. This extension controls how XAML pages are processed and how the XAP file is created. The structure of a Silverlight application as generated by Visual Studio includes the entry point for the application (the App.xaml and App.xaml.cs files), an empty UserControl (Page), an empty application manifest, the AssemblyInfo source file, and of course the project file. Let's look at using MSBuild to build this application. On disk, these files are organized as shown here:

```
chapter13\App.xaml
chapter13\App.xaml.cs
chapter13\chapter13.csproj
chapter13\Page.xaml
chapter13\Page.xaml.cs
chapter13\Properties
chapter13\Properties\AppManifest.xml
chapter13\Properties\AssemblyInfo.cs
```

Simply executing msbuild.exe with the project file specified as the command line parameter causes MSBuild to execute, compiling and packaging this application. The output from msbuild.exe looks like this:

```
C:\book\code\chapter13>msbuild chapter13.csproj
Microsoft (R) Build Engine Version 3.5.30428.1
[Microsoft .NET Framework, Version 2.0.50727.3031]
Copyright (C) Microsoft Corporation 2007. All rights reserved.
Build started 7/7/2008 10:43:22 PM.
Project "C:\book\code\chapter13\chapter13.csproj" on node 0 (default targets).
  Processing 0 edmx files
  Finished processing 0 edmx files
PrepareForBuild:
  Creating directory "Bin\Debug\".
```

```
  Creating directory "obj\Debug\".
CopyFilesToOutputDirectory:
  Copying file from "obj\Debug\chapter13.dll" to "Bin\Debug\chapter13.dll".
  chapter13 -> C:\book\code\chapter13\Bin\Debug\chapter13.dll
  Copying file from "obj\Debug\chapter13.pdb" to "Bin\Debug\chapter13.pdb".
CreateSilverlightAppManifest:
  Begin application manifest generation
  Application manifest generation completed successfully
XapPackager:
  Begin Xap packaging
  Packaging chapter13.dll
  Packaging AppManifest.xaml
  Xap packaging completed successfully
CreateHtmlTestPage:
  Creating test page
  Test page created successfully
Done Building Project "C:\book\code\chapter13\chapter13.csproj" (default targets).
Build succeeded.
    0 Warning(s)
    0 Error(s)
Time Elapsed 00:00:01.04
```

The actual compilation and creation of the DLL and PDB files is done after the `PrepareForBuild` task. After the compilation, a Silverlight-specific application manifest is created, and the contents are packaged into a XAP file. If you examine the contents of the `obj\Debug` directory, you will see the following files:

```
App.g.cs
chapter13.csproj.FileListAbsolute.txt
chapter13.dll
chapter13.g.resources
chapter13.pdb
Page.g.cs
ResolveAssemblyReference.cache
XapCacheFile.xml
```

The `App.g.cs` and `Page.g.cs` files are generated based on their corresponding XAML files and should not be edited. These files contain the generated partial class definition for their corresponding class. Much like with Windows Forms, these generated files include the implementation of `InitializeComponent` and objects for any XAML elements with an `x:Name` attribute defined. The DLL and PDB files are the important parts of the output, and exactly what you should be used to from .NET—the code compiled to an assembly and a symbol file for debugging purposes. The `XapCacheFile.xml` file is the Silverlight application manifest and contains instructions for the XAP packaging utility, such as the files to include in the XAP and where to place the generated XAP file.

```
<xapCache source="C:\book\code\ chapter13\Bin\Debug\chapter13.xap"
        lastWriteTime="7/7/2008 10:43:23 PM">
  <file source="C:\book\code\ chapter13\obj\Debug\chapter13.dll"
```

```
          archivePath="chapter13.dll"
          lastWriteTime="7/7/2008 10:43:22 PM" />
  <file source="C:\book\code\ chapter13\Bin\Debug\AppManifest.xaml"
          archivePath="AppManifest.xaml"
          lastWriteTime="7/7/2008 10:43:23 PM" />
</xapCache>
```

While using Visual Studio project files as the configuration files with MSBuild is a useful approach, sometimes you might need to use the native MSBuild file format. While it does share a lot with the Visual Studio project file format, there are a few differences. Let's take a look at an MSBuild file that goes a lot further than the preceding simple example. This build file is suitable for this chapter's code; therefore, it includes directives to compile library assemblies and the application, and include resources or content files. The file, build.proj, is annotated with line numbers and broken up for ease of discussion. Repetitive elements have been removed in the interest of space and clarity, but all line numbers match the build.proj included in this chapter's code. Of course, these line numbers would not appear in an actual MSBuild project file.

```
001: <Project
002:   ToolsVersion="3.5"
003:   DefaultTargets="Build"
004:   xmlns="http://schemas.microsoft.com/developer/msbuild/2003">
005:
006:   <!-- Application Configuration -->
007:   <PropertyGroup>
008:     <TargetFrameworkVersion>v3.5</TargetFrameworkVersion>
009:     <SchemaVersion>2.0</SchemaVersion>
010:     <NoStdLib>true</NoStdLib>
011:     <NoStdCfg>true</NoStdCfg>
```

The Project is the root element for MSBuild configuration files. The TargetFrameworkVersion is set to 3.5, but keep in mind that this has no connection to .NET 3.5 on Windows. This version number is reflective of the time when Silverlight was released (.NET 3.5 is the latest release and includes WCF and the updated MSBuild, as described here).

```
013:     <RootNamespace>chapter13</RootNamespace>
014:     <AssemblyName>chapter13</AssemblyName>
015:     <OutputType>Library</OutputType>
016:     <OutputPath>ClientBin</OutputPath>
```

The RootNamespace, as its name implies, specifies the root namespace used in the source code being built. The AssemblyName specifies the file name used for the built assembly. Since both Silverlight applications and Silverlight libraries are DLLs, the OutputType will always be set to Library. The OutputPath specifies the directory where the output files of tasks from this configuration file are placed.

```
018:     <SilverlightAppEntry>chapter13.App</SilverlightAppEntry>
```

This specifies the class that inherits from the IntelliSense class and thus serves as the entry point for the Silverlight application. Without this, the packaged XAP won't be valid and won't successfully start in Silverlight.

```
020:     <SilverlightManifestTemplate>
                         Properties\AppManifest.xml</SilverlightManifestTemplate>
021:     <GenerateSilverlightManifest>true</GenerateSilverlightManifest>
```

These two properties are required in order to generate a Silverlight manifest file that includes the details of the XAP file. If you don't specify these, no Silverlight manifest is generated, and if you specify the next two properties, the constructed XAP file will contain only the DLL from the build process instead of all the files it should.

```
023:     <XapOutputs>true</XapOutputs>
024:     <XapFilename>chapter13.xap</XapFilename>
```

These two properties instruct MSBuild to create a XAP file with the specified name. The XAP file is placed in the directory specified in the OutputPath property. If these properties are not specified, no XAP file will be produced.

```
025:     </PropertyGroup>
026:
027:     <!-- Silverlight assembly references required by code -->
028:     <ItemGroup>
029:       <Reference Include="mscorlib" />
030:       <Reference Include="system" />
031:       <Reference Include="System.Windows" />
032:       <Reference Include="System.Core" />
033:       <Reference Include="System.Net" />
034:       <Reference Include="System.Windows.Browser" />
```

This ItemGroup section shows the set of Silverlight assemblies that are required to build a default Silverlight application that results from creating a new Silverlight project in Visual Studio. If the application being built uses assemblies other than these, this section is where they get added.

```
035:     <Reference Include=
                  "chapter13library, Version=1.0.0.0, Culture=neutral,
                                          processorArchitecture=MSIL">
036:       <SpecificVersion>False</SpecificVersion>
037:       <HintPath>libs\chapter13library.dll</HintPath>
038:     </Reference>
```

This is the first Silverlight class library. The HintPath specifies where this library is located.

```
039:     <Reference Include=
                  "chapter13library2, Version=1.0.0.0, Culture=neutral,
                                          processorArchitecture=MSIL">
040:       <SpecificVersion>False</SpecificVersion>
041:       <HintPath>libs\chapter13library2.dll</HintPath>
042:       <Private>False</Private>
```

This is the other class library. Setting the value of the Private property to False is what prevents this assembly from being included in the XAP file.

```
043:        </Reference>
044:      </ItemGroup>
045:
046:      <!-- Files to build application class -->
047:      <ItemGroup>
048:        <Compile Include="App.xaml.cs">
049:          <DependentUpon>App.xaml</DependentUpon>
050:        </Compile>
051:        <Compile Include="Page.xaml.cs">
052:          <DependentUpon>Page.xaml</DependentUpon>
053:        </Compile>
```

This is the format used to compile the code-behind files for each XAML page. Since each XAML page is marked as a dependency, the next ItemGroup's contents are built first.

```
075:        <Compile Include="Properties\AssemblyInfo.cs" />
076:      </ItemGroup>
077:      <ItemGroup>
078:        <ApplicationDefinition Include="App.xaml">
079:          <Generator>MSBuild:MarkupCompilePass1</Generator>
080:          <SubType>Designer</SubType>
081:        </ApplicationDefinition>
082:        <Page Include="Page.xaml">
083:          <Generator>MSBuild:MarkupCompilePass1</Generator>
084:          <SubType>Designer</SubType>
085:        </Page>
```

This section includes the part of the build process that turns a XAML page, such as Page.xaml, into its corresponding generated partial class for the code-behind, such as Page.g.cs. There's one entry here for each XAML file in the project.

```
114:      </ItemGroup>
115:      <ItemGroup>
116:        <Resource Include="ball_blue.png" />
117:      </ItemGroup>
```

This Resource element specifies that the resource file is placed into the Silverlight application assembly.

```
118:      <ItemGroup>
119:        <Content Include="ball_red.png" />
120:      </ItemGroup>
```

The Content element specifies that the resource file should be packaged in a XAP file that is created at the end of the build process.

```
122:      <!--
123:        The file that is used by MSBuild to Build C# Silverlight Applications, and
124:        which specifies the C# compiler. Note that $(MSBuildExtensionsPath) is the
125:        path to the Program Files\MSBuild folder.
126:      -->
```

```
127:    <Import Project=
                        "$(MSBuildExtensionsPath)\Microsoft\Silverlight\v2.0\
                         Microsoft.Silverlight.CSharp.targets" />
128: </Project>
```

This part is required to import the Silverlight-related tasks into the build for use by MSBuild. The Silverlight-related tasks used in this build file include compiling XAML and creating a XAP file.

Silverlight Assemblies

Certain assemblies are not automatically available for Silverlight applications. Only the core runtime assemblies, installed to $(ProgramFiles)\Microsoft Silverlight\(*version #*), are present on client computers. The reason these assemblies form a core is to keep the Silverlight plug-in relatively small. Just a few of the assemblies in this directory are mscorlib (IO, reflection, collections, etc.), System (support classes), System.Xml (XML parsing), System.Windows (controls, animation, 2D drawing, etc.), System.Core (LINQ), System.Windows.Browser (DOM access and host interoperability), and System.ServiceModel (services). This set of classes should provide a significant amount of what Silverlight applications need. If you need more, though, you must install the Silverlight SDK and distribute assemblies from the SDK with your application.

The assemblies included with the Silverlight SDK fall into two categories: client and server. Since these are not part of the core, these assemblies must be packaged as part of the XAP file that is downloaded by the client. The client assemblies include dynamic language support (IronPython, IronRuby, managed JScript), more controls in System.Windows.Controls.Extended (e.g., the Calendar and Tab controls), and other assemblies to support syndication, more XML functionality, and so on. There is only one server assembly, System.Web.Silverlight, and its main feature is a media player capable of fine-grained control over media. These assemblies are located in $(ProgramFiles)\Microsoft SDKs\Silverlight\v2.0\Libraries by default.

The MSDN documentation specifies which assembly a class is in. Consult the documentation if Visual Studio cannot build your application because an assembly reference is missing.

■Note The library assemblies are packaged with the XAP file, so make sure your application only references those assemblies that it needs. It is important to keep the size of the XAP file as small as possible to provide a positive user experience. Other strategies for improving the user experience are to download library assemblies on demand (if your application doesn't need them right away) or provide a splash screen (using the splashScreenSource) since it will load much faster than the XAP.

Summary

This chapter covered packaging and deployment of Silverlight applications and libraries. The XAP file is the main unit of deployment when delivering Silverlight applications to the user. A XAP file can include the main Silverlight application assembly, resources such as images and video, and library assemblies. I discussed the OBJECT tag, showing how to place a Silverlight application on a web page and describing the various Silverlight plug-in configuration options available. You saw how to use resources and libraries from Silverlight, including how to package them and how to download them on demand. Finally, any complete software engineering process has a build process, so you saw how to leverage MSBuild to include Silverlight in the build. You've now reached the end of the journey through how Silverlight works and learned all you need to build applications. In the final segment of this book, all these pieces will come together into a real application.

■ ■ ■

CHAPTER 14

Advanced Topics

While this book has covered a significant amount of Silverlight, there is much more to it. This chapter aims to provide information on some of these other topics. The biggest topic yet to be covered is the multithreading support that Silverlight provides. Used properly, threading is a great way to provide a smooth user experience by doing work such as lengthy calculations or downloading files while the user interface remains responsive. Another useful technique for certain applications is the use of a *timer*—a way to execute some code on a certain periodic schedule (e.g., every 10 seconds). This chapter concludes with how to dynamically load assemblies and even dynamically add XAML to your user interface.

Threading

Silverlight is a *multithreaded* environment, which means multiple sequences of code can execute simultaneously. You've already encountered this in the asynchronous nature of network communication. The main application thread makes a call to the `BeginGetResponse` method of `HttpWebRequest`, and then your code doesn't need to sit around waiting for a response. The actual network communication happens on a different thread, and when a response from the server is received, the method specified as the asynchronous callback is invoked. In Silverlight, this specific callback actually happens on a thread other than the main application thread. The main application thread is usually referred to as the user interface thread, since this is the thread where all user interface–related code lives (e.g., code that creates the user interface, code for handling events, etc.). Figure 14-1 shows an illustration of two threads of execution: the user interface thread and a worker thread that is used for the network communication. The worker thread representation is shifted down to illustrate the time when the worker thread is created.

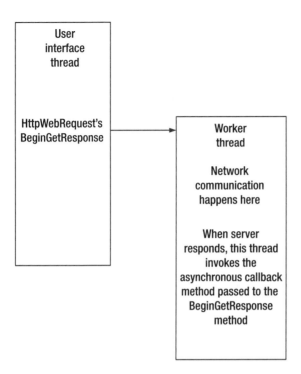

Figure 14-1. *Illustration of user interface thread and worker thread*

If you build web applications solely using technologies such as HTML, JScript, and Ajax, you can't take advantage of threading in the underlying operating system. Using multiple threads allows you to build more complex applications that have a high degree of responsiveness to users. With multiple cores and multiple processors in computers these days, it would be surprising if Silverlight did not provide support for using threads. Of course, using threads introduces new sets of problems for developers. First, you want to be careful to not overuse threads. Since ultimately each thread is backed by an operating system thread, there are a limited number of threads you can use, as each thread requires memory and costs CPU time. Another significant problem occurs any time several threads want to access the same data. If two threads want to modify a shared piece of data, such as an integer variable, it's possible to see unexpected behavior if one thread modifies the variable while the other thread is in the middle of a modification operation. This is known as a *race condition*, since both threads are in a race to access the shared data, and it's unpredictable which will "win." Race conditions are only one type of potential threading issue. If you need to use threads in your Silverlight application, use them carefully. Of course, the benefit of threads can outweigh the inherent problems when used properly.

The Thread Class

The System.Threading.Thread class is the managed class that wraps a thread in the underlying operating system. This is the class you use when you manually create threads or when you want to do something like put a thread to sleep. The properties of the Thread class are shown in Table 14-1.

Table 14-1. *Properties of the System.Threading.Thread Class*

Property	Type	Description
CurrentCulture	CultureInfo	Gets/sets the culture for the current thread.
CurrentThread	static Thread	Gets the currently active thread.
CurrentUICulture	CultureInfo	Gets/sets the culture used by the resource manager when accessing culture-specific resources at runtime.
IsAlive	bool	true if the thread is currently running normally and not aborted/stopped.
IsBackground	bool	true if the thread is a background thread. Background threads do not prevent the Silverlight runtime from shutting down; therefore, they may be killed abruptly without completing.
ManagedThreadId	Int32	Unique identifier assigned to the managed thread.
Name	string	Gets/sets the name of the thread.
ThreadState	System.Threading.ThreadState	Gets the current state of the thread.

The most useful methods of the Thread class are shown in Table 14-2.

Table 14-2. *Methods of the System.Threading.Thread Class*

Method	Description
Abort	Causes a ThreadAbortException to occur in the thread. The thread will usually terminate. It will transition to the AbortRequested state and ultimately to the Aborted state.
Join	Blocks the calling thread until the thread that Join is invoked on is finished. This is useful when the calling thread must wait for results or other events to complete before proceeding.
Sleep	Static method. Puts the calling thread to sleep for a specified time span or number of milliseconds. While sleeping, the thread will not consume any processor time.
Start	Starts the thread. You can optionally pass an object to the Start method that the thread's work method will use.

A thread can be in one of several states, as shown in Figure 14-2. Note that the Background state is not mutually exclusive to the other states. It's possible for a thread to be a background thread and to be running, for example. Both of these states can be discovered by consulting the ThreadState property of a thread.

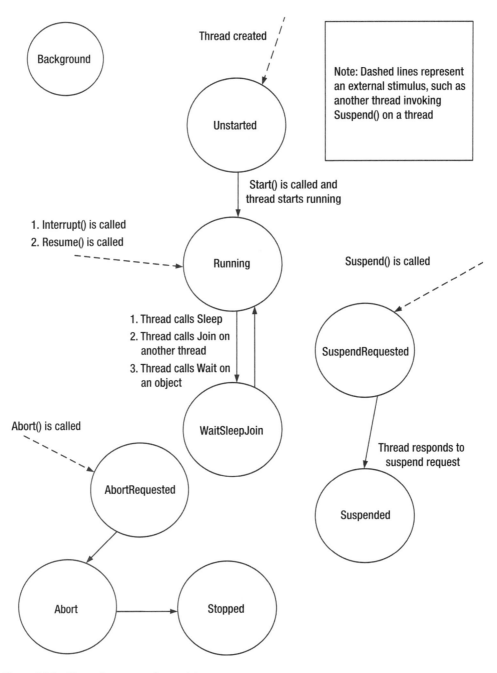

Figure 14-2. *Thread states and transitions*

Creating and Managing Threads

If you want to execute some code on an alternate thread, you can place the code to execute in its own method and then pass this method to the Thread class's constructor (by wrapping the method in a ThreadStart object). We'll use the following method to simulate some work:

```
public void doSomething()
{
    Thread.Sleep(5000); // 5 seconds
    Dispatcher.BeginInvoke(delegate() { statusText.Text = "Work done."; });
}
```

The code for this chapter contains a simple interface used to start a thread executing the doSomething method. You can repeatedly click a button to see the current state of the thread. You should see the state go from Running to WaitSleepJoin and finally to Stopped after the 5-second sleep period is over. Here's the event handler for the first button that creates and starts the thread:

```
private void startThreadButton_Click(object sender, RoutedEventArgs e)
{
    currentThread = new Thread(new ThreadStart(doSomething));
    currentThread.Start();
    statusText.Text = "Thread created and started";
    threadStateText.Text = currentThread.ThreadState.ToString();
}
```

The Thread constructor uses the ThreadStart class to wrap the method that does the work. There is an alternate class, ParameterizedThreadStart, that is used when you want to pass an object to the method that performs the work. This object gets passed to the Start method, which subsequently passes it to the method wrapped by ParameterizedThreadStart. A method suitable for use with ParameterizedThreadStart takes a single object as a parameter.

```
public void gotoSleep(object time)
{
    int timeToSleep = (int)time;
    Thread.Sleep(timeToSleep);
}
```

Starting the thread is accomplished using code similar to the nonparameterized ThreadStart class; however, the parameter is passed to the Start method:

```
currentThread = new Thread(new ParameterizedThreadStart(gotoSleep));
currentThread.Start(7500);
```

While this is an effective way to create a thread to do some processing, it has several problems. The main problem is that creating a thread is expensive, and if you continue to create threads like this, your application's performance might be impacted, since the environment handles the creation and eventually the cleanup of threads. To address this problem, you should use something called the *thread pool*, which contains a number of already created threads ready to jump into action and do some work.

The thread pool automatically handles the allocation, creation, and cleanup of threads. If your application requires a larger number of threads than the thread pool already has, then new threads are created and added to the pool. If your application requires fewer threads than the pool has, however, your application won't incur the cost of creation of new threads, since they are already available in the pool. Another advantage to the thread pool is that if at one point your application requires a large number of threads, but later on it doesn't, the unused threads will automatically clean themselves up until the pool contains a number of threads closer to what your application currently requires. You interact with the thread pool using the System.Threading.ThreadPool class. You never create an instance of the thread pool, since it is completely managed by the environment (the Silverlight plug-in), so all methods are static. The ThreadPool class provides methods to get and set the minimum and maximum number of threads, but you'll usually leave this up to the thread pool itself. The vast majority of the time the thread pool will better manage thread counts than you can. The most useful method to you is the QueueUserWorkItem method.

The simplest way to use QueueUserWorkItem is to pass it a method that does the work. This is similar to passing a method to a ThreadStart class constructor, but it requires less work and frees you from having to interact with the thread directly.

```
private void startThreadButton_Click(object sender, RoutedEventArgs e)
{
    ThreadPool.QueueUserWorkItem(doSomething);
    statusText.Text = "Work queued for a thread pool thread";
}
```

Although this code functions similar to manually creating and using a thread, you can't get state information about the thread since there is no Thread object. The work is sent to a background thread, and then the application just carries on.

Let's say you have a user interface with a TextBox, named resultTextBox, that displays the contents of something you download using HttpWebRequest. Error handling and details of reading the response stream are left out for simplicity since they aren't needed for this illustration.

```
void responseHandler(IAsyncResult asyncResult)
{
    HttpWebResponse response = (HttpWebResponse)request.EndGetResponse(asyncResult);
    StreamReader reader = new StreamReader(response.GetResponseStream());
    string result = "";
    // read and process file
    resultTextBox.Text = result;
}
```

If you attempt to run this code, you'll get an error about cross-thread access not being allowed. This problem with modifying resultTextBox directly from the response handler is due to the response handler executing on a different thread. Only the main user interface thread can modify user interface elements. What you need, then, is a way to get the user interface thread to make the user interface modification. This happens using something called the Dispatcher.

The Dispatcher

The DependencyObject acts as the base object for many classes in Silverlight. One important aspect of this class, however, is its single property, Dispatcher. Objects can only be modified on the thread they are created on. Each object, therefore, has a Dispatcher property that provides two important pieces of functionality. First, you can test whether an object can be modified from the current thread by calling the CheckAccess method. If the current thread is the same as the one the Dispatcher belongs to, CheckAccess will return true. The other important functionality is the ability to queue some code to execute on the Dispatcher's thread. This is how we go about solving the cross-thread access problem when modifying user interface objects. The method used to execute some code on the Dispatcher's thread is called BeginInvoke. Figure 14-3 shows the relationship of two threads and the Dispatcher object.

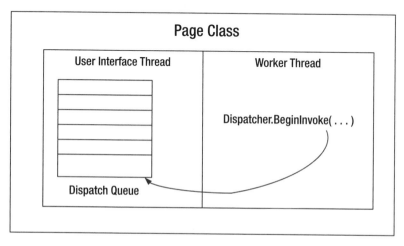

Figure 14-3. *A worker thread using the Dispatcher to queue code to execute on the main thread*

Let's rewrite the responseHandler to properly interact with the user interface by using the Dispatcher property:

```
void responseHandler(IAsyncResult asyncResult)
{
    HttpWebResponse response = (HttpWebResponse)request.EndGetResponse(asyncResult);
    StreamReader reader = new StreamReader(response.GetResponseStream());
    string result = "";
    // read and process file
    Dispatcher.BeginInvoke(delegate() { resultTextBox.Text = output; });
}
```

This usage of BeginInvoke creates an anonymous, zero-parameter method by using the delegate keyword. You can also execute a method that has parameters by using the alternate form of BeginInvoke, which takes an array of parameters as its second parameter. In this case, we call BeginInvoke directly because part of the defined behavior of HttpWebResponse is that the response handler is invoked on a thread other than the original calling thread. If you're in a situation where the invoking thread might be the user interface thread or a different thread, you can use CheckAccess combined with BeginInvoke in order to modify the user interface:

```
void modifyUserInterface()
{
    if(Dispatcher.CheckAccess())
    {
        resultTextBox.Text = "modified from UI thread";
    } else {
        Dispatcher.BeginInvoke(
            delegate() {
                outputTB.Text = "modified from non-UI thread";
            }
        );
    }
}
```

Of course, while you'll primarily use the Dispatcher to modify the user interface, it is also useful for modifying any data that is associated with a different thread. As illustrated in Figure 14-3, each thread has a dispatch queue. This is where the code you specify in a BeginInvoke method goes. Each call to BeginInvoke adds a unit of work to the dispatch queue.

The BackgroundWorker Class

If you need to perform work on a separate thread, the easiest way to do this is by using the BackgroundWorker class. This class makes it easy to do work (such as a long download) on a separate thread so your user interface stays responsive. This class also provides events for reporting progress of the work. Its properties are shown in Table 14-3.

Table 14-3. *Properties of the System.ComponentModel.BackgroudWorker Class*

Property	Type	Description
CancellationPending	bool	true when the application attempts to cancel the BackgroundWorker via a call to the CancelAsync method.
IsBusy	bool	true when the BackgroundWorker's task is in progress (after the call to RunWorkerAsync, and as long as the task isn't complete or cancelled).
WorkerReportsProgress	bool	true when the BackgroundWorker is configured to report progress via the ProgressChanged event handler.
WorkerSupportsCancellation	bool	true when the BackgroundWorker is capable of being cancelled via CancelAsync.

The BackgroundWorker has three events: DoWork, ProgressChanged, and RunWorkerCompleted. Normally, a method you register with an event is invoked when the event is raised. This same mechanism, however, is used by the DoWork event. In this case, what is normally an event handler instead contains code that makes up the work that will be performed by the BackgroundWorker. ProgressChanged is used to register a method that can handle progress change notification—most useful for displaying a status indicator on the user interface, since the method call happens on the initiating thread (most commonly the user interface thread). The RunWorkerCompleted event is raised when the work is complete.

Let's explore just how the BackgroundWorker operates. Figure 14-4 shows a demonstration with three buttons. Clicking each button will start a new BackgroundWorker configured with some information to tell it how long to execute, and where to send data (the TextBlock next to the button) as it executes and when it completes.

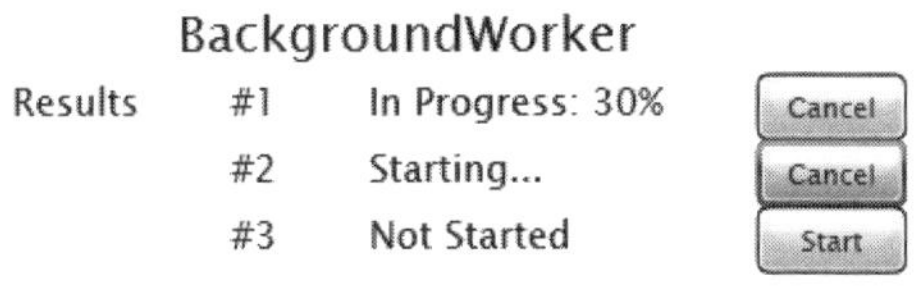

BackgroundWorker

Results	#1	In Progress: 30%	Cancel
	#2	Starting...	Cancel
	#3	Not Started	Start

Figure 14-4. *BackgroundWorker demonstration*

Before we can make use of the BackgroundWorker, we must define a method that encapsulates the work that we want done on a background thread. This method supports cancellation, and takes an integer argument (contained in the CustomWorkerArgs instance that is passed in via the DoWorkEventArgs object) that controls how long the method takes to execute. The long-running operation is simulated via Thread.Sleep:

```
public void performLengthyOperation(object sender, DoWorkEventArgs e)
{
    BackgroundWorker bw = (BackgroundWorker)sender;
    CustomWorkerArgs args = (CustomWorkerArgs)e.Argument;
    e.Result = args;
    for (int i = 1; i <= 10; i++)
    {
        if (bw.CancellationPending)
        {
            e.Cancel = true;
            break;
        }
        else
        {
            Thread.Sleep(args.sleepTime / 10);
            bw.ReportProgress(i * 10, args);
        }
    }
}
```

The DoWorkEventArgs object defines several useful properties: Argument, which contains an arbitrary object that was passed to RunWorkerAsync; Cancel, which you set to true to cancel the work (generally done when CancellationPending is set to true); and Result, which is used to store an object that can be processed by the RunWorkerCompleted event handler. Since this configuration of BackgroundWorker supports cancellation (something we must explicitly implement in the method that performs work), the CancellationPending property is checked and the loop aborted prematurely if it is true. The ReportProgress method takes two parameters: an integer representing percentage completion, and optionally a user state, used to communicate some form of information to the progress event handler.

The CustomWorkerArgs class simply holds an integer representing an index (so we can easily access the button/text block associated with a BackgroundWorker) and an integer for sleepTime (the total time the worker method should take to execute). Using a class like this is how you can communicate as much information as needed to the BackgroundWorker.

```
class CustomWorkerArgs
{
    public int index;
    public int sleepTime;
}
```

Since the various event handlers for BackgroundWorker include a sender (the BackgroundWorker instance), we can hold a reference to this worker at the class level and compare the instances instead of passing the index via CustomWorkerArgs. In fact, in one case (when the worker is cancelled or throws an exception), this is mandated. However, this information is included in the CustomWorkerArgs class in order to show where information can be accessed and used in the BackgroundWorker's event handlers. We keep an array of BackgroundWorker instances at the class level, along with an array of Buttons and an array of TextBlocks. The Button, in XAML, stores the appropriate index in the Tag attribute. A single Button event handler is used to start a BackgroundWorker.

```
private void buttonTask_Click(object sender, RoutedEventArgs e)
{
    // Tag used to get index for button/text blocks
    int index = Convert.ToInt32(((Button)sender).Tag);
    if (workers[index] != null)
    {
        resultBoxes[index].Text = "Cancelling...";
        workers[index].CancelAsync();
        bwButtons[index].Content = "Start";
    }
    else
    {
        BackgroundWorker worker = new BackgroundWorker();
        worker.WorkerReportsProgress = true;
        worker.WorkerSupportsCancellation = true;
        worker.ProgressChanged +=
                new ProgressChangedEventHandler(worker_ProgressChanged);
        worker.RunWorkerCompleted +=
                new RunWorkerCompletedEventHandler(worker_RunWorkerCompleted);
        worker.DoWork += new DoWorkEventHandler(performLengthyOperation);
        CustomWorkerArgs args = new CustomWorkerArgs();
```

```
            args.index = index;
            args.sleepTime = 25000;
            bwButtons[index].Content = "Cancel";
            resultBoxes[index].Text = "Starting...";
            workers[index] = worker;
            worker.RunWorkerAsync(args);
        }
    }
}
```

The index is retrieved via the Tag attribute, and then the corresponding worker entry in the workers array is checked. This entry is set to null when the BackgroundWorker completes (or errors or is cancelled), so if you find it not null, then the worker is active and working. Otherwise, a new BackgroundWorker is created. This is where we set WorkReportsProgress and WorkerSupportsCancellation to true. Again, these properties should only be set to true when you construct the method that does work to explicitly handle the cancel condition and to report progress.

Next, the event handlers are registered. Let's take a closer look at these. DoWork is registered with the method that actually does the work. In this case, this is the performLengthyOperation that we already implemented. The rest of this method creates a CustomWorkerArgs instance, configures it, and passes it to the BackgroundWorker in the RunWorkerAsync method. RunWorkerAsync is what starts the actual work, provided DoWork is registered with the work method.

The progress handler is straightforward. The UserState property of ProgressChangedEventArgs contains the object originally passed to RunWorkerAsync. The source of this property, however, is the second (optional) parameter to the ReportProgress method of BackgroundWorker. If you need to pass something custom specifically to the progress report handler, you can do it using the UserState property.

```
void worker_ProgressChanged(object sender, ProgressChangedEventArgs e)
{
    int index = ((CustomWorkerArgs)e.UserState).index;
    resultBoxes[index].Text = "In progress: " + e.ProgressPercentage + "%";
}
```

The RunWorkerCompleted event handler is much more interesting. Here, we must check whether the background worker was cancelled or if it had an error. If either of these conditions are true, you can't use the Result property of the RunWorkerCompletedEventArgs, or else your code will throw an exception.

```
void worker_RunWorkerCompleted(object sender, RunWorkerCompletedEventArgs e)
{
    BackgroundWorker bw = (BackgroundWorker)sender;
    int index;
    if (e.Error != null || e.Cancelled)
    {
        // if there's an Error or this worker was cancelled,
        // we can't access Result without throwing an exception
```

```
        if (bw == workers[0])
            index = 0;
        else if (bw == workers[1])
            index = 1;
        else
            index = 2;
        if (e.Error != null)
            resultBoxes[index].Text = "Exception: " + e.Error.Message;
        else
            resultBoxes[index].Text = Cancelled";
    }
    else
    {
        index = ((CustomWorkerArgs)e.Result).index;
        resultBoxes[index].Text = "Completed";
    }
    bwButtons[index].Content = "Start";
    workers[index] = null;
}
```

If there is no error and the worker was not cancelled, the Result property can be accessed. The else block illustrates accessing Result, providing a quick way to arrive at the right text block.

Remember that all of these event handlers happen in the thread that created the BackgroundWorker. Since these workers were created on the user interface thread, it's possible to directly access the various text blocks to set their Text property to something appropriate. There are two big advantages to using the BackgroundWorker. First, it makes it easy to do work on a background thread without needing to worry about manually creating and managing a thread. Second, the various event handlers happen on the calling thread, making modification of a user interface easy without needing to use a Dispatcher.

Working with Shared Data

One of the trickiest problems when it comes to working with multiple threads is using shared resources—typically, shared memory in the form of objects or primitive types. When it comes to shared data, one potential issue is known as a race condition. Figure 14-5 illustrates two threads attempting to increment a single integer variable named value. However, a simple increment is split into smaller operations behind the scenes: the value of the variable is read, incremented, and stored back into the variable.

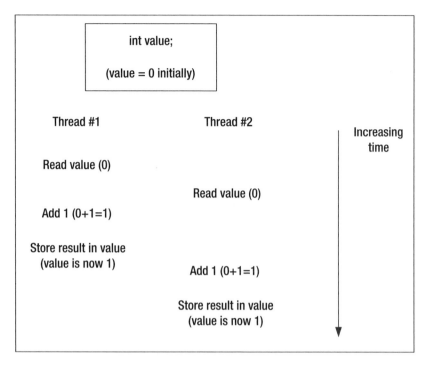

Figure 14-5. *Two threads incrementing a shared variable*

After each thread is done executing, you would expect the value of the integer variable to be 2, not 1. Unfortunately, while the second thread did read the value, the read happened before the first thread was done with its increment. This means both threads think the value was 0 and increment it to 1. The second thread clobbers the increment done by the first thread.

What we want is a way to ensure that all the tiny pieces of the increment (the read, the increment, and the write-back) work as a single unit. This increment then acts as an atomic operation—an operation (or sequence of operations) that works together and isn't preempted by another thread. This atomicity is achieved by using synchronization mechanisms. Actually, the increment and decrement are such common operations that the Silverlight base class framework provides a specialized increment and decrement that are guaranteed to happen without another thread preempting them. These convenience operations, and a few others, are provided by the System.Threading.Interlocked class. The methods of Interlocked are shown in Table 14-4. All methods are static.

Table 14-4. *Methods of the System.Threading.Interlocked Class*

Method	Description
Add	Adds two 32-bit or two 64-bit integers and stores the result in the memory location of the first integer (pass first integer by reference).
CompareExchange	Compares two values (integers or arbitrary types via a generic version) and replaces the value in the memory location of the first parameter with the second parameter if the first parameter is equal to the third parameter (a value used in comparison with first parameter).
Decrement	Decrements a 32-bit or 64-bit integer by 1.
Exchange	Exchanges two values (32-bit or 64-bit integers, or arbitrary types via a generic version). The exchange occurs by setting the memory of the first parameter to the value of the second parameter, and then the original value stored at the memory of the first parameter is returned from the method.
Increment	Increments a 32-bit or 64-bit integer by 1.

The Interlocked class can be extremely useful if you need to only make use of an operation it accounts for. You don't need to do anything other than invoke Interlocked.Increment (ref number) if you want to add 1 to an integer variable without needing to worry about other threads getting in the way. If you want to do something beyond a simple increment or add or comparison, you need a mechanism to turn an arbitrary set of operations into an atomic operation that can't be affected by other threads.

This atomicity is achieved by using a *synchronization mechanism*. A synchronization mechanism is a way for a thread to gain exclusive access to something (possibly one or more resources), locking out all other threads. When a thread is done with its work, it sends a signal essentially saying "I'm done" and letting other threads then obtain access to the shared resources.

One of these synchronization mechanisms is known as a *monitor*. Every object instance has a monitor associated with it. You can view a monitor as a token that only a single thread can own at any given time. If there are multiple threads attempting to gain access to a monitor, only the first thread that successfully requests it gets it. Other threads then line up, waiting for the first thread to release the monitor. The C# language provides a keyword, lock, that makes it easy to obtain a lock on an object's monitor.

If you need to control access to resources within a class, it's recommended you create a private object instance to use as a lock. This solves several problems with the design of the monitors in the CLR, including ensuring that the lock cannot be obtained by an outside class. If you were to obtain a lock on the current object instance via this, an outside class could also request a lock on the same instance. In practice, this looks like the following if we attempt to write a simple list (that uses an array internally). This is a simple list without error handling to illustrate how to use this synchronization functionality.

```
class ThreadSafeList
{
    private Object m_lock = new Object();
    private int[] listItems;
    private int count;
    public ThreadSafeList()
    {
        listItems = new int[100];
```

```
        count = 0;
    }
    public void Add(int num)
    {
        lock(m_lock)
        {
            // if list is full, allocate more space
            // otherwise, just add to end...
            listItems[count] = num;
            count++;
        }
    }
    public void RemoveAt(int index)
    {
        lock(m_lock)
        {
            for(int i=index; i<count; i++)
            {
                listItems[i] = listeItems[i+1];
            }
            count--;
        }
    }
}
```

Using the lock keyword ensures that only a single thread has access to the internals of the list (the listItems array and the count variable) at any given time. If you removed the lock requests and let several threads add items to and remove items from the list, it probably won't take long for something to go wrong, such as phantom values showing up in the list or the count variable not accurately reflecting the proper size of the list.

There are other synchronization mechanisms you can use in your code, such as AutoResetEvent. This class was used in Chapter 4 to create a synchronous socket. The AutoResetEvent class works by signaling. An instance of this class can either be signaled or not signaled. When not signaled, any thread that calls the Wait method of the AutoResetEvent class will block. Conceptually, the thread is waiting for a specific event to signal. An instance of AutoResetEvent is signaled when its Set method is called. Let's look at the ReceiveAsString method from the SynchronousSocket class from Chapter 3:

```
public string ReceiveAsString()
{
    if (!this.Connected)
    {
        throw new Exception("Not connected.");
    }
    SocketAsyncEventArgs asyncEventArgs = new SocketAsyncEventArgs();
    byte[] response = new byte[1024];
    asyncEventArgs.SetBuffer(response, 0, response.Length);
    asyncEventArgs.Completed +=
```

```
            new EventHandler<SocketAsyncEventArgs>(SocketOperationCompleted);
    AutoResetEvent receiveEvent = new AutoResetEvent(false);
    asyncEventArgs.UserToken = receiveEvent;
    _socket.ReceiveAsync(asyncEventArgs);
    receiveEvent.WaitOne();
    receiveEvent.Close();
    if (asyncEventArgs.SocketError == SocketError.Success)
    {
        return (Encoding.UTF8.GetString(asyncEventArgs.Buffer,
                    asyncEventArgs.Offset, asyncEventArgs.BytesTransferred));
    }
    else
    {
        throw this.Error;
    }
}
```

The relevant part of this code is the creation of AutoResetEvent (initially in the nonsignaled state, specified by passing false to the constructor), invoking the asynchronous receive method, and then blocking by waiting for the event to signal via WaitOne. The call to Close just cleans up this particular AutoResetEvent since it isn't needed beyond this single method call. The AutoResetEvent instance is passed to the method that acts as the callback for the receive operation via the UserToken property of SocketAsyncEventArgs. The callback method, SocketOperationCompleted, gets ahold of the AutoResetEvent instance and signals it.

```
protected void SocketOperationCompleted(object sender, SocketAsyncEventArgs e)
{
    if (e.SocketError != SocketError.Success)
    {
        this.Error = new SocketException((int)e.SocketError);
    }
    ((AutoResetEvent)e.UserToken).Set();
}
```

Once signaled, the ReceiveAsString method can proceed, since it now has a result from the socket receive operation completing. While this is an effective way to impose synchronous semantics on asynchronous operations, you should in general not take this approach without considering the design of the application. A synchronous socket can be useful for quick bursts of communication, but if you're implementing a file downloader via sockets, the user interface will completely block; therefore, you should use the standard asynchronous functionality of sockets.

Using Timers

Timing can be quite useful in applications, such as to time-code execution, influence animations (such as when a certain animation starts), or perform or other application-specific functions, such as using a stage timer in a game. The two most useful timer classes in Silverlight are DispatcherTimer, a timer integrated with the dispatch queue, and Timer, from the System.Threading namespace. The major difference between these two timers is where the work method that occurs periodically is executed. The Timer class executes the work method on a separate thread, leaving the user interface responsive, but requiring use of the Dispatcher to change the user interface. The DispatcherTimer, however, does not have this restriction since it executes on the same thread. This makes it much easier to use. Figure 14-6 shows an interface used to experiment with both of these timers.

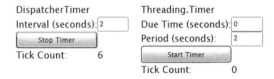

Figure 14-6. *DispatcherTimer and Timer classs demonstrations*

The DispatcherTimer

The DispatcherTimer works by hooking its Tick event up to a method that will be called on a periodic basis. You specify how often the Tick event is raised by passing a TimeSpan to the DispatcherTimer constructor, or by setting the Interval property to the TimeSpan. The timer is then started via the Start method and stopped via the Stop method. Here's code that counts to 20 in 1-second intervals, displaying each number on the user interface:

```
private int count = 0;
private void startTimer_Click(object sender, RoutedEventArgs e)
{
    DispatcherTimer timer = new DispatcherTimer();
    timer.Interval = new TimeSpan(0, 0, 1);
    timer.Tick += new EventHandler(timer_Tick);
    timer.Start();
}
void timer_Tick(object sender, EventArgs e)
{
    count++;
    outputText.Text = "Tick count: " + count;
    if (count == 20)
        ((DispatcherTimer)sender).Stop();
}
```

The System.Threading Timer

The Timer in the System.Threading namespace does basically the same thing, but the work (in the form of a callback method passed to Timer) is done on a thread from the thread pool. The method that does work on a periodic basis is specified as a parameter to the Timer constructor. There are five overloads of this constructor, each providing a different way to specify how often the work method is invoked. You can also optionally pass extra state information. The most important parameter to each constructor is `TimerCallback`, used to wrap the method that does the work. The `dueTime` parameter is used to specify delay before the timer starts, and the `period` parameter is used to specify delay between each subsequent invocation of the callback. If `dueTime` or `period` are set to infinite, they are effectively disabled (an infinite due time, for example, causes the timer to never start). A due time of zero causes the timer to start immediately, and a period of zero causes the work method to get invoked only once.

`Timer(TimerCallback)`: Creates a timer with an infinite due time and infinite period, preventing the timer from invoking the callback. Use the `Change` method to set a new due time/period. The state object is the `Timer` itself.

`Timer(TimerCallback, object state, Int32 dueTime, Int32 period)`: Creates a timer with a custom state object (useful for passing information to the work method), and a due time and period in milliseconds.

`Timer(TimerCallback, object state, Int64 dueTime, Int64 period)`: Same as the `Int32` version, but provides the ability to specify lengths of time that can't be represented in a 32-bit integer.

`Timer(TimerCallback, object state, TimeSpan dueTime, TimeSpan period)`: Same as the `Int32` version, but uses a `TimeSpan` to make it easier to specify lengths of time such as seconds or minutes.

`Timer(TimerCallback, object state, UInt32 dueTime, UInt32 period)`: Same as the `Int32` version, but instead uses unsigned integers to represent the due time and period.

■**Caution** Each time the `Timer`'s period elapses, the work method passed to the `TimerCallback` is invoked. This work is then executed by a thread from the thread pool. If the work method takes longer to execute than the period, it is likely that the work method will be executed by two threads from the thread pool at the same time. You must ensure that the work method can tolerate this scenario. This can also happen if the threads in the pool are exhausted and the work method is queued multiple times, waiting for threads from the pool to become available.

There is only one useful method on the `Timer` class: `Change`. The `Change` method is used to change the due time and interval of the timer, and has four overloads that match the four ways to specify due time and period in the constructor. The work method takes a single object parameter that corresponds to the `state` parameter passed to the constructor (or the `Timer` object itself if the first form of the constructor was used).

```
private void doSomething(object state)
{
    Dispatcher.BeginInvoke(
        delegate() {
            timerOutputText.Text =
                (Convert.ToInt32(timerOutputText.Text) + 1).ToString();
        });
}
```

Since the work method happens on a different thread, the `Dispatcher` must be used to make changes to the user interface. A button on the user interface is again hooked up to a method that starts/stops the timer.

```
private void timerButton_Click(object sender, RoutedEventArgs e)
{
    if (threadTimer != null)
    {
        threadTimer.Change(0, Timeout.Infinite);
        timerButton.Content = "Start Timer";
    }
    else
    {
        if (threadTimer != null)
            threadTimer.Change(Convert.ToInt32(dueTimeTextBox.Text) * 1000,
                                Convert.ToInt32(periodTextBox.Text) * 1000);
        else
            threadTimer = new Timer(new TimerCallback(doSomething), null,
                            Convert.ToInt32(dueTimeTextBox.Text) * 1000,
                            Convert.ToInt32(periodTextBox.Text) * 1000);
        timerButton.Content = "Stop Timer";
    }
}
```

We instruct the timer to stop by setting the period to `Timeout.Infinite`. The `Change` method is used to restart the timer also. This is the only way to interact with the `Timer` after it has been created, except for destroying it via `Dispose`.

Dynamically Loading Applications

There are two mechanisms Silverlight provides for dynamically loading applications. Assemblies can be stored outside an application's XAP file and downloaded on demand, and then loaded into the Silverlight environment via a tiny subset of the Reflection support from .NET. The other approach is to create or download XAML and add it to the visual tree. You can create fragments of XAML, stored in strings, and convert these to an object by using the `XamlReader.Load` method.

You saw the first approach in Chapter 13. You can download an assembly using `WebClient` and then pass the result stream to the `Load` method of `AssemblyPart` in order to get an `Assembly` object you can use.

```
AssemblyPart part = new AssemblyPart();
Assembly asm = part.Load(e.Result);
```

You can then use this assembly, such as for invoking `CreateInstance` to create instances of classes within the assembly. The other approach, using `XamlReader`, provides a mechanism to dynamically parse XAML at runtime and possibly add the resulting object (or tree of objects) to the user interface. Let's take a simple TextBlock stored in a XAML file in the web site (i.e., not distributed in the XAP) and then download and display it. The file contains a TextBlock by itself.

```
<TextBlock xmlns="http://schemas.microsoft.com/winfx/2006/xaml/presentation"
                Text="Downloaded Fragment"
                Margin="20" Foreground="Red" FontSize="16"/>
```

In order for this disembodied XAML to successfully parse via XamlReader.Load, it must meet the following criteria:

- It must be well formed. This should go without saying, but in the interest of being complete, the XAML must be well-formed XML and XAML. If an element name is misspelled or an end tag is missing, parsing will fail.

- It must have a single root element. Any XAML fragment can only have a single root element. It's easy to load a single TextBlock, but if you want to load a more complex tree of objects, they must be in a root element such as Canvas or Grid.

- The root element must specify the default XAML namescope. No matter what object you use for the root, you must add the xmlns, as shown in the preceding TextBlock. This provides the link between the XAML structure and the XAML fragment to the parser. You can specify other namescopes if there is a need.

We'll use WebClient to download this file. The DownloadStringCompleted event handler invokes XamlReader.Load to parse the downloaded file, cast it to the right class, and then add it to the user interface.

```
private void downloadFragmentButton_Click(object sender, RoutedEventArgs e)
{
    WebClient wc = new WebClient();
    wc.DownloadStringCompleted +=
        new DownloadStringCompletedEventHandler(wc_DownloadStringCompleted);
    wc.DownloadStringAsync(
        new Uri("/chapter14Web/XamlFragment.xaml", UriKind.Relative));
}
void wc_DownloadStringCompleted(object sender,
                                DownloadStringCompletedEventArgs e)
{
    TextBlock tb = (TextBlock)XamlReader.Load(e.Result);
    downloadedFragmentBorder.Child = tb;
}
```

Figure 14-7 shows what the downloaded fragment looks like after being added to the bottom Border control.

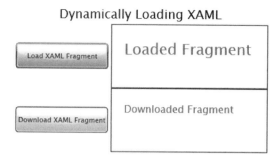

Figure 14-7. *Dynamically loaded XAML*

Summary

This chapter delved into some of the advanced aspects of Silverlight. You probably won't use them in every application, but when you do need them, you're now familiar. The biggest topic was the multithreading support provided by Silverlight. While you can manually create and use threads, it's much better to either leverage the thread pool or use the BackgroundWorker class to do work on a thread other than the main application thread. You also saw two timers provided by Silverlight, the DispatcherTimer and the Timer from the System.Threading namespace. Finally, you saw how to parse XAML at runtime and even load it into the user interface.

Chapter 15 will complete your journey through Silverlight by combining many of the topics you've encountered in this book. You'll see the design and implementation of a real application, showing just what Silverlight is capable of when put to use.

CHAPTER 15

■■■

Case Study: Campus Explorer

This chapter explores the rationale, design, and implementation of a Silverlight application that could conceivably exist on the Web. This application features an interactive map, information, images, and video of different parts of a university campus. The finished application is shown in Figure 15-1.

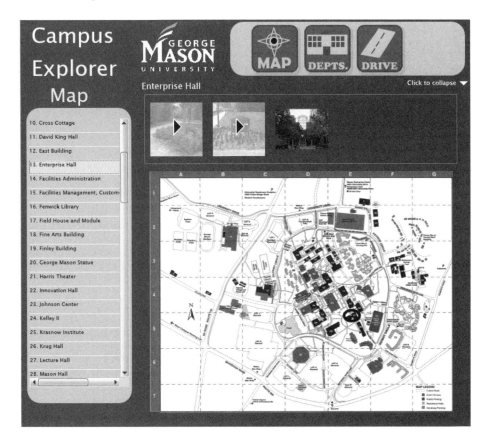

Figure 15-1. *A view of the finished Campus Explorer application*

Application Features

George Mason University has decided it wants to introduce a new feature on its main web site to help prospective students and other visitors explore the campus. The university currently has several campus maps that can be viewed online or downloaded and printed. While useful (especially when on campus), there is no connection to what the campus actually looks like. Additionally, other aspects of the university, such as academic departments, must be looked up separately and then manually located on the map (first by finding the building's number and then where this building is on the map).

The people representing George Mason University have asked for the following features in the first version of an application:

- Display the existing map.

- Show all buildings on a single campus and allow users to select a building and highlight it on the map.

- Show all departments within the university, and when a user selects a department, display information about the department and highlight the building that houses the department's main offices.

- When a building is the focus of the user's attention, show any images/video associated with it in thumbnail form.

- When a user selects an image or video thumbnail, reveal a more detailed view (for videos, the user can play/pause/resume/stop the video).

- Show a list of main roads visitors can take to get to the university, and when one is selected, highlight the route on the map (possibly with additional information on the map such as directional arrows, text assistance, etc.).

- Ensure the application can work on both Windows and OS X, and within different browsers, ensuring all visitors to the web site can make use of the interactive map.

Silverlight is an excellent choice to address these requested features because it is cross-platform, natural to develop on for .NET programmers, and has great support for handling images and video.

Design of the Application

The Campus Explorer must present different views of information and provide a good deal of interactivity for exploring a campus map. All this must be represented in some way so the application can display information to the user and know where to get media files such as video.

User Interface Design

A reduced version of a highly detailed map must be visible at all times. Users must be able to see a list of buildings on the map, departments in the school, and driving directions. When focusing on a building, users must be able to see any media attached to it. All these aspects must be considered when designing the user interface. Figure 15-2 shows the outline of the user interface that will be built.

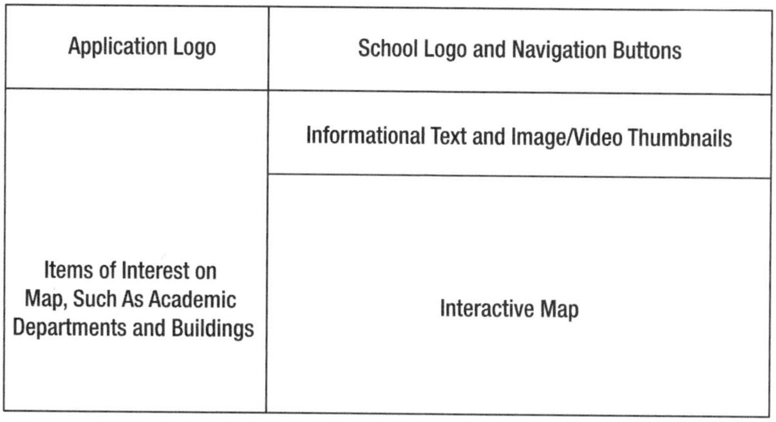

Application Logo	School Logo and Navigation Buttons
	Informational Text and Image/Video Thumbnails
Items of Interest on Map, Such As Academic Departments and Buildings	Interactive Map

Figure 15-2. *Outline of the Campus Explorer application*

This user interface is implemented using several XAML files. There is a XAML page for the main application, one for the map, and another for the video thumbnails. Any functionality that is limited to a page can stay within that page, such as the navigation buttons at the top and the navigation options at left. These fit more as part of the page code than code for a reusable element.

Data Representation

The data representation must be determined before the implementation can begin. After gathering information about what needs to be stored and processed by the application, the following facts are defined:

- A school has a name and initials.

- A school has one or more campuses.

- A school has one or more academic departments.

- A department has a name, an abbreviation, a description, and a building number.

- A campus has a name.

- A campus has a map.

- A campus map has a name, a full-size image (path to image, width, and height), and a reduced-size image (path to image, width and height).

- A campus map has zero or more annotations.

- A map annotation has a name, a description, a path to an image, and a category.

- A campus has one or more buildings.

- A building has a name.

- A building has associated map information.

- A building's map information has a building number, a grid cell, and a building location that can be highlighted on the map.

- A building has zero or more images and zero or more videos.

- Images/video for buildings have a caption, a path to the media, a width, and a height.

Figure 15-3 shows a data model that represents the preceding information. This model will turn into a set of classes corresponding to the structure of an XML file.

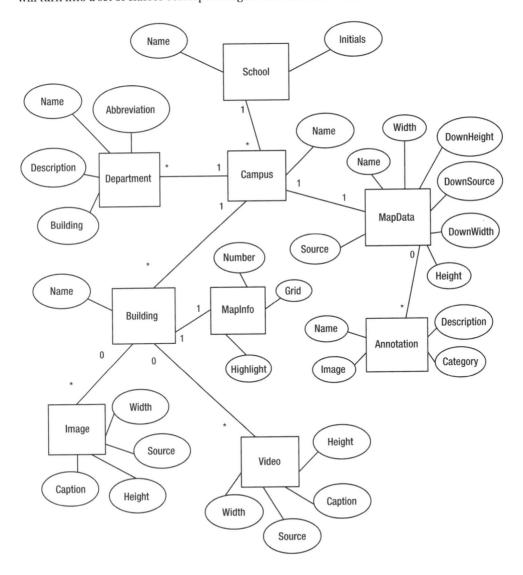

Figure 15-3. *Data model*

The use of classes provides an easy way to serialize an XML file, enable data binding, and expose a `DisplayText` property to help make the XAML a bit cleaner. A piece of the XML file looks like this:

```xml
<?xml version="1.0" encoding="utf-8"?>
<school name="George Mason University" initials="GMU">
  <departments>
    <department abbreviation="CS" name="Computer Science"
                      building="44" description="..."/>
  </departments>
  <campuses>
    <campus name="Fairfax">
        <mapdata name="Fairfax Campus" source="fairfax.png"
                      width="2400" height="2000"
                      downsource="fairfax_down.png"
                      downwidth="600" downheight="500">
            <annotations>
                <annotation name="From 66"
                              category="Driving Directions" description="..."
                              image="annotations/fairfax_directions_66.png"/>
            </annotations>
        </mapdata>
        <buildings>
            <building name="Enterprise Hall">
                <mapinfo number="13" highlight="1470,1040,170,120" grid="E5"/>
                <images>
                    <image caption="Stairs to center of campus"
                            source="/images/EnterpriseBasement.png"
                            width="100" height="100"/>
                </images>
                <videos>
                    <video caption="Outside Main Entrance Floor"
                              source="/videos/EnterpriseMainEntrance.wmv"
                              width="100" height="100"/>
                    <video caption="Outside Bottom Floor"
                              source="/videos/EnterpriseBottomFloor.wmv"
                              width="100" height="100"/>
                </videos>
            </building>
        </buildings>
    </campus>
  </campuses>
</school>
```

Packaging of the Application

There are three general categories of files that are sent to the client: the Silverlight application, the school data (the XML file and map information), and media files for the school (images/video). The XAP file containing the application is downloaded to the client when a user browses to the application on a web site. This must be done regardless, though it's possible to cache the XAP file on the client browser.

The school data is downloaded after the application initializes. This is done for three main reasons. First, the user interface (even if it's a progress bar) is displayed faster, giving the user a better experience. Second, the school's data can be saved to isolated storage, also improving the user's experience (faster loading next time they visit the application). This also carries with it the benefit of less server traffic for users who visit the application repeatedly. If you use isolated storage, you must implement a version check to see if the server has updated data. Third, this places school-specific information outside the Silverlight application, making it easier to structure a generalized application that can be productized and sold to other universities.

The third category of files contains images and video of different parts of a campus. These are packaged as part of the web site. The paths to these files are stored in the XML data file. This also provides a way to store the media in Silverlight Streaming and reference those paths. For simplicity, the included media is packaged with the web site for this chapter.

Application Implementation

Let's now take a look at how the different aspects of this application are implemented.

Helper Methods

Any application usually has some form of utility methods—code useful in many different parts of the application. Sometimes these are stored in their own class. This application only has one method that is useful in different parts of the application, and since it makes sense as a way to augment the Application class, it takes the form of an *extension method*, a feature introduced in C# 3.0. Here's the implementation of this extension method, GetHostAddress— an easy way to retrieve the path to the server where the Silverlight application lives, but suitable for referencing media contained in the web site:

```
public static class ApplicationExtensions
{
    public static string GetHostAddress(this Application app)
    {
        return (app.Host.Source.AbsoluteUri.Substring(0,
            app.Host.Source.AbsoluteUri.IndexOf(
                app.Host.Source.AbsolutePath)));
    }
}
```

The GetHostAddress is useful for referencing images/video located on the host web site. You use it like this:

```
video.Source = new Uri(App.Current.GetHostAddress() + "/test.wmv",
                                   UriKind.Absolute);
```

This extension method does not return a string with a trailing slash, and the method must be modified if the web site/web application hosting the Silverlight application is under a directory within the web site. For example, this method won't work with `http://localhost:51161/chapter15web`, but it will work with `http://localhost:51161/`. This is because the virtual directory piece isn't presented in the `app.Host` object in a way we can identify it.

XAML Organization

There are four XAML files that make up this application (not including `App.xaml`). `MainPage.xaml` features the main user interface. `Map.xaml` includes the interactive map and the informational panel. `VideoThumbnail.xaml` is used to display a video with a play button overlay in `Map.xaml`. `ErrorFrame.xaml` catches and displays unhandled exceptions, providing a smoother user experience than a browser error.

MainPage

`MainPage.xaml` contains the main parts of the application. An instance of this XAML is wrapped by the `ErrorFrame` from Chapter 12. `MainPage.xaml` contains everything except the interactive map and its associated informational panel (that contains text or images/video). The ListBox's appearance is changed by using a control template, as are the navigation buttons at the top of the user interface. A user control can be placed onto a XAML page by exposing the XML namespace, and is done in `MainPage.xaml` to put the `Map.xaml` control on the page:

```
<UserControl x:Class="chapter15.MainPage"
    xmlns="http://schemas.microsoft.com/winfx/2006/xaml/presentation"
    xmlns:x="http://schemas.microsoft.com/winfx/2006/xaml"
    xmlns:ce="clr-namespace:chapter15">
    <!-- ... -->
    <ce:Map Grid.Row="1" Grid.Column="1" x:Name="mapControl"/>
    <!-- ... -->
</UserControl>
```

MainPage.xaml also includes a pop-up that covers the entire interface while data is downloaded. The frosted effect of the entire interface is achieved by using `Opacity`.

```
<Popup x:Name="startupPopup">
    <Canvas Background="White" Opacity="0.7"
            Width="860" Height="815">
        <TextBlock x:Name="dataDownloadProgressText" Text=""
                   Canvas.Left="400" Canvas.Top="400"/>
    </Canvas>
</Popup>
```

Map Interaction ListBox

The left side of the application contains a list of items such as the buildings on the map, departments from the school, or a group of annotations such as driving directions. The default ListBox appearance doesn't fit as well into this application as it should, so it was modified. As discussed in Chapter 8, the best way to go about changing a control's appearance is by using

Expression Blend to either create an empty control template (if you want to work with a clean slate) or edit the existing control template (if you want to make minor tweaks or have existing XAML that can guide you). Changing the appearance of the ListBox for this application requires defining a new control template both for the ListBox and for the items in the ListBox. The ListBox control template is changed to remove the border around it:

```
<Style x:Key="ListBoxStyle1" TargetType="ListBox">
    <Setter Property="Template">
        <Setter.Value>
            <ControlTemplate TargetType="ListBox">
                <Grid>
                    <ScrollViewer x:Name="ScrollViewer"
                                  BorderThickness="0"
                                  Padding="{TemplateBinding Padding}">
                        <ItemsPresenter/>
                    </ScrollViewer>
                </Grid>
            </ControlTemplate>
        </Setter.Value>
    </Setter>
</Style>
```

The ListBoxItem's control template is changed by removing many of the storyboard animations, making the items appear flatter in order to blend in more with the visual appearance of the application. The entire control template is too long to show in this chapter, but here is the new XAML for the MouseOver state. The Opacity property is altered to display the mouseover highlight since the item's content is underneath.

```
<vsm:VisualState x:Name="MouseOver">
    <Storyboard>
        <DoubleAnimationUsingKeyFrames
                Storyboard.TargetName="HoverOverlay"
                Storyboard.TargetProperty="(UIElement.Opacity)">
            <SplineDoubleKeyFrame KeyTime="00:00:00" Value="0.75"/>
        </DoubleAnimationUsingKeyFrames>
    </Storyboard>
</vsm:VisualState>
```

There is a single ListBox that uses this control template (by way of a style). The ListBox uses data binding to easily populate the items collection. Since there is a control template for the ListBox and a control template for ListBoxItem, the ItemContainerStyle of the ListBox is used to specify the style (containing the control template) for the items.

```
<ListBox x:Name="mapItemsListBox"
         ItemsSource="{Binding Mode=OneWay}"
         Width="190" Height="500"
         Canvas.Left="15" Canvas.Top="75"
         Style="{StaticResource ListBoxStyle1}"
         SelectionChanged="mapItemsListBox_SelectionChanged"
```

```
                ItemContainerStyle="{StaticResource ListBoxItemStyle1}">
        <ListBox.ItemTemplate>
            <DataTemplate>
                <StackPanel Orientation="Horizontal">
                    <TextBlock Text="{Binding Path=DisplayText}" Height="25"
                               Foreground="Black" FontSize="10"
                               VerticalAlignment="Top"/>
                </StackPanel>
            </DataTemplate>
        </ListBox.ItemTemplate>
    </ListBox>
```

Any object with a `DisplayText` property can be used for data binding with this ListBox. For example, the `Department` class features the following `DisplayText`:

```
public class Department
{
    [XmlAttribute("name")]
    public string name { get; set; }
    public string DisplayText
    {
        get
        {
            return (this.name);
        }
    }
    // ...
}
```

This approach makes it easy to only specify the ListBox once in the XAML; then, behind the scenes, the `DataContext` property is set accordingly. This could also be accomplished by changing the `DataContext` and the data binding within the item template.

Map.xaml

The `Map.xaml` page contains four main elements: the informational panel at top (featuring text/images/video), the reduced-size map on the user interface, the zoomed map, and a pop-up for viewing a larger image/video. Let's look closer at these aspects of the map interface.

Map Zoom

The core of the application is the interactive map. The most interesting feature is the ability to zoom into a particular point on the map. The map zoom is accomplished using two images and what you might call a trick. The high-resolution map is a 2400×2000 PNG file. If this were the only image used, letting Silverlight shrink the map into a smaller space would potentially look terrible. Instead, the image is shrunk in a graphics program such as Paint.NET. The two big advantages to having the lower-resolution version are that you can ensure it looks good, and Silverlight won't have to do the extra work of shrinking the image into a smaller space. For this application, the 2400×2000 map is shrunk to 600×500. This maintains the aspect ratio of the image while ensuring the image is small enough to fit on the main user interface. These two images are placed into the data package downloaded by the application.

When a user presses and holds the left mouse button, a zoomed slice of the map appears, along with some informational text. The zoomed slice is a 200×200 rectangle taken from the 2400×2000 image. Figure 15-4 shows what the smaller rectangle shown on top of the 600×500 image looks like in outline form, and Figure 15-5 shows what this looks like in the application.

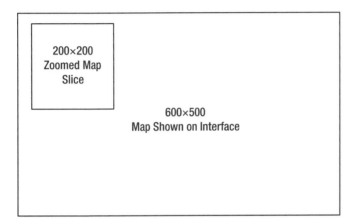

Figure 15-4. *Representation of zoom rectangle on top of reduced-size map*

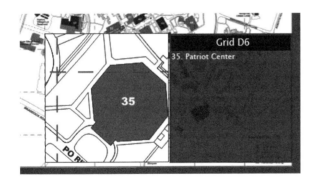

Figure 15-5. *The zoomed slice of the map shown on top of the main map*

The zoomed slice is actually an image with its source set to the full-size map image, and the Clip property is used to isolate the 200×200 rectangle:

```
<Image x:Name="zoomedMapImage"
       Width="2400" Height="2000" Visibility="Collapsed">
    <Image.Clip>
        <RectangleGeometry Rect="0,0,200,200">
            <RectangleGeometry.Transform>
                <TranslateTransform X="0" Y="0"
                    x:Name="zoomedMapClipTransform"/>
```

```
            </RectangleGeometry.Transform>
        </RectangleGeometry>
    </Image.Clip>
    <Image.RenderTransform>
        <TranslateTransform X="0" Y="0"
                    x:Name="zoomedMapTransform" />
    </Image.RenderTransform>
</Image>
```

The zoomed slice is centered on the point where the mouse is clicked. The initial mouse click is handled by the following method:

```
private void mapCanvas_MouseLeftButtonDown(object sender,
                                    MouseButtonEventArgs e)
{
    zoomedMapImage.Visibility = Visibility.Visible;
    zoomBorder.Visibility = Visibility.Visible;
    gridInfoBorder.Visibility = Visibility.Visible;
    setZoomedPosition(e.GetPosition(mapCanvas));
}
```

This method makes the appropriate elements of the zoomed slice and associated grid information visible, and then translates the position of the mouse to a point within the mapCanvas (the top-left of the mapCanvas is 0,0, and this ensures the mouse position is relative to this point). The setZoomedPosition method does all the work of calculating the correct slice to show and determining what buildings are within the current grid cell.

```
private void setZoomedPosition(Point p)
{
    // ...
}
```

Let's look at what the setZoomedPosition does, a piece at a time. The position of the image (the zoomed slice) is set as follows:

```
zoomedMapImage.SetValue(Canvas.LeftProperty, p.X-100);
zoomedMapImage.SetValue(Canvas.TopProperty, p.Y-100);
```

Since it's a 200×200 slice, subtracting 100 from each coordinate centers the slice. Next, the clip must be set so that the image displays the correct slice. This is a matter of converting the position of the mouse from the local coordinate system (a point within the 600×500 image) to the larger map's coordinate system (a point within the 2400×2000 image).

```
zoomedMapClipTransform.X = ((p.X) / 600) * 2400 - 100;
zoomedMapClipTransform.Y = ((p.Y) / 500) * 2000 - 100;
```

This clips the full-size image to where we want it. Subtracting 100 must be done since the slice is centered. This isn't all that is needed, however. The image itself must be placed into position based on where the mouse was clicked. This is why there's an additional Translate transform on the image. Once the clip region is set, this slice must be moved into position so the top left of the slice is the top left of the visible rectangle that contains the slice on the user interface. This is accomplished by setting the Translate transform to the opposite of the Translate transform used for the clipping:

```
zoomedMapTransform.X = -1 * zoomedMapClipTransform.X;
zoomedMapTransform.Y = -1 * zoomedMapClipTransform.Y;
```

It may help to visualize a physical map on a desk with a rectangular magnifying glass that is in a fixed location above the map. First, the rectangle of interest must be identified (this is the crop, isolating a small section of the map), and then the map itself must be moved beneath the magnifying glass so that the correct piece of the map is directly beneath the magnifier. Allowing the user to hold down the left mouse button and drag the zoomed slice around is accomplished by handling the MouseMove event of the Canvas that holds the map. This event handler passes the mouse position to the setPosition method that performs the calculations and placement of the slice:

```
private void mapCanvas_MouseMove(object sender, MouseEventArgs e)
{
    setZoomedPosition(e.GetPosition(mapCanvas));
}
```

The rest of setZoomedPosition positions the informational pane that is attached to the zoomed map slice and populates it with a list of building names within the current grid cell.

Highlighting Buildings

The data contains information on the location of each building in order for the application to highlight it on the map. This highlighting is accomplished via a black ellipse in the XAML that is only visible when a building is highlighted:

```
<Ellipse Stroke="Black" StrokeThickness="5" x:Name="highlight"
                                Visibility="Collapsed"/>
```

The ellipse's Visibility property is set to Visible and placed on the user interface according to the map information stored along with the buildings:

```
private void highlightBuilding(Building building)
{
    if (!string.IsNullOrEmpty(building.mapinfo.highlight))
    {
        string[] pieces = building.mapinfo.highlight.Split(',');
        highlight.Visibility = Visibility.Visible;
        highlight.SetValue(Canvas.LeftProperty, Convert.ToDouble(pieces[0]));
        highlight.SetValue(Canvas.TopProperty, Convert.ToDouble(pieces[1]));
        highlight.Width = Convert.ToDouble(pieces[2]);
        highlight.Height = Convert.ToDouble(pieces[3]);
    }
}
```

Map Annotations

A map annotation is some form of decoration that adds information to the map. While annotations can be viewed as a generalized concept, this application uses them just for driving directions. There are mainly two approaches to creating annotations. The first is by leveraging drawing primitives from Silverlight, such as the TextBlock for text, and shapes such as lines and ellipses to paint information onto the surface of the map. This approach would either require a specialized use of Expression Blend (to create XAML on top of the map image and then export this XAML) or a custom tool (to either draw the annotations onto a map image or convert XAML from Expression Blend into another format if required).

The other approach, and the one taken with this application, is to start with the original map image, open it in a graphics editor such as Paint.NET, and draw annotations on a new layer, leaving the original map alone on the initial layer. The original layer containing the map can then be deleted, leaving the annotations on a largely transparent image. When this image is displayed after the original map, the annotations appear on top. By working with the original full-size map, the annotations can easily be displayed on the 600×500 surface and on the zoomed slices from the 2400×2000 image.

The Map class defines the showAnnotation method that takes the path to the annotation:

```
public void showAnnotation(string annotationImageSource)
{
    clear();
    BitmapImage imageSource = new BitmapImage();
    imageSource.SetSource(SchoolData.GetMapAnnotation(annotationImageSource));
    annotationMapMini.Source = imageSource;
    annotationMapMini.Visibility = Visibility.Visible;
}
```

The annotationMapMini is placed right after the main map image shown on the user interface. This ensures that when the annotation image is shown it appears on top of the main map:

```
<Image x:Name="mainMap" Width="600" Height="500"
            Canvas.Left="0" Canvas.Top="0"/>
<Image x:Name="annotationMapMini" Width="600" Height="500"
            Canvas.Left="0" Canvas.Top="0" Visibility="Collapsed"/>
```

Since most of the annotation image is transparent, the file size generally isn't too large. There was one problem encountered in the development of this part, however, The color space in the PNG was stored in an indexed format that is incompatible with Silverlight with respect to transparency. The image appeared fine but the transparent parts weren't transparent. This was addressed by converting the PNG from an indexed color space to RGBA. One easy way to do this is with ImageMagick (you can download this from www.imagemagick.org/). The following invocation of the convert.exe program changes a PNG to RGBA:

```
convert.exe <source image> -channel RGBA <destination image>
```

Informational Panel

The informational panel located immediately above the map features a single line of text that is always visible, and optionally additional text or images/video below it. You can see what this panel looks like in Figure 15-6 when it features some media.

Figure 15-6. *The upper panel containing images/video*

The right side of the first line also contains an arrow allowing users to collapse this panel if they don't want to see the extra information. The arrow is a single image that a Rotate transform can be applied to.

```
<StackPanel Orientation="Horizontal" Canvas.Left="518" Canvas.Top="0" >
    <TextBlock Text="Click to collapse" x:Name="arrowLabel"
            Foreground="White" FontSize="12" Margin="0 0 5 0"/>
    <Image Source="arrow_down.png" x:Name="arrowButton" Width="18" Height="18"
        MouseLeftButtonUp="arrow_MouseLeftButtonUp">
        <Image.RenderTransform>
            <RotateTransform Angle="0" CenterX="9" CenterY="9"
                                    x:Name="arrowRotation"/>
        </Image.RenderTransform>
    </Image>
</StackPanel>
```

When the arrow is clicked, the animation happens and the rotational angle of the arrow image is set:

```
private void arrow_MouseLeftButtonUp(object sender, MouseButtonEventArgs e)
{
    if (upperPanelExpanded)
    {
        scrollUp.Begin();
        arrowRotation.Angle = 90;
        infoText.Visibility = Visibility.Collapsed;
        mediaScrollViewer.Visibility = Visibility.Collapsed;
        arrowLabel.Text = "Click to expand";
        upperPanelExpanded = false;
    }
    else
    {
        scrollDown.Begin();
```

```
        arrowRotation.Angle = 0;
        infoText.Visibility = informationalTextVisibility;
        mediaScrollViewer.Visibility = mediaListVisibility;
        arrowLabel.Text = "Click to collapse";
        upperPanelExpanded = true;
    }
}
```

This arrow could be implemented as a custom control template for Button, but its appearance is so simple that the additional visual states for the Button are more than we need.

The container for images/video associated with a building on campus is simply an empty StackPanel inside a ScrollViewer. This makes it easy to provide scrolling behavior in case there are more images/videos than can be seen at a single time.

```
<ScrollViewer HorizontalScrollBarVisibility="Auto"
              VerticalScrollBarVisibility="Disabled"
              Height="130" Canvas.Left="15" Canvas.Top="30" Width="600"
              Visibility="Collapsed" x:Name="mediaScrollViewer">
    <StackPanel Orientation="Horizontal" x:Name="mediaStackPanel"/>
</ScrollViewer>
```

When a building is selected (either by the user selecting a building or department), any videos/images associated with it are added to the mediaStackPanel. Here's the code that handles all the video. Remember that the video and images are stored on the web site, not as part of the Silverlight application.

```
mediaStackPanel.Children.Clear();
if (SchoolData.school.campuses[0].buildings[i].videos != null &&
    SchoolData.school.campuses[0].buildings[i].videos.Count > 0)
{
    for (int j = 0;
            j < SchoolData.school.campuses[0].buildings[i].videos.Count;
            j++)
    {
        VideoThumbnail video = new VideoThumbnail();
        video.Source = new Uri(App.Current.GetHostAddress() +
            SchoolData.school.campuses[0].buildings[i].videos[j].source,
            UriKind.Absolute);
        video.MouseLeftButtonUp += media_MouseLeftButtonUp;
        video.Margin = new Thickness(10, 0, 10, 0);
        video.Tag = j;
        mediaStackPanel.Children.Add(video);
    }
}
```

Whenever an image or video is clicked, the media_MouseLeftButtonUp event handler is invoked. This event handler displays either the image or video and causes a pop-up to open. The pop-up is defined in XAML and contains the header text, the content (image or video), and control buttons (play/pause for video, and always a close button).

```
<Popup Canvas.Left="20" Canvas.Top="40"
       Width="300" Height="300" x:Name="imagePopup">
    <Border BorderBrush="Black" BorderThickness="1"
            Background="Black">
        <Grid>
            <Grid.RowDefinitions>
                <RowDefinition Height="24"/>
                <RowDefinition Height="*"/>
                <RowDefinition Height="Auto"/>
            </Grid.RowDefinitions>
            <TextBlock x:Name="zoomedMediaHeader"
                       HorizontalAlignment="Center"
                       Text="Front Entrance" Foreground="Red"/>
            <Image x:Name="zoomedImage" Width="300" Height="300"
                   Grid.Row="1" Visibility="Collapsed"/>
            <MediaElement x:Name="zoomedVideo" AutoPlay="False"
                          Width="300" Height="300" Grid.Row="1"
                          Visibility="Visible"/>
            <StackPanel HorizontalAlignment="Center" Grid.Row="2"
                        Orientation="Horizontal" Height="24">
                <Button x:Name="videoPlayStopButton" Content="PLAY"
                        Margin="2" Click="videoPlayStopButton_Click"/>
                <Button x:Name="videoPauseResumeButton" Content="PAUSE"
                        Margin="2" Click="videoPauseResumeButton_Click"/>
                <Button x:Name="popupButton" Content="CLOSE"
                        Click="popupButton_Click" Margin="2"/>
            </StackPanel>
        </Grid>
    </Border>
</Popup>
```

This informational panel can be collapsed or expanded, and is a great place to add some subtle animation. This is accomplished via two storyboards in the resource dictionary for the Map control:

```
<UserControl.Resources>
    <Storyboard x:Name="scrollUp" Storyboard.TargetName="upperPanel"
                Storyboard.TargetProperty="Height">
        <DoubleAnimationUsingKeyFrames>
            <LinearDoubleKeyFrame KeyTime="0:0:0" Value="170"/>
            <LinearDoubleKeyFrame KeyTime="0:0:0.2" Value="30"/>
        </DoubleAnimationUsingKeyFrames>
    </Storyboard>
    <Storyboard x:Name="scrollDown" Storyboard.TargetName="upperPanel"
                Storyboard.TargetProperty="Height">
        <DoubleAnimationUsingKeyFrames>
            <LinearDoubleKeyFrame KeyTime="0:0:0" Value="30"/>
            <LinearDoubleKeyFrame KeyTime="0:0:0.2" Value="170"/>
```

```
            </DoubleAnimationUsingKeyFrames>
        </Storyboard>
    </UserControl.Resources>
```

Summary

This chapter described the design and implementation of a Silverlight application that could conceivably exist on the Web. There are definitely enhancements that can be made to this application, such as linking the interactive map with courses and student schedules, and providing additional information that can be pointed out on the map. There were relatively few problems encountered when developing this application, illustrating the fact that Silverlight provides a great degree of what we need as software developers to build rich applications. There is a lot of expressiveness provided by Silverlight, and now it's your turn to make use of this new platform from Microsoft.

Index

threading and, 39
in XAML, 16–17
user roles, 238–239, 243–244
UserAgent property, 217
UserControl element, 64, 69–70
UserToken property, 88, 89

V

ValidatedOnException, 99
ValueChanged event, 60
var keyword, 110
VB .NET, 207
versioning, 280–281
VerticalAlignment property, 43
video, 125–138
video player, 129–130
VideoBrush class, 158, 159
virtual machines, 2
visibility keyword, 75
Visibility property, 40, 69
Visual State Manager (VSM), 171–172
Visual Studio, debugging with, 263–267
Visual Studio 2008, 5
VisualStateManager class, 174, 179, 181
VisualTransition class, 175

W

WCF. *See* Windows Communication
    Foundation
web application projects, 7
web pages
    hosting Silverlight on, 278–284
    user interface elements, 164–166
web service binding, 74
web services
    client service proxy for, 76–80
    creating simple, 74–75
    for network communication, 74–94
WebClient class, 81–83, 94
Width property, 43, 20
windowless parameter, 279
Windows, supported browsers, 271
Windows Communication Foundation
    (WCF), 74–75
Windows Forms, control layout in, 43

Windows Media Encoder, 133
Windows Presentation Foundation (WPF),
    1, 3
Windows Presentation
    Foundation/Everywhere (WPF/E), 3
worker thread, 293
Write method, 114
WriteByte method, 114
WriteLine method, 264

X

x scope, 18
XAML (Extensible Application Markup
    Language), 1, 3, 36
    as dialect of XML, 17
    class implementation, 30–31
    dependency property system, 18–23
    for dynamically loading applications,
        311–313
    introduction to, 13–30
    markup extensions, 24–30
    namespaces, 18
    type converters, 23–24
XAML files, 5–9, 276
XAML pages, navigating between, 68–70
XamlReader, 311
XAML_Viewer class, 69–70
.xap file extension, 7, 275
XAP files, 7, 241, 249
XapCacheFile.xml file, 286
x:Key property, 26, 166
x:Name property, 168
XML
    classes for working with, 97
    parsing, 107–108
    serializing, 108–109
    XAML as dialect of, 17
XmlReader class, 107
XmlReader.Create method, 107
XmlSerializer, 108–109
XmlWriter class, 108

Z

ZIP files, downloading images stored in,
    138–140

You Need the Companion eBook

Your purchase of this book entitles you to buy the companion PDF-version eBook for only $10. Take the weightless companion with you anywhere.

We believe this Apress title will prove so indispensable that you'll want to carry it with you everywhere, which is why we are offering the companion eBook (in PDF format) for $10 to customers who purchase this book now. Convenient and fully searchable, the PDF version of any content-rich, page-heavy Apress book makes a valuable addition to your programming library. You can easily find and copy code — or perform examples by quickly toggling between instructions and the application. Even simultaneously tackling a donut, diet soda, and complex code becomes simplified with hands-free eBooks!

Once you purchase your book, getting the $10 companion eBook is simple:

❶ Visit **www.apress.com/promo/tendollars/**.

❷ Complete a basic registration form to receive a randomly generated question about this title.

❸ Answer the question correctly in 60 seconds, and you will receive a promotional code to redeem for the $10.00 eBook.

2855 TELEGRAPH AVENUE | SUITE 600 | BERKELEY, CA 94705

Offer valid through 04/09.